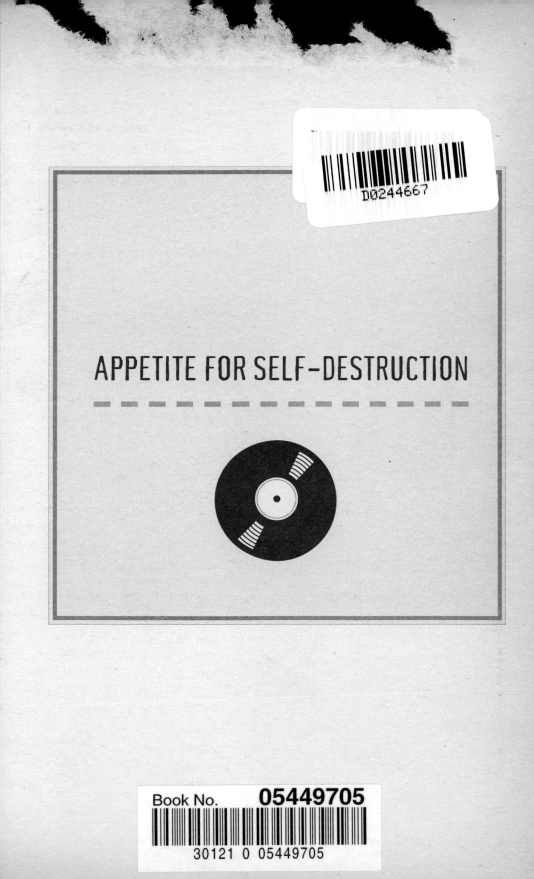

APPETITE FOR SELF-DESTRUCTION

APPETITE FOR
SELF-DESTRUCTION

The Spectacular Crash of the Record Industry

in the Digital Age

SIMON &
SCHUSTER

London · New York · Sydney · Toronto

A CBS COMPANY

First published in Great Britain by Simon & Schuster UK Ltd, 2009
A CBS COMPANY

1 3 5 7 9 10 8 6 4 2

Simon & Schuster UK Ltd
1st Floor
222 Gray's Inn Road
London WC1X 8HB

www.simonandschuster.co.uk

Simon & Schuster Australia
Sydney

A CIP catalogue record for this book
is available from the British Library.

ISBN: 978-1-84737-136-2

Book design by Ellen R. Sasahara

Printed in the UK by CPI Mackays, Chatham ME5 8TD

For Melissa and Rose

"A strategic inflection point is a time in the life of a business when its fundamentals are about to change. . . . Strategic inflection points can be caused by technological change but they are more than technological change . . . A strategic inflection point can be deadly when unattended to. Companies that begin a decline as a result of its changes rarely recover their previous greatness. But strategic inflection points do not always lead to disaster. When the way business is being conducted changes, it creates opportunities for players who are adept at operating in the new way."

—Andrew S. Grove, *Only the Paranoid Survive*

"Look out, honey, 'cause I'm using technology
Ain't got time to make no apology."

—Iggy Pop and James Williamson, "Search and Destroy"

Contents

Cast of Characters

CBS Records

Walter Yetnikoff, president, 1975–1987

Tommy Mottola, president, 1988

William Paley, CBS Inc., CEO, 1986–1995; died 2003

Laurence Tisch, CBS Inc., president, director, chairman of the board, 1988–1990; died 2003

Dick Asher, deputy president, 1979–1983

Frank Dileo, promotion director, Epic Records, 1979–1984; manager, Michael Jackson, 1984–1990

George Vradenburg, senior VP, general counsel, 1980–1991

Jerry Shulman, market researcher, VP of marketing, Legacy founder, general manager, 1973–1999

Bob Sherwood, Columbia Records president, 1988–1990

Sony Music Entertainment, purchased CBS Records, 1988

Walter Yetnikoff, chairman, 1987–1990

Michael "Mickey" Schulhof, chairman, 1991–1995

Tommy Mottola, president, 1989–1998; chairman and CEO, 1995–2003

Don Ienner, president, Columbia Records, 1989–2003; president, US division, 2003–2006; chairman, 2006

Michele Anthony, senior vice president, executive vice president, chief operating officer, 1990–2004; president and chief operating officer, 2004–2006

Al Smith, senior vice president, 1992–2004

Fred Ehrlich, Columbia Records, vice president, general manager, 1988–1994; VP, general manager, president, new technology and business development, 1994–2003

David W. Stebbings, technology director, also for CBS Records, mid–1980s–1995

Jeff Ayeroff, copresident, WORK Group, 1994–1998

Jordan Harris, copresident, WORK Group, 1994–1999

John Grady, Sony Music Nashville, president, 2002–2006

Phil Wiser, chief technology officer, 2001–2005

Mark Ghuneim, Columbia Records, VP, 1993–2003; senior VP of online and emerging technologies, 2003–2004

Sony Corp.

Akio Morita, cofounder, as Tokyo Telecommunications Engineering Corporation, 1946; died 1999

Norio Ohga, various positions, including president, chairman, CEO, 1958–2003; served as chairman, Sony Music Entertainment, 1990–1991

Michael "Mickey" Schulhof, joined mid-1970s; president, CEO, 1993–1996

Toshitada Doi, headed digital team, beginning in 1980; later executive VP

Marc Finer, director of product communications, late 1970s–1988

John Briesch, VP audio marketing, 1981–present

Nobuyuki Idei, CEO, 1999–2005; chairman, 2003–2005

Sir Howard Stringer, chairman and CEO, American division, 1998–present; overall CEO, 2005–present

Phil Wiser, chief technology officer, 2005–2006

Sony BMG

Rob Stringer, UK division, chairman, CEO, 2004–2006; president, Sony Music, 2006–present

Michael Smellie, BMG, chief operating officer, 2001–2004; chief operating officer, 2004–2005

Andrew Lack, chairman and CEO, Sony Music, 2003–2004; chief executive officer, 2004–2005; nonexecutive chairman, 2005–present

Rolf Schmidt-Holz, nonexecutive chairman, 2004–2005; chief executive officer, 2005–present

Thomas Hesse, BMG, chief strategic officer, 2002–2004; president, global digital business, 2004–present

Steve Greenberg, president, Columbia Records, 2005–2006

Joe DiMuro, BMG and RCA Records, senior VP, 1998–2004; executive VP of strategic marketing, 2004–2006

Warner Music/Warner Communications

Steve Ross, Warner Communications, CEO, president, chairman, 1972–1990; Time Warner, CEO, 1990–1992; died 1992

Mo Ostin, president, Reprise, then Warner Music, 1967–1995

Joe Smith, Warner, president, 1972–1975; Elektra Records, chairman, 1975–1983

Doug Morris, Atlantic Records, president, 1980–1990; cochairman and co-chief executive officer, 1990–1994; Warner Music, president, chairman, 1994–1995

Ahmet Ertegun, Atlantic Records, founder, 1947; died 2006

Jac Holzman, Elektra Records, founder, 1950; Warner Bros. Records, senior VP, chief technologist, 1973–1982; Warner Music, consultant, Cordless Records creator, 2005–present

Elliot Goldman, Warner Communications, senior VP, 1982–1985

Bob Krasnow, Elektra Records, president, 1983–1994

Howie Klein, Reprise Records, president, 1996–2001

Stan Cornyn, various positions, including senior vice president and founder/CEO of new media, 1958–1990

Bob Merlis, publicist, senior VP of worldwide communications, early 1970s–2001

Jeff Gold, executive VP, general manager, 1990–1998

Robert Morgado, chairman and CEO, 1985–1995

Michael Fuchs, chairman and CEO, 1995

Danny Goldberg, chairman, 1995; Atlantic Records, president, 1994–1995, senior vice president, 1992–1994

Roger Ames, chairman and CEO, 1999–2004

Paul Vidich, vice president, strategy, business development, and technology, 1987–2004

Kevin Gage, vice president, strategic technology and new media, 2000–2005

Edgar Bronfman Jr., chairman, chief executive officer, 2004–present

AOL Time Warner

Gerald Levin, Time Warner, chairman and CEO, 1993–2001; AOL Time Warner, CEO, 2001–2002

Bob Pittman, chief operating officer, 2001–2002

Barry Schuler, AOL, chairman and CEO, 2000–2003

William J. Raduchel, senior vice president and chief technology officer, 2001–2002

George Vradenburg, general counsel, executive VP for global and strategic policy, 1997–2002

EMI Records Group

Joe Smith, president and CEO, 1987–1993

Charles Koppelman, chairman and CEO, 1994–1997

Eric Nicoli, executive chairman, 1999–2007

Ted Cohen, senior vice president of digital development and distribution, 2000–2006

Barney Wragg, head of digital, 2006–2007

Guy Hands, chairman, 2007–present

BMG

Clive Davis, Arista Records, founder, 1974, president, 1974–2000; RCA Records, president, 2003–2004; North American division, chairman and CEO, 2004–2008; chief creative officer, 2008–present

Strauss Zelnick, president and CEO, 1994–2000

Bob Jamieson, RCA Music Group, chairman and CEO, 1997–2000; North American division, president and CEO, 2001–2004

Bob Buziak, RCA Music Group, president, 1990–1994

Bill Allen, recording studio maintenance engineer, director of new technology, other positions, 1987–2001

Zomba/Jive

Clive Calder, cofounder, 1975; chairman and CEO, 1975–2002

Ralph Simon, cofounder, 1975; left company, 1990

Barry Weiss, president and CEO, 2002–2008; chairman, BMG, 2008–present

Steve Lunt, VP of A&R, late 1970s–2005

Stuart Watson, Zomba International, managing director, 1999–2002

David McPherson, A&R director and VP, 1994–1998

Bertelsmann

Thomas Middelhoff, chairman and CEO, 1997–2002

Andreas Schmidt, president of e-commerce group, 2000–2001

A&M

Herb Alpert, cofounder, 1962; left company, 1993

Jerry Moss, cofounder, 1962; left company, 1999

Gil Friesen, general manager, president, 1964–1993

Al Cafaro, numerous positions, including chairman and CEO, 1976–1999

Jim Guerinot, general manager, 1992–1994
Jeff Gold, assistant to the president, vice president of marketing and creative services, 1981–1990

PolyGram

David Braun, president, US, 1980–1981
Jan Timmer, president, Philips, 1983–1996
Cor Boonstra, president, Philips, 1996–2001
Alain Levy, president and CEO, 1991–1998
Jan Cook, VP, chief financial officer, 1985–1998; CEO, 1998

Universal Music Group

Edgar Bronfman Jr., the Seagram Co., president, 1989–2000; Vivendi Universal, executive vice chairman, 2000–2002; on board of directors through 2003
Doug Morris, chairman and CEO, 1995–present
Zach Horowitz, president and chief operating officer, 1998–present
Albhy Galuten, senior vice president, advanced technology, 1995–2005
David Geffen, founder, Geffen Records, 1980; sold to MCA, 1990
Jimmy Iovine, Interscope, cofounder, 1989; chairman, 1989–present
Debbie Southwood-Smith, A&R, various labels, including Interscope, 1985–2005
Mark Williams, A&R executive, Interscope, through 2007
Courtney Holt, vice president of marketing, head of new media and strategic marketing, 1999–2006
Erin Yasgar, new-media executive, Interscope, 1998–2002

Napster, 1999–2002

Shawn Fanning, cofounder
John Fanning, founding chairman, original CEO
Sean Parker, cofounder
Jordan Ritter, cofounder, engineer
Eileen Richardson, CEO, 1999–2000
Bill Bales, chief operating officer
Yosi Amram, investor
Jordan Mendelson, engineer
Ali Aydar, engineer
Eddie Kessler, VP of engineering
John Hummer, investor
Hank Barry, CEO, 2000–2001

Konrad Hilbers, CEO, 2001–2002
Lyn Jensen, chief financial officer
Milt Olin, chief operating officer
Liz Brooks, marketer

Kazaa, 2000–2005

Niklas Zennström and Janus Friis, founder
Nikki Hemming, Sharman Networks, CEO, part owner
Kevin Bermeister, Brilliant Digital Entertainment, Altnet, CEO
Phil Morle, chief technology officer
Mick Liubinskas, marketing director

RIAA, Recording Industry Association of America

Hilary Rosen, chairman, 1998–2003
Cary Sherman, general counsel, 1997–2003; president, 2003–present
Frank Creighton, head of piracy enforcement, 1987–2003
David W. Stebbings, senior vice president for technology, 1995–2000

Apple

Steve Jobs, cofounder, 1976; chairman and CEO, 1976–1985,
    1997–present
Steve Wozniak, cofounder, 1976–1981
Tony Fadell, member of iPod engineering team, 2001–2004; vice
    president of iPod engineering, 2004–2006; senior vice president of
    iPod division, 2006–present
Jonathan Rubinstein, senior vice president of hardware and iPod
    engineering, 1997–2006
Vinnie Chieco, freelance copywriter

Prologue
1979–1982

Disco Crashes the Record Business, Michael Jackson Saves the Day, and MTV *Really* Saves the Day

ONE MAN almost destroyed the music industry in the late '70s.

His name was Steve Dahl, and he was a roundish Chicago rock disc jockey with huge glasses and a shaggy bowl cut. In a maniacally nasal voice, he pioneered shock radio with his outrageous stunts. Once, during the 1979 Iran hostage crisis, he made random on-air calls to Iran and savagely mocked the first person with a foreign accent to answer. But the WLUP-FM DJ didn't find widespread recognition until he started smashing Donna Summer records in the studio, calling to arms a crazed group of followers he dubbed the Insane Coho Lips.*

Dahl's hatred for disco ran deep and personal. He had taken a long road to his first Chicago job, dropping out of high school at age sixteen to work at an underground station near his home in La Cañada, California. He scored a few DJ gigs and married a young woman who'd called one night to request Leonard Cohen's "Suzanne." Naturally, they divorced. But when he was nineteen, less than a year after they'd split up, Dahl sat in his Subaru in front of her house, waiting all night for her to come out. This was the 1970s, so rather than having him arrested for stalking, she used personal connections to land him a morning-show job at a struggling station as far away as possible, in Detroit.

Almost overnight, Dahl turned his new station's ratings around.

---

*The name came from a street gang at the time called "The Insane Unknowns" and a fleet of coho salmon at Burnham Harbor in Chicago, which Dahl was driving by when he heard a report about gangs on the radio. "Lips" was a non sequitur.

Big-time Chicago rock stations came calling, and Dahl accepted a job at WDAI, where he worked until it abruptly switched formats in 1978, dropping Led Zeppelin and the Rolling Stones and transforming into "Disco 'DAI." Pictures of the Village People started appearing in its promo ads. Dahl, a rock guy, had no choice but to quit. He accepted a morning-show job at another Chicago rock station, WLUP.

"I was just mad at my previous employer," the now-white-haired, still-Hawaiian-shirt-wearing Dahl says. "And Midwesterners didn't want that intimidating [disco] lifestyle shoved down their throats." The antidisco campaign became the centerpiece of Dahl's morning show with cohost Garry Meier. They invited listeners to call in with their most hated disco songs; after airing a snippet, Dahl and Meier would drag the needle across the record and queue the sound of an explosion. The show was wildly popular. When the duo offered membership cards to a kill-disco organization, ten thousand listeners called the station within a week to sign up. Dahl took the show on the road, packing a suburban Chicago nightclub with a "death to disco" rally. But what was so intimidating about people dancing in nightclubs? Why did rock fans in Chicago hate disco so much?

Because it *sucked.* That's why.

The songs, the dancing, the roller-skating, the disco balls, the heavy makeup—it was all so massive, so goofy, and over the top. Andy Warhol, Studio 54, *Skatetown, USA*, "Disco Duck"—people were getting sick of this stuff. Besides, in order to make it with a lady, during the disco craze, a guy had to *learn how to dance.* And wear a fancy suit! It was an outrage. (It's also possible these rock fans hated disco because black and gay people liked it, although nobody talked about that in public.) Whatever the reason, the backlash was inevitable. Disco needed to be destroyed, and Dahl appointed himself the pied piper for this enraged crowd. He found a compatriot in twenty-eight-year-old Mike Veeck, a failed rock guitarist. "I loathed disco," Veeck said later.

Veeck happened to have an excellent forum for what would become the decisive event in Dahl's campaign: Comiskey Park, home of the Chicago White Sox. He was the son of then–Sox owner Bill Veeck, a seventy-five-year-old baseball legend. (When he owned the Cleveland Indians, the elder Veeck made Larry Doby the first black player in the American League.) With his father's permission, Mike Veeck and Dahl hatched a plan. On July 12, 1979, the White Sox were to play a night doubleheader against the Detroit Tigers at Comiskey. In the days leading up to the game, Dahl announced on the air that White Sox fans could enter the park for just 98 cents if they brought a disco record. Sister Sledge, Bee Gees, "I Will Survive"—it didn't matter. Everything would be obliterated.

The Sox averaged sixteen thousand fans at their home games that year, and they expected a few thousand people more than usual because of Dahl's stunt. They were completely unprepared for the army of fifty-nine thousand fans who showed up at the first game, carrying stacks of Bee Gees albums in their arms. Another fifteen thousand spilled along the surrounding South Side streets. They wore Led Zeppelin and Black Sabbath T-shirts, smashed bottles on the ground, smoked God-knows-what and chanted their almighty rallying cry: *"Disco sucks!"* In the stands, sharp-edged records flew like Frisbees. The players were clearly unsettled. The Tigers' Ron LeFlore wore his batting helmet in center field during the first game.

Dahl was surprised. And nervous. He had prepared for a monumental failure, not thousands of minions waiting for him to lead. Wearing a green army helmet the size of a fishbowl and a matching jacket with wide lapels, looking like a hippie Colonel Klink, Dahl arrived in center field in a military Jeep between the two games.

"I didn't think that anyone would even show up," Dahl says today. The Sox fireworks crew had rigged crates of records to explode with dynamite. He managed a few incomprehensible screams and his best anti-disco catchphrase from the radio (borrowed from a popular *Second City* TV sketch of the time): "That blowed up *real* good!" It worked. Unwittingly, he rallied ten thousand fans to storm the field, climbing down the foul poles and turning the record explosion in center field into a raging bonfire. Sox officials hesitated to call in the cops for fear of stirring things up even further. They allowed fans to linger, shredding the dirt and turf beyond recognition. The senior Veeck and legendary baseball announcer Harry Caray impotently attempted to exhort people back to their seats over the loudspeaker. For thirty-seven minutes, Sox fans, disco haters, and all-purpose rabble-rousers united in a massive jamboree of public destruction.

One such Sox fan was a twenty-one-year-old South Sider who'd been sitting in the upper deck with six or seven of his friends from the neighborhood. One by one, they jumped over the barrier, then climbed fifteen feet down to the field. They were delighted to discover they could slide unmolested into third base and casually pick up bats and other paraphernalia their favorite players had left behind. The man was Michael Clarke Duncan, a stockroom employee at the Carson Pirie Scott department store downtown. You may recognize the name: He later broke into Hollywood and earned an Oscar nomination for his work as the hulking, doomed prisoner in *The Green Mile*, costarring Tom Hanks. None of the many TV newsclips of the scene captures Duncan, which is surprising, given that he stood 6'5", wore a huge Afro, and was one of the few black people on the field.

Duncan was also perhaps the only disco fan on the Comiskey field that night. "I loved disco music back then!" recalls Duncan, now fifty-one, a veteran of more than seventy movies, including *The Island* and *Sin City*. "I had the four-inch-wide shoes, the belt buckle, the tight pants with no pockets." He'd been to tons of all-night-dancing clubs, and his sister often let him borrow her stacks of Donna Summer records.

"After Steve Dahl did that, nobody wanted to wear the platform shoes in the following weeks. Nobody wanted to wear the bell-bottoms," Duncan says. "People were like, 'Ah, that's getting kind of old now, things are kind of changing.'"

Dahl, who went to work the next morning expecting to be fired, wound up a bigger celebrity than ever. The week of the demolition, July 8 to 14, Chic's "Good Times" hit the Top 10—one of six disco songs to do so. On August 18, three disco singles were in the Top 10. By September 22, the number dropped to zero. "It seemed pretty immediate. Bars that had gone disco immediately seemed to turn back into rock 'n' roll clubs. Live music began to thrive again," Dahl says. "All I know is that the Bee Gees and KC, of KC and the Sunshine Band, are still mad at me."

Disco sucks! Disco sucks!

It was the new mantra of white America. As a thirteen-year-old suburban Who fan, I myself carried a gold D.R.E.A.D. card, which stood for Detroit Rock-and-rollers Engaged in the Abolition of Disco. The local rock station, WRIF-FM, gave them out at concerts. My older brother, a station intern, brought them home by the boxload. Back then, they were hard-to-find totems of coolness. I must have owned three hundred of the damn things, not counting the fifty or so I gave out to kids on the block who suddenly wanted to be my best friends.

Almost thirty years later, the idea of furiously hating disco seems ridiculous. I dumped my D.R.E.A.D. cards in the trash during college, and I now hear Donna Summer and Chic as links in the musical chain between early-'70s funk and soul and the beginnings of rap music. Vicki Sue Robinson's "Turn the Beat Around"? Hot Chocolate's "You Sexy Thing"? It's incredible to me that rock fans would actually *riot* for the right to hear REO Speedwagon and Foreigner on their local airwaves instead. Anyway, disco's grooves never really died, they just went underground, in the form of house music and other big-city warehouse happenings of the early '80s. (That's not to mention every wedding in the universe, including my own, where the Village People's "Y.M.C.A." has been a dance-floor prerequisite.) Steve "Silk" Hurley, who as a high school DJ was souping up Chicago dances at the time of Dahl's demolition, remembers wanting to track down the records that hadn't blown up real good. "Most DJs never stopped," says Hurley, a Grammy-winning remixer and veteran DJ. "It didn't affect me at all. I thought it was a joke."

But in 1979, disco had rammed headlong into the wall of the brick house. "People were trying to murder it," says Gloria Gaynor, who had the misfortune of peaking, with "I Will Survive," in the year of the backlash. "Someone was saying, 'I'm bringing in rock acts and every time I try to promote my record they're putting Gloria Gaynor or Donna Summer in my slot. And this sucks. *Disco* sucks.' I began to think it was an economic decision."

The reason disco died *was* economic, but it wasn't really a decision. As always, record labels went where the sales were, and for much of the late 1970s, that was disco. Soon, the boom made executives complacent when they should have been scouting for new talent. "The labels should have lost *more* money. They should have fucking *closed* for what they did," says Nicky Siano, who used to DJ in drag as two thousand dancers writhed all night at his influential The Gallery club in New York City. "Between 1974 and 1977, any record that had the word *disco* on it would just *sell*. People didn't have to hear it. They just took it and bought it. When the record companies saw that happening, they put any old piece of garbage in that wrapper. People started getting burnt, and they got really pissed off. And they stopped buying."

When disco fans stopped buying, record stores around the United States suddenly found themselves inundated with millions of unwanted LPs. The stores had to return them to the labels. It was a recipe for music-business disaster, and in 1979, labels started to crash. Sales plummeted that year by almost 11 percent after more than a decade of growth. The first to go down, in spectacular fashion, was over-the-top Casablanca Records.

Casablanca had been founded six years earlier by Neil Bogart, who had an ear for fads and a gift for burning through a lot of money. Born Neil Bogatz, he was a postal worker's son who learned show business by singing and dancing in the Catskills. His first industry job was ad salesman for the trade journal *Cash Box*, and by the end of the '60s, he'd worked his way up to president of a new label, Buddah Records. In its first year, Buddah made $5.6 million, thanks to bubblegum hits like the Ohio Express's "Yummy, Yummy, Yummy" and the 1910 Fruit Gum Company's "Indian Giver."

Bogart's specialty was elaborate, shameless promotions—some worked and some imploded. While at Buddah, he tailed a prominent radio program director through the streets of New York City in a rented limousine, using a loudspeaker on top of the car to blast the names of his acts. He also signed one of the most unique recording acts of 1969, the New York Mets, and dragged the entire team, many of them drunk, into the studio for an all-night session after they won the World Series. Buddah managed to release this album the day of the city's ticker-tape parade for the Miracle Mets, and an album of gimmick songs like a version of the *Damn Yankees* show tune "You Gotta Have Heart" sold nearly 1.3 million copies. Bogart also botched a new act, Elephant's Memory, a rock band that would later back John Lennon during his politically active phase in the early 1970s. Bogart surrounded the band at one showcase with inflatable elephants and various barnyard animals, and was surprised when they drew derision from the crowd.

Bogart flirted with bankruptcy until the mid-1970s, when he met Italian producer Giorgio Moroder, who introduced him to a gospel-turned-disco singer named Donna Summer. With singles like Summer's "Love to Love You Baby," Casablanca rode the disco boom hard, going platinum on just about every record it threw into the marketplace. But more than songs or sales, Casablanca was legendary for its excesses. Quaalude dealing was rampant, as were elaborate food fights at the fancy restaurant across the street. Bogart equipped all fourteen of its executives with brand-new Mercedeses. He presented Donna Summer, when she flew from Germany to New York to promote her *Love to Love You Baby* album, with a life-size cake that looked exactly like her. It was even the same *size*. The cake, according to Fredric Dannen's book *Hit Men*, took two seats in a cross-country airplane and a freezer ambulance to get to Summer's performance at the Penta discotheque in New York. The company's executives were out of their minds. Promo man Danny Davis, who didn't do drugs of any kind, famously recalled talking to a radio programmer on the phone while a colleague trashed the stuff on his desk with a golf club, then lit the desk on fire.

"Almost anything could have happened at Casablanca," says Bill Aucoin, who managed Casablanca's most famous rock act, KISS, in those early days. "The first offices were a converted home with a pool house. If you went to the pool house at any time, day or night, as a record promoter or a DJ, you probably could get laid at any moment."

"[The office] was being used for nonsocial purposes," is David Braun's euphemism of choice. He would know. A veteran music business attorney who represented Bob Dylan and Michael Jackson, Braun moved from Los Angeles to New York to become president of Poly-Gram Records in 1981. PolyGram had purchased half of Casablanca for $10 million in 1977, thinking the disco hits would continue. Unfortunately for the label, Summer broke her contract and fled to industry mogul David Geffen's new record company. KISS's hits dried up—for a while. New acts like over-the-top rock band Angel, whose members would emerge from pods on stage, possibly inspiring a key scene in *This Is Spinal Tap*, never caught on. Then there was the tricky little matter of Casablanca executives shipping hundreds of thousands of records at a time, with little regard for public demand, and being unprepared when stores returned them. (This problem was common in the industry.) And as Steve Dahl's demolition suggested, the public suddenly wasn't quite as enamored of disco as it used to be. Braun had to clean up Bogart's $30 million mess. These missteps almost killed PolyGram Records, whose market share had jumped from 5 percent to 20 percent in the disco era. For a few years, it had been the world's largest record label.

Casablanca imploded, and so did the industry. (And so did Bogart, who died in 1982 at age 38 of cancer.) Although record companies' sales had climbed from just under $1 billion a year in 1959 to a *Saturday Night Fever*–fueled record of $4.1 billion in 1978, the antidisco backlash lingered from 1979 to 1982. CBS Records laid off two thousand employees and drastically cut its artist roster and budgets. Susan Blond, a publicity executive at CBS-owned Epic Records, says the company lost three hundred employees on her first day. Her staff eventually disappeared entirely. Blond's boss, CBS' flamboyant attack-dog chairman, Walter Yetnikoff, declared the industry "in the intensive care ward."

But then came the savior.

THE FORMER MOTOWN child superstar arrived in a black leather jacket spilling over with belt buckles. He danced like a backwards angel, screeched and squealed, and—inexplicably—wore one white glove. In late 1982, Michael Jackson almost magically restored the music industry's superstar clout by releasing one record.

Jackson didn't do it on his own. The most important music business guy behind the success of *Thriller* was Yetnikoff, a coke-addicted, fast-living, bomb-throwing, disrespectful, disloyal provocateur. He grew up in Brooklyn, the son of a painter with a hot temper and a sympathetic mother who cleaned his wounds whenever his father knocked him around. His grandparents were Jewish immigrants from Austria or Poland—they were never quite clear which—and they spoke Polish and Yiddish around the house. They called Walter "Velvel," his Yiddish name. With his mother's encouragement, Yetnikoff picked up garbage and made city deliveries on nights and weekends to put himself through Columbia Law School. His first job out of college was at a New York law firm, Rosenman & Colin, where he met a young lawyer named Clive Davis. Harvard-educated and imaginative, Davis had tired of the legal business and taken a job as counsel for CBS Records down the street. Davis called Yetnikoff in early 1961 to offer him a job.

The head of CBS was Goddard Lieberson, an Eastman School of Music–trained man in impeccable tweed suits. He and Yetnikoff couldn't have been more different, but the crude Yetnikoff befriended the erudite Lieberson. Though Yetnikoff called Lieberson "Potted Lieberfarb" behind his back, the relationship stuck, and Velvel climbed through the CBS ranks around the same time the Beatles turned rock 'n' roll into a gigantic worldwide commodity. Through the 1970s, following Davis's lead, Yetnikoff grew rich off Miles Davis, Bruce Springsteen, Earth, Wind, and Fire, and Barbra Streisand. By the 1980s, in his own words, he'd grown into a "wild man," the bearded, squinty-eyed tough talker whose autobiography, *Howling at the Moon*, begins with this (fictional) sentence: "After her third orgasm, Jackie O looked at me with a mixture of gratitude and awe."

Yetnikoff was smart. To win the respect of Mick Jagger at a Paris wine bar, he calculated the value-added tax in France on a cocktail napkin. Jagger, a London School of Economics dropout, subsequently signed the Rolling Stones to a CBS record deal. Yetnikoff was also known for throwing outrageous tantrums. One of his legendary office exchanges with Larry Tisch, head of CBS Records's parent company, television monolith CBS Inc., ended with Yetnikoff threatening bodily harm and pounding his fist on the table. During a 1975 contract renegotiation with Paul Simon and his attorney, the mogul and the singer-songwriter's aggressive bargaining escalated into a full-blown argument, and Yetnikoff banned Simon from CBS Records's building for life. "Walter Yetnikoff was crazy and wild and weird like a fox," says George Vradenburg, former general counsel for CBS Inc. "He could yell and scream and throw things, and at the same time wink at me."

And Yetnikoff was fiercely loyal to his artists. He helped a post-*Thriller* Jackson weasel out of a promised duet with his brother Jermaine. Yetnikoff once referred to Bruce Springsteen's very serious 1982 masterpiece *Nebraska* as *Omaha*—in front of him, no less—but agreed to release it, even if it didn't sell, to make Springsteen happy. Which he did. (And it didn't sell.)

He cheated on his wife with his secretary. He cheated on his wife with a fellow music-business type he called Boom Boom. He snorted copious amounts of coke. He openly rebelled against his superiors at CBS. He tried to get Mike Wallace of CBS's *60 Minutes* fired for investigating the music business. He engineered coups. "If anything," he said after an NBC payola exposé, which pegged him as a cokehead, "I became more defiant, more arrogant, more contemptuous of my adversaries."

But as the fast-living Yetnikoff suffered through the record industry's postdisco crash, he was growing antsy. Jackson's last album, *Off the Wall*, which had sold 8 million copies in 1979, was one of the few bright lights in a terrible year. Soon that minor gold rush had faded. By the end of 1981, CBS Records took in a little more than $1 billion, its worst yearly earnings since 1971. So Yetnikoff pressured his biggest star. With just months left in 1982, he gave Jackson and producer Quincy Jones a deadline: Finish a new album, and make it a blockbuster, by Christmas. They weren't happy about having to rush, but they obeyed and finished the final *Thriller* mixes in a month. They turned them in to Epic Records, for release just before Thanksgiving.

"I told you I'd do it," Jackson told Yetnikoff. "I told you I'd outdo *Off the Wall*."

Yetnikoff responded: "You delivered. You delivered like a mother-fucker."

Jackson: "Please don't use that word, Walter."

Yetnikoff: "You delivered like an angel. Archangel Michael."

Jackson: "That's better. Now will you promote it?"

Yetnikoff: "Like a motherfucker."

Thriller, like *Off the Wall* before it, wasn't just brilliant music—it was brilliant business. Michael Jackson had effectively replaced disco by absorbing the dying genre into his own brand of dance music. Steve Dahl's Chicago demolition-turned-riot may have killed disco commercially, but the fans were still alive—and Jackson was a master of providing the slinky rhythms to warm their hearts. The melodies catch in your head in the perfect way. The bass lines sound like poisonous snakes. The rebellious anger in "Beat It" and "Billie Jean" is palpable but never over the top.

It was the right album at the right time: All seven of its singles landed in the Top 10, the album lasted a ridiculous thirty-seven weeks at No. 1 on the *Billboard* charts, and it went on to sell more than 51 million copies—the best-selling album in the world until the Eagles' *Their Greatest Hits* surpassed it (in the United States, anyway) in 2000. *Thriller* singlehandedly rescued CBS from its late '70s doldrums—the company's net income jumped 26 percent in 1983, to $187 million—pushing fans back into record stores and propping up the industry.

"*Thriller* was like Moses carrying all the Jews across the Red Sea,"* says Lee Solters, a veteran Los Angeles music publicist who worked on the album's campaign. "He rescued the music industry. The music industry suddenly became alive again." And as *Thriller* climbed the charts, it awarded even more power to Yetnikoff, the star maker with a direct pipeline into the reclusive Jackson's mysterious personal life.

Thriller's singles took off on the radio, beginning with Top 40 stations and crossing over to rock thanks to Eddie Van Halen's guitar solo on "Beat It." Then Jackson's people produced a video for "Billie Jean." It was sharp and clean, with Jackson in a pink shirt and red bow tie

---

* Michael Jackson's personal life has largely buried what made him such a magnetic performer in the *Thriller* era. Even on eBay, it's almost impossible to dig up copies of the old, celebratory Michael books: *Moonwalk*, a ghostwritten autobiography, is so long out of print that my attempt to purchase it on Amazon produced instead *Moonwalker*, a kids' coloring book and concert-film tie-in, in which a leather-jacketed Jackson saves the universe from aliens.

dancing all over the mean streets, and seemed perfect for a new music cable channel that had made instant stars out of nobodies like the Stray Cats and Billy Idol.

But there was a problem: MTV didn't play videos by black artists.

MILES DAVIS COMPLAINED about the lack of black stars on the video channel, formed in 1981, which was rapidly growing its influence and power within the record industry. So did Stevie Wonder. Rick James, who had a smash radio hit with "Super Freak," publicly railed that MTV was "taking black people back four hundred years." Nobody at MTV adequately explained this unspoken policy in public. The closest thing to a defense came from the channel's only black VJ, J. J. Jackson, who told Davis at a party that the channel's format was rock 'n' roll, and most rock stations didn't play black artists, either, other than the late Jimi Hendrix.

Michael Jackson smashed through MTV's color line, but it was Yetnikoff who solved the problem behind the scenes. "I was the instigator, I guess," recalls Ron Weisner, Jackson's early comanager. "I took the finished 'Billie Jean' to MTV and they refused to air it. So I went to Columbia Records. Walter Yetnikoff and I went to [powerful CBS Inc. chief] Bill Paley. He called MTV and said, 'This video is on the air by end of business today or else Columbia Records is no longer in business with you.' One day changed the whole thing."

MTV cofounder Bob Pittman remembers the history a little differently. Then again, that story has been told and retold so many times, by so many people with conflicting interests and clashing egos, that it's impossible to nail down the facts. "I'll give you my story, which I hope is the true story, but God only knows," says Pittman, who would later be a top executive for AOL Time Warner and today runs a New York City media-investment firm called the Pilot Group. He'd heard about Rick James's complaints, but the "Super Freak" video, with its very kinky girls in Lycra and lace, didn't meet MTV's pre-Madonna standards. "It seems ridiculous today," Pittman admits. In fact, he says, the channel couldn't wait to play the *Thriller* videos.

Either way, the combination of MTV and Michael Jackson was a one-two commercial punch that began the resuscitation of the record industry. When MTV first went on the air on August 1, 1981, with the Buggles' "Video Killed the Radio Star," it was the product of a unique brain trust of frustrated and slumming music-business types waiting for something big and interesting to come along. John Lack, a thirty-three-year-old rock fan and former CBS news radio executive, first came up with the idea. Marketing whiz Tom Freston was an advertising executive who'd worked on the G.I. Joe account before fleeing the toy business to hike through the Sahara with a girlfriend, then landed in Asia to run a fabric-export company. And John Sykes, who had been working at Epic Records, was responsible for the wildly effective promotional ideas. During MTV's early days, he offered a teen Van Halen fan forty-eight hours of "pure decadence" (i.e., Jack Daniel's and groupies) with the band. The slickest of the group, by far, was Pittman, son of a Mississippi Methodist minister. He'd begun his career as a fifteen-year-old DJ and worked up to program director for a planned cable-TV experiment called the Movie Channel.

Lack received a visit one day from Elektra Records founder and Warner Music executive Jac Holzman, who showed up in his office with a stack of videotapes. Some were of Holzman's old discovery, the Doors, who'd recorded an amateurish $1,000 film for "Break On Through" and aired it on afternoon TV dance shows. Others were surprisingly innovative clips, like "Rio," a psychedelic collection of rainbow-colored effects set to music by Michael Nesmith, formerly of the Monkees.

The clips gave Lack an idea. *The* idea. Music on television had been around for years in the form of weekly shows, from *American Bandstand* to *Album Tracks*. But nobody had ever attempted a twenty-four-hour music-video channel. Everything happened quickly after that. Lack, Sykes, Pittman, and Freston put on suits and ties, fired up Olivia Newton-John videos for middle-of-the-road executives at parent companies Warner and American Express and came out of the meetings with $25 million in financial backing. They scooped up as many old videos as they could find, and tried to coax all the major record label executives to send them new ones—for free. That part of the plan was not popular.

"John Sykes and I would go out to the record companies, and we would take a whole presentation: 'Look, the record companies are in the doldrums. The pitch is, you're losing money for the first time in decades, radio stations have very tight playlists, and when they do play your new stuff they don't identify what it is,'" Pittman recalls. "We said, 'We're going to play more music than they are, and when we play it we're going to put on the name of the artist, the album name, the song name, and the label. And it'll cost you nothing to give them to us. If this happens to work, we will change the record industry.'"

A few label chiefs were actually enthusiastic. Doug Morris, head of Atlantic Records at the time, signed on right away. Warner Bros. Records's Mo Ostin and Elektra Records's Joe Smith soon followed his lead. So did Gil Friesen, then president of the influential independent label A&M. But Sid Sheinberg, president of MCA-Universal, declared at an industry convention: "This guy Lack is out of his fucking mind." CBS's Yetnikoff shared Sheinberg's view—he still rued the day record labels had started giving radio their music for free some fifty years earlier. But eventually Yetnikoff's underlings and CBS's biggest-name artists started pressuring Yetnikoff. He had no choice but to sign on.

"I was a skeptic," says Joe Smith, now in his late seventies, retired and living in Beverly Hills. "I said, 'Now, why would anybody want to buy their record off of a video?' You're never that eager to give away your product to anybody." But labels agreed to part with a few small videos, and when an unknown band, Duran Duran, became a superstar purely through MTV airplay, Smith was convinced. "We said, 'Whoa! There's something happening here.' They convinced me. [Veteran songwriter] Van Dyke Parks, the head of [Warner's] video department—he was a lunatic, stoned twenty-six hours a day, he was making videos with Randy Newman and some of our other artists. We were investing money like crazy." Before long, David Bowie, Mick Jagger, and Pete Townshend were lining up to shout "I want my MTV!" on the air. Soon, other artists were jumping on board, too, like Tom Petty, Peter Gabriel, Talking Heads, and, most dramatically, a young Bay City, Michigan, singer and dancer named Madonna Louise Ciccone.

MUSIC STARS WERE huge again. They were *on TV*! The money from record sales, which had dropped precipitously in 1979 and wobbled up and down through the early 1980s, jumped 4.7 percent in 1983. Out of disco's ashes had risen a new sales monster, *Thriller,* which established the video-driven blueprint for fellow superstars Madonna, Bruce Springsteen, and Prince. "Like everything else, when the tide comes in, all the ships go up," says Dick Asher, who at the time was a top CBS Records executive and long-suffering Walter Yetnikoff underling. "It was not only good for CBS but good for the whole industry."

Asher didn't know it yet, but while the record industry had built gold-standard software (the music) and a revolutionary new international marketing tool (MTV), it still needed new hardware. And that was coming.

Veteran artist attorney David Braun began the 1980s by negotiating, on behalf of Michael Jackson, an unprecedented 42 percent of the wholesale price on each US album sold. The deal with CBS Records was extraordinary, given most superstars received 10 percent to 20 percent at the time. In 1981, Braun quit his law firm to become president of PolyGram Records. He lasted less than a year. He had spent so much of his career trying to secure the biggest possible advances for his artists, and hadn't seriously considered the constraints record labels were under when they'd tried to tamp down his numbers. As head of a major label, he was suddenly learning those constraints firsthand—and he didn't like them. But one day, during his short time at PolyGram, he showed up twenty minutes late to a historic meeting. Back then the label was owned by Philips and Siemens, two European companies that specialized in home electronics. An emissary from Siemens showed up at precisely 9:00 one morning to meet with the PolyGram staff about a small, round, shiny, silver object that stored data digitally. Nothing special, right? Braun had been on the phone with some artist managers, and by the time he straggled into the meeting, the Siemens guy was just about finished. "Unlike the Americans, when the Germans say 9:00, they *mean* 9:00," Braun says.

That meeting was the beginning of the compact disc business, although it wasn't like record companies saw the future and jumped in right away. Several label chiefs, including Walter Yetnikoff and Sid Sheinberg, had their misgivings. But once they did: boom. "I left as the compact disc was coming in," Braun says. "And the CD saved the industry."

Chapter 1
1983–1986

Jerry Shulman's Frisbee: How the Compact Disc Rebuilt the Record Business

JAMES T. RUSSELL hated the pops and crackles in his Bach, Beethoven, and Bartók records.

It was the early 1960s. Rock 'n' roll was young. Frank Sinatra was still the King of Pop. Russell clung to the classical recordings he'd been buying since high school. Not a single radio station played this type of music in Richland, Washington, where Russell lived. He became obsessed with preserving his LPs so they wouldn't deteriorate into static. Like some audiophiles of the time, he tried using a cactus spine instead of a steel stylus on his record player. That worked OK, but he still heard the infernal snapping and crackling. "I'd been tinkering with how to get better sound out of an LP for fifteen years," he says. "I decided: 'This isn't going to work. We need a better record.'"

Russell was no ordinary audiophile. Born in Bremerton, Washington, he had become fascinated with radios during grade school—building them, listening to them, figuring out how the electricity worked inside. One day his older sister suggested he would enjoy physics in high school. And sure enough: "Pow!" he recalls. "That was the *world*. Everything is based on physics. And that was that." At Reed College in Portland, he plunged into anything involving instruments—computers, optics, chemistry—although he got a degree in physics, naturally. His first job out of college was at the Atomic Energy Commission's Hanford Nuclear Plant. Russell's job was basically to help engineers when they ran into technical snags. Soon he started inventing stuff, like computer controls for a test reactor.

In 1965, Battelle Memorial Institute took over from General Electric as the manager of Russell's lab. He had hardly been shy over the previous few years, in complaining about the Bach and Beethoven records—or broadcasting his determination to do something about them. Fortunately, his new bosses were slightly more receptive to his crazy ideas, even if they had nothing to do with nuclear physics.

Russell's home hi-fi, like all music systems of the time, was based on analog sound—a needle inscribed each curvy sound wave into the grooves of a vinyl record. Taken together, and played on a phonograph with a stylus moving in the groove, these waves added up to music. But the phonograph had no way of keeping out dust and other foreign particles. Which meant static—Russell's nemesis. He juggled the possibilities in his mind. He visualized exactly what he wanted to build. Then he wrote it all down, in an official Battelle lab notebook.

He had one big idea to solve the problem. *Optics.* Who needed a needle? Russell would use a beam of light to read his new musical discs. Still, he wasn't the first inventor to run into frustration with this idea. The whole "mechanical-optical structure," as he called it, was too complicated to work in the average living room. And the costs, for hi-fi enthusiasts, could have added up to $15,000 or $20,000. That was far too expensive.

What he needed was a cheap way to record music onto a disc the size of a 45 rpm single. He considered several techniques, including one involving frequency modulation, commonly used in FM radio, but they all relied on old-fashioned analog technology. The static would still drive him crazy. Then he came across another helpful science: *pulse-code modulation*, or PCM. An ITT scientist was the first to suggest this idea in 1937, and the legendary Bell Laboratories electrical engineer Claude E. Shannon developed the blueprint for future use in the late 1940s. When Russell started his own experiments, the telephone industry was already tinkering with PCM. The idea was to take an analog signal, like something you'd hear on a record player or the radio, and convert it into a series of microscopic blips—ones and zeroes. It turned out to be the key technology for digitizing sound. With digital, a symphony could be recorded not as cumbersome sound waves but as groups of tiny binary dots.

This technology eventually became known as "red book," the heart of every compact disc. Play combinations of these tiny ones and zeroes 44,100 times per second and you start to hear music.

Russell knew it would be a long road to build this kind of musical disc. "Just about each time I came up with a solution to the problem at hand," he says, "there were more problems to solve." To turn a symphony score into digital bits, for example, he would need to create hundreds of thousands of these bits. They would never fit on a disc small enough for home hi-fis. So he decided to make the bits incredibly tiny—the size of a micron, or one-millionth of a meter. That would require a microscope. And even if he did manage to come up with such a disc, he'd have to devise an intricate error-correction system so each disc could play all the music flawlessly. But if he did . . . imagine the possibilities. Records that sounded just as perfect every time you played them. Needles that didn't wear out. Discs that didn't scratch or warp over time.

One Saturday when he had the house to himself and he could really focus on his work, everything clicked—optics, pulse-code modulation, digital, a precision-mechanical system, microns, plastic discs. "Well," Russell says, "it seemed pretty straightforward to me at the time."

He proposed the big idea to his bosses at Battelle on March 9, 1965, and they told him to go for it. Over the next year and a half, he would build a contraption that worked roughly like the compact disc players that still sit in cars and living rooms around the world. In an early Battelle public-relations photograph of Russell standing next to his machine, both of them look like relics from another era. Russell has dark, slicked-back hair, a widow's peak, glasses, a dark suit coat, and a thickly knotted tie. The machine next to him is a foot and a half long and a foot tall, made of thick pieces of metal. It could be a CT scan for a small animal—large and boxy on one end, with a cylindrical piece in the middle and various wires and rods extending to a point on the other. The "discs" are clear, rectangular glass plates the size of paperback novels. "It's all very well that I built a patent, but there's lots of patents out there that are worthless," he says. "The fact that we were able to build a laboratory prototype added enormous credence to the whole idea."

Russell is careful not to refer to himself as the inventor of the compact disc. In fact, the early history is somewhat confusing. Russell acknowledges that two electronics giants, Sony and Philips, came up with their own discs independently, sometime after he invented the technology. But back in September 1966, when Russell filed the sixth patent of his forty-year, fifty-three-patent career, he became the first inventor to create the fundamental technology that would lie at the heart of every compact disc. The US Patent Office gave him the patent in 1970. It is unclear just how closely the Sony and Philips engineers paid attention to Russell's work. In any event, decades later, the owner of his patents would establish that Russell was the first to get this far with CD technology, winning a huge US court ruling in the early 1990s.

But instead of wealth and fame, all James T. Russell received as a reward was a stack of patent papers and, from his employer, a one-foot-tall crystal obelisk recognizing his work in optical-digital recording technology. So why don't all the people who keep hundreds of CDs lovingly alphabetized throughout their homes remember Russell as the Thomas Edison of the digital age? "Long, sad story," says the retired physicist, seventy-five, from the basement lab of his home in Bellevue, Washington.

In the early 1970s, the funding dried up at Battelle. Nobody had the cash to help an obsessive nuclear physicist invent a better record. "It was very frustrating," Russell recalls. He pitched it to companies, and was told that his invention involved too many different high-tech ideas that couldn't possibly be compatible. Besides, if it was so great, IBM would have already done it.

Russell didn't want to give up on his idea, despite five years of frustration. And although strapped for cash, Battelle didn't want to give up, either. In fall 1971, a New York venture capitalist, Eli Jacobs, responded to a request from the lab and contacted Russell about his invention. The two agreed to sidestep into video, and Russell successfully grafted digital recordings of TV shows onto glass plates similar to the audio ones he'd come up with several years earlier. (Russell still keeps a stack of these plates in his basement lab.) They sent out 2,500 brochures inviting everybody to Richland—the press and big companies with pockets deep enough to license the technology. More than one hundred people accepted the invitation. In 1974, Philips and Sony sent reps to his lab. The Philips guy told Russell the company wasn't working on optical-digital technology and, in his opinion, never would. A few months later, an Eli Jacobs rep flew to Eindhoven, Holland, to try to sell the invention to Philips, the huge Dutch electronics company that would help bring the compact disc to the worldwide market. What he was describing, the Philips people told him, was great for computers, but it just wouldn't work for entertainment.

What Russell didn't know was that, in 1974, Sony and Philips were in fact working jointly on their own versions of the technology he had already patented. Using lasers developed at MIT and Bell Labs in the 1960s, both companies independently hit upon a way of recording and listening to digital music. Sony had built a refrigerator-sized, several-hundred-pound contraption called the X-12DTC. It was even bigger and clumsier than Russell's awkward-looking device.

"[Russell] was one of the pioneers. He did excellent work essentially all alone," says K. A. "Kees" Schouhamer Immink, a longtime engineer for Philips. "Philips just had bigger pockets. They could invest billions of dollars just to do that."

By the 1980s, Russell's optical-digital technology was completely out of his hands. Battelle had licensed his patents to Eli Jacobs. When Jacobs's Digital Recording ran out of money, the venture capitalist sold all of his company's patents—including Russell's—to a Toronto start-up for $1 million in 1985.

The executives at this company, Optical Recording Corporation, knew what they had. ORC's savvy, opportunistic owner, John Adamson, saw that Russell's patents—now *his* patents—could be worth hundreds of millions of dollars. He brought the patent papers and a couple of attorneys to dozens of meetings with Sony and Philips reps in Tarrytown, New York, Tokyo, Osaka, and elsewhere. Naturally, the lawyers from these gigantic electronics companies argued that their own patents came first. Although Adamson's company was quickly running out of money and close to bankruptcy, his people persevered. In February 1988, well into the CD era, they convinced Sony and Philips to pay him royalties; by the end of that year, ORC was flush with $10 million.

Buttressed with cash and confidence, Adamson and his lawyers shifted their focus to CD manufacturers—major record labels—beginning with massive Time Warner and its subsidiary, Warner Music. ORC sued for patent infringement in 1990. The media conglomerate's lawyers were fierce. "Nobody's ever recognized [Russell] as being an inventor of the CD," Michael Rackman, a patent attorney who represented Time Warner, says today. "Let's suppose that I invent a new way to communicate, and you invent a tank and you put my communications in the tank. Are you going to say I invented the tank?" But the jury was unconvinced. In 1992, it ruled for the Toronto company and ordered Time Warner to pay $30 million. Other record labels then agreed to pay royalties, for sums Adamson won't disclose. Not a bad return for ORC's original investment in James T. Russell's patents.

Russell, however, received not a cent.

Today, Russell spends his time inventing new devices, consulting for companies, and playing with his seven grandchildren. He dreams about cities with lots stacked upon lots poking more than half a mile into the sky. Why not? Digital was once considered a loopy idea, too.

On its official website, Philips credits its own engineers for inventing the CD. Sony Corp.'s official 1996 history *Genryu* credits researcher Heitaro Nakajima, who "must have been one of the first to actually produce digital sound." But documents from the Patent Office and US District Court in Wilmington, Delaware, clearly establish Russell as the first person to come up with the blueprint. As he predicted in 1966, this would lead to the very same world-changing technology used in DVDs and CD-ROMs. Russell, who lives in a hilltop house that overlooks the Cascade Mountains, is not bitter. "But a little credit would have been nice," he says. "And maybe a little money."

UNLIKE JAMES T. RUSSELL, the engineers at Sony Corp. had a powerful benefactor who immediately recognized the beauty—and the dollar signs—in digital optical technology. His name was Norio Ohga, and he hadn't intended to go into business. He was an opera singer, studying at the Tokyo National University of Fine Arts and Music. One day in the early 1950s, Tokyo Telecommunications showed up at his college to record a symphony with a newfangled tape recorder. Ohga had never seen anything like it. He was so smitten with the new technology that he went before the faculty senate and persuaded the university to buy one of these machines for 140,000 yen—the equivalent of a year's tuition for most students on campus. It was a highly unusual situation—students rarely addressed the faculty this way—but Ohga won them over with his charm and confidence.

Soon he started a correspondence with Tokyo Telecommunications. He wrote up technical diagrams to improve its tape recorder. Impressed and taken aback, founders Masaru Ibuka and Akio Morita invited Ohga to join the company. They courted him for a few years, as he focused on his singing and traveled through Asia and Europe. In 1959, he relented.

Ohga would rise through the ranks at the company, which eventually became Sony Corp. Given his classical music background, he took a particular interest in his engineers' work with digital recording. When he learned they were developing an "audio laser disc," he immediately made it a top company priority. In fact, one of Sony's top researchers, Heitaro Nakajima, had been working on digital audio since roughly 1967, when he headed the technical division of NHK, Japan's public broadcasting company. He accepted a job at Sony in the early 1970s, and (perhaps unbeknownst to him) followed Russell's tracks for the next several years. By 1976, Sony's team of engineers had come up with the X-12DTC digital-recording behemoth—too big, of course. Within another two years they presented Ohga with a laser audio disc about the size of an LP record, holding 13 hours and 20 minutes of digital sound. Ohga immediately recognized it would cost the company more than $1 million to produce just one. He told the engineers to try again.

Meanwhile, Philips was making progress on the same idea. The company was still reeling from Laservision, its videodisc system, a titanic commercial flop. The company put out about 400 players, and received 200 returns by disappointed customers who'd been under the mistaken impression that it could record TV shows. (Would that we could go back in time and introduce desperate *All in the Family* fanatics to TiVo.) Philips's engineers had long pooh-poohed audio in favor of video, but after the Laservision debacle they were ready to try something different.

Ohga, seeing Sony's engineers couldn't solve certain problems on their own, like reducing the cumbersome size of every disc, decided to team up with one of his company's top competitors. He renewed an old friendship with Philips technical executive L. F. Ottens, and the two decided to collaborate. Soon a group of eight Sony and Philips engineers began meeting monthly in Tokyo and Eindhoven. At first they didn't get along. They haggled over who got to patent which technology, how many bits they should graft onto every disc, and whether the disc should match the length of a cassette tape or fit into the pocket of a suit jacket. They argued over maximum storage—an hour was considered standard, but Ohga would not budge on seventy-five minutes. "Ohga had a long discussion with [company founder Akio] Morita, and they both agreed: You could not introduce a CD that could not play Beethoven's Ninth in its entirety," recalls Mickey Schulhof, the American executive whom Sony sent to Eindhoven to work with lead Sony engineer Toshitada Doi and his Philips colleagues.

One October day, in Eindhoven, the engineers were in a conference room squabbling when the clear skies outside suddenly went gray. Thunder started blasting. One of the Philips scientists joked that the thunder represented their superiors' disapproval with all the arguing. Discussion wasn't quite so heated after that. The Philips people introduced the Sony people to Dutch gin. The Sony people introduced the Philips people to hot and cold sake. As anybody who owns the Red Hot Chili Peppers' epic *Bloodsugarsexmagik* on CD can attest, Ohga got his way on disc length—74 minutes, 42 seconds. Philips won on the physical width of the disc—12 centimeters.

"The meetings were absolutely fantastic," says Kees Immink, a member of the Philips team. "Our management let us just sit in one room and come out with ideas. You have coffee together. You have lunch together. We are still friends. Even after twenty-five years we have good days."

Ohga declared October 1982 the final deadline for introducing the disc and a joint Sony-Philips player to the consumer market. The deadline meant the team had to solve all kinds of tricky technical problems at the last minute, but they persevered. Sony's audio engineers brought bedding to their labs so they could work day and night. One of the first steps, in the middle of 1981, was unveiling a player with a catchy in-joke for a nickname—*goronta*, a Japanese term for "bulky" or "unwieldy."

The digital revolution was under way. But there was one more hurdle. The electronics people had to talk the world's biggest record executives into it.

NORIO OHGA KNEW record label executives weren't exactly going to welcome the compact disc like the Second Coming of the Beatles. They'd been getting rich for four decades off LPs, and this industry had a track record of brutally opposing advances like the 78 rpm single and, yes, the vinyl record itself. So Ohga arrived at the International Music Industry Conference, sponsored by *Billboard* magazine in Athens in May 1981, with the biggest guns he could think of. He had persuaded his favorite symphony conductor and early CD adopter, Herbert von Karajan of the Berlin Philharmonic, to let Sony digitally record several performances. Von Karajan was thrilled, calling it "superior to anything achievable with analog technology." Ohga brought these recordings to the conference and was confident he could win over even the stodgiest executive.

He was wrong. "Hostile. Very hostile," recalls Jan Timmer, the newly appointed head of Philips's software company, PolyGram Records, and one of the most effective champions of the compact disc. "I was fortunate there weren't any rotten tomatoes in the room. Otherwise, they would have thrown them at me." CBS's Yetnikoff, despite his ties to Sony, was especially furious. So were the executives from EMI Music, another prominent major label, which owned storied Capitol Records and the Beatles' catalog. In his book *Sony*, John Nathan refers to Jerry Moss, head of A&M Records, the fiercely independent label executive who had turned Carole King, the Carpenters, and the Police into international superstars, as "screaming" his opposition. "I made a bit of a small statement at the meeting," Moss says, almost sheepishly, today. "I liked the hardware and the whole ease of the CD. And I generally applauded the idea that Sony and Philips were getting together on this one piece of machinery. But I thought they could have done something to stop piracy." Piracy was the record industry's issue of the day. Throughout 1982, as the record and electronics industries were grappling with the technology that would fundamentally change their business and make them rich for decades, *Billboard* routinely trumpeted piracy headlines at the top of page one.

The electronics companies were determined. The stakes were high. Sony was reeling from its Betamax loss to VHS in the videocassette-format wars, and would in 1984 endure the worst sales year in its history. Philips was an electronics behemoth, with operations in sixty-five countries and revenues of $18.2 billion in 1980, but a *Business Week* story the following year reported the company "so far has not demonstrated that it will prove equal to the challenges facing it at home, much less abroad." The heads of these companies had enough vision to know the small, shiny disc would bail them out, possibly for years to come. They also knew they needed software to go with the CD hardware, or the whole enterprise would fall apart.

That meant music. And that meant record labels.

The stakes were high for record labels, too. In order to adopt the CD, they would have to shut down multimillion-dollar LP plants that had been operating for decades, which meant layoffs. They would have to reissue their entire catalogs in digital form. (Cassettes, for the time being, would survive; label executives believed two "carriers," an expensive one and a cheaper one, were the most the public could possibly handle without feeling swamped or confused.) They would have to persuade retailers to replace every wooden LP rack in every store with smaller racks that accommodated compact discs. And they would have to change the artwork.

There was hope, however. Label executives were nervous about the LP. They, too, didn't like the warping and popping. A majority of the most powerful label chiefs could see the CD was the future. But they remained gun-shy, after years of investing heavily in high-tech debacles like quadraphonic sound, a production style in which different instruments came out of four separate speakers rather than the standard stereo or mono. By the early 1980s, even the sturdy 8-track tape was looking like a clumsy relic of another era. "We were confused years earlier by quadraphonic sound. That just died," recalls Joe Smith, then chairman of Elektra Records. "But here was this marvelous technology. The sound was perfect."

Sony's Ohga did not let up. He used profits from the joint CBS/Sony Records venture in Japan to build the very first CD plant, for $30 million, in the Shizuoka Prefecture region along the Pacific coast. He wanted to build more than one, but CBS's executives were unhelpful at best and belligerent at worst. Walter Yetnikoff, the bearded, Yiddish-smack-talking dervish, led the opposition. He was once Ohga's closest friend but, in part because of his CD opposition, wound up one of his greatest enemies.

The heads of the major record labels argued about digital technology at Recording Industry Association of America meetings: Yetnikoff was there. So was Jac Holzman, founder of Elektra Records, who had discovered the Doors and Queen. As the chief technologist for Warner Communications in the early 1970s, as well as a board member for the Atari video-game system and a director of Pioneer Electronics, he showed up at an RIAA meeting one day in late 1981 or early 1982 (nobody can remember) as the de facto tech guru. Joe Smith, who chaired the meetings, said to Holzman: "Give us an outline of what the hell we can expect to happen here with the CD."

Holzman gave a brief pitch, then took a few questions. One came from Jay Lasker, head of ABC-Paramount Records, an old-school record guy who had started out in Decca's sales department after leaving the US Army in 1945. "Sometimes," Lasker declared, "I turn on the television set and I get a lot of clouds. Is there something else I'm not plugging in?"

There was a pause. Holzman was momentarily confused. *Cable television?* Finally, Smith spoke up. "He's not the repairman!" he screamed. "He can't answer why you get clouds on your television set!'"

Holzman finally answered the question anyhow. "It depends,"

he said, "on whether he is living in a house he owns or in an apartment." Lasker would not be the last record mogul baffled by digital technology.

SOMETIME IN 1981, Marc Finer, Sony Corp.'s director of product communications, started showing up at the big record labels. Finer was hardly an imposing figure—about 5'11", brown hair, glasses, usually wearing a conservative suit and tie—but he carried a mysterious, attention-getting object to label conference rooms filled with Walter Yetnikoffs and their high-powered associates. It was the Sony CDP-101, a player launched in Japan and not yet available on the US market. The album Finer chose was Billy Joel's 1978 album *52nd Street*—the very first CD title, released in Japan—and he won the room with the very first song, "Honesty." "It was a guaranteed showstopper to every label we played it to," Finer says. "Everybody talked about and pointed to the very clear benefits of CDs—the absence of record noise, greater portability. But ironically, one of the most impressive aspects of the demo was watching that little drawer open and close."

The labels' resistance was about to crumble. The first two to give way were PolyGram and CBS, which made sense, because Philips owned PolyGram and CBS had been in a joint agreement with Sony to sell records in Japan since 1968. But some at CBS still put up resistance, especially Yetnikoff, the chairman. In Norio Ohga's account, Yetnikoff aggressively opposed the new technology from the beginning. He didn't want to build expensive plants. He didn't want the technology to allow pristine pirated copies of CDs on cassette tapes. Akio Morita, Sony's charismatic chairman and cofounder, lobbied Yetnikoff during regular meetings at the CBS offices in New York City. It wasn't absolutely necessary to get Yetnikoff on board. Ultimately, Ohga would go over his head to the more receptive CBS Inc. president, Thomas Wyman (whom Yetnikoff called "Super Goy"). But his acceptance of the CD was crucial to win over the rest of the record label's employees.

John Briesch, Sony's vice president of audio marketing at the time, was present at many of these meetings between Yetnikoff and Morita. "[Yetnikoff] was pretty tough," Briesch remembers. "I can imagine a lot of four-letter words—he used more than I'd ever heard of."

The CBS people who worked under Yetnikoff recall a sort of contradictory enthusiasm for the revolutionary new technology. At the time, Jerry Shulman was director of market research for the record label, which meant he did a lot of studies and looked at a lot of data and nobody at CBS Records had any idea what he was doing. One day, Yetnikoff unexpectedly called Shulman into his office, where a bunch of Sony and CBS executives were milling around. "I have no idea what they're talking about," Yetnikoff told Shulman, "but this will be your project." Shulman was young and could talk high-tech. He was qualified. He became CBS's point person for the CD.

It wasn't easy. CBS's sales reps, in the middle of a poor-selling year during the terrible transition between the postdisco crash and Michael Jackson's *Thriller*, were so swamped with LPs and cassettes that they barely had time to listen when Shulman showed up in their offices. "They saw themselves as content providers and had no vested interest," Shulman says. The reps called the CD "Jerry Shulman's Frisbee."

Sales reps were hardly the only Luddites in the music business. Arista Records founder Clive Davis, who was on the cusp of making one of his greatest discoveries, Whitney Houston, wasn't a big CD fan at first. Capitol and EMI had no intention of reissuing the Beatles' catalog. (These reissued, remastered, Beatles-approved CDs finally arrived in 1986, with much fanfare.) And word was starting to leak out to producers and musicians that it was suddenly possible to make a recording so perfect that engineers would have to adjust the studio microphones to account for footsteps and other background noise. Many of them predicted this technology would be a pain in the ass. Pricey, too. "The expense of digital equipment is horrendous, and I don't see any price breakthroughs in the short-term," the chief engineer of a top New York studio told *Billboard* in early 1982. Every other engineer in the lengthy article concurred.

The most aggressive detractors formed Musicians Against Digital, and rocker Neil Young spoke for the digital-equals-soulless camp: "The mind has been tricked, but the heart is sad." "We had a number of major acts at Warner labels, whether it was the Cars or Fleetwood Mac—none of these artists were prepared to put music on compact disc. They were sort of afraid of it," recalls Alan Perper, a Warner distribution executive, who, like CBS's Shulman, became the label's CD point person. "Keith Jarrett did one of the very first jazz CDs, and you could hear air-conditioning running in the background, chairs moving around. You could hear him grunting and moaning and going, 'Yeah!'"

Who needed digital? Why not stick with what works? "The retailers' point of view was, 'Look, we're carrying Michael Jackson in an LP and a cassette—and now you want us to carry it in a third version? Fuck you!'" Shulman says. "'And also, we're not going to change our fixtures in the stores—we have twelve-by-twelve-inch bins for LPs and our cassettes are behind the counter.'"

Shulman came up with an early solution, and he isn't proud of it: the blister pack. This was the clear, oblong wrapper that encased the disc in the bottom compartment and the liner notes in the top. "That was me," he admits. "It cut everyone's fingers to shreds when you cut it open." His idea was to showcase the sleek, shiny, silver disc for all record buyers to see. Even better, two of the blister packs could sit side-by-side in traditional LP bins. These would evolve into a cardboard package called the longbox.

It wasn't only the big companies that stood to profit from CDs. In 1982, Rob Simonds was a buyer at Schoolkids Records in Ann Arbor, Michigan, specializing in Japanese imports. He was a young, bearded fan of Yes's *Tales from Topographic Oceans* who lived and breathed music. He even spent an entire summer learning how to translate Japanese printing into English so he could read the labels of the records he imported. In so doing, he built up a strong local market among hippie rock fans and college students. Then the compact disc changed his life. "I was the first one of the people that I knew who discovered the CD, because I actually brought in a Sony player from Japan in one of my record orders," Simonds recalls. "The only thing I could play on it for the first six months was the demonstration disc."

Simonds immediately started showing it off to his friends around Ann Arbor, and he figured that if they were this fascinated with the new technology, other people would be, too. He turned his CD hobby into a business, supplying record stores around the States with any titles he could get his hands on from Japan—at first, strange Japanese classical and pop albums and, inexplicably, the entire *oeuvre* of schlocky German big-bandleader James Last. When each of these CDs sold out, the stores begged Simonds for more. He soon wound up partnering with three experienced music businessmen—his brother-in-law, Don Rose, who ran a record store and a small label; Doug Lexa, another importer of Japanese records; and Arthur Mann, a lawyer who'd helped Bon Jovi sign his first major record deal. Together, they formed one of the very first CD-focused record labels, Rykodisc.

By this time, PolyGram Records, still reeling from the collapse of disco and its misguided investment in Neil Bogart's Casablanca Records, had hired a new president. A large, bald native of Holland who had joined Philips in 1952 as an accountant, Jan Timmer was entrepreneurial and had a way of being both friendly and persuasive. He was almost as pushy as Sony's Ohga in championing the CD to labels and record stores.

Timmer was smart enough to realize that PolyGram's music catalog, while strong, especially in classical, wasn't enough to prop up the compact disc all over the world. The label needed a partner. He set his sights on Warner Communications. The storied record label, whose assets included the catalogs of Frank Sinatra and the Grateful Dead and hot new artists like Van Halen and Dire Straits, was receptive. Many of the company's top executives—including record division chief David Horowitz, who owned one of the very first CD players—immediately saw the CD as the future.* As a result, Warner executives were among the most enthusiastic supporters of the new format at the decidedly low-tech RIAA meetings.

The powerful chairman of Warner Communications, Steve Ross, was no Luddite, either. When Warner owned the Atari video game company in the early 1980s, Ross could be found late at night in front of his television set, struggling to beat back electronic aliens. One day in late 1982, Ross dispatched a vice president, Elliot Goldman, to Hamburg, Germany, to meet with PolyGram's Timmer. Warner wanted to plunge into the CD business. By Ross's way of thinking, if CDs really were the future, and CBS and PolyGram were already in on it, Warner could be shut out. They had to find a way in.

Goldman and Timmer hit it off. Earnestly, Timmer made his pitch.

---

* Not every Warner executive was enamored of the CD. In his memoir *Exploding*, then–Warner Music creative director Stan Cornyn writes, "At first, in '82, most folks in the American record business had figured that the CD was some kind of foreign trick." Robert Heiblim, president of the electronics company Denon at the time, recalls Cornyn, who had a reputation as a new-technology buff, being surprisingly skeptical. Heiblim also encountered especially harsh resistance from Atlantic's Ahmet Ertegun and executives at Arista (run by Clive Davis at the time) and A&M. Responds Cornyn: "I have been in the record industry known as a sassy speaker. So I may have sassed at one point onstage." Early on, Cornyn viewed the CD as one of an endless line of technologies pitched to labels as the next big thing. Later, David Horowitz called several Warner executives around his big blue conference table in New York to emphasize the CD. He deputized Cornyn to push it. "Therefore, I was slightly less sassy," Cornyn says.

The CD was the future, he said, and he wanted it to have all the Warner music on it—Frank Sinatra, Neil Young, everyone. He suggested Warner do its manufacturing through Philips. And he suggested Warner pay a three-cent royalty on each CD. Goldman was with him until that last bit.

"I looked at Jan," Goldman recalls, "and I said, 'Jan, you must be joking. You're telling us you want Warner Communications to put its music on the CD, which will establish the CD, and you want us to *pay a royalty*? There's no chance in the world that would happen.' I said this very nicely."

Timmer had to think about it. Whatever happened next is open to dispute. Timmer insists Warner agreed to the royalty. "Yes! Yes!" Timmer says today. "That was, of course, a significant royalty for us—Sony and Philips. We spent all that money developing this new product, and three cents was, after all, peanuts to the record industry." Goldman fiercely disputes his friend's "faulty" recollection. "Trust me, there was no royalty paid to Philips on CDs manufactured," he says. Warner tech guru Jac Holzman, who was also present at the Hamburg talks, didn't respond to an email question about them.

Stan Cornyn, the longtime Warner executive who wrote *Exploding: The Highs, Hits, Hype, Heroes and Hustlers of the Warner Music Group*, wasn't at the German "schloss," as he calls it in the book. But he knows how the royalty discussion turned out. "Yes, royalty happened," the retired Cornyn says in a phone interview. "What they did was shove it away from us record labels and push it over to the pressing plants. Most of us owned the pressing plants. So, in fact, the corporation paid it. As far as I know—which is a very limiting qualification—it never expired. It was a key factor for Sony and Philips to make money after all these years." The royalty stands today.

In any case, the next day Timmer called Goldman to accept the offer. Warner was in the CD business. To celebrate, Timmer took Goldman and Holzman to one of his favorite restaurants, in the hills outside Hamburg. Toward the end of dinner, Goldman made another tiny suggestion. Why not merge the two companies, Warner and PolyGram? That would establish a new powerhouse record label just as the CD was about to take off.

Unfortunately, CBS's Walter Yetnikoff was a competitor, and he hated the idea. So much that he embarked on a public campaign of lobbying congressmen, hiring attorneys, and making threats in the press.

Yetnikoff won. The Federal Trade Commission nixed the merger due to antitrust concerns.

Billboard reported numerous front-page stories on the planned merger. *Billboard*, however, carried no coverage of the *other* decision Goldman and Timmer made in Hamburg. The Warner-PolyGram merger would have been big. The CD was about to rescue the industry, and the royalty decision would cost labels hundreds of millions of dollars over the next twenty-five years.

IN 1982, the CD marketing guys kept pushing. Sony's Marc Finer and John Briesch helped Chicago's huge classical station WFMT create the first-ever all-digital broadcast. Emil Petrone of PolyGram worked with small classical labels like Telarc to ship their masters to Japan and get the CDs distributed to US stores. All three men kept meeting with top record executives in their posh offices, pleading with them to make the shift from LP to CD as quickly as possible. The big guns were trotted out to make sweeping, hyperbolic predictions. Akio Morita declared the CD would "breathe new life" into the music and hi-fi businesses and replace the analog disc. Jan Timmer said both formats would exist side-by-side for ten to fifteen years, but the CD would emerge victorious. Jac Holzman likened the easy-to-use CD player to a microwave oven. "Just stick the thing in the slot and program it any way you like," he said.

Sony reps sent Stevie Wonder, Phil Collins, Grover Washington Jr., and Barbra Streisand demo CDs of their work remastered in digital. They loved it. Toshitada Doi, who headed up the Sony-Philips research team, traveled from Japan to Hollywood searching for customers. A jazz saxophonist and fan of Charlie Parker, Doi bonded with Wonder over Sony's new $150,000 digital recorder. (The prevailing recording technology in those days was 24-track analog and cost $20,000 to $30,000.) Wonder bought a recorder for his Wonderland Studio. Billy Joel, whose album *52nd Street* had been the first pop CD released in Japan, endorsed the technology. So did his producer, Phil Ramone, the studio veteran who'd worked with everyone from Barry Manilow to the Ramones. "It was what I was wanting to happen. It was as you hear it in the control room," Ramone says today.

The turning point came in 1983. It was inevitable, really. The CD just sounded better than the LP, no matter how much its detractors complain to this day about losing the rich, warm analog sound. Together, the labels' CD point people, like CBS's Shulman and Warner's Perper, as well as Finer, Briesch, and Petrone, formed the Compact Disc Group to lobby the industry and the public. The group's membership swelled to dozens of people, representing more than fifty companies, and they promoted the CD in increasingly sexy ways. They toured nightclubs, demonstrating CDs directly to fans. "We ran around the country like a bunch of vagabonds," Perper recalls. "You'd think we were trying to get elected to the presidency." They successfully lobbied MTV, convincing cofounder Bob Pittman to exercise his clout with the major record labels.

For the big labels, the sales numbers were starting to become very persuasive. In Japan, which had launched the CD in October 1982, demand for the players was far outstripping supply. By January 1983, Sony had to double its capacity, to 10,000 players a month. The company's one CD plant in Shizuoka Prefecture, south of Tokyo, ramped up to 300,000 CDs a month. Or so the company said—it was still hard to manufacture a whole lot of CDs at once, especially given early problems with error correction that would take another year or so to work out. By March, CDs were available in Europe. A small record store in Hartford, Connecticut, Capitol Record Shop, went to an all-CD format, importing titles from Japan and Europe for $24.95 apiece. A Sony executive predicted the company would manufacture 10 million CDs a year by mid-1984. Windham Hill, a tiny new age record label, decided to put out three new CD titles.

"CD" became the big buzzword, a synonym for "sleek" and "sexy." The players still cost $1,000, but the public was getting excited. *Rolling Stone* printed a January 1983 article titled "The Digital Revolution: Will the Compact Disc Make the LP Obsolete?"

But the hype was not why the hold-out record labels (and retailers) finally came around. The true reason had to do with one number: $16.95. This was the opening price for a CD.

For years, labels had been stuck selling LPs for top prices of $8.98. Tom Petty's label, MCA, had tried to boost the price for his 1981 album *Hard Promises* to $9.98. *Nine ninety-eight!* An outrage! The fan-friendly Petty waged such a public stink, even threatening to put huge $8.98 stickers on the front of the record, that MCA had no choice but to back off. (Petty's album became a Top 10 hit.)

So labels and record stores were forced into keeping LP prices extremely affordable for consumers, which didn't make the executives happy. The CD was an opportunity to change consumers' expectations about what music should cost. It was more expensive to manufacture, and record labels immediately saw that they could tack on more pennies to the wholesale prices in order to improve their profit margins.

They also saw the CD as a chance to rejigger artists' contracts. The first thing labels did, as artist attorneys and managers from that time recall all too vividly, was reduce the artist's royalty by 20 percent. Labels also boosted what they called the "packaging reduction" from 10 percent or 15 percent in the LP days to a very standard 20 percent. There were other reductions from what artists made, too, like the always-mysterious free-goods allowance, which even experienced music business lawyers can't really define. After labels factored in these newfangled deductions, a typical artist received roughly 81 cents per disc. Under the LP system, artists made a little more than 75 cents per disc. So labels sold CDs for almost $8 more than LPs at stores, but typical artists made just six cents more per record. When they realized just how aggressively fans would replace their LP collections with CDs, label attorneys asked older "catalog acts" to sign new contracts with drastically reduced royalty rates. Some signed, some didn't.

"They did it under the guise of [the CD] being a 'new technology.' But although CDs came out in 1982 or 1983, in some cases that reduction lasts to this day," says Jay Cooper, a veteran artist attorney who made Tina Turner's comeback record deal in the 1980s and has represented Lionel Richie, Etta James, and Sheryl Crow. "Oh, they got away with it! The reality is, unless you're representing a *super* superstar, record companies have all the power. As the attorney, [artists] come to you and say, 'I gotta have this deal!' In many cases, they'll sign anything." Mickey Schulhof, a top Sony executive who worked closely with CBS Records executives at the time, says these new kinds of record label CD contracts had important long-term implications: "That's not an insignificant reason for the improvement overall in the economics of the record industry."*

---

*To research this chapter, I visited former label executive Joe Smith, the good-natured raconteur, 1950s disc jockey, and should-have-been stand-up comic. (At one industry function, he reportedly made the following inspired introduction of the great Seymour Stein of Sire Records, who turned the Ramones, Blondie, Talking Heads, and Madonna into stars: "He is to the record industry what surfing is to the state of Kansas.") For an hour, I listened to Smith on a luxurious couch in front of the largest

Although the initial $16.95 price dropped at first, eventually labels kept raising prices, despite retailers' objections. For one stretch, every Christmas, Tower Records' Russ Solomon recalls, CDs went up—from $13.98 to $14.98 to $16 to $17 to $18. "Every year they'd do this and [retailers] would say, 'Goddamnit! People aren't gonna buy it at this price.' . . . And their argument was at the time that it'd cost a lot more to make the CD and they had more spoilage and all that kind of crap. Which may have been kind of true in the very, very beginning—about six months." So did record chains complain? "That's exactly right," Solomon says ruefully. "You *complained*. If you don't mind having a conversation with a wall! They'd *laugh*."

IN 1983, after working for years for RCA Records, Jim Frische went to Sony to be the general manager of manufacturing. Almost immediately, he met with his boss in Japan, who gave him his first mission through an English translator: *Reopen Terre Haute*. For twenty-eight years, a 100-square-foot, two-building plant in Terre Haute, Indiana, had pressed CBS LPs, but the company had recently closed it down to save costs. Now CBS and Sony wanted to turn it into a CD-pressing plant. It was Sony's vision that a booming overall US market for CDs was good for the record and electronics industries, so the company intended to share Terre Haute with any other record label that wanted to put out the new technology (and pay for it, of course). (Mickey Schulhof, Sony's top US executive, had been the catalyst for purchasing the CBS-owned building. He regularly piloted a company jet to Terre Haute to oversee production of 100,000 discs per month—and more as the new technology took off in the marketplace.)

When Frische first walked into the abandoned Terre Haute facility during the very hot summer of 1983, he must have felt like the tenant who suddenly discovers cockroaches in his perfect new apartment. He and a fellow Sony executive were standing in a wide puddle of water in the middle of the cavernous plant. The floors were dirt. And Frische, as head of the plant newly christened the Digital Audio Disc Corporation,

---

flat-screen television set I've ever seen in my life. Afterward, I stood in the large foyer of his beautiful home in Beverly Hills, preparing to leave. The retired, seventy-eight-year-old head of Warner, Elektra, and EMI shook my hand and said, "The business ain't full of Martin Luther Kings."

had to transform this building into a state-of-the-art "clean room." LP plants smell like burning vinyl and workers are accustomed to tramping dirt all over the place. Not so CD plants. "The environment is totally controlled, like a hospital operating room. You completely control the flow of air in and out of that room," says Frische, who is retired and no longer has to commute three hours a day between his longtime home in Indianapolis and the Terre Haute plant. "The dirtiest thing you can put in that clean room is a person. There are these 'air showers'—you have to go through a series of doorways and put on smocks."

Workers had to gut the place and put on a new roof, and they finished in less than a year, under relentless pressure from the Sony executives in Japan. Sony was tired of shipping CDs overseas to meet booming demand in the United States.

Not everybody celebrated. After the plant's grand opening in 1984, a group of about sixteen executives from CBS and Sony headed to Terre Haute, donned smocks, and toured the clean rooms. The plant had cost $20 million—half from Sony and half from CBS—to convert from an old-fashioned LP-pressing plant to a CD clean room. Almost everybody in the group was enthusiastic. Walter Yetnikoff, however, started murmuring to himself, as one witness recalls. The volume of his voice went up and down, until finally he blurted: "Ten million *fucking* dollars for *this*?"

By numerous Sony accounts, in the early days of the CD, Yetnikoff never fully came around. In 1982, CBS was in trouble. Disco was dead, and *Thriller* had yet to arrive. One of the biggest record companies in the world was leaking money—profits had dropped more than half from 1981 to 1982, from $58.9 million to $22.2 million. It's easy to see why Yetnikoff was a little reluctant to go around spending tens of millions on technology based on ones and zeroes he couldn't even see.

But Yetnikoff has his own recollections of those days. "I had been predicting . . . that compact discs, a new innovation in which our Japanese partner Sony was heavily invested," he writes in his 2004 autobiography, *Howling at the Moon*, "would revolutionize the industry." Like Jerry Moss, he was just a little worried about piracy.

Yetnikoff's hindsight was 20/20. CBS's Terre Haute facility, which opened in 1984 with a capacity of 300,000 CDs per month, was producing 850,000 CDs and 1.1 million DVDs per day twenty years later. In 1983, CDs made the US record industry just $17.2 million. In 1984, that figure would jump to $103.3 million—an increase of more than 500 percent. That was just the beginning. By 1999, sales of this unbreakable technology would bring in more than $12.8 billion, just in America. Rob Simonds's company, Rykodisc, was a beneficiary of this windfall. After landing deals with enthusiastic artists like Frank Zappa, Elvis Costello, and David Bowie, the label with the light-green CD cases grossed $100,000 in 1985 and $7 million in 1988.

"Suddenly, everybody had to go in and buy a whole new record collection," says Howie Klein, head of Warner Music–owned Reprise Records in the 1980s and 1990s. "The CD became the thing—it was no longer about the cassette, it was no longer about vinyl records. That is the single thing that made the record industry absolutely roll in cash. Cash came in like you would not believe. All this money came in and suddenly everybody wanted a piece—whether it was very, very high salaries for upper management or [for] artists." The boom would last for a long, long time, making the scruffiest of grunge musicians and the most profane of rap stars incredibly rich. Record executives would make tens of millions of dollars, buy obscenely expensive homes, and drive around in bulletproof limos. Most important, Wall Street would start to pay attention.

Big Music's Big Mistakes, Part 1

The CD Longbox

The longbox was 6 inches wide, 12 inches tall, and made entirely of cardboard. It usually came wrapped in cellophane. Consumers had to rip it apart with their bare hands to access the compact disc inside.* And it was impossible to recycle. In 1990, Terry Friedman, a Democrat in the California Assembly, declared it responsible for killing 10,000 to 20,000 California trees every year. "This went on for *years*—this wastefulness of making boxes and putting CDs inside them," says Jordan Harris, who ran Virgin Records US and Sony's Work label until he quit the industry in 1999 and formed OZOcar, a high-end New York City hybrid-car service.

In the early 1980s, when Sony and Philips executives were trying every trick they could think of to push record labels to switch from the LP to the CD, they had to pick their battles carefully. Record stores were a sensitive support base—after all, they actually had to sell the things. Many were deeply skeptical of the CD. They were worried about theft, and they didn't want to tear down their sturdy, wooden, *expensive* record racks and build

---

*Albert Brooks's character in 1991's *Defending Your Life* memorably meets his demise attempting to tear open longboxes while driving.

new ones for something like $9,000 to $10,000 for every 5,000-album store. Distribution chiefs like Henry Droz of Warner and Paul Smith of CBS didn't want to go to war with the retailers. Raising Tower Records's wholesale prices against founder Russ Solomon's wishes was one thing, but this was a revolution. And nobody wanted to lose floor space at the Tower on the Sunset Strip when they had a new Bruce Springsteen CD to sell. CD-pushing executives at Sony and Philips were relieved. A box—*is that all?* "We're not insensitive," Harry Losk, of Philips-owned PolyGram, declared gleefully at the time. Thus the labels designed the longboxes so that two of them would fit into a space created to house a 12-inch record.

This was a long time before Al Gore released *An Inconvenient Truth.* Who cared about a few cardboard boxes? Within a decade, though, even executives within the record industry were starting to wonder what the hell they were doing with these useless monoliths. Mike Bone, an Island Records president who had once sent dead rats to journalists as a promotional tool for the English rock band Boomtown Rats' first album, declared himself a responsible member of a group called Ban the Box. He proclaimed the longbox "garbage" and offered to put up his own money to subsidize the group, which included the Grateful Dead, R.E.M., Nirvana manager Danny Goldberg, and Island and Rhino Records executives. Ex–Talking Head David Byrne affixed a sticker to every copy of his 1992 CD *Uh-Oh*: "This is garbage. This box, that is. The American record business insists on it though. If you agree that it's wasteful, let your store management know how you feel." Raffi, the popular kids' singer, refused to put his album out in a longbox, while rocker Peter Gabriel insisted on releasing a greatest-hits CD in its own plastic jewel box. Perhaps the cleverest statement came from Spinal Tap, whose *Break Like the Wind* CD came out in an *extra*-long longbox—a deliberately phallic 18 inches.

Retailers and their allies at major labels fought back. Sal Licata, EMI's president, argued in a 1992 *Billboard* op-ed titled "Why We Should Keep the CD Longbox" that the box was a marketing tool filled with "visual stimuli" and "consumer-appealing presentation." Tower's Solomon declared a California State Assembly ban-the-longbox bill "totally unnecessary." And so it lived on, killing forest after forest, as US compact disc sales jumped from 17.2 million in 1983 to 286.5 million in 1990. Behind the scenes, however, numerous executives of the early 1990s fumed—and schemed.

Jeff Gold, a Warner Music vice president, tried just about everything to get rid of it. First, he talked to Warner's sales executives. As expected, they didn't want to piss off the retailers. Then he went to meetings of Warner's longtime distribution company, WEA, and stood up, articulating his cause to a sizable crowd. Distribution chief Henry Droz responded with a familiar mantra: "It would cost retailers a *fortune* to reconfigure bins for these things." Gold sat down. "I was the dummy who tried to sell it on 'let's be good corporate citizens,'" he says.

For a while, Gold tried to work with the longboxes. He went to the artists. R.E.M.'s *Out of Time* was about to come out, and Gold approached the band's manager, Bertis Downs, asking to transform the longbox into a political petition. Downs agreed. So days after the CD came out, a new group, Rock the Vote, received 10,000 signed longboxes supporting the Motor Voter Bill, which made it faster and easier for Americans to register for elections. Rock the Vote made a huge production of delivering them to Congress, which passed the bill. (The first President Bush vetoed it; President Clinton signed it later into law.) "We actually turned this thing from useless to slightly useful," Gold says.

Finally it dawned on Gold that in this business, only one thing could kill the longbox: money. Gold met with Murray Gitlin, then Warner's chief executive officer, and asked how much longboxes cost in a given year. A little less than $25 million, he was told. (Each longbox cost 24 cents to make, and Warner's annual sales were about $90 million.) So Gold schlepped to another WEA distribution meeting and suggested cutting the longbox, saving $25 million and giving half the savings to record stores. "That resonated," Gold says. "There was this kind of magic moment of recognition."

Finally, the longbox died in April 1993. The fact that it took so long was symbolic of the decentralized record industry's inability to do anything quickly. Anything, of course, except sign talent and sell CDs.

Chapter 2
1984–1999

How Big Spenders Got Rich in the Post-CD Boom

GIL FRIESEN sits on a $1,000 Frank Gehry Wiggle chair atop an Odegard rug in his beautifully white, rectangular, and modern home in the posh Brentwood area of Los Angeles. His living room is about the size of a two-car garage; it's airy and uncluttered and seems to go on forever. On the other side of the room, behind Friesen, is a wall-sized Ross Bleckner painting, of white dots arranged in a huge astronomical spiral. Around the corner from the painting is a wall of three 10-foot-tall windows with eucalyptus trees brushing against them on the outside. Beyond the trees are a small pool and a hillside, panoramic view of Beverly Hills and much of Los Angeles.

Friesen is tall and straight, wearing a pink dress shirt and slacks. With his slicked-back white hair and a salt-and-pepper goatee containing the slightest hint of scraggle, he looks a bit like actor Dennis Hopper. Here, in his home, it is distracting to talk to him about the record business, in which he worked for more than thirty years, mostly as number-three executive for the independent label A&M Records, because the art and literature scattered tastefully throughout his living room is so captivating. Greeting guests at the front door, for example, is a headless, fluorescent blue bust of a woman's torso and hips by the late French postwar sculptor Yves Klein. The wide, low table in front of Friesen is covered with thick books, and as he talks about distributors and retailers, words seem to leap out from the titles—*Karl Lagerfeld, Jazz, Leni Riefenstahl, Africa.*

Friesen, in his early seventies, is what you'd call an old-school record man. He talks for an hour about how the business grew from a bunch of guys shipping records out of warehouses to a streamlined global marketplace of compact discs. He started out in the mailroom of Capitol Records—a job he discovered as a UCLA student in the late 1950s, scouring the want ads for something interesting to do. For the next few months, he worked near the back door in the famous tower shaped like a stack of records at Hollywood and Vine. Frank Sinatra and Nat "King" Cole walked in and out. Friesen watched recording sessions. He worked his way into a full-time job, first in accounting (which he hated), then in promotions (which he liked).

In 1960, the great disc jockey Alan Freed showed up in Los Angeles to work for a local radio station, KDAY. These were Freed's declining years. Although he had broken Chuck Berry and Bo Diddley on the radio just a few years earlier, and become one of rock 'n' roll's forefathers of promotion, his years of indulging in "$50 handshakes" caught up with him, wrecking his career after the infamous payola scandal of the late 1950s. KDAY managers were so afraid of controversy that they refused to let him put on local rock shows. None of this mattered to Friesen, who had a Peggy Lee record to promote. He sent a telegram to Freed welcoming him to town, and Freed took a liking to the young promo man. Freed didn't last long in LA—he would station-hop to Miami, New York, and Palm Springs before dying in 1965, of cirrhosis of the liver and other causes.

But Freed did one important thing during his time in LA: He introduced Gil Friesen to Jerry Moss. Back then, Moss was a record promoter who schlepped singles like the Crests' "Sixteen Candles" to radio stations on the coasts. The two bonded at the Hollywood Boulevard coffee shop where all the promo men hung out. They agreed it was hilarious when Freed, the rock 'n' roll legend, turned Friesen's Kingston Trio folk single "El Matador" into a KDAY Pick of the Week. "We became instant friends," Friesen recalls.

Moss had just formed a small company, Carnival Records, with another friend, trumpeter Herb Alpert. Together, Alpert and Moss put out the musician's instrumental "Tell It to the Birds." They sold the master for $750 and used the money to build a recording studio in Alpert's 419 Westbourne Drive garage. Meanwhile, Friesen was jumping from job to job. He handled West Coast sales and promo for Kapp Records, picking up crates of records like crooner Jack Jones's "Wives and Lovers" from warehouses and dragging them to radio stations throughout California. In 1964, Friesen went to England, looking for a hit—as manager for P. J. Proby, a ponytailed pop singer best known for "Niki Hoeky" and for wearing tight trousers on stage. Friesen sums up that experience in a word: "unsuccessful." On a trip to Europe to make an international distribution deal for A&M, Moss went to England, contacted Friesen, and rescued him from that kind of life.

By then, Alpert and Moss had changed the name of their garage label to A&M Records. Famously, they had taken some time off from making records to attend a bullfight in Tijuana, Mexico, and the spectacle inspired Alpert to create a new sound: "Spanish flair." Alpert and the Tijuana Brass put out "The Lonely Bull" in 1962, and it took off, selling 700,000 copies and giving Herb and Jerry a moneymaking streak that would continue for almost four decades. On November 17, 1964, Moss hired Friesen, initially to handle Alpert's touring activity, later as label president. He became the ampersand in A&M.

This trio of executives would turn A&M Records into one of the most successful independent labels in history. Their policy was simple: Sign great artists and let them do their thing. They started with Sergio Mendes and Brazil '66, hit a gold mine with Peter Frampton's 10-million-selling *Frampton Comes Alive!* in 1976, and turned raw talents like the Carpenters, Joe Cocker, and the Flying Burrito Brothers—and later Janet Jackson, the Police, Bryan Adams, and Soundgarden—into polished stars.

As A&M grew, so did the record business. The company tried to stay independent—owned by Moss and Alpert, not giant corporations like CBS or General Electric—but by the late 1970s that was becoming more and more difficult. Moss and Friesen, the money guys, clung for years to an archaic American network of mom-and-pop distributors. They shipped crates of records from warehouses to retailers between orders for televisions and washer-dryers. This system allowed for a lot of hanky-panky. Labels would ship far more records to the distributors than they would actually sell; they'd "ship gold," or 500,000 copies, allowing them to claim big hits, but huge crates would come back later as returns. Labels and distributors also routinely called record stores, begging or bribing managers to switch an album from No. 2 to No. 1 so they could claim the top record in that market. But soon old-school guys were dying out all over the country. A&M found itself with crates of unsold records in warehouses in Los Angeles and Chicago—an unacceptable, money-leaking situation. "There was a period of time at A&M there where it looked very shaky," recalls former label executive Al

Cafaro. So Moss signed a deal with a major label, RCA, to distribute its records worldwide. "I knew my product was going to get sold, and I knew I was going to get paid," Moss says. "I didn't have to worry about distribution, and I could really concentrate on the artists."

The business was evolving from small-time guys who packed their products into crates themselves to an international network of distribution executives with MBAs. "I remember I was so intimidated that I went to Harvard and took a short business course," Friesen says. Thus, when the compact disc came along to change the business forever, he was prepared. But not at first.

Like everybody else, Jerry Moss, who had literally screamed his opposition to the CD at a 1981 industry conference in Athens, Greece, came around when he smelled the money. By 1987, Friesen was saluting CDs in the pages of *Rolling Stone*: "They're the most exciting innovation the record business has had in this decade." Today, sitting on his Wiggle chair, Friesen remembers the post-CD era as a time of huge profits, cash flow, and unprecedented Wall Street interest. "That's when the record business began to appear in the business section of newspapers—previously it wasn't even second to the movie business," he says. "The music business began to live large."

Friesen is staring at the ceiling of his living room, deep in thought in response to a question. He has been living in this 1953 home, originally built by Swiss architect Marc Peter Jr., since he bought it in 1985 for $1.45 million. Beginning in the 1990s, Friesen hired Richard Meier and Michael Palladino, who together had designed LA's state-of-the-art Getty Center, to add an entirely new second floor as part of an elaborate expansion project. They were responsible for the look of this living room—windows, eucalyptus trees, the whole relaxed and airy feeling. All told, the improvements added $4.9 million to the value of Friesen's home, according to the Los Angeles County Assessor's Office.

The question at hand: How did the CD-fueled growth in the record business change Friesen's life, personally? "Well," he says after a long moment, "I bought this house."

THE CD BOOM lasted from 1984 to 2000. In the first year, sales jumped 625 percent, to 5.8 million; in the last year, with Britney Spears, 'NSync, Eminem, and the Backstreet Boys setting retail records that may stand forever, CD sales reached an unprecedented 942 million. "The business grew pretty dramatically. There was plenty of dough and people started spending it," recalls Bob Buziak, president of RCA Records from 1986 to 1990. "You would have to spend $1 million to find out if you had a hit."

In 1992, Barbra Streisand signed a Sony album-and-movie deal for $40 million. Not to be outdone, Madonna landed a Warner deal for $60 million. Michael Jackson took a $30 million advance from Sony, including a valuable new wrinkle—a share of the profits from every CD, beginning with *Dangerous.* Gil Friesen and A&M ponied up $50 million to win a 1991 bidding war for its most reliable superstar, Janet Jackson. Even ZZ Top, the Texas blues trio whose 1980s "Legs" heyday turned out to be short-lived, scored an RCA deal for $35 million to $50 million. "I made some of the largest deals that have ever been made," says attorney Donald S. Passman, who represented Mariah Carey, Janet Jackson, and others. "People would say, 'How can you do that to the companies?' I go, 'Look, they're the ones that want to make the deals. Nobody put a gun to their heads.' The only thing stupid would be not taking it." Videos were another enormous expense. Budgets were small at first, but by the early 1990s they were up to $300,000 or $400,000. At decade's end, says prolific director Dave Meyers, who made Jay-Z's "Dirt Off Your Shoulder," "An average budget for me was maybe close to $1 million."

It was a great time for rock stars and executives, who had just muddled through the postdisco crash from 1979 to 1983. The 1970s had been filled with expensive drugs and exorbitant fashions, and nobody wanted it to end. Conserving money and making prudent budget decisions? This wasn't how things worked in the rock 'n' roll business!

Fortunately, a new generation of musicians was more than happy to rediscover the old decadence. They became megastars just as the CD was taking off, and even today it's hard to recall their success without a mental picture of their albums on shiny, silver pieces of plastic. Their genre would come to be known as "hair metal." Their form of rebellion was not so much in the music but the lifestyle: drugs, groupies, fast cars, and, of course, hairspray.

There is a scene in Mötley Crüe's hilarious and disturbing group autobiography, *The Dirt,* in which drummer Tommy Lee recalls "chilling in the Caymans" as friends of their manager walked in and out of their apartment carrying suitcases full of cash and cocaine. These one-named gentlemen—"Jerry," "Leigh," "Tony"—were in town to launder money. One day Leigh showed up with a suitcase and promised coke-heads Lee and singer Vince Neil they could keep the contents of his $1,000 leather briefcase if they could pick the lock. Lee accomplished the trick with a butcher knife from the kitchen. The rock stars discovered dozens of coke-filled plastic bags and plunged in, face-first, ruining the stash. Eventually manager Doc McGhee walked into the apartment, had a fit, and kicked out Lee and Neil. "I think we ended up paying for all the drugs we destroyed out of our royalties," Lee said.

Metal bands weren't the only music stars fixated on expensive haircuts during the CD boom. By the end of their run up the pop charts in the early 1990s, the gorgeous singing trio Wilson Phillips was spending $7,000 on hair and makeup for promotional appearances. Carnie and Wendy Wilson were the daughters of Beach Boy Brian Wilson, and Chynna Phillips's parents were John and Michelle Phillips of the Mamas and the Papas. Not long after the women formed a band, major labels bid for the right to sign them. SBK, an independent, was willing to throw the most money around, snagging the young women with a $500,000 advance. The label's cofounder, music-industry veteran Charles Koppelman, had a habit of showing up at Wilson Phillips concerts in a Bentley with "CAK" vanity plates and a blazer with a Cuban cigar tucked behind a pocket square.

"CDs were selling like crazy and the companies had tremendous cash flow—and it gave them the opportunity to spend a lot more money on artists and marketing," says Koppelman, now chairman of Martha Stewart Omnimedia. "One could spend a couple of million bucks—easy—on a new artist launch."

Just how much did SBK, backed by the major label EMI, spend on Wilson Phillips? Arma Andon, one of the band's original managers, breaks down the numbers:

—$500,000, hiring big-name producer Glen Ballard and making debut record, *Wilson Phillips*

—$50,000, CD artwork

—$1.5 million, videos for the five singles, including "Hold On" and "Release Me"

—$600,000, tour support

—$1 million, radio promotion, such as flying the band to perform at local station-sponsored festivals

—$2 million, record store advertising and product placement
   fees

—$5.65 million, total

OF COURSE, SOME of this money came out of Wilson Phillips's own
record royalties. Had the band *not* sold 8 million copies of its debut
CD worldwide, it could have easily stumbled into a quagmire of unre-
couped-royalty debt to SBK. Hundreds of would-be pop stars succumbed to this fate. Wilson Phillips did not, in part because its record
label was willing to spend as much as it took to turn them into megastars.
The plan worked—for a while. "You've got to understand: If you hit a
home run, there's a big payoff down the line," says Andon, who was
simultaneously the band's comanager and an SBK senior vice president.
"It was a great investment."

Wilson Phillips dragged out the success of the first album for almost
two years. Its 1992 follow-up, *Flesh and Blood*, sold just 750,000 copies,
and the band's summer tour stiffed. Then the trio broke up. Chynna
Phillips's solo album, *Naked and Sacred*? Stiffed. Albums by the two
sisters as the Wilsons? Stiffed. Phillips married a Baldwin. Carnie Wilson had gastric bypass surgery—which we know firsthand, because she
did it live on the internet in 1999. They reunited five years later for
an album of other people's songs. As for Charles Koppelman, he did
OK. He sold SBK to EMI-Capitol and became chairman of that major
label in 1993. When he left the company four years later in an executive
shake-up, EMI bought out his contract for $50 million.

From the early 1980s through the mid-1990s, it seemed like every-
body in the music business was a Charles Koppelman. "I spent money!
I spent money! And I loved it!" says Michael Alago, an A&R scout at
Elektra Records and other big labels for twenty-three years. One night
in 1986, Alago took one of his discoveries, Metallica, to a typically fancy
$1,000 dinner at tony New York City restaurant Sparks Steak House.
Afterward, Elektra's chief financial officer, Aaron Levy, told Alago
never again to use his corporate credit card for such frivolous expenses.
"I was like, 'OK, Aaron, I won't do it anymore,'" Alago recalls. "Then a
week later someone else was in town and there goes that corporate card
again."

As a twentysomething A&R rep for A&M Records in the early 1990s,
Debbie Southwood-Smith stayed at the Four Seasons for band-scout-
ing trips around the country—*every week*. Which was nothing com-

pared to the dough Southwood-Smith and her colleagues spent to woo bands. Sebadoh, whose sound was so raw that critics dubbed it "lo-fi," prompted a major label bidding war during the Nirvana-and-Soundgarden era. "They're bastions of indie rock, and here A&M and Geffen are renting them beautiful cars and putting them up at the Chateau Marmont. They ended up not signing to either one of us," Southwood-Smith recalls. "[Punk band] D-Generation had suites at the Hilton in Los Angeles that overlooked the pool. They would throw these huge parties. It was like you would hear about in the old days of rock 'n' roll. Chairs in the swimming pool. The craziest stuff was happening. There was definitely a lot more money."

Big Music was blowing up. Wall Street wanted in. Bertelsmann, a 151-year-old German book publishing company founded by a do-it-yourself printer named Carl, swooped in to buy RCA Records from General Electric for $300 million in 1986. Chief financial officers from all over the world were starting to look at record companies—or, even better, CD companies—as an easy and fun way to pump up their bottom lines. "The all-vinyl business had its ups and downs. This one, it just seemed to grow without any end in sight," recalls Bob Merlis, a former publicist and corporate spokesman for Warner Music. "That's when the multinationals got all excited about the music business. And that's when the business changed from this homegrown kind of thing to 'we have to do better this next quarter from the last quarter or our parent companies will be upset.'"

RCA and its all-American logo—Nipper the dog looking quizzically into a phonograph—going to the Germans was one thing. Could CBS Records, the all-American home of the Boss and the King of Pop and whatever Barbra Streisand was, really go to the Japanese? That's what the trades were saying, and the rumors turned out to be true.

Walter Yetnikoff was the catalyst.

In 1988, the CBS Records chairman had two problems. First, his legendary consumption of drugs and alcohol prompted one of his biggest rivals, MCA's Irving Azoff, to declare in an industry speech that CBS had a drug addict at the helm. But Yetnikoff was perhaps even more addicted to power, and a straight-shooting New Jersey billionaire named Laurence Tisch was standing in his way. Two years earlier, Tisch, owner of the Loews Corporation, had taken over a controlling interest in the label's parent, CBS Inc. At first, Yetnikoff encouraged Tisch—even tried to charm him—because he couldn't stand his previous boss at CBS Inc., Thomas Wyman, the president. But as ex–CBS Inc. general counsel George Vradenburg recalls: "When Larry got in, Larry really did not talk to Yetnikoff, and Yetnikoff felt a bit betrayed. [Yetnikoff] ended up disliking Larry perhaps more intensively than he disliked Tom Wyman." Yetnikoff called Tisch "the Evil Dwarf."

Tisch never quite understood the record business. As head of CBS Inc., he thought he could plunge into the record label, sidle up to the top executives and managers, and work his influence subtly, from within. But Yetnikoff got in his way, preventing Tisch from getting close to anybody. "[Tisch] thought the business relied too much on personalities and loyalties, and he wasn't confident that he understood the business," Vradenburg says. "To some extent, he had that little concern at the back of his head that the business wasn't clean. The people in it were not people that wore three-piece suits. They had not come out of any business that Larry had been associated with. There was this sense that this business had problems with drugs, independent [radio] promotion and bribery and kickbacks. There wasn't anything specific. . . . But there was always that worry."

Yetnikoff was shocked to discover Tisch wanted to sell CBS Records to Nelson Peltz, another billionaire, whose fortune was not in music or entertainment but in the food business. Yetnikoff stomped into Tisch's office, employing some of his best expletives. Tisch calmly suggested that Yetnikoff could buy CBS Records for the same price he offered Peltz—$1.25 billion. In cash. The gears in Yetnikoff's law school–trained brain started whirring. He knew he couldn't do anything without Sony, which had owned CBS–Sony Records since executives from the two companies established a joint venture in the late 1960s. That company was booming, thanks in part to the CD's popularity in Japan. So Yetnikoff contacted Mickey Schulhof, then the highest-ranking American official at Sony. Of course, Yetnikoff didn't like him either. He called him "Meekee."

Unlike Yetnikoff, Schulhof was not a record man. He had degrees in physics from Cornell, Brandeis, and Grinnell, but went into business at age thirty. His résumé gave him the background for a manufacturing job at CBS Records, and he oversaw things like recording studios and inventory control—"the noncreative side," he says. Clive Davis, the

CBS executive who'd hired him, realized Schulhof was up for something more technical and introduced him to Harvey Schein, then the US president for Sony.

Schein hired Schulhof as an assistant in 1974, and within three months, Sony's charismatic chairman, Akio Morita, was asking to meet this new American employee he'd been hearing so much about. Morita, too, was a physicist. The two men bonded. Per Morita's instructions, Schulhof successfully built a Sony speaker factory in Delano, Pennsylvania. He also bonded with Morita's number two, Norio Ohga, who, like Schulhof, was an amateur pilot. The executives became Sony's power troika for the next two decades, zooming around the world for business and personal trips on the company's various Falcon jets. "Whatever you discussed with [Schulhof], he could answer you like a specialist, a professional," Ohga says. "When you try to discuss music with most people, or airplanes with most people, the conversation doesn't go very far. With Mickey, if we spoke of airplanes he was on the level of an airline pilot, and since he was a real learner, if I asked him to look into something he'd come back in a flash with the most detailed report you can imagine. No matter what the subject, he'd be there and master it."

Yetnikoff, who was not so cultured but just as smart, was naturally threatened by this kind of personality, as well as by Schulhof's proximity to Japanese power players he, too, considered friends. Nonetheless, in spring 1986 he called Schulhof, suggesting Sony buy CBS Records outright. To his surprise, Schulhof responded positively. "I called Morita at home and he said, 'Of course. Now is the golden time. We know software is important,'" Schulhof recalls. Yetnikoff and Schulhof knew Sony was desperate to expand into the US music business. In part, this was because of the CD, whose profits were jumping at that time to previously unimaginable heights. But it was also because Sony was preparing to release hardware like Digital Audio Tape, or DAT, and the MiniDisc, and its executives believed these formats could be almost as lucrative as the CD. When Sony had gotten burned before, with the ill-fated Betamax format, it was in part because the electronics giant had no movie software to supplement its hardware. Sony executives didn't want to make that mistake again.

For the next year, Sony and CBS haggled. Schulhof met with a lawyer and a financial adviser at 7:30 one morning at the Mayfair Regis. The three then showed up at Yetnikoff's house on Fifty-sixth Street.

Yetnikoff, who was given to all-night drinking, dragged himself out of bed at 8:30 a.m., put on a bathrobe, instructed his wife to prepare especially potent coffee, and proceeded to extract an agreement that would bring him a fee of something like $20 million. They were all set to pull the trigger. Then William Paley, the legendary chairman of CBS Inc., who was known for his whims, decided the sale wasn't such a good idea. He strongly discouraged CBS's board, including Tisch, from going through with it. They were ready to vote "no."

Fate intervened. On October 19, 1987—Black Monday—the stock market crashed. Billionaire Tisch freaked out, fearing his financial future wasn't so secure after all. Paley or no Paley, he called Schulhof the next day and wanted to know if Sony's offer—$2 billion—still stood. Schulhof called Morita. "He said, 'If the company was worth $2 billion yesterday, it's still worth $2 billion today. My opinion hasn't changed,'" Schulhof recalls. "We bought CBS Records." In 1988, Yetnikoff finally succeeded in his quest, as he put it, to have somebody "install me as Super Czar and make me superrich."

What Yetnikoff didn't know was that an old friend, hyper-ambitious Thomas D. Mottola Jr., was quietly consolidating his power at CBS, positioning himself to take over the moment Yetnikoff slipped. Given Yetnikoff's drug-and-alcohol problems and his increasing lack of public discretion, Mottola and his allies felt certain that time was coming— soon. It would be a monumental power grab, one that would shape the way Sony's music companies, Epic and Columbia, would operate for more than a dozen years.

AT EIGHT YEARS OLD, Tommy Mottola of New Rochelle, New York, was a talented trumpet player. It won him a private school scholarship, but then he got bored and switched to the guitar. He had a rebel spirit, ditching school and running away from the military academy to which his parents had sent him when he decided he wasn't a fan of attending his private school. Mottola's mom and dad finally gave in, letting him come home if he behaved. He didn't exactly keep his side of the deal, playing in a rock band, racing cars, and partying so hard that an old friend later called him "the baddest boy in New Rochelle." Instead of focusing on school, he focused on girls. He dated Lisa Clark, daughter of powerful ABC Records founder Sam Clark, in the highfalutin' neighboring town of Harrison, then married her in 1971. Through a connection with his father-in-law, Mottola snagged small parts in four film flops, then tried to make it as a singer under the name "T. D. Valentine." He was terrible, but the experience gave him connections in the music business, and he was working as a song plugger for music publisher Chappell when he got his first break.

It was in the form of a hunky but weirdly dressed duo—one short guy with dark hair, one six-foot-plus guy with long, wavy, blond hair and platform shoes—called Hall and Oates. They could *sing*. Using his newfound industry connections, Mottola promised Daryl Hall and John Oates a record deal if they dumped their current manager and hired him instead. Like many young stars in the history of the record industry, they quickly went into debt ($230,000 in their case) to the first label that signed them. Then they switched to RCA Records, borrowed some more money, and . . . well, anybody who listened to the radio in the 1980s knows the rest. They catapulted Mottola into the record business. He named his management company Don Tommy Enterprises, which some in the business speculated was due to Mottola's fascination with the Mob. (Mottola was said to have been introduced to infamous boss Vincent "the Chin" Gigante.) Either way, he wore gold chains and purple leather jackets and looked cool.

Mottola soon changed the name of his company to Champion Entertainment, and through Hall and Oates's lawyer, Allen Grubman, he befriended CBS chairman Walter Yetnikoff. Some in the company came to call him "Walter's personal valet."

Yetnikoff liked Mottola so much that he promoted him to take over CBS's US labels, replacing veteran Al Teller. "Al was a Harvard MBA, very uptight, businesslike—every 'T' crossed and 'I' dotted and all that sort of thing. Not the most loved guy, but he loved music," recalls Bob Sherwood, a longtime CBS executive who ran Columbia Records for a year and a half during the transition to Sony. "Tommy was a manager. Céline Dion owes a lot more to him than [to] her voice coach. He saw this rough-hewn woman from Canada and turned her into a superstar. Tommy and I worked well together, but he had been a very abrasive manager—which the successful ones ultimately are."

One night in 1988, while attending a party for CBS blues singer Brenda K. Starr, Mottola received a demo tape from a mysterious benefactor. He stuck it in his limo's cassette deck and immediately knew he was hearing a star. Eighteen-year-old Mariah Carey and her multi-octave* voice had already received an offer from Warner's Mo Ostin for $300,000.

But Mottola received authorization from Yetnikoff to up the offer by $50,000, and he signed Carey. He also pushed her then-boyfriend, a producer, out of the picture, although neither Mottola nor Carey has ever said how. Mottola was married at the time, but he nonetheless canoodled with Carey around New York nightclubs. Soon he was divorced.

Yetnikoff continued to support his friend. He had given Mottola a $3 million bonus after just a few months in Teller's old job, and in 1990 arranged to have Mottola paid $15 million over five years, not counting bonuses. "One of the more interesting facts about Tommy is that he's extremely smart," Yetnikoff told a reporter. "He's hidden that from the world until recently." What Yetnikoff didn't know was that by the end of 1990, Mottola was fraternizing with his boss's long-term enemies. Yetnikoff was right—Mottola was extremely smart. He proved a master of power politics at Sony Music Entertainment. He saw cracks in the powerful chairman's foundation. For example, just two years after the Sony takeover, Yetnikoff was in rehab. He was in the process of divorcing his long-suffering wife, Cynthia. Warner had displaced Yetnikoff's previously dominant company in market share, building up new acts like R.E.M. and Anita Baker, whereas Sony's biggest labels, Columbia and Epic, relied on older stars like Jackson and Springsteen. And it wasn't like anybody had any sympathy. He'd built up incredible ill will over two decades of childish behavior, making enemies everywhere he went. Sometime back, Yetnikoff had supposedly pissed off fellow record mogul David Geffen by asking one of his assistants whether the openly gay Geffen would teach Yetnikoff's girlfriend the finer points of oral sex. Geffen started talking to his old friends, Bruce Springsteen's manager, Jon Landau, and Michael Jackson himself, pushing them farther away from Yetnikoff. Landau issued a statement: "Neither Bruce nor I have had a significant conversation with [Yetnikoff] in nearly two years."

---

*Mariah Carey's eight-octave range is something of a canard. Media reports have placed her between four and eight octaves over the years, and I once made the mistake in a *Rocky Mountain News* concert review of repeating this information, leading to a flurry of emails between the managing editor and the entertainment editor. Snopes.com, the urban-myth-debunking website, believes eight octaves are impossible and Carey's range is probably closer to four. I guess it's just better to say, "She's a good singer."

Mottola formed an alliance with Geffen and Allen Grubman. The influential industry lawyer had recently tried to strong-arm Yetnikoff into signing a massive new contract for Michael Jackson, a client he'd recently taken over, but Yetnikoff blew up and banned Grubman, once his friend and confidant, from the building. (Jackson remained with Sony Music.) On advice from Geffen and Grubman, Mottola started schmoozing the Sony executives—most effectively, by befriending Akio Morita's aspiring pop-star goddaughter, Seiko Matsuda. Leaks appeared in the *Wall Street Journal* saying Yetnikoff was on his way out. Soon, Frank Dileo, a former Epic Records vice president of promotions, Yetnikoff's close friend, and Michael Jackson's manager, found himself the final link between Yetnikoff and his top artists. "Once they blow me out, Walter's vulnerable," Dileo remembers thinking. Shortly after that, Jackson abruptly fired Dileo. Yetnikoff suddenly had no artist connections.

Yetnikoff fell. Hard. Ohga, who had stayed at Yetnikoff's house and swam at his pool numerous times during his visits to New York, interrupted a vacation to meet with his Sony Music chief at his office. He patiently explained to Yetnikoff that he was tired of his public outbursts and lack of finesse with Sony's biggest stars. He put Yetnikoff on sabbatical, then pressured him to cut off his three-year contract. (Yetnikoff managed to retain $25 million in the settlement.) "I'm sorry, Walter," Ohga said, "but this hurts me more than it hurts you." Ohga did not shake his old friend's hand. After the Sony chief left with his attorney, a security guard showed up and asked Yetnikoff to leave through the side door. While Yetnikoff cleared out, Ohga was in the next room, symbolically handing over the reins to Mottola. (To Mottola's frustration, he wouldn't officially take over Sony Music until 1991, about a year after Yetnikoff left the company; at first, Ohga himself became chair of the music group and allowed Mickey Schulhof to run the daily operations as Mottola's boss.) After the purge, a reporter asked Yetnikoff what he would do. "Count my money," he replied. "And, believe me, that's going to take some time."

While Yetnikoff was counting, Mottola was spending. "He was riding that job for all it was worth," says an industry source from that time. Finally in charge of Sony Music, ex-manager Mottola gave Aerosmith, recently dropped by Geffen, a $25 million deal. He spent $800,000 to produce Carey's debut album, $500,000 to redo her first video, and another $1 million on general promotion. The *New York Times* called him "Sony Music's Mr. Big Spender" in a front-page headline. In June

1993, he married Carey in a massively overblown Manhattan wedding, in which the bride wore a 27-foot train and Springsteen, Tony Bennett, Ozzy Osbourne, and Robert De Niro were among the stars in attendance. The couple moved into a $10 million estate with a 20,000-square-foot house in Harrison, New York, surrounded by golf courses and country clubs. It was equipped with the works: shooting range, electronic security doors, 64-channel recording studio, indoor swimming pool, and Ralph Lauren as a neighbor.

Well before the wedding, Sony Music Entertainment employees fired up their publicity, marketing, and promotion machines to focus almost exclusively on Carey. "The eight-hundred-pound gorilla in the room was the fact that they were having a relationship and everybody in the world knew it," Bob Sherwood recalls. "There's not anybody with a brain who wasn't going to put maximum effort into her." During a contract negotiation in the early 1990s, Michael Jackson called an old friend, Mickey Schulhof, to complain that his sales slump was due to Mottola putting disproportionate resources into Carey's career. Yet, as Sherwood points out, the Carey-Mottola-Sony triumvirate paid off. Her Sony CDs would sell 55 million copies in the United States alone, putting her in the Top 20 of all time.

By 1992, though, given the hits from Carey, Dion, and Michael Bolton, Sony had a pop-only reputation. Springsteen had split with the E Street Band. Disturbing revelations about dalliances with young boys were starting to dog Michael Jackson. Sony Music, once a giant in the form of CBS Records, looked weak compared to competitors like Warner and even EMI. It wasn't that Sony Music was doing poorly, in general. The company's operating profits, according to the *New York Times,* jumped by 60 percent between 1987 and 1991. But its top rival, Warner, *doubled* its profits during the same period. This was unacceptable in a hyper-competitive business. Mottola would soon change all that. At one point Michele Anthony, the hard-nosed attorney for rock acts such as Guns N' Roses and Alice in Chains, told Mottola over dinner: "I wouldn't sign a rock act with Sony if my life depended on it. You guys are arrogant and out of touch, and your company has been living off the fat of its superstar roster for so long you don't have a clue how to develop a new act." Mottola hired Anthony, who started bringing hit rock acts to the label. Before long, Sony's high advances to top artists prompted huge bidding wars, helping to set the lavish new deals for Michael Jackson and Aerosmith as the industry standard.

"Nobody likes to overspend when you're on the corporate side," Schulhof says. "But I knew what Tommy was spending. I never had a problem with it, and I don't think what he spent was disproportionate with what others were spending at the time in the industry."

Mottola's personal expenses, including travel, ballooned to $10 million a year. Three of his five assistants made $180,000 a year. Employees received $550 Gucci bags for the holidays. Mottola's brain trust, including Anthony and rising Columbia chief Don Ienner, rode to the top of the Sony Building in New York in a special freight elevator, and drivers shuttled them around the city in new Mercedeses. They became Mottola's *famiglia*, as *New York* magazine later put it in a profile. Jeff Ayeroff, a longtime Warner Music executive in LA who joined New York–based Sony Music in 1994, as cofounder of the Work label, says: "It was sort of like the West Coast was liberal and the East Coast was take-no-prisoners. These guys were very aggressive and very smart and did whatever it took." When Work signed a young actress, Jennifer Lopez, Mottola instructed his people to open their wallets. "He let us spend more money on marketing than anybody else would have," Ayeroff recalls. J. Lo's 1999 debut *On the 6* went triple platinum.

Nobody worried about money at Sony. "I didn't look at the financials. I wasn't entrepreneurial, and I wasn't running the company," recalls Michael Goldstone, a talent whiz who linked an unknown San Diego singer, Eddie Vedder, with an established Seattle rock band and signed them to Epic as Pearl Jam. "I was this A&R gunslinger going out and finding bands." Pearl Jam and another of Goldstone's discoveries, Rage Against the Machine, became superstars. So did Ricky Martin, J. Lo (who was rumored to have gone out with Mottola after he broke up with Carey), Destiny's Child, the Dixie Chicks, and Shakira. It didn't matter how much the label spent as long as the hits kept coming.

ALTHOUGH A VETERAN Sony executive described Mottola's company to *New York* as "a real oligarchy," Bob Sherwood says the chairman and his people aspired to rebuild the label in Warner's laid-back image. "They wanted to move Columbia from being a New York–based, relatively uptight, suit-and-tie kind of label to a more Warner look," he says. "Tommy brought lots of Warner executives. They liked a more freeflowing style." To be sure, Warner's chairman, the goateed and erudite Mo Ostin, had built a record label where freewheeling executives could thrive. None other than Frank Sinatra had hired Ostin in 1963 to run his new label, Reprise, and Ostin had spent the better part of three decades signing artists on instinct, including Jimi Hendrix, Joni Mitchell, the Kinks, Frank Zappa, and Neil Young, and letting them do their thing over time. "Mo loved talent magnets like Geffen, [Elektra chief Bob] Krasnow, and [longtime Warner Music executive Lenny] Waronker," writes retired Warner executive Stan Cornyn in *Exploding*. "He collected them like his wife, Evelyn, collected fine scarves."

To illustrate the point, one day in 1983, one of Krasnow's hotshot A&R executives, Michael Alago, walked into his office talking up a new, eardrum-shattering heavy-metal band that had almost zero chance of ever getting on the radio. Krasnow really had no idea what Alago was talking about, but he authorized him to sign Metallica anyhow. "He trusted my instincts. Sometimes he said, 'You're crazy, we're not doing it,'" Alago says. "But he knew that I knew we were on to something." Metallica's Elektra albums, beginning with *Kill 'Em All*, would combine forces with Guns N' Roses to begin pushing hair metal off the charts. (Later, a succession of grunge bands would finish the job.) Although they started as long-haired teenagers hawking tapes, Metallica would sell 58 million albums by late 2008, just 2.5 million less than Michael Jackson, in the United States.

But Warner Music, by the early 1990s, was moving in a more corporate direction, just like every other major label during the CD boom. In this new world, patient, instinctive, aging talent aficionados like Ostin and Krasnow were rapidly becoming obsolete.

This Warner shift began, as most things at Warner did, with company chairman Steve Ross. Born Steven Jay Rechnitz in Brooklyn, son of Jewish immigrants, Ross married into money in 1954. He became the head of his father-in-law's company, Kinney Parking, as it was expanding from funeral homes to parking lots. By the late 1960s, Ross had made a lot of money, but he didn't want to spend the rest of his life worrying about funeral homes and parking lots. He identified a bunch of growth areas, and the one that interested him most was "leisure time." So he expanded, first by buying National Periodical Publications, the company that owned *MAD* magazine, and then by acquiring a huge talent agency, Warner–Seven Arts. One of the company's most valuable assets was a record label, Warner Reprise. Another asset was Atlantic Records, owned by perhaps the most famous record industry talent scout ever, Ahmet Ertegun, who (thanks to a hefty paycheck) agreed to be part of the $400 million deal. (Sinatra, as founder of Reprise, received $22.5 million—his biggest-ever single check at that time.)

Ross's style was to pay top executives like Ostin and Ertegun lavishly and leave them alone. The company thrived this way for years, and employees of the Burbank record label grew to, if not exactly love, then respect New York City–based Ross as a sort of benevolent corporate grandfather. "There were many people there in key positions that had been there a very long time," recalls Jorge Hinojosa, manager of Warner's first rap star, Ice-T. "Even the [Burbank] building was nicer than the other buildings. It was like this ski chalet—interesting wood and interesting design. It was a beautiful place."

So employees more or less trusted Ross when, in 1986, he started indulging merger pitches from Time Inc., the magazine empire. Ross was especially interested because of one of Time's assets, cable TV, which he saw as a growth industry at least as promising as "leisure" had been in the late 1960s. Time executives were impressed with money-making Warner Music. "At Time Warner, the record company was, cash on cash, the best business in the company," says Michael Fuchs, an executive of Time Warner–owned HBO who was instrumental in merging the companies. "Quarters when we used to make our presentation, the music guys would stand up and we'd go, 'Holy shit!' We couldn't believe it, how good their business was." After haggling for almost four years with Time executives, Ross agreed in 1990 to merge the two companies into Time Warner, with a stock market value of more than $15 billion and annual revenue of more than $10 billion. (The merger also started with $16 billion in debt.) Ross became CEO.

In late 1992, Ross, sixty-five, died unexpectedly of prostate cancer. Gerald Levin, a brilliant manager with a photographic memory, stepped in to become the company's chief executive officer. Levin, however, knew little about the record business. Pressured by debt, he and other corporate types started to demand that the music unit function like every other unit. "It was a pretty benign place when Steve Ross was alive and Mo reported to him," says Jeff Gold, Warner Music's executive vice president and general manager for much of the 1990s. "When they sold to Time, especially after Steve Ross died, all of a sudden people are looking at your quarterly results more closely. . . . If you sell fifty million records one year and seventy [million] the next year because of a couple of fluke records, then they say, 'All right, how are you going to sell eighty?' And it just wasn't a business that worked that way." Under

Levin, corporate types like Robert Morgado began to rise at Warner Music, while longtime executives like Mo Ostin found their influence diminished, an irritating development for the company's lower-level but experienced record men like Doug Morris and Danny Goldberg of Atlantic.

Levin's vision for Warner Music was "do no harm." Every Time Warner executive understood cable TV was the Almighty Future, and all the music and movie divisions had to do was quietly make money and not create a ruckus.

So it was interesting timing when Warner artist Ice-T, one of the most profane, funny, and forceful rappers of all time, chose to make a heavy metal record with his new band, Body Count. One song on this record, "Cop Killer," juxtaposed chilling gunshot noises against first-person lyrics encouraging violence against police officers. "What do you want to be when you grow up?" Ice-T asked ominously. "Good choice." Of course, the song was political—a response to police brutality in LA, a problem that had recently caused public outrage with the videotaped beating of Rodney King at the hands of the LA Police Department.

The story of "Cop Killer" began when Ice-T dropped off his new *Body Count* record to Warner executives. To a person—well, except for Russ Thyret, the label's executive vice president of marketing and promotion, who worried about the response from police groups and radio programmers—the staff loved it. They were also fond of Ice-T, whose menacing public persona masked the warm, savvy, charismatic businessman who'd sold more than 2 million albums for Seymour Stein's Sire Records with little overhead. Back then, hip-hop was a street genre, and a few well-placed singles at key Los Angeles or Chicago radio stations gave artists the credibility they needed for heavy sales. Ice was a master of this approach, and he was also hot, having just coheadlined the first Lollapalooza festival around the United States in summer 1991. *Body Count* came out March 30, 1992. The first single, "There Goes the Neighborhood," was about to hit MTV.

Then, in late April, a jury acquitted the three officers accused of beating Rodney King, and riots broke out all over Los Angeles. Racial tensions heated up across the country, and "Cop Killer" blew up into front-page headlines. It's hard to pinpoint the exact date that "the fucking 'Cop Killer' fuse gets lit," as Hinojosa remembers it, but he knows it was a few days before he and Ice boarded a private Warner jet to meet with label executives in New York to sign a new record deal. Madonna had just received $60 million for a multimedia deal including books and movies, and Ice-T and Hinojosa were fantasizing about a similar deal worth $10 million. But Warner executives' tone had abruptly changed. "By the time we land in New York, the talk [at the meeting with Warner] wasn't about 'how can we capitalize on this shit we're doing?' It was like, 'This "Cop Killer" shit is kind of messed-up,'" Hinojosa says. "We got dressed to go to a party. We didn't realize we were going to a funeral." Time Warner was in crisis management mode.

The controversy dragged on, through the end of 1992. Picketers marched in front of the company building, carrying "Time Warner Puts Profits Over Police Lives" signs. Warner Music execs received death threats. Police groups boycotted the company. Stockholder Charlton Heston stood up at a meeting and recited Ice-T lyrics such as "I'm 'bout to dust some cops off!" like Moses reading the Ten Commandments. His powerful peers threatened to withdraw stock. Ice posed in a policeman's uniform on the cover of *Rolling Stone*. He provocatively asked reporters why songs like Johnny Cash's "Folsom Prison Blues," with the line "I shot a man in Reno just to watch him die," didn't get the same kind of response. At first, Time Warner supported Ice-T as an artist with the right to free speech. Then the company caved, putting out a version of *Body Count* (with Ice's authorization) minus the "Cop Killer" track. Executives backed off their impassioned free-speech defense. For the cover of Ice-T's *next* album, *Home Invasion*, he wanted to use a cartoon design of a teenager listening to rap and enjoying Malcolm X's autobiography as exaggerated ghetto bad guys break into houses, brandish large guns, and grope scantily clad women. He brought it to Warner's cuddly, chalet-style offices in Burbank. Executives debated the cover but decided they couldn't support it. Ice-T knew what time it was. In a letter to Warner, he announced his split from the label. He put out 1993's *Home Invasion*, provocative cover and all, on an independent hip-hop label, Priority Records. *Time*'s reviewer, a Time Warner employee, called the album "balanced and coherent."

Warner's capitulation to public pressure over a work of art was symbolic of larger problems within the company. Robert Morgado, whom *Master of the Game* author Connie Bruck described as Steve Ross's "hatchet man," was slowly flexing his muscle, pushing for changes at the various labels where Ross had been basically hands-off since, well, forever. "No one ever replaced [Ross] in terms of being able to balance the complex cast of characters—all of whom derived some sense of direction from him," remembers Danny Goldberg, who would briefly head the label after the Time-Warner merger. "Once [Ross] died, Morgado tried to make it a more conventional structure, with everyone reporting to him. And Mo never got along with him. And [Morgado] never got along with Doug Morris, either."

Ostin couldn't take it. In early 1994, he left the label after thirty-one years. Morgado initially promoted Morris from head of Atlantic to head of Warner's US operations overall, thinking he could control the younger executive. Instead, Morgado kicked off an epic, label-wide power struggle, which *The Wall Street Journal* called "open warfare." Elektra's veteran executive, Bob Krasnow, not one to easily accept reporting to new people, raised a stink and left the company. The office shouting matches between Morris and Morgado reverberated along yards and yards of corporate hallways. The company divided into factions. In 1995, Time Warner's Levin felt Morgado had alienated too many of Warner's music executives and fired him.* Later, over lunch, Morris would tell Morgado he regretted the last eighteen months. The two shook hands. "To observers, it was like tacking a happy ending on to *King Lear*," Stan Cornyn wrote. But it wasn't over yet.

Michael Fuchs, a longtime HBO executive and Time Warner power player, took over. He started to see cracks in Warner Music's foundation. He had slightly more polish than Morgado, but he had a nasty habit of telling longtime record executives—including Morris—what they didn't want to hear. "When I got there [Warner Music], the wheels had begun to fall off a little bit," Fuchs says. "They'd had about ten years of the CD boom, and when the money rolls in like that there's a tendency to live big and everything seemed quite easy. I can't attest to what it was like before that. But when things began to slow down, it became evident that these businesses were not being run very tightly." Fuchs started "moving the furniture around right away," as he puts it. He fired Morris, shut down expensive label experiments—like a direct-mail operation that never really went anywhere—and made cutting fat out of budgets a hallmark of his leadership. But he got no further than Morgado. Levin fired Fuchs, too, in November 1995, after six months.

---

* Morgado did not respond to an interview request for this book; when he left in 1995, he touted the company's "strong growth trajectory" in a Time Warner press release, from $1 billion in revenues in 1985 to almost $4 billion.

Just before he left, though, Fuchs helped Levin make a historic decision. It seems quaint today, after fifteen years of explicitly violent and sexual hip-hop from Snoop Dogg to Young Jeezy, but in 1996, Time Warner was unwilling to irritate its moralistic shareholders in the post–"Cop Killer" era. C. DeLores Tucker, spotlight-loving head of the National Political Congress of Black Women, made sure of that. She owned ten shares of Time Warner stock and showed up at a May 1996 shareholders' meeting at City Center in New York. In a seventeen-minute speech that made headlines everywhere, Tucker denounced Interscope Records, a division of Warner Music, for its violent and misogynistic hip-hop music. A third of the crowd spontaneously applauded, including Henry Luce III, son of legendary Time Inc. founder Henry Luce. Under pressure, Levin and Fuchs divested from Interscope. Jimmy Iovine and Ted Field, owners of the hip-hop label, bought their 50 percent stake back from Warner, then turned around and sold the label to MCA for $200 million. "[Warner Music] couldn't take the heat and decided to get rid of Interscope," says Roger Ames, who became Warner Music chairman in 1999. "Certainly, for that period, their record company suffered by being owned by Time Warner."

As for Interscope, it would fare quite well, breaking artists like Eminem, 50 Cent, Gwen Stefani, and The Game over the next decade.

BY THE EARLY 1990S, it was getting harder for anybody to compete with major labels like Sony and Warner, who were spending tens of millions of their massive CD profits to turn talented new artists into Michael Jackson–style hit machines. Even A&M, the independent label that had started in Alpert's garage in 1962, was struggling. "Big advances were starting to be more of a key fix in this game," recalls Jerry Moss, the label's cofounder.

In 1989, Moss and his partner, Herb Alpert, decided twenty-seven years of independence was enough. Their storied label was in the midst of a dismal year—its biggest single was "Rock On," a cover song by hunky *The Young and the Restless* star Michael Damian. Moss was friendly with the head of PolyGram, David Fine, and he approached him about buying A&M.

Fine was receptive. After buying troubled Casablanca Records in the late 1970s, PolyGram had spent much of the postdisco crash in free fall. But the CD bailed out the company, in part because the public was suddenly eager to buy old content—from the Supremes to Bob Marley to A&M stalwarts like Joe Cocker and the Police. PolyGram became the proverbial big, hungry fish. It ate Island Records, the maverick record company that had turned Bob Marley and U2 into stars. It ate Motown, which no longer resembled the legendary Detroit company of Marvin Gaye and the Supremes but still had a huge catalog. And it ate A&M, for a reported $500 million in 1989. "We had the opportunity to get fresh new repertoire in the company," says Jan Cook, PolyGram's finance chief at the time. "A&M had a whole catalog roster that was not to be sneezed at."

The sale wasn't supposed to change much at A&M. Jerry Moss stayed on, working with his friend David Fine, and theoretically he would continue to bring Stings and Janet Jacksons onto the roster. But Moss and Friesen started to feud more than usual. Over twenty-five years, they had drifted to their own sweet spots within the company, Friesen with marketing and day-to-day management and Moss with sales. Often, though, Moss would pop up out of nowhere to undercut a Friesen decision. "From my perspective, Gil was a terrific leader, very involved, very forward-thinking, very engaged—and really had to work around things. It was not unusual for Jerry to sort of stick his nose into Gil's office and just question what was going on," recalls Al Cafaro, who would later run the company. "I think that was something that Gil struggled with." After the Poly-Gram sale, the long-standing relationship between Moss and Friesen changed. Moss became PolyGram's official contact at A&M. Friesen, who had essentially been running the company forever, chafed at the new structure. The company divided into Moss factions and Friesen factions. Friesen approached PolyGram execs and declared he was in charge. According to one insider, Moss interpreted this move as disloyal. By the end of 1990, Friesen had resigned, under pressure from A&M's board, which included Jerry Moss and Herb Alpert.

Neither Moss nor Friesen is willing to go into much detail about this period. "We had a different philosophical approach to where the company should go," Moss says. They remained estranged until the Rock and Roll Hall of Fame inducted the Police in 2003. "That was great fun," Moss says. "I'll always give old friends the benefit of the doubt."

Moss, too, left A&M after PolyGram's leadership changed. David Fine was out. French record executive Alain Levy was in. "All of a sudden I had a new boss, who wasn't laughing at my jokes," Moss says wryly.

The company heated up again, briefly, under Cafaro, as Soundgarden, Janet Jackson, and Sting took off, but A&M would never regain its former glory as the weird hit indie label that grew out of Herb Alpert's garage.

A&M was hardly the only independent to sell out during the CD boom. In 1990, David Geffen sold his namesake record label to the music-and-movies corporation MCA for $545 million. Later that year, Sony's Japanese competitor, Matsushita, bought its own software company—MCA—for $1.6 billion. Nirvana's Kurt Cobain may have worn a "Corporate Rock Magazines Still Suck" T-shirt on the cover of *Rolling Stone* in 1992, but Nirvana's record label, Geffen, was being rolled up into bigger and bigger corporations.

Edgar Bronfman Jr., a songwriter and longtime music and movie fan, paid close attention to these mergers. Bronfman was the third-generation heir of the Seagram Co., the massive Montreal distillery of Chivas Regal, Crown Royal, Captain Morgan rum, and Tropicana fruit juice. At first, Bronfman chose not to follow his father, Edgar Bronfman Sr., into the family business. Instead, he wrote songs with a partner, Bruce Roberts, including Dionne Warwick's soupy 1985 ballad "Whisper in the Dark." (Bronfman Jr.'s *nom de rock* was "Junior Miles," and he gets several songwriting credits on *Intimacy,* Roberts's 1995 album for Atlantic Records.) Bronfman also dabbled in Hollywood, producing movies like 1982's *The Border*, which flopped despite costars Jack Nicholson and Harvey Keitel. That same year, with no entertainment successes to speak of, Bronfman finally accepted a job from his father to be Seagram's assistant to the office of the president. Within a few years, his father made him chairman.

So Bronfman accepted that his destiny was not to be the next Neil Sedaka. But there was still a chance to be the next Steve Ross. Bronfman waited for the right moment to jump in. He focused on the storied MCA, which owned masters by the Who and B.B. King but had in recent hitless years earned a reputation as the "Music Cemetery of America." In March 1995, Bronfman pushed the Seagram board to buy MCA for $5.7 billion. This was not, as some have speculated, because Bronfman the songwriter wanted a pathway into the music business. Bronfman says he merely wished to diversify the company into a more stable North American industry. "As far as I know, the board at Seagram may have been entirely and blissfully ignorant of my songwriting career," Bronfman says today.

* * *

BRONFMAN STRIPPED OFF the MCA name, which he deemed overly corporate, and replaced it with a more familiar one that symbolized his rebuilding efforts—Universal. Hollywood jeered—what business did this entitled liquor-and-oil baron have in movies and music?—but Bronfman wasn't finished. The Seagram tycoon also had his eye on PolyGram.

Purchasing A&M, Island, and Motown, in addition to reaping big European profits off its vast classical music catalog, made PolyGram the world's biggest music company by 1998, with hits by country star Shania Twain, rappers Jay-Z and DMX, and teen pop trio Hanson. But its young film division had not quite turned the corner to profitability. And the company's chief executive, Alain Levy, believed film was the future. Levy had convinced Jan Timmer, head of his parent company, Philips, that PolyGram should invest heavily in building a credible film division. But Timmer retired in 1996, and his successor, Cor Boonstra, who came from the international food conglomerate Sara Lee, didn't know from the film business. "Levy took the position that 'I'm doing a great job with the biggest record company in the world, this is what I'm doing, these are the reasons I'm doing it, leave me alone,'" says Al Cafaro, the A&M chief who worked for Levy after PolyGram bought his company. "And Boonstra didn't like that."

One day in 1998, Hollywood-obsessed Levy flew from London to Los Angeles to meet with Bronfman. They were to discuss PolyGram buying Universal's film division, owned at the time by Bronfman's Seagram Co. Bronfman, however, may have known something Levy didn't know. At that very moment, Seagram was in the process of buying PolyGram. "I don't think [Boonstra] had Alain Levy much in the loop," says a source close to the negotiations. Although Bronfman says he's pretty sure Levy knew he was buying the company when he first met him, many PolyGram executives of the time had no idea the cataclysmic merger was coming. "We were certainly taken by surprise," recalls longtime PolyGram finance chief Jan Cook.*

At the time, Cook was fifty-nine. He had been planning to retire

---

*Whether Levy knew about the Seagram sale during his meeting with Bronfman is in dispute among various sources. Cook believes he didn't, while Bronfman thinks he did. Levy did not respond to several interview requests.

within the next four or five years. He was at his second home, in Portu-
gal, when he received a call from PolyGram's president: *Could you fly
to New York City right away to complete some paperwork?* Seagram
just bought the company. "Using private jets and the Concorde and
such things, I was able to get there in thirty-six hours," Cook recalls.
He did the due diligence, but he wasn't happy about it. To Cook, the
company had been sold out from under him. Seagram offered him the
chief financial officer position with its newly renamed Universal Music
Group. "But what you get with this merger, all the people were going to
be axed," he says. "And I didn't want to be the guy who was doing that to
my colleagues and the employees I'd worked with and trusted to build
the company. I said, 'No, thank you very much,' and retired." Seagram
fired 980 PolyGram employees and cut 200 acts from its music roster.
The company abruptly closed fifty-three-year-old Mercury Records,
former home of Dinah Washington and Bon Jovi, and merged Geffen
and A&M with Interscope, the onetime gangsta rap pariah label. "They
swallowed up my company, and I was gone," says Mark Kates, the Geffen A&R executive who worked with Nirvana, Teenage Fanclub, and
Sonic Youth and signed Beck and Weezer. "Seagram is a company
based on selling the same amount of fluid to the same part of the world
to the same amount of people every year. That's great, but the record
business could not be more different than that." Geffen had been the
most successful rock label of the early 1990s, but it was no longer the
future. That belonged to hip-hop and pop. Interscope Records. And
Universal.

If ever there was a record label built for economic success in 1998, it
was the Universal Music Group. Bronfman's wheeling and dealing put
him in control of some of the most storied record labels of all time—
A&M, PolyGram, Island, Geffen, Interscope, and Motown, to name a
few—stocked with modern hit makers from U2 to Dr. Dre and a catalog including Bob Marley, Nirvana, the Supremes, the Who, and Hank
Williams Sr. He also had two of the top music executives. "These are
record men like the old days," former RCA president Bob Buziak says.
"Doug Morris and Jimmy Iovine, you could say, are the Jerry Mosses
and Ahmet Erteguns." In other words, nothing could go wrong at the
Universal Music Group, as long as CDs kept selling. And what could
possibly stop them?

Big Music's Big Mistakes, Part 2

Independent Radio Promotion

The 1960 payola scandal that wrecked pioneering rock 'n' roll DJ Alan Freed's career—he and seven others were indicted for bribery, and he died five years later—was hardly the end of payola. Federal laws regarding this kind of bribery were weak and almost impossible to enforce, and in 1979, the Federal Communications Commission watered them down even more, decreeing that "social exchanges between friends are not payola." So record companies kept doing it—spending more and more money every year.

The indie promo racket attracted very questionable characters to the music business, which had never exactly had a squeaky clean reputation. One was Fred DiSipio, a skinny, 5'7" Philadelphian with a high-pitched voice and a gigantic bodyguard known as Big Mike. *Nobody* crossed DiSipio and Big Mike. DiSipio had been a war hero on the USS *Gambier Bay* during World War II, and he started his career managing singers like future talk show host Mike Douglas and crooner Al Martino.

In the 1980s, DiSipio was a key figure in what record label types called "the Network," a loose affiliation of indie radio promoters who took payments of $60 million to $80 million a year from major labels and used them to lean on radio program directors. In this way, hits were made. But it was an expensive way—according to Fredric Dannen's investigative classic *Hit Men,* the record industry spent more than 30 percent of its pretax profits on independent radio promotion.

Hit Men opens with a 1980 experiment by Dick Asher, then CBS Records's deputy president. Asher was an ex-Marine. He was practical. He liked balanced budgets. He had been head of CBS's international division for years, signing smash artists such as Julio Iglesias. The company's top executives brought him over to cut costs. And he couldn't help but notice the annual millions in the indie promo column. Asher chose one of the biggest rock bands in the world, Pink Floyd, as an unwitting guinea pig. Asher decided not to pay the Network to push Pink Floyd's sure-thing single, "Another Brick in the Wall, Part Two." It wouldn't matter, he figured. *The Wall* was huge, even without radio play, and Pink Floyd's concert tour was setting sales records. But guess what? Nobody played the song. Eventually Pink Floyd's manager contacted Asher and begged for mercy. A moral crusade was well and good, but *where was the radio hit?* Asher backed down. Floyd got its smash single.

For this and other crusades, Asher walked into a feud with his boss, Walter Yetnikoff, who knew many of the promo men personally and looked the other way at the gigantic budget items. Tension between the two stubborn men blew up into profanity-laced shouting matches at the CBS offices and soon led to Asher's downfall. Yetnikoff fired him in 1983. "I wasn't a whistleblower. I wasn't," says Asher, a retired music business consultant who lives in Boca Raton, Florida. "I reached a point where I didn't want CBS involved in something. If any part of CBS were caught in any illegal activity, the government could pull their licenses."

On February 24, 1986, DiSipio showed up on television—for the wrong reasons. For months, *NBC Nightly News* had been investigating independent radio promotion and its alleged ties to the Mafia. A month earlier, reporter Brian Ross had been the beneficiary of one of the more remarkable coincidences in TV journalism history. Ross was sitting in the lobby of New York's Helmsley Hotel, waiting to interview a source, when Mafia figures John Gotti, Joseph N. Gallo, and Frank DeCicco suddenly appeared before him, bodyguards in tow, and took the elevator to a penthouse room. Following not far behind were two of the biggest members of the Network—Joe Isgro (the West Coast man) and Fred DiSipio (East Coast). Ross frantically called his producer, Ira Silverman, and they managed to snag the live footage of Isgro, DiSipio, and the Mob figures coming back out of the hotel. It would dominate the network's report a month later.

Predictably, *NBC Nightly News*'s "The New Payola" freaked out the industry. It became an albatross, something record executives had to answer for at shareholder meetings. When the story broke, label executives said they were shocked—*shocked*—that people would believe such a thing went on in their companies. Privately, many of these executives were psyched. They suddenly had a moral and legal reason to kill their outlandish budget items for indie promo. Yetnikoff, who had helped squash an internal Recording Industry Association of America investigation on the same subject, defended indie promotion in several interviews. He thought the whole business was funny and arranged to have the theme from *The Godfather* playing at a CBS function. "I'm not saying no indie [radio promoter] ever did anything wrong, but there's nothing inherently bad about trying to *influence*, is there?" Yetnikoff told *Esquire* in an extraordinary article in which he slams cocktails at a nightclub with Mick Jagger and the Eurythmics' Dave Stewart. Payola ended in a cluster of late-1980s grand jury and Senate hearings, some led by Al Gore. As always, though, pay-to-play bounced back. Only the names changed.*

Born and raised in Cincinnati, Bill Scull had answered a newspaper ad in 1970 for a job involving records. He thought it meant financial records. But the job was with an independent record distributor, one of those guys who bought crates of vinyl records from labels like Columbia and Epic and sold them to music stores. Every city had an indie distributor at the time—big ones like Cleveland and Chicago had two. Unassuming, of medium height, sporting square glasses and slicked-back hair, Scull turned out to be good at shaking hands, making connections, and turning business contacts into lifelong friends. "He's always doing

---

* DiSipio quickly disappeared. Isgro was sentenced in 2000 to 50 months in prison for loan-sharking; when he got out, the *Hoffa* producer secured the movie rights to the story of 1920s mobster Lucky Luciano.

promotion, no matter what it is," says Craig Diable, who worked Warner Music radio promo in the Midwest for years. "If he meets the chef of a restaurant, the next thing you know, Billy's like, 'You need tickets? You need CDs? Let me know.' The guy says, 'You don't call for reservations— you call *me*.' And this guy's got him all set up. That's what Billy does."

Scull's next job was at a small label, Metromedia. A colleague quit and Scull wound up with the Miami account. Before long he represented the South, too. He'd fly into his towns, and indie distributors would pick him up and show him a good time. Scull climbed the ladder of record labels, from Metromedia to Polydor to Elektra to Arista. Then he started to meet guys in Cincinnati and Cleveland who worked in independent radio promotion. They took payments from record labels and gave some of it to radio stations.

Scull was tight with these radio program directors in the Midwest. He had partied with them for years. In 1980, Scull decided to switch from record promotion to independent radio promotion. Instead of pulling down a salary from labels to push records directly to station programmers, he'd work for himself. He'd be a middleman. "I thought, 'There's no independent promotion person in Cincinnati. I've been doing this ten years. I'm going to take a shot,'" he recalls. He opened his business in his upstairs bedroom, with one telephone. Ariola Records, a small label, was the first to pay him—$1,000 for adding Amii Stewart's "Knock on Wood" to a local playlist. More and more small labels started hiring him.

Soon he decided to hit up the big-time labels—Capitol, Columbia, Warner.

And that's when a record executive told him he'd better check in with Fred DiSipio. "I called Fred," Scull recalls. "Turns out he not only had Capitol, he had Columbia, Epic, Warner Bros. All of a sudden, I had a whole lot of records and ten or fifteen stations. Fred started sending me a lot of money. FedExed every week. It was awesome. Beyond my wildest dreams. I would get, like, $10,000 or $15,000 depending on what kind of a week it was. And that's how it got started."

Scull was well positioned throughout the *NBC Nightly News* debacle, which extricated DiSipio and Isgro from the music industry for good, give or take a few lawsuits and harsh words. He had kept a low profile in Cincinnati, opening Tri State Promotions and building up clout over time with his radio connections. In Chicago, Jeff McClusky, whom the *Chicago Tribune* called "an earnest, non-blustery, teetotaling family man who works 12-hour days and knows just about everybody who matters in the industry," became Scull's biggest rival. "Fred went away. The old guys that had been doing this—they all kind of went away. Their business was a different business. They had a handful of people who they had these relationships with," Scull says. "It became a lot more corporate and a lot more aboveboard. And Jeff McClusky and our company really became the large companies." McClusky went so far as to contact FCC attorneys, making sure his business model as a middleman was legal. What he did, he says, was no different than a peanut butter manufacturer paying for positioning at a grocery store. In any event, Congress never intervened.

In fact, Congress relaxed its radio restrictions during the mid-1990s, allowing fewer and fewer media companies to own more and more of the stations. By 2001, three giant broadcasters, Clear Channel, Citadel, and Cumulus, owned 60 of the top US stations. The indie promoters started going straight to the companies, rather than the individual program directors. McClusky, for example, arranged an exclusive deal with Cumulus Media, which reported revenues of more than $1 million a year it received from record companies via indie promoters in its annual reports. In 2001, Bill McGathy, another indie promoter, successfully bid $3.25 million for the rights to represent Clear Channel and the hundred-plus US stations it owned. "Drugs and hookers are out; detailed invoices are in," wrote Eric Boehlert, an investigative music business reporter for Salon.com who covered indie radio promotion extensively. Scull, McClusky, and the others in the indie promo racket would take as much as $300 million in "legal payola" every year from record labels by the late 1990s. They'd turn around and give program directors money and record labels access to the program directors. Once, McClusky paid $2,000 out of his own pocket for fifty premium seats to a Backstreet Boys concert in Buffalo, New York. He snagged the tickets through his connections with the Boys' management company, the Firm. He then gave them to a Top 40 program director in Rochester, New York, to build a lasting relationship and open the door for future single "adds."

It was not uncommon for Scull to make $50,000 in a week from record labels, 60 or 70 percent of which he would give to radio stations. That's almost $1.7 million every year in profit—not as much as the $27 million DiSipio was said to have amassed in *Hit Men*, but still a decent living. "From the mid-'80s to the late '90s, the labels were really, as we say, 'donkey strong.' They were full of cash. They were at their peak," Scull says. "Because they had the money, they signed more acts than any time previously. The large labels, because they had the catalog, were the rich ones—the Sonys, the RCAs, the Capitols." The labels couldn't figure out how *not* to pay him. "Probably [labels'] biggest expense was indie pro-motion," says Tim Hurst, a former Midwest radio-promo man for Warner's Reprise Records. "The labels just thought they had to keep up with the Joneses. If the next-door neighbor had indie promotion, and they didn't, they would have gotten screwed."

Whether teetotaling Jeff McClusky or allegedly Mob-tied Fred DiSipio was at the center of the action, indie promo was like a drug for the labels: They were addicted to paying multimillion-dollar chunks of their annual budgets to these middlemen, and they couldn't figure out how to stop it. This worked out just fine in the donkey-strong music business economy, but when the money ran out, it was a disaster. Labels managed to extri-cate themselves from their arrangements to pay promoters like McClusky and Scull tens of millions of dollars a year. Big radio companies, like Clear Channel, decided they didn't need the hassle of being linked to pay-to-play in the public eye. So in the early 2000s, the indie promo men finally went away, for the most part. But that created a problem: The radio people at major labels found themselves with no legal, reliable means of getting songs on the radio. (They didn't have Bill Scull's connections with program directors, for example.) And they couldn't keep their jobs without a steady stream of hit radio singles. They were trapped. Left to their own devices, many of them resorted to bribery. It took a crusading New York attorney general with gubernatorial ambitions—Eliot Spitzer, who, as it turned out, had a dirty secret of his own—to remove pay-to-play for good from the record industry. In the process, Spitzer killed pay-to-play. And he further crippled the business.

———

Big Music's Big Mistakes, Part 3

Digital Audio Tape

For decades, the Recording Industry Association of America, or RIAA, had a simple job: certifying records that sold 500,000 copies as "gold," and records that sold 1 million as "platinum." The trade group for the major labels changed with the times, though, and by the late 1970s it had a fulltime staff devoted to fighting counterfeiters and bootleggers. By the end of the next decade, news reports estimated losses to music, video, book, and software piracy were $270 billion in a year. It was typical for RIAA officials to work with police on raids—like one in 1985 on a printing plant in Bell, California, outside Los Angeles, which captured 160,000 bogus labels for hit groups like Air Supply and Kool and the Gang. The counterfeiters had intended to affix these labels to inferior copies of records and sell them on the streets—potentially taking away as much as $1 million from the music business, executives said. Three men at the plant were arrested.

Into this paranoid world stumbled the Digital Audio Tape.

Developed by Sony Corp. in the mid-1980s, DAT was to the clunky old cassette what the CD was to vinyl. Like the CD, the magnetic tape was digital, which meant sound was recorded in a series of ones and zeroes, eliminating cassette hiss. Sony was in a hurry. Its executives perceived the DAT, as well as spinoff formats like its own MiniDisc and Philips's Digital Compact Cassette, as the future of the record business. Selling one format—CD—was working just fine. Selling *two* products—CD and DAT—would make everybody even richer. Preparing for a 1987 launch, Sony lined up support from Denon, Matsushita, and others and released players for $1,000 to $1,500.

But there was a problem, which boiled down to one verb: *record*. The major labels didn't like that word very much. They hadn't liked it with the cassette, either, but cassettes made inferior copies of records and CDs, and "copying the copy" with tapes was a recipe for frustratingly sludgy sound. By contrast, the DAT was digital, so it could make a perfect copy every time. Sony marketers were proud of their sleek, easy-to-use, high-sound-quality tape, and they rolled out a campaign similar to the one that had worked so well for the CD. They were met not with hugs and flowers but with glares and threats from the labels. "They proceeded to claim that DAT would be the end of the world, cause cancer, and create global warming," says John Briesch, president of Sony's consumer audio-video group.

The biggest label cheeses—CBS's Walter Yetnikoff, Warner's Mo Ostin, Arista's Clive Davis—flew to Canada to meet with electronics-industry bigwigs for a summit on the new technology. This would become known as the "Maneuver in Vancouver." Unbeknownst to "the Japanese," as then-EMI executive Joe Smith refers to the electronics reps,

CBS Records's high-tech people had come up with their own solution to the DAT problem. They created Copycode, a tiny circuit that would cut notes out of the music if anybody tried to record a CD onto a DAT. The electronics reps were told all DATs must come equipped with this new copy-protection technology. *Or else.* Miffed at this crude display of record industry clout, the Japanese walked out. In response, the labels refused to license their music to DAT. Nobody would be able to buy a Springsteen or Madonna DAT in a store.

Sony pressed on, but the DAT wasn't about to get anywhere without the record industry's support. So in 1989, reps from consumer electronics companies met label executives in Athens, Greece, to hammer out a compromise—nobody would have to pay labels a royalty if they sold a DAT device, but they would have to equip them with a widget known as the Serial Copy Management System. This would allow people to copy music—once. What they couldn't do was copy the copies. In 1990, the world's biggest publishers—songwriters and other businesspeople who make money off songwriting royalties—piled on. Led by Sammy "High Hopes" Cahn, a group of one hundred prominent publishers filed suit against Sony, demanding royalty payments for the devices. Sony had no choice but to concede. Thus did Congress pass the Audio Home Recording Act, riddled with loopholes, which President George H. W. Bush signed in early 1992. By then, though, the DAT had lost excitement in the marketplace. "We killed the DAT machine," Joe Smith recalls.

But there is an important footnote to the DAT's tragic story. When Congress was working with the recording industry to create the Audio Home Recording Act, lawyers for computer companies demanded an exemption. Americans, they said, had the unalienable right to back up data on CD-ROMs. "I said, 'Here's the deal: You either cut us out of this, or we're going to throw our bodies across the tracks,'" says Jim Burger, a lawyer who represented Apple Computer and other high-tech companies at the time. The record industry fiercely opposed this exemption, but its lawyers and lobbyists realized the legislation wouldn't pass without a compromise. So it was decided computer companies could sell PCs with built-in recording devices. IBM and the others would pay no royalties to record labels, nor would they add a chip restricting the number of copies. "They blew it," Sony's DAT marketer, Marc Finer, says of label lobbyists who allowed the exemption without a major fight. "Completely."

It took a few years for the implications of this loophole to sink in. In 1994, Andy Schneidkraut, owner of Albums on the Hill, a twenty-year-old record store at the bottom of a staircase at the University of Colorado in Boulder, had his best year ever. He sold 1,800 copies of the Dave Matthews Band's *Under the Table and Dreaming* CD to legions of college students. Life was good. But his exuberance was short-lived. By the end of the 1990s, he was lucky to sell 200 copies of *any* record. Why? Two words: *ripping* and *burning.* CU students began to show up on campus with their own PCs, all equipped with the CD-rewrite drives exempted by the Audio

Home Recording Act. No longer did every Dave Matthews Band fan drop by Albums for a $16.99 CD. *One* fan would drop by for the CD and burn copies for the other fifty kids on his dorm hall. Schneidkraut considered selling those ubiquitous packages of CD-Rs, which seemed to get cheaper and cheaper every day. But he couldn't bring himself to do it. "It was like a knife in my back—if someone would come up and say, 'I'd like the new Dave Matthews, and can I get twenty-five blank CDs please?'" says Schneidkraut, who still holds court behind the counter at Albums, where annual revenues have dropped from $600,000 to $240,000. "It was too painful."

It was particularly galling to Steve Gottlieb, president of the independent label TVT Records, to walk down the aisle of an Office Depot or Best Buy and find a row of name-brand, Microsoft Windows—equipped personal computers containing CD burners and storage capacity to hold thousands of songs. "It was clear that the computer companies—Dell, Apple, Compaq—had done market research and determined that a great way to reinvigorate laptop sales and computer sales is to bundle them with the implicit proposition that you could have all the music you want, free," Gottlieb complains. "And what's the music industry response to this? 'We don't sue big companies.'" But before the implications of ripping and burning truly sank in—for better or for worse—the record industry would enjoy another renaissance. For a few glorious years, in the late 1990s and early 2000s, it seemed like teen pop would last forever.

Chapter 3
1998–2001

The Teen Pop Bubble: Boy Bands and Britney
Make the Business Bigger Than Ever—
But Not for Long

THE MOMENT Erik Bradley knew boy bands were taking over the world came on June 28, 1998, at the New World Music Theatre near Chicago. 'NSync, the hunky young pop stars who'd just had a radio hit with "I Want You Back," were opening the outdoor show. Bradley was backstage. The band was hanging out in its trailer before its brief set. Bradley smelled something odd. It seemed to be coming from a large metal fence, covered with a blue plastic tarp, which separated the fans from the performers. Then he realized desperate fans were using lighters to *burn holes* in the tarp so they could get a better look at Justin Timberlake, Lance Bass, and the rest. "It was *maniacal*," says Bradley, program director for Chicago's B-96, a Top 40 radio station that played the crap out of boy bands for the better part of four years. "It shows you how bad they wanted to see them. It was really, really huge."

For Tom Calderone, the moment was April 14 of the same year, during 'NSync's first MTV appearance, set in a new Times Square studio. The channel was still ensconced in grunge and hip-hop, and this squeaky clean group of dancing white kids wasn't exactly what producers craved for their new countdown show *MTV Live*. "We were like, 'All right, they seem to have a track record with Disney, they're female-themed, let's give it a shot,'" says Calderone, then the channel's executive vice president for music and talent. "All I remember was five thousand kids outside on the sidewalk screaming. We got a phone call from HR saying, 'The *New York Times* is complaining because it's so loud—how long is this show going to last?'" *A long time*, as it turned out. Within five months, *MTV Live* would morph into *Total Request Live* and become the primary outlet for 'NSync, the Backstreet Boys, Britney Spears, Christina Aguilera, and their vast battalions of sign-painting teens.

The B-96 Summer Bash and *MTV Live* were just the beginning. From roughly 1997 through 2001, teen pop was a massive worldwide record industry sales machine. The Backstreet Boys' 1999 album *Millennium* set an all-time record by selling 1.13 million copies in its first week; Britney Spears's *Oops! . . . I Did It Again* leaped over that mark a year later, selling 1.3 million; and 'NSync would establish a new first-week record, once and for all, in late 2000, with 2.4 million. All told, these three acts alone would sell 96 million CDs in the United States—more than the Eagles, the Rolling Stones, or Michael Jackson. The CD boom of the 1980s and 1990s peaked spectacularly during this era. "People keep asking me, 'What are you going to do when the pop bubble bursts, as it always has in the past?'" complained Larry Rudolph, Britney Spears's manager and attorney, to the *Los Angeles Times.* At the time, the answer seemed obvious: *Never gonna happen.*

Yet teen pop, by its very nature, is destined to crash after a few years, when its fans go to college, get jobs, raise families, and tear down their boy-band posters. It happened with Paul Anka, Fabian, the Bay City Rollers, New Kids on the Block, and Debbie Gibson, and it would happen with Backstreet Boys and 'NSync. There were a few structural problems within the record industry, too. 'NSync's "Bye Bye Bye," the Backstreet Boys' "I Want It That Way," and Britney's "Oops! . . . I Did It Again" were breezy and lovable bubblegum singles, worthy of airplay in any era, but there were just two or three of these on every big teen pop album. At the time, labels offered no cheap single format. A Backstreet fan *had* to buy the $15 *Millennium* CD in 1999 to own "I Want It That Way." (Just as a hip-hop fan had to buy Nelly's entire CD for the "Country Grammar" single or Sisqo's entire CD for "Thong Song.") It was no coincidence, then, that Napster, the free file-sharing service, popped up on the internet at precisely this time. The least frustrating way to obtain "I Want It That Way" in 1999 or 2000 was to download it for free. Illegally.

Labels had been expanding—hiring new staff, spending unprecedented millions on bands—throughout the 1980s and 1990s. They had no reason to think it would stop during the teen pop era, which made everybody rich, not just the executives who worked with Britney and Backstreet. Eminem, Shania Twain, Céline Dion, and Limp Bizkit took off in this period, Carlos Santana came back, and even artists better known for their concerts, like Phish and the Dave Matthews Band, were able to go multiplatinum. Labels were fat and happy, although some executives worried about a market peak. "You have the huge infrastructure of people . . . on a ton of different floors and all of a sudden you're stuck with these huge costs. And it's harder to cut people than it is to hire them," says Lyor Cohen, chairman of the Warner Music Group. "All these companies did was try to find fabricated shit* so they didn't go through having to let people go. Then you go into an era of fabricated, highly promoted, highly advertised stuff—it's very flimsy, it sells very quickly, and we're also hurting our credibility with the long-term music lover. And then [the fans] go away to college." Teen pop was one last squeeze of the sponge to get the world to spend millions and millions of dollars on compact discs. It wouldn't last.

Just before it self-destructed, though, two men would make a *lot* of money off boy bands and Britney Spears. Their names were Lou Pearlman and Clive Calder. When teen pop inevitably crashed, one survived. The other did not.

LOUIS J. PEARLMAN and Clive Calder had a few things in common. They both played in rock 'n' roll bands as teenagers. They both were self-made men with a talent for recognizing what sells—Pearlman as a blimp manufacturer, Calder as a record label talent scout. They both liked to talk. A *lot*. "As busy as [Calder] was, you couldn't get him off the phone in under half an hour," remembers Gary Stiffelman, attorney for Justin Timberlake. "It was amazing—he could talk your fucking ear off. All I could think of was, 'Doesn't he have something better to do?'" They both had thinning hair as they approached middle age in the late 1990s. Pearlman's red locks were turning wispy, complementing the multiple chins that made him look like a roly-poly cartoon character. Calder's

---

* I will let the reader decide whether Cohen's comment is "rockist"—defined by Kelefa Sanneh in the October 31, 2004, *New York Times* as an unfair slam against well-crafted pop music because it somehow isn't "authentic" enough. Sanneh wrote, "Rockism means idolizing the authentic old legend (or underground hero) while mocking the latest pop star; lionizing punk while barely tolerating disco; loving the live show and hating the music video; extolling the growling performer while hating the lip-syncher."

bald pate, with gray on the sides, gave him a comforting, charismatic dignity. Most important, both Pearlman and Calder saw the teen pop boom coming and invested in acts such as the Backstreet Boys, Britney Spears, and 'NSync before anybody else.

In almost every other aspect, however, they were completely different. Pearlman craved the limelight, posing in magazines with his hunky protégés, transforming himself into a personality every bit as big as that of Justin Timberlake or Nick Carter. Calder, meanwhile, was pathologically private. In thirty-three years in the music business, he gave only one interview, in 1996, to the British trade *Music Business International.* Where Pearlman used shady accounting to afford his living-large lifestyle, Calder kept meticulous records and was, to others in the business during the CD boom, shockingly frugal. "Clive was more no-frills, no-bullshit, just get it done. Lou was more 'Heeeey, everybody, let's have a good time!'" says David McPherson, a former A&R executive for Jive Records, who worked closely with both men during the teen pop boom. "Lou was the happy, jolly guy, nonthreatening, just a nice guy that you didn't want to let down or piss off. I've never seen him mad. I've never seen him yell at anybody. Whereas Clive—I've seen him mad, I've seen him just *yell.*"

Born in Johannesburg, South Africa, in 1946, Clive Calder, who is white, grew up fascinated with black music during apartheid. In the 1960s, he wore sideburns and played Motown covers in white bands such as Calder's Collection and the In Crowd. He performed for five hours almost every night. He convinced the Johannesburg office of EMI Music, the British major label, to give him a job in A&R. Being a South African talent scout was a hard way of life, especially given the complications of apartheid: When EMI tried to sell made-in-America records to South African buyers, the label had to remove photos of black musicians from the album sleeves. And Calder took heavy risks finding singers to make new records. "There are many cities in South Africa where I never knew the white areas, but I knew every shebeen, every hall, every club in the black areas," Calder said in his one interview. At age twenty-four, he was, according to *Rolling Stone*, "fanatically self-disciplined, socially remote, charming when he had to be, ruthless when he didn't." He didn't drink or dance. Tax manuals made up his bedside reading.

Calder was a long-haired hippie in the most reactionary country in the world. There was no flower power in South Africa in the 1960s. He signed bands to EMI and branched into concert promotion. The police and right-wingers harassed him and his psychedelic-rock clients, breaking up an outdoor festival he organized. Malawi, a nearby African country, wouldn't allow his rock tour to cross the border unless he cut his hair; immigration officials watched as a roadside barber did the job. His love of Motown, combined with the twisted laws of South Africa, moved him to switch from rock to soul music. At the time, blacks were allowed to listen only to black music and whites only to white music. Music by black Americans was the only exception, giving US soul megastars such as Percy Sledge a disproportionate level of local stardom.

Calder met a kindred musical spirit, Ralph Simon, keyboardist for a rival band known as the Bassmen, in the late 1960s. The two formed CCP Records around 1970 to focus on local singers. They put out "Candlelight," a catchy, English-language pop single by a black singer, Richard Jon Smith, and radio censors had to admit it was so bland it didn't violate any rules. The song went to No. 11 in South Africa, and soon Calder had recruited an entire hit factory worth of black pop singers who wore Afros and platform boots and looked like they could have been in the Jackson 5. David McPherson, one of Calder's A&R men years later, believes Calder honed his gold-standard "ears" at this time, creating South African hits under elaborate restrictions.

"South Africa was segregated. At the time, black artists kind of had to use the studio when whites had to go home at night," recalls Jonathan Butler, a Cape Town–born singer who recorded for Calder when he was twelve, then moved to London and earned a Grammy nomination for his 1987 soft-R&B hit "Lies." "At night time, when I went to a colored neighborhood, Clive goes to his white area and that's it. At midnight, if a black guy was found in that neighborhood, you'd probably be arrested. It wasn't so for the whites—the whites could come into any neighborhood and drive around.

"Many of us were excited about living our dream," he continues. "Clive and Ralph were very liberal in their views and the way they ran their company. They were visionaries."

They met another visionary, although he didn't look like one: Robert John "Mutt" Lange, a long-haired Rhodesian producer who had recorded cover songs for one small discount label. Calder became his manager. The ambitious trio—Calder, Simon, and Lange—decided in 1974 they had to get out of South Africa. "We were politically very much opposed to the old apartheid regime," Simon recalls. "That really led to literally giving up everything—and with what little money we had scraped together, buying airline tickets to go to London." Having left their families behind, Calder and Simon opened the Zomba Music Group in 1976, named after a Malawi town, and they found themselves at ground zero of the British punk rock movement. They didn't exactly fit—Simon Draper, a cofounder of Virgin Records, told *Rolling Stone* Calder was "slightly off the pace, a little uncool, didn't dress quite correctly, hadn't exactly got the tempo." But he was quite good at networking—and making money.

Calder and Simon decided publishing—the part of the music business that takes a tiny songwriter's cut for every song sold via album or single—was where the money was. They set out to find songwriters. The first came from a French producer, Henri Belolo, who delivered a group he helped create, the Village People, after twelve UK labels turned them down. Zomba became the disco stars' British sub-publisher. Calder and Simon agreed they had to keep as much control of Zomba as possible and use major labels simply to distribute records. It helped that Mutt Lange was the real thing—a big-time producer who worked with new wavers Boomtown Rats and Graham Parker before producing AC/DC's 1979 classic *Highway to Hell*. Zomba used its Lange connection to meet and manage a wide range of producers and songwriters, and asked every performer who came through to sign a publishing deal.

In 1977, Calder and Simon opened a New York City office. One of the first people to respond to their inquiries was Clive Davis, the legendary record executive who had been fired from Columbia and recently formed the smaller Arista Records. He gave the South Africans a distribution deal. They signed singer Billy Ocean. Their songwriters started to hit big. Publishing profits kicked in. Zomba built a studio and expanded into gospel labels, marketing, distribution, and music equipment. By 1990, Zomba was worth $225 million, with fifty companies, including fast-growing Jive Records. In contrast to the rest of the record business at the time, frills were verboten. "The Jive offices were crummy, cardboard desks," says attorney Gary Stiffelman. "They just really did everything on the cheap." Eventually, Calder came to see Ralph Simon as a frill. Calder and his old South African mate had a "very bad" falling-out, Simon remembers. Simon would later tell *Forbes* his partner "has a ruthlessness that knows no boundaries." Today, this is all he'll say by way of specifics: "For a variety of reasons we had different views on ethics."

That was around the same time Calder took a chance on a style of music everybody else in Big Music was ignoring: hip-hop.

In 1982, Calder, the longtime aficionado of hit black music, agreed to meet with a young, just-out-of-college clubgoer named Barry Weiss. His father, Hy Weiss, had been one of those 1950s New York indie label owners who stuck $50 in his palm and gave nudge-and-a-wink handshakes to payola-accepting radio programmers. Calder liked Barry Weiss right away. For his job interview, Calder made Weiss take him out for a night on the town. Weiss stepped up. He knew bouncers and doormen at gay clubs, hip-hop clubs, and black clubs all over the city, and he scored admissions for the duo all night long. He was hired. Weiss had a knack for scouring record-sales charts in cities all over the United States and coming across regional talent that hadn't yet broken around the country—rap pioneers like DJ Jazzy Jeff and the Fresh Prince, Boogie Down Productions, Kool Moe Dee.

"Do you know any rappers?" Calder asked Weiss one day. Weiss didn't, but he knew about Mr. Magic, a well-known New York DJ who was instrumental in breaking the genre on the air. Calder asked one of the writers for his publishing company, Thomas Dolby (later famous for "She Blinded Me with Science"), to create the catchy, repetitive part of the song known in industry parlance as "the hook." Mr. Magic was to rap on the track. But the DJ called at the last minute because he got a job on WBLS and his agent told him he couldn't rap and DJ at the same time. Weiss, still twenty-three and new to the company, freaked out. Fortunately, Mr. Magic knew another guy.

An unknown, Jalil Hutchins, agreed to take Mr. Magic's place in the studio. Further raising Barry Weiss's stress level, Hutchins showed up with no rhymes and another unknown rapper, simply called Ecstasy. It took two days, but Jalil and Ecstasy came up with "Magic's Wand," which turned into a huge hit single. Weiss named the group Houdini. Calder changed it to Whodini. Weiss booked them for a concert in Akron, Ohio. He served as their road manager. "We had rooms next to each other, and all I know is there was noise all night," recalls Weiss, today the top executive for Sony's BMG-turned-Zomba Music. "I heard champagne popping. I was not invited."

Calder flew Whodini to London to record an album. "I never had been on a plane in my *life*," Hutchins says. "In '82, no cats in my neighborhood were going to *London*." Then Calder sent the band, now a trio with DJ Grandmaster Dee, to Germany to record with the great producer Konrad "Conny" Plank, who had started out as a sound man for Marlene Dietrich but had recently made albums with Devo and Ultravox. A stream trickled underneath Plank's studio. Platinum albums lined the walls of the bathroom. These were luxuries Whodini had never seen before, and the trio was shocked. Calder occasionally dropped in, wearing jeans and a dress shirt, sharing his own ideas, but he left the band to its creative instincts—and Whodini came through with "Rap Machine" and "Nasty Lady," two songs from their classic debut *Whodini*. But the experience ultimately killed the band. "I got a big problem in my career now, from the way Clive Calder developed me," Hutchins says today, with dashed hopes of expensive German studios and hotshot producers evident in his regretful voice. "Because he spoiled me. And nobody else does it like that." Hutchins's primary regret is not buying stock in Zomba when he had the chance. Today, Whodini tours sporadically on the old-school circuit.

Hip-hop was well and good, but Calder quickly realized that to *really* make money he needed something else. He needed pop stars— big ones. He needed Lou Pearlman.

LOUIS J. PEARLMAN started his career as a rock star, albeit a small one. His parents took him to his first concert when he was thirteen—the Doors opened for Simon and Garfunkel at Forest Hills Tennis Stadium, near his hometown of Flushing, New York, in 1967. He was there to see his cousin, Art Garfunkel, but what really blew him away was the Doors. Inspired, the young guitarist and his pals at J.H.S. 185, Edward Bleeker Junior High School formed a band. They were called the Starlighters, then Flyer, and they played Doors and Beatles covers and an especially grooving version of Iron Butterfly's "In-a-Gadda-Da-Vida." They recorded a few tracks, but broke up in 1971 because every member wanted to be the lead singer.

Pearlman's dad was a Brooklyn dry cleaner who delivered clothes in a red-and-white Dodge station wagon to customers all over Long Island. Herman "Hy" Pearlman just barely made enough money through Pleasant Laundry to support his family of three in a one-bedroom apartment. Lou started working at age eight, with a $20-a-month lemonade stand, then graduated to bike repair, paper routes, and coffee-and-donut delivery.

At age ten, he looked into the sky and his life changed. "It was the first time I ever saw a blimp," he said, years later. "It told me to have a good year." The next day he walked to the Flushing commuter airport to talk his way into riding in one. He hung around the base so often that the Goodyear people eventually hired him as a crew member.

Aircraft became his calling. After graduating from Queens College, he started two New York companies—one to take tourists up in helicopters, another to charter airplanes. They made him a lot of money. In 1982, he pulled out his savings, borrowed money from friends and relatives and, with $250,000, started Airship International, a blimp company that provided advertising for McDonald's and Metropolitan Life Insurance. *Sports Illustrated* called him "Baron Blimp."

Pearlman's flying businesses gave him connections, and not just for life insurance. By the late 1980s, "Air Lou," as he came to be called, had spun off a fast-growing charter jet company, which had made a name for itself hauling rock stars from concert to concert—Paul McCartney, the Rolling Stones, Michael Jackson, and Madonna were among the passengers. None of them excited him so much as an unfamiliar name he noticed in a logbook in late 1989: *New Kids on the Block.* Pearlman discovered the popular boy band was filling stadiums around the world. "I thought the New Kids must be raking it in if they could afford to pay $250,000 a month for one of our planes," he later wrote in his autobiography. They'd made $200 million in concert sales and $800 million in merchandise revenues. Their svengali was Maurice Starr, who'd built the smash R&B band New Edition before they sued to break their contract.

Hmm, thought Pearlman. In 1989, the timing wasn't right for a new boy band—yet. He had to wait for the New Kids to peak. And he had to wait out the post–New Kids era, which belonged to Nirvana, grunge music, alternative rock, and college students. Over the next seven or eight years, the pendulum of pop music tastes would swing back to pop—Hanson and the Spice Girls were ascendant, and Ricky Martin was on the brink of graduating from *his* boy band, Menudo. "You could tell the alternative age was over and the cycle just came back for pop music," says Paris D'Jon, who discovered the boy band 98 Degrees.

With the New Kids on his mind, Pearlman hired an old friend, Gloria Sicoli, an ex-singer with talent-spotting expertise. They tried out forty young men at his house in the summer of 1992. All of them pretty much sucked, except for Alexander James McLean, fourteen, a veteran of local talent contests, musicals, and theater productions. AJ arrived with his mother and sang three New Kids songs to a backup tape while Pearlman watched from a couch. AJ was talented. So was his friend, Tony Donetti, who passed the audition—but then Pearlman's people lost his phone number. During a second round of auditions, in the aircraft parts warehouse of Pearlman's company, Trans Continental, Donetti resurfaced as "Howie Dorough." He had been using a stage name on his agent's recommendation.

They found more local talent—Nick Carter, then twelve, who had a rebellious look and shaggy blond hair and had performed with the Tampa Bay Buccaneer cheerleaders for two years; Kevin Richardson, a model and actor who'd been a Ninja Turtle and Aladdin at Disney World; and Richardson's tenor-singing cousin, Brian Littrell. They'd audition other members, who wouldn't stick around, but these five named themselves the Backstreet Boys after a flea market across the street from the T.G.I. Friday's in Orlando. By May 8, 1993, they were playing SeaWorld, in Orlando, before three thousand screaming girls.

Pearlman contacted New Kids manager Johnny Wright, who with his wife Donna had to hear the Backstreet Boys sing over the phone before agreeing to manage them. For a star-making operation, the Trans Continental home base was surprisingly plain. "We were living in Orlando in a nondescript office park, where we were doing all our business," recalls Jay Marose, who signed on as vice president of marketing and promotions after working on a Chicago campaign for Fruit of the Loom underwear. "My office looked out across an asphalt parking lot at Johnny's office, and the other side was the studio. You would have just driven by. That's what kept us pretty normal. You would go bowling, and the movie theaters would give us free passes. There was nothing to do. I had these seventeen-year-olds going, 'What should we do tonight?' We were just sitting around staring at each other."

The offices were a sanctuary from the rest of the world, which had started to take notice—loudly. "The pitch of fourteen thousand girls?" Marose asks, answering his own question with a burst of laughter. Those screams would act as a résumé for the band.

Pearlman saw right away that he needed a major record label to take the Backstreet Boys to the next level of fame and money. He used his considerable salesmanship to make contact with A&R scouts and attempt to talk them into seeing the Boys live. Unfortunately for Pearlman, the scouts were deep into alternative rock at the time. It took Donna Wright's voicemail, containing the high-pitched din of thousands of kids at a Cleveland concert, to capture the attention of David McPherson at Mercury Records. Intrigued, he accepted one of Pearlman's numerous invitations to see the Boys live—this time, at a high school in Hickory, North Carolina. At the concert, McPherson had a revelation. Hipsters might be obsessed with Stone Temple Pilots and Pearl Jam, he thought, but this is what kids are really listening to. He signed them to a deal at Mercury, but his label superiors didn't really understand the band, so the Backstreet Boys languished without any hits.

Around that time, in 1993, McPherson made contact with Calder and showed up at Zomba for a job interview. Calder asked McPherson what he was working on. McPherson mentioned a couple of R&B acts he thought Calder would think were cool.

Calder wasn't too impressed. Then McPherson mentioned the Backstreet Boys. "He was like, 'You know what? Groups like this are big overseas, and this group could help me expand my operations overseas—and, maybe, if they get big, all over the world,'" McPherson says. "It took a lot of money and a lot of time and a lot of A&R and marketing in a climate where you were crazy to spend that on a group like them. A group like that was unpopular, an uncool thing in a business where cool means a *lot*." McPherson was hired. Mercury bought out the Backstreet Boys' contract for $35,000, then dropped the band. Then the Boys signed with Jive Records, the Zomba imprint that specialized in pop, hip-hop, and R&B.

Clive Calder and Lou Pearlman needed each other, at least at first. Pearlman put together the Backstreet Boys and then 'NSync. Calder had the resources to break them around the world. They weren't best friends, but they had a cordial business relationship. "One of the reasons they got along was because Clive was always in control. It was a perfect symbiotic relationship," McPherson says. "Lou didn't care about the details. He didn't care how many songs were going to be on the album and who was going to produce those songs and what outfits the group was going to wear. He had spent so much time trying to get these guys signed—and no one signed them—that when he found willing suitors in myself and Clive Calder, all he had to do was sit back and go for the ride. Man, he was happy! Some people in that situation would try to control this and control that. He didn't care. He just wanted to be there for the pictures and the parties and the accolades and the plaque presentations. He knew Clive was going to take care of the business."

Calder, McPherson, and their Zomba colleagues had two strategies. First, Backstreet needed songs. Calder sent them to Sweden to record with a group of producers discovered by an aggressive scout in Zomba's Dutch offices. Dag Volle, also known as Ace of Base songwriter-producer Denniz PoP, was among them; Martin Sandberg, who renamed himself Max Martin, was PoP's protégé. Backstreet recorded their first three songs, including "We've Got It Going On," at the producers' studio.

Next, Calder thought: *We have to get them in front of the kids.* Aside from the occasional Disney World show, American crowds weren't always interested. After Pearlman booked them to open for a wet T-shirt contest, the crowd pelted them with ice cubes. "We've Got It Going On" couldn't get on the radio, and it peaked at No. 65 on the *Billboard* Hot 100 chart. They needed seasoning. The breakthrough was in Germany, a country with government-controlled radio that never quite plunged into alternative rock and hardcore hip-hop. The Boys sold out concerts, scored hit videos, and turned "We've Got It Going On" into an overseas smash. Their success spread around Europe.

Calder called an old friend, Stuart Watson. He ran SWAT Enterprises, a consultancy that specialized in breaking acts in Asia. Watson listened to four Backstreet Boys songs and knew they were hits. He demanded Calder send the band to Asia, and Calder agreed. The band did promotional show after promotional show, from Singapore to Korea, and posed endlessly for magazine photo sessions. Using the 1980s publicity plan for teen singer Tiffany, Watson put the Boys in malls. Within three weeks, the band sold 1 million CDs in Asia. Later, a Montreal program director, on vacation in France, heard the band and returned home to put them on the radio. Barry Weiss, Jive's president, set up a Montreal concert; fifty thousand showed up. Girls screamed. Weiss called Calder from the show and held up the phone. Weiss and Calder both knew what was next: America.

"They brought them to Chicago, to the station, on a tour bus," recalls Erik Bradley, program director for B-96, the Top 40 radio station WBBM-FM in Chicago. "They came by and met everybody and were so nice and amazingly seasoned for being young people. They sang a cappella in the lobby." The Boys showed up at a dinner in New Orleans, hosted by EMI Music, and schmoozed with independent radio promoters like Bill Scull of Tri State Promotions in Cincinnati. "Unlike rock bands, these bands were perfect for radio stations to do promotions with," Scull says. "They totally appealed to the Top 40 demographic—fifteen to eighteen to twenty-five years old, the female demo. They were cute and they were fun and they could dance! Every radio station wanted them to show up for the birthday bash, the Halloween party, the Christmas show, whatever. We did all sorts of things with them like that." The Boys worked their boyish charm all over the place. They broke in America in 1997, starting a rush of debut CD sales that would ultimately total 14 million.

More good fortune arrived for Jive Records in 1996: a fifteen-year-old girl who had recently moved to New York from Orlando, where, with Justin Timberlake and JC Chasez, she had been a Mouseketeer on *The Mickey Mouse Club.* With help from her mother and a local attorney, Larry Rudolph, Britney Spears was aggressive and ambitious and sent a demo tape of her cover of a Toni Braxton song to record labels all over the city. None heard anything even remotely commercial in her voice. Jive, however, was actively seeking a female star to push to the Backstreet Boys audience. "We were looking for a Debbie Gibson, if you like," says Steve Lunt, a Jive A&R man at the time. "[Spears's demo tape] was in one of those karaoke studios where you lay your vocal over an imitation of somebody else's track. It was totally awful. She was singing totally in the wrong register. But when she got to the end, her voice went up to the sort of 'girlie range,' and you heard the kind of soul she had." The accompanying photos were cute, too.

Lunt took the material to Calder. He agreed to a deal, with a caveat: *Be cautious.* If Calder didn't hear a hit in six months, Spears would be just another teen with big dreams.

Lunt went to work. The standard operating procedure at Zomba was to keep everything in-house. Lunt hooked Spears up with a number of songwriters in the company's publishing division, but they mostly focused on R&B. Finally, in the fifth month, he found Eric Foster White, a pop songwriter and producer. Singer and producer clicked immediately, and White linked Britney with a 1986 Jets tune, "You Got It All," penned by Rupert Holmes of "Escape (The Piña Colada Song)" fame. "Sweet and innocent and catchy. A little bit R&B but still basically sweet pop," recalls Lunt, now an A&R vice president for Atlantic Records. "When Clive heard that in the A&R meeting, he said, 'OK, we've got something.' Up until that, it was in doubt." Calder and Lunt then contacted Max Martin, the Swedish pop producer who'd worked with Backstreet, and asked him to fly to New York. Spears, Martin, and

Lunt went to dinner and hit it off. Martin and Spears flew back to Sweden and, within two days, sent back a demo—" . . . Baby One More Time."

"We at Jive said, 'This is a fuckin' smash,'" Lunt recalls. In all, Spears cut six songs in Sweden. Then she returned to the States and started working the key radio stations. Jive's top radio-promotion executive, Jack Sadder, brought her one day to Star 100.7 in San Diego to talk to one of his longtime contacts, music director Michael Steele. Because Steele didn't have a cassette deck in his office, Sadder convinced him to listen to Spears's tape in the car. "We go out in the parking lot. It's just hot as hell in Southern California, probably one hundred degrees that day. I get in the driver's seat. Jack's in the passenger seat. This little fifteen-year-old is in the backseat of my car. I want to go to lunch," Steele recalls. "It's ' . . . Baby One More Time.' I go, 'Yeah, this is all right.' We go back into the station, and thirty days later she was No. 1."

As Calder predicted, Backstreet and Britney fed off each other in the marketplace. Pearlman had a piece of the Backstreet Boys, and as they became more successful thanks to Jive Records's machinations, their manager became richer. "Baron Blimp" left blimps behind—his public company, International Ltd., had crashed twice and the stock had dropped from $6 to 3 cents per share—and threw himself into music. Trans Continental grew fast, spending tons of money on studios, training, and touring. Pearlman's Orlando lifestyle became extravagant, as he would later chronicle in a promotional videotape called *Lou Pearlman Living Large*. The title was especially catchy given Air Lou's heft. He lived in a $12 million mansion down the street from ex-Magic basketball star Shaquille O'Neal. He also lived in a Mediterranean mansion in suburban Windermere, off Lake Butler, where he kept boats and Jet Skis. He rode in a blue Rolls-Royce with a chauffeur. He made political contributions to Republicans, owned a small piece of the local arena football team, the Orlando Predators, and showed off a diamond-studded Rolex to guests. He was single and, though he didn't even drink, he couldn't get enough of entertaining. "He was arrogant and thought he was the smartest guy in the room, but he could be very charming," says Bob Jamieson, ex-head of RCA Records and, later, its parent company BMG North America. "But there was always an element of him that made you second-guess. You felt uncomfortable."

It's hard to imagine a more successful act than the Backstreet Boys circa 1997, but Pearlman needed something else. "You can't make money on an airline with just one airplane," he told the *Los Angeles Times*. According to Pearlman, it was his idea to begin auditions for a second group—but this is where the story starts to get ugly. And full of contradictions.

In Pearlman's version, he auditioned five new boys, beginning with Chris Kirkpatrick, an Orlando doo-wop singer and Outback Steakhouse employee who yearned to form his own band. Kirkpatrick had a friend of a friend named Justin Timberlake, who had a shockingly deep baritone for a teenager and an impressive résumé, from *Star Search* to *The Mickey Mouse Club*. Fellow Mouseketeer JC Chasez and a mutual friend, Joey Fatone, joined within a few weeks. Justin's voice coach brought in Lance Bass. Together, the boys scrambled letters in their names and came up with 'NSync. The auditions and 'NSync's name were all Pearlman's idea. Timberlake's mother, Lynn Harless, had another version of the story, which vehemently contradicted Pearlman's recollection. "[Pearlman] did not 'select' the members of 'NSync," she would declare in a court affidavit. "The members of 'NSync found each other. . . . Mr. Pearlman did not 'audition' these singers; we all did. The name 'NSync was not Mr. Pearlman's idea but mine."

A feud between the two Trans Continental groups—soon to be the world's biggest pop stars—set in. "We brought in another brother and they saw it as an abandonment," said Johnny Wright, who became manager for 'NSync, which was OK with Backstreet until their new rivals followed their blueprint in Germany and Asia and became just as famous as their predecessors. "And that ended up putting me in a position I did not want to be in where the groups are now competing head to head in a race to the top."

The idea for a second superstar boy band—whether it came from Pearlman or not—turned out pretty well commercially. But there were cracks in the foundation of Pearlman's boy-band empire. The first came from the Backstreet Boys themselves. They were tired. They acted less like boys and more like pop stars. *Professionals.* They showed up in Pearlman's office one day in August 1997 with entourages—girlfriends, brothers, uncles. The *Wall Street Journal* reported "name-calling" that day and quoted Johnny Wright: "The meeting was not on a positive note." In May 1998, at the height of their success, when they'd earned his company $200 million in revenues, the Boys filed suit against Pearlman. They insisted they had earned $300,000 during the same period Pearlman made $10 million. They called themselves "indentured servants." They were also, sources told the media, a little miffed at having to compete with 'NSync within the same management company. Pearlman settled with the band. They got more control over recording, merchandising, and touring. Pearlman saved face—or so he told the media later. He negotiated a sort of monetary "sixth Backstreet Boy" role for himself, and in 1999, the *Wall Street Journal* estimated he took in $20 million of the band's overall profits just in that one year. "It would be nice to have them as my five sons," Pearlman said. "Instead, it's five sons with lawyers in between."

Backstreet saw "Big Papa," as he called himself, as anything but fatherly. "Here were some guys that sold twenty-plus million albums on their first record and barely had anything to show for it," says Peter Katsis, senior vice president of music for the Firm, which represented hard-rock bands Korn and Limp Bizkit and took over the Boys' management. "Each guy maybe had a nice house in the Orlando area and a couple of bucks in the bank—but certainly nothing reflecting what they should have been able to make."

The Firm inherited the Boys' Into the Millennium tour, planned for late 1999, and its managers were shocked at the behind-the-scenes disarray and B-level concert professionals they inherited from Pearlman's company. "Total *Spinal Tap* shit," Katsis recalls. The stage was to be five feet tall. The show was to include nine wardrobe changes. "So," he asked, "these guys are going to *crawl* under this five-foot-high stage to do *nine* wardrobe changes?" Katsis fired a lot of people. The tour sold 765,000 tickets in just a few hours, filling every venue on the docket for thirty-nine cities. It drew 2 million fans in the end.

'NSync didn't take long to catch up with the Backstreet Boys—in terms of both CD and ticket sales *and* friction with Lou Pearlman. Big Papa marketed them in the Boys' image, as a singing-and-dancing team starring the Friendly One, the Cute One, the Rebellious One, and so on. Like the Backstreet Boys and a lot of young, inexperienced stars at the beginnings of their careers, 'NSync signed a contract that allowed their manager to make tons of money off their success. In early 1997, JC Chasez realized the band was selling millions of records in Germany as well as boxloads of T-shirts and other merchandise throughout their European tour. The band complained, demanding accounting for CD sales. On August 1, Pearlman gave each member a paltry advance of $10,000. Chasez contacted a lawyer relative, who looked at the band's contracts and found problems. She referred them to an experienced music business attorney, Adam Ritholz, who had worked for CBS Records and represented singer-songwriter Lisa Loeb and R&B star Maxwell.

Ritholz studied the contracts. He learned Trans Continental took 50 percent of the band's CD royalties, 50 percent of T-shirt and other merchandise sales, and 30 percent of touring revenues—a far greater share than the standard manager's 10 to 15 percent. He requested more documents from Trans Continental's attorneys. He learned Pearlman had formed 'NSync Productions Inc., listing his home as the place of business and giving himself the power to make decisions on behalf of the band. The band was reluctant to go against its Big Papa but demanded a meeting with him at a Trans Continental office in May 1999. They were there all day—maybe ten hours. Pearlman lectured the band. His lawyers tried to scare them: *If they continued along this path, they'd endanger their careers.* One by one, each member of 'NSync stood up and walked out of Pearlman's office.

In his negotiations with Pearlman, Ritholz tried to enlist the band's record label, RCA, to help the band extricate itself from Trans Continental. By Ritholz's way of thinking, the label and its parent company, BMG, which at the time was the second-biggest label in the United States, could put far more pressure on Pearlman than five young men and their attorney ever could. He figured the label, wanting to take care of its hot-selling assets, would agree. Instead, he was shocked to discover that Strauss Zelnick, then the chairman of BMG, refused to abandon Pearlman. "He said to me, 'I have a certain principled way of doing things. This is the girl I brought to the dance—she may not be the prettiest girl, but she's the girl I'm going home with,'" Ritholz says. "It was a very significant misjudgment on his part." As Ritholz recalls it, Zelnick asked to meet with the band in person—at a Times Square hotel room in July 1999. No lawyers were allowed to attend, but Ritholz found out later that Zelnick insisted that he would "do anything in his power" to make sure RCA put out the band's next CD. Once again, 'NSync walked out.*

---

* Others remember the meeting a different way, saying Zelnick tried to mediate the dispute between Pearlman and the band. "It was actually a relatively friendly meeting," says a source privy to the talks. "Lou gave the boys hugs. They were angry at Lou because they felt he was taking too much of the economics and they had made a bunch of demands. The boys laid out very aggressive terms, perhaps even reasonable, but Lou was not prepared to go there. Ultimately the meeting was disappointing for the boys."

Ritholz soon realized Pearlman's company had unintentionally given the band a huge loophole. Early on, Trans Continental agreed to release an 'NSync album in the United States within a year after its recording. But the band's self-titled debut came out in Germany—and took almost two years to arrive in the United States. "We took the position that the agreement was therefore terminated and 'NSync was free to make another deal," Ritholz says. As for BMG, it seems the label's German subsidiary, Ariola, had never made 'NSync sign a standard "inducement letter," which would have held them to their label contract even if they broke with their management company. 'NSync gave notice. Although Lou Pearlman and RCA Records didn't see it this way, the band that was about to sell 11 million copies of 2000's *No Strings Attached* in the United States became a free agent.

At first, Clive Calder didn't want any part of 'NSync's dispute with Lou Pearlman. The head of BMG Entertainment, Zelnick, was a friend who'd supported Calder's crazy boy-band notions from the very beginning. Zelnick had authorized the Backstreet Boys' maiden voyage in Germany, after all. Plus, BMG owned 20 percent of Zomba and distributed the labels' CDs worldwide. Calder didn't want to damage that relationship. But he quickly realized he could spin the 1999 'NSync trial into solid gold.

Clive Calder learned this very important bit of information by coincidence. Ritholz had been negotiating with many labels, but he wasn't even considering Calder's Jive/Zomba operation. The label already had the Backstreet Boys, and 'NSync didn't want to work at the same company as its rival. In late July 1999, Ritholz was on the phone with a London-based Zomba executive regarding a producer he represented. Calder knew Ritholz, happened to be in the London office, and jumped on the line. "What's going on?" he asked pleasantly. Ritholz told him of 'NSync's status. Calder couldn't believe it. Maybe he would be interested in signing the band, he told the attorney. Ritholz then convinced 'NSync that having two superstar boy bands on one label wouldn't be a problem—lots of labels have enough resources for multiple R&B singers or alt-rock bands who compete for the same radio play. In about a month, the negotiations went forward and 'NSync signed with Calder's company.

That was too much for Strauss Zelnick.

Back in 1994, Zelnick had been a confident, straightlaced, thirty-seven-year-old wunderkind with a Harvard MBA and a star-studded résumé, including ownership of the video-game company Crystal Dynamics and executive titles at 20th Century Fox and Columbia Pictures. His wife called him "MKIA"—"Mr. Know It All." Bertelsmann recruited him to be president of its record label, BMG Entertainment, whose biggest holdings at the time included R&B stars TLC and diva Whitney Houston. "I had virtually no record business experience," Zelnick says. "My style was, up-front, to acknowledge and admit my lack of experience. I always maintained healthy respect for those who were vastly more experienced than I."

Zelnick would remain the top BMG executive for the next seven years, and he gradually absorbed music business culture. (Zelnick, however, never lost his folksy corporate style: He gave twelve-packs of his homemade barbecue sauce, Strauss in the House, to friends, complete with his picture on the bottles and BMG's address on the back.) Within a few years he would find himself working out at a gym with a trainer named Tyrese, an aspiring R&B singer who would soon become a star for his label. Zelnick would also happily sing along as teen star Pink jumped on a table at a Beverly Wilshire presidential suite label party to perform "There You Go."

It seemed as if Zelnick could do nothing wrong during his first five years at BMG. The label's worldwide sales increased 7 percent, to $4.6 billion. Its US market share jumped from fourth (out of five major record labels at the time) to second, behind powerhouse Universal Music.

But Zelnick's long music business honeymoon ended abruptly in 1999. First, he took the fall for pushing out BMG's best-known record executive, sixty-six-year-old Arista founder Clive Davis, just after Davis had engineered Carlos Santana's 5-million-selling *Supernatural* comeback. But as Bertelsmann's board knew well, Davis spent money to make money, profit margins were low, and he annoyed the company's top brass by not grooming a successor. Zelnick picked another well-known label executive, Antonio "LA" Reid of LaFace Records, as Davis's replacement. Davis did not go quietly. He told everybody he knew in the music business that he was being pushed out. Barry Manilow called the move "mean-spirited," and Santana and Aretha Franklin threatened to leave the label. (They didn't.) Davis went on to form J Records, discover Alicia Keys, sign a contract with *American Idol*, and return to his old label as the head of BMG North America. (Zelnick wouldn't comment on the Davis escapade.)

Zelnick, too, was responsible for BMG's break with the company's Clive Number Two—Calder. When 'NSync abandoned BMG's ship, choosing Calder's Zomba as their new label, Zelnick was suddenly in a terrible position. He didn't want to lose the band, which was at the time the label's biggest-selling act. And he didn't want to anger Calder, whose label was a money machine for BMG. Yet Zelnick chose to cast his lot with Pearlman and sue the band—as well as Calder and Zomba—for breach of contract. He alienated Calder, once his ally. Then he was forced to settle with the band. Zelnick wouldn't talk about the case, but a source close to BMG at the time speculates why Zelnick made his decision: "Lou is a bad guy. He treated the guys badly. But BMG had a deal with him and [Pearlman] lived up to it. He had not breached it."

The BMG–Trans Continental lawsuit against Zomba, the band, and Calder himself was for $150 million in damages. The trial lasted two and a half months, but it seemed like forever. The band and its old, estranged friends from Trans Continental found themselves in US District Court in Orlando on Christmas Eve 1998. "Justin and I were texting each other about our suits—because we'd never seen each other in suits," says Jay Marose, head of marketing for Trans Continental. The band settled with Pearlman's company just after Christmas 1998, for an undisclosed amount. "That was the most stressful time of my career," says Bob Jamieson, then chairman of BMG North America. "I don't want to talk about that. It's too far gone and brings up a lot of pain."

On January 12, 1999, Jive Records put out 'NSync's new single: "Bye Bye Bye."

Swooping in to grab 'NSync from BMG was merely part one of Calder's long-term plan. That made him tons of revenue, as the band's debut Jive album would be the record-setting *No Strings Attached*. Part two was even more involved—and savvy. Calder had set the table for it in the early 1990s, when he sold huge chunks of Zomba's profitable publishing and record divisions to BMG. In 1996, BMG execs and Calder made a deal involving a "put option"—an agreement for BMG to buy Zomba for a certain price at a later date. Negotiated before Jive's 'NSync bonanza, this price was reportedly three times Zomba's profits during a three-year period. By the early 2000s, that price was suddenly—and unexpectedly to BMG—very high. Calder could sell anytime he liked. Or not.

Masterfully, Calder held out until precisely the right moment. *No*

Strings Attached came out in early 2000 and sold 11 million copies in the United States alone. (That in itself was a lot of revenue that BMG, having lost the band to Calder, didn't get.) In June 2002, after 'NSync, Britney Spears, and the Backstreet Boys had set international records for album sales, Calder must have been pretty sure this type of music was reaching its peak. He called BMG and declared he wanted to sell. The price, based on the 1996 formula, was $2.74 billion. BMG could afford it. Its parent company, German publishing behemoth Bertelsmann, had recently sold a share in America Online Europe back to AOL Time Warner for more than $7 billion.

As *Rolling Stone* reported at the time, Island Records's Chris Blackwell, who discovered Bob Marley and U2, received $300 million when he sold his company. David Geffen got just $550 million. Richard Branson, jet-setting airline magnate and music industry genius, received a paltry $950 million for Virgin.

"The most impressive man ever in the music business, if you ask me," the Firm's Peter Katsis says of Calder. "Here's this guy who built all this stuff up and knew exactly what to do with it, knew exactly how far to take it, knew exactly when to sell his company."

Ruthless is a word many in the record business have used to describe Clive Calder, who pops up in *Forbes* magazine every year as something like the 317th richest person on the planet. But his sell-out to BMG may not have been motivated purely by ruthlessness. An old friend says Calder's attitude changed, perceptibly, one terrible day in 2001. It seems Calder used to be able to see the World Trade Center from Zomba's offices. "Anyone who knew him knew that he tended to put work before family," says ex-Jive A&R man Steve Lunt, who has known Calder since the late 1970s, when his English rock band City Boy signed with Zomba. "After 9/11, there were subtle changes to that equation. He would start taking vacations. He would go on boat trips with his wife and kids. It wasn't long after that when he made that huge deal. He realized, ultimately, there were other things more important to his life. I'm sure he's currently dedicating himself to those as we speak." Clive Calder lives, reclusively as ever, in the Cayman Islands.

LOU PEARLMAN LOST his two jewels, but he kept hustling. He still had other teen pop acts—C Note, Innosense, LFO. He shifted to reality television, appearing on MTV's *Making the Band* series about assembling the next Backstreet Boys or 'NSync. The result of this experiment, O-Town, was named after Trans Continental's $6 million recording studio, and the group sold more than 1 million copies of its debut. But Pearlman never regained his old touch. "He was never hands-on. He would always pawn you off to another guy who was working with the company at the time," says Raul Molina, a singer for C Note, a bilingual singing-and-rapping group marketed, a bit against its will, as a boy band. "They never really had any music experience."

Pearlman nonetheless micromanaged C Note. "Watch, at the end of the next song, David [Perez] will unbutton his shirt and they'll go crazy," Pearlman told *Los Angeles Times* reporter Geoff Boucher during a fairgrounds concert in 1999. Sure enough, singer Perez unbuttoned his shirt at the end of the next song and the girls went crazy. But C Note didn't agree with Pearlman's decisions. He insisted they add a blue-eyed, blond-haired white boy to the all-Hispanic lineup—which they did, reluctantly. When their label, Epic, scored the band a float with Jennifer Lopez for the Puerto Rican Day parade in New York City—ideal for their bilingual audience—Pearlman nixed the plan. He sent them to an Adidas-sponsored show at Bryant Park instead. The parade drew 2 million spectators.

"He's one of these salesmen who could sell anything to anybody," says Molina, twenty-eight, now recording with a new, post-Pearlman version of the band. "We'd go into a meeting and be ready to tell him: '*This* is what we need to do!' And before we knew it, it was all turned around. The sky was green and the grass was blue. We ended up signing even the same contracts 'NSync and Backstreet Boys signed. At that point, we didn't know any better."

Then the teen pop bubble burst, as every teen pop bubble does. Fans grew up. The next generation of kids—the little brothers and sisters of the boy-band fanatics—just didn't have the same emotional connection to these superstar acts. Not only that, the acts were obviously getting older, with no choice but to remake themselves into the more sophisticated crooners you might hear on adult-contemporary radio stations. The transition did not go well for most of them. Record sales plummeted for the Backstreet Boys. Nick Carter left the group. His solo album went nowhere. Britney Spears, of course, transformed from schoolgirl to snake-wielding burlesque dancer to Kevin Federline's wife to head-shaving mom to MTV awards show bust to suicide risk to sitcom guest star. Only Justin Timberlake made the transition; after he split from

'NSync, he released 2002's *Justified* (on Zomba, of course), which would turn him into one of the world's biggest pop stars. Years later, teen pop came back—in the form of *Hannah Montana, High School Musical*, the Jonas Brothers, and other smash TV shows, albums, and concert tours by stars on the Disney Channel and other Disney-owned properties.

Pearlman survived the end of teen pop by forming corporations— talent agencies,* artist management firms, airlines. He wooed investors for Employee Investment Savings Accounts. He reminded them of his glory days with 'NSync and the Backstreet Boys and showed them the massive car collection and Jet Skis he kept at his suburban Orlando mansion. A lot of people, sadly, succumbed to his charm. Manhattan dentist Steven Sarin met Pearlman through a connection with his Florida retirement home. Pearlman called Sarin and his wife every year on their birthdays and invited their whole family to various teen pop concerts. They invested their life savings. Joseph Chow, an engineering professor at the University of Illinois-Chicago, dumped more than $14 million into Trans Continental entities—in exchange for hanging out with Pearlman in the 1990s.

Even to sophisticated investors, Pearlman had an irresistible charm. "He was certainly very friendly," says Jennifer Chow, Joseph's daughter, who dutifully went to Backstreet Boys concerts with her father even though, in her early twenties, she liked Nirvana better. "He would always say, 'I'm trying to make new things happen! Break boundaries! Take things to the next level!' He was very excited and animated." Over the years, Pearlman treated former Chicago freight company owner David Mathis to lunch with Britney Spears, introduced him to stars like Sylvester Stallone, and accompanied him on a Budweiser blimp ride. "He told us he had 412 airplanes, the company had a value of $1.8 billion, and the IPO was coming out at $17.50 a share," Mathis told the *St. Petersburg Times* in 2007. "It was totally convincing."

The problem for Pearlman, an accounting major at Queens Col-

---

* In 2003, after Florida officials investigated hundreds of complaints about Pearlman's Trans Continental Talent Inc. website, I interviewed Pearlman by phone for *Rolling Stone*. The complaints came from actors, singers, and others who said the website charged them $1,500 apiece and did little more than post their résumés online—if that. Friendly but rushed, Pearlman denied all the charges. "Trans Continental is a big company and stands by our name and reputation," he said, blaming the media for sensationalizing the complaints. "People who know us know the story. It doesn't help the image, but it hasn't hurt me."

lege, was accounting. Basically, he didn't do any. In what investors later called a Ponzi scheme, Pearlman shuffled funds from one of his corporations to the next, paying bills without keeping track of which company owned what. Sarin, the Manhattan dentist, lost his life savings. His wife cried every day.

Mathis, the Chicago freight-company owner, claimed a loss of $2.8 million. Chow, the engineering professor, died in 2002, leaving his children to deal with his defaulted Trans Continental investments. In 2007, the Florida Office of Financial Regulation declared Pearlman may have duped about 1,800 investors out of $317 million. The FBI raided his home and Trans Continental offices in Orlando. Banks seized his assets. Investors sued by the dozens. Pearlman declared bankruptcy.

For months, Pearlman went missing. He wrote a letter to an Orlando newspaper saying he was busy in Germany promoting a new boy band, US5. In 2007, a federal grand jury indicted him on three counts of bank fraud. Creditors liquidated his assets in an Orlando auction. They sold a platinum *Millennium* album for $2,300 and Pearlman's honorary key to the City of Orlando for $1,400. Officials finally captured him in late June, where he was registered in an Indonesian hotel under the name "A. Incognito Johnson." He returned home to Orlando and, in March 2008, acknowledged he oversaw schemes that fraudulently took $300 million from investors and banks. He pleaded guilty to several federal charges: conspiracy, money laundering, and making false statements during a bankruptcy proceeding. On May 21, 2008, a US district judge sentenced him to twenty-five years in prison, with a chance of reducing his time by one month for every $1 million he paid back to investors. "I'm truly sorry, your honor, to all the people who have been hurt by my actions," Pearlman said in the courtroom, wearing an orange jumpsuit and leg shackles. Further ugly revelations came with Pearlman's fall. In *Vanity Fair*, a census taker named Alan Gross declared *himself* the subject of Pearlman's famous early history about becoming obsessed with blimps and hitching a ride with the blimp hangar people in the 1960s. "The stories he tells?" Gross said. "They're not about Lou. They're about me." As Gross told it, he and Pearlman were childhood neighbors in the Mitchell Garden Apartments in Flushing; Gross saw the blimps from his window, made friends with the blimp operators, and became a gofer at the blimp hangar. Pearlman merely adopted Gross's stories as his own. And if that weren't creepy enough, *Vanity Fair*'s reporting revealed Pearlman allegedly showed some of his young male singers porn movies, wrestled naked with them in their beds, and created a culture where sex with the boss was expected, almost inevitable. Pearlman has denied the claims.

"Karma's a bitch," 'NSync's Lance Bass said.

ONETIME WUNDERKIND STRAUSS Zelnick would last at BMG for only another year after the 'NSync settlement. By late 2000, Zelnick and his boss, Bertelsmann chief executive officer Thomas Middelhoff, had worked together for more than six years. They liked each other. But one day, Zelnick was sleeping at home after a strenuous oral-surgery session, and he received a phone call from Middelhoff that would be the beginning of the end. He told Zelnick that Bertelsmann was about to invest millions of dollars in a small Silicon Valley startup that allowed music fans all over the world to share songs online for free. Zelnick felt blindsided. "How could the music group not know about this?" he said. As Middelhoff well knew, Zelnick considered this business model to be outright theft of copyrighted music. Middelhoff held the opposite belief. He felt Napster would save the record industry.

Big Music's Big Mistakes, Part 4

Killing the Single

In 1959, when Terry McManus was twelve, he bought a 39-cent copy of Jerry Lee Lewis's single "I'll Sail My Ship Alone" from a drugstore in Birmingham, Alabama. Later, when the Beatles and Beach Boys started putting out arty albums like *Sgt. Pepper's Lonely Hearts Club Band* and *Pet Sounds,* he went along with them, shelling out $3.99 apiece. For years afterward, he used singles as a cheap way to decide which albums to buy. But as the major labels started to make more money than ever off CDs in the 1980s and 1990s, McManus began noticing he couldn't find a single anymore. "Here is where the North American music industry made its greatest mistake of the twentieth century," McManus, a veteran Canadian producer and songwriter, wrote in a *Billboard* op-ed. "When it stopped making vinyl singles and offered nothing to replace them, the industry stopped a whole generation from picking up the record-buying habit."

McManus was prescient. He wrote his *Billboard* piece in 1997, two years before millions of music fans would learn how to get singles their own way—for free—via the internet. "If you think about water that's trying to reach the surface—it comes up in one place and you plug it up. And you go, 'OK, that's plugged up, my water problem is finished.' It's not. It's still seeking a way to rise to the surface," says McManus, now a music business professor at Fanshawe College in London, Ontario, Canada. "As soon as Napster opened up, the single came roaring back up. I call Napster 'the revenge of the single.'"

Why did the business phase out the single?

"Very simple," says Jim Caparro of the Entertainment Distribution Company, who was, in the 1990s, president of Island Def Jam Records: Not enough profit. The single cost too much to produce and didn't make up enough in sales. For years, major labels used singles as cheap or free promotional tools. They'd give them away to radio stations, persuading programmers to air their songs. They'd gussy them up and give them out at concerts. "The industry was looking for excuses to get out of it," Caparro recalls. "You had these arguments that singles were cannibalizing album sales. So they killed the single."

By the late 1990s, the record business had boiled down much of the business to a simple formula: 2 good songs + 10 or 12 mediocre songs = 1 $15 CD, meaning billions of dollars in overall sales. Cassettes, too, gradually fell victim to this formula, and were phased out. Attempts to resuscitate the singles market, like the "cassingle" and a shorter version of a record known as the EP, ultimately failed. "They tried everything," says ex-Tower executive Stan Goman. Instead of singles, Tower started displaying candy bars and other tchotchkes at the counter for impulse shoppers to buy for less than $1. "It's no coincidence that the decline of cassettes and the rise of CD burning arose simultaneously," says Steve Gottlieb, president of the independent label TVT Records. "People realized the only viable way to buy music was $16.99, because CD was the only viable format."

In the short term, dozens of artists and labels made mountains of cash off this formula. Remember OMC's "How Bizarre"? Chumbawamba's "Tubthumping"? These were one-hit wonders, but the acts were lucky enough to make records in an era when fans had no other choice but to buy the album in order to get the single. "If you only sold hand lotion in five-gallon bottles, pretty soon people would be tired of it," says Albhy Galuten, a well-known producer who later became Universal Music Group's senior vice president of advanced technology. "You can't go around forcing people to buy something they don't want."

Yet that was precisely the direction the record industry wanted to go in. CDs were big. How could major labels make them *huge*? The answer was to sell more CDs, at bigger record stores. Music chains like Tower and Wherehouse were well and good, but for *huge,* labels had to go to Wal-Mart. Or Best Buy, Target, or Circuit City. But there was a fatal flaw in that strategy.

Big Music's Big Mistakes, Part 5

Pumping Up the Big Boxes

From the mid-1980s to the mid-1990s, on a stretch of busy highway in Merrillville, Indiana, Hegewisch Records occupied a small, nondescript hut of a building, next to a gravel parking lot, in a part of town that epitomized suburbia—strip malls on every corner, endless traffic, especially during holiday shopping season, and Chili's, Taco Bells, and T.G.I. Friday's stretching as far as anybody could see. Inside the store, Red Red Meat CDs were displayed as prominently as Madonna CDs on the racks. "Guitarist Wanted" fliers papered the small, narrow entryway, next to worn copies of the *Illinois Entertainer* and other thin newspapers devoted to the local rock scene. Hipsters who played in bands on the side stood behind the counter in horn-rimmed glasses and bowl cuts. This Hegewisch was part of a three-store chain, and it survived by selling an eclectic mix of rock, pop, and jazz CDs.

One day in 1992, a Best Buy came to town, across and about a quarter-mile down US 30 from Hegewisch. Circuit City showed up a year later. It wasn't so bad at first—dishwashers and computers didn't exactly compete with music. But soon Best Buy started marketing its CDs and cutting prices more aggressively than ever. It would take a loss on hit CDs, drawing music fans into the store to buy much more profitable toaster ovens. This was an awesome development for consumers. The Beatles' *Anthology 2* cost $27.99 at Hegewisch and $22.99—with a free, limited-edition interview disc—at Best Buy. It was ridiculous for Hegewisch. "We can't keep up with that," Dave Diaz, the store's twenty-nine-year-old manager, said at the time. The Merrillville Hegewisch closed in 1995. The other two stores in the chain hung on until 2003.

Best Buy started selling CDs at all its stores in 1986, as a way of supplementing its core business, stereo equipment. Best Buy's CD sections took off as CD sales exploded; its stores were stocking 40,000 to 60,000 titles by the mid-1990s. Not only that, Best Buy could afford to drop the prices on CDs, even the hot new titles, when Tower and Hegewisch were stuck selling them for the usual prices in order to make a profit. (Although numerous record label executives say Best Buy's music economics involved taking a loss on a wide swath of CD titles, the company's executives insist they always made money from music. "The reality is all of our businesses have to be profit contributors," says Gary Arnold, the chain's senior entertainment officer.) Consumers were thrilled, because CDs were cheaper than ever. Labels were happy, too, until they realized just how much they had to compromise to sell millions of CDs in these stores.

In 1996, Best Buy and Wal-Mart sold more than 154 million units out of more than 616 million overall, according to Nielsen SoundScan. With their newfound clout, these chains started dictating terms. Wal-Mart pushed back against explicit lyrics and album covers—in 1993, the company refused to stock Nirvana's *In Utero* due to back-cover artwork depicting human fetuses. Nirvana's then-label, Geffen Records, decided not to censor the artwork and just live with the lack of sales at Wal-Mart's 1,964 stores. Labels would compromise within three years, producing "clean versions" of certain hip-hop records and airbrushing racy images out of CD covers so Wal-Mart would stock them.

Best Buy was far less moralistic but developed hefty financial requirements to stock albums. The chain demanded $40,000 to $50,000 from labels to push CDs in house ads and on displays and racks, sources say. This practice changed record stores forever. Tower Records, for one, went ballistic. "Frigging Best Buy!" says Stan Goman, Tower's former chief operating officer. "That was it." For years, Tower Records had a policy of not accepting money to display CDs prominently on store shelves. Store managers made those decisions based on what was selling and what they thought was good. It was a fair policy, but it was a dinosaur. Eventually, Tower couldn't resist the competitive pressure—and caved. "I couldn't believe it—all this stuff I never heard of on end-caps in the store," Goman says. "You wind up displaying all this *crap*. I had a fight on a daily basis with that. I said, 'What the hell are we taking this money for?' When the big boxes got in, they just used the same strategy that they used with everybody else, which was common in the grocery industry. We had a different philosophy. It ended up blowing up in our face a little bit."

But the label distribution execs didn't want to kill off Hegewisch, or Tower Records, or Sam Goody. These stores had been loyal customers for decades, and sold a lot of records. If they sold *Anthology 2* for $5 more, that, too, was good for the record companies, right? So the major labels came up with a policy: "Minimum Advertised Price," or MAP. Any store that sold CDs above a certain price would receive a financial boost from the record labels in the form of newspaper or television advertising. Newbury Comics in New England sold 'NSync's CD *No Strings Attached* in its first week for $11.88. A week later, to get the free ad money, Newbury raised the price to $14.99. "The MAP thing was great," says Terry Currier, owner of two Music Millennium stores in Portland, Oregon. "It gave everybody a fair shake to not be bulldogged by the big retailers and not have to give away the product." But it didn't last.

In 2000, after MAP had been in place for almost eight years, the Federal Trade Commission accused the labels of price-fixing, and the FTC declared they were penalizing some record stores, like Best Buy and Wal-Mart, for selling CDs too cheaply. Best Buy's Arnold never understood the labels' logic: What's wrong with selling CDs too cheaply? The major record labels had been doing it for years through bargain-basement mail-order deals like Columbia House. "Nobody ever explained that to us," Arnold says. "If you are so concerned about the perceived value of your product, how can you place it available twelve-for-a-penny?" The government cracked down hard. From 1996 to 1999, the FTC announced, CD purchasers paid a collective $480 million more than they should have, thanks to these MAP policies at record stores. The commission leaned on the five major record labels, which agreed to drop the practice.

Further humiliation was in store for the labels. Forty-one states, from New York to Arizona, filed suit, alleging price-fixing and collusion. The labels' lawyers had no choice but to settle. Although they didn't officially admit any wrongdoing, labels agreed to pay $20 to anybody who bought any one of the 4.1 billion CDs sold between 1995 and 2000. They also agreed to donate 5.5 million CDs—worth about $75.5 million—to schools and libraries around the country. Would these free CDs include big sellers like Bruce Springsteen and Beyoncé? Not a chance! In 2002, the Louisville Free Public Library in Kentucky was not exactly thrilled to receive as part of this settlement 171 free CDs, including *Martha Stewart Living: Spooky Scary Sounds for Halloween*, Linda Eder's *Christmas Stays the Same,* Lee Greenwood's *American Patriot,* and six copies of Ricky Martin's *Sound Loaded.* "It's better than a poke in the eye with a sharp stick—but not much," Craig Buthod, the Louisville library's director, said at the time. "I'd have to say this looks like leftovers."

Before long, mass retailers like Best Buy and Wal-Mart would account for more than 65 percent of all the CDs sold in the United States. Tower and Musicland would go bankrupt. If labels wanted to continue selling millions of CDs, they *had* to rely on Best Buy and Wal-Mart. Eventually, big boxes would drastically reduce their shelf space. But in the meantime, Napster was on the way.

Chapter 4
1998–2001

A Nineteen-Year-Old Takes Down the Industry—with the Help of Tiny Music, and a Few Questionable Big Music Decisions

IN 2007, Doug Morris, sixty-eight-year-old chief executive officer of the Universal Music Group, the world's largest record company, gave an interview to *Wired* magazine that left many in the record industry frowning in stunned silence. He was talking about major labels in the late 1990s and why he and his contemporaries didn't plunge into internet music more quickly. "There's no one in the record company that's a technologist," he said. "That's a misconception writers make all the time, that the record industry missed this. They didn't. They just didn't know what to do. It's like if you were suddenly asked to operate on your dog to remove his kidney. What would you do?" Responded the *Wired* writer: "Personally, I would hire a vet." Morris shot back: "We didn't know who to hire. I wouldn't be able to recognize a good technology person—anyone with a good bullshit story would have gotten past me."

Granted, record labels didn't have high-tech staffs on the level of Apple Computer or Sun Microsystems. But Morris's memory of his own staff at the time was disturbingly out of touch. "There were only like forty people trying to get Doug's attention," says Erin Yasgar, who headed Universal's first new-media department, beginning in 1998. "We were all like, 'Pay attention to us!'" Also at Universal were internet experts like Albhy Galuten, the Grammy-winning *Saturday Night Fever* soundtrack producer who later created the first Enhanced CD to include video and software, and Courtney Holt, who had marketed Universal artists online since the dial-up days of America Online and

CompuServe. These high-tech experts were scattered throughout all the major labels.

It was the CD that first turned record people who otherwise might not have known a bit from a byte into New Media Executives. One of the very first ones was Stan Cornyn, longtime vice president of Warner Music, a creative and funny guy who in the 1960s had penned famous and influential industry ads like "Joni Mitchell is 90% Virgin." In the mid-1980s, the bespectacled Warner veteran started a new division called the Record Group, whose function was, as he recalls in *Exploding*, "make-whatever-you-can-dream-up." His small staff tinkered for months, losing money, developing business models for CD+Graphics, Laserdisc, and a new video format called CD-V. "Bill Gates came by my office, saw our work, and pretended to be interested," Cornyn writes. "I realized he'd never make it in showbiz." None of this digital ephemera came remotely close to matching the success of the compact disc.

Once executives figured out how to use AOL and Netscape, their days of tinkering in label labs, trying to add new functions to shiny pieces of plastic, were over. In late 1993, a panicked secretary strode into Warner vice president Jeff Gold's office to deliver an urgent message: Depeche Mode's new *Songs of Faith and Devotion* CD had just leaked to fans in online chat rooms! "Oh no!" Gold declared to himself in a panic, picking up the phone, preparing to implement all kinds of high-tech emergency response plans. Then he paused: "*Chat rooms?*" He opened a CompuServe account to check them out, and it wasn't long before he became addicted. Gold called his friend Marc Geiger, who had founded the Lollapalooza rock festival and was then head of new media for Rick Rubin's American Recordings. The two met regularly at Geiger's house in Los Angeles and lurked on fans' online conversations. Then they went back to work and made some calls. Working with CompuServe and AOL, Gold and Geiger ran Thursday-night talk shows, with Perry Farrell of Jane's Addiction, among others, and posted exclusive sound clips and contests. At one point, Gold showed Mo Ostin, Warner's respected old-school record man, what he and Geiger were up to after hours. "Fantastic," Ostin said dryly, "but don't forget your real job."

Yes, contrary to Morris's recollections, major labels employed technologists. Some, like Geiger and Gold, were amateur tinkerers who simply thought computers were cool. Others, like Paul Vidich of Warner

Bros., were business-strategy types who saw internet music as a huge sales and marketing opportunity—Vidich and his staff went so far as to set up the Madison Project, a high-level experiment to sell music files over Time Warner cable television systems in San Diego in 1999. Fred Ehrlich, Sony Music's head of new technology, spent the dot-com boom investing millions of his company's money in promising ventures like eUniverse. When the dot-coms crashed, Sony abandoned ship, divesting its 20 percent stake in eUniverse. That company morphed, essentially, into MySpace. "A lot of those investments wound up being very successful a couple of years later," Ehrlich says today. It was only certain people in charge who thought like Doug Morris.

When Netscape went public in 1994, introducing the World Wide Web to the public and ushering in the internet boom, top executives at major labels were largely unmoved. Starry-eyed visionaries from high-tech startups kept showing up in their offices, presenting business plans and, invariably, asking for free content. "I met with people until I was blue in the face, from the dot-com industry," remembers John Grady, head of Mercury Records in Nashville in the late 1990s. "After a while, it grew rather tiresome. That's sort of the taste everybody had in their mouth from it." These would-be dot-com millionaires tried to push old-school record men to sell music online, change the business model, plunge into the new world. They made little progress. One of the most credible dot-com guys, in the eyes of the music business, anyhow, was Rob Glaser. By December 1995, he had already started RealNetworks, which was growing fast as the premier online-audio service on the internet, one that turned dry National Public Radio news reports into essential audio content for web surfers. He contacted numerous label execs, trying to make a content deal. Everybody was nice—he had lunches with Al Smith and Fred Ehrlich of Sony Music and cigar-chomping Charles Koppelman of EMI. He hung out with MCA executives on a private jet. Each exec seemed to enjoy the meetings but had no interest in doing business. They were making big money. They had the Spice Girls. They had all the time in the world. Why change?

THE STORY OF Napster does not begin with Shawn Fanning, the nineteen-year-old Metallica fan with big headphones who invented this revolutionary file-sharing software in his college dorm room. It actually begins in the dark ages of the late 1970s, with a group of easygoing, bespectacled German audio engineers working on their PhD theses at the University of Erlangen-Nuremberg.

Back then, Professor Dieter Seitzer was trying to transmit speech more quickly and efficiently over phone lines—both via traditional copper wires and the Integrated Services Digital Network, or ISDN, which many scientists perceived as the future of telephone systems. While working on this problem, Seitzer decided it might be even more interesting to send tiny music files over phone lines. But he was so ahead of his time that a confused German bureaucrat denied him a patent. The word the examiner used was "impossible." Seitzer took that as a personal challenge and immediately assigned one of his PhD students to project shrink-the-music.

The student, Karlheinz Brandenburg, soon devoted his doctoral thesis to audio compression. He joined a team of ten to fifteen audio researchers who would spend the next twelve years working on Seitzer's problem. Brandenburg was the research team leader—sort of. "Everybody contributed ideas," he says. "It was not me implementing and the others having ideas."

Thus began a convoluted process, involving dozens of scientists from the Erlangen-Nuremberg team, Bell Laboratories, Philips Electronics, and several other companies working separately and together, to create a compressed audio file that would become known as the MP3. To make this idea work, the researchers had to tap into an existing science—*psychoacoustics*—that had been applied to loudspeakers, telephone networks, and other high-tech sound developments from as early as the 1930s. (It's unclear which of the research teams was the first to adapt this science to audio compression; the idea had been floating around in academic German papers for years.) Psychoacoustics has to do with how the human brain perceives sound, and, more important, which sounds the brain leaves out. For example, whenever two identical sounds hit the ear from two different directions, a human will hear it as a single sound coming from the first direction. This is called the *Haas effect*, and understanding such phenomena allowed the German team, in essence, to throw out the sounds human ears don't hear and keep the important ones.

This was complicated—and cumbersome, especially at first. The best track Brandenburg and the German engineers could find for research purposes was Suzanne Vega's hit "Tom's Diner," which contained no noise other than the singer-songwriter's voice. The researchers used state-of-the-art equipment of the time, like the digital signal processors that Bell Labs had first released in 1979, to take tiny samples of every second of music on a digital audio disc. The team reasoned that if CDs used 16 bits of data to sample music 44,100 times per second, which comes out to roughly 1.5 megabits per second, a compressed version of the music could use a much smaller number—say, 128,000 bits per second. The question was where to allocate those bits in sampling the music. Maybe a particularly important middle C would take up a few hundred bits; a high-frequency sound undetectable to the human ear might wind up using no bits at all. (These techniques would eventually lead MP3 critics, from rocker Neil Young to digital music pioneer James T. Russell, to bemoan the loss of sound quality.) Combining psychoacoustics and long-established concepts like Huffman coding and Fast Fourier Transforms, the team wrote software encoders and decoders to compress the audio files. But they were limited by the high-tech realities of the time. They could test only twenty seconds of music at a time, due to the limited capacity of hard-drive storage, and they had trouble finding enough university computing time to spend four hours on each twenty-second passage. Not only that, it was the age of low-capacity, 3.5-inch floppy discs.

They labored for more than a decade on the project, meticulously working out the kinks and taking advantage of advances in storage capacity and the growing availability of personal computers. For a long time, nobody had any idea that this obscure German research project would turn into anything more than an obscure German research project. "In 1988 somebody asked me what will become of this," Brandenburg told the BBC News. "And I said it could just end up in libraries like so many other PhD theses."

By 1991, the engineers had enough resources to perfect the MP3. They successfully compressed "Tom's Diner" into the format and developed a standard player for computers. They began to share resources with a prominent German research society, the Fraunhofer Institute for Integrated Circuits, and together they focused on turning their invention into a worldwide hit. They wrote a proposal to the Geneva-based International Organization for Standardization, which tells the world, for example, how many tubes and valves belong in car tires and the minimum amount of platinum required for platinum jewelry. One of the many subgroups of the ISO, as the organization is widely known, is the Moving Picture Experts Group, or MPEG, which formed in 1988 to create standards for digital multimedia formats. By then, the scientists from Philips, Bell Labs, and the other companies working on the same idea had come up with similar inventions and were furiously trying to make them work. At the time, all these scientists were still thinking *telephone.* But the internet would soon become far more exciting than the phone.

In all, fourteen different groups submitted their technologies to MPEG. And this is where the history of the MP3 becomes even murkier. "It's not a straightforward story, unfortunately,"* says German team member Bernhard Grill, who specializes in algorithm and software design. In 1991, MPEG merged four of the proposals and eventually turned the compression technology into a standard with the catchy little name of ISO-MPEG-1 Audio Layer 3. That's MP3, for short. Two variations, MP2 and MP1, worked better for video.

At the time, nobody in the record industry had a clue any of this was going on. Executives at Sony Music, Warner, and the rest didn't know MP3 existed, let alone that it contained no copy protection. Nor did they know that any music fan in the world could stick a CD into a recordable drive on a computer and rip every song into a compressed, easy-to-store form, then burn the MP3 to a blank CD, or post it for free on the internet, or even trade it via email. The Fraunhofer team tried to warn the industry in the early 1990s, but didn't get anywhere. "There was not that much interest at that time. Oh, there were some meetings, but not with the top hierarchy," Grill says. "They didn't realize how fast the internet would grow. No one saw it coming that fast."

As the 1990s wore on, and the internet started to blow up, the MP3 slowly turned into an underground hit. One fan discovered it, then

---

* This is an understatement. On its website, Fraunhofer calls this team "inventors of the MP3," and media often refer to Karlheinz Brandenburg as "the father of the MP3." The truth is not so simple. A bunch of companies earned patents for contributing ideas and technology to the format. One of these was Bell Labs, where Brandenburg worked briefly in the late 1980s. Then Alacatel-Lucent bought Bell Labs's MP3 patents. Then the company insisted on receiving royalty payments, just like the Fraunhofer Institute, which gets $2,500 for every video game that uses the MP3 format. So when Microsoft paid $16 million to license the technology for including MP3s in its Windows Media Player, Alcatel-Lucent's lawyers sued. They won a $1.52 billion judgment, although a federal judge in San Francisco set aside the ruling in August 2007. "I never call myself the inventor of MP3, because there's a lot of people," Brandenburg says in an interview. "I know on whose shoulders I stand. But on the other hand, I certainly had a lot to do with the development of MP3."

another, then another. Two of them were Rob Lord and Jeff Patterson, then computer-science majors at the laid-back campus of the University of California–Santa Cruz. Patterson had a band, the Ugly Mugs. Lord was an indie rock and electronic music fan who happened to be studying psychoacoustic audio compression. Lord found the MPEG specifications online. With help from friends at Sun Microsystems and elsewhere, they landed free server space and taught themselves how to encode music in the MP2 compression format. They posted Ugly Mugs songs on internet newsgroups. They were surprised to hear from fans in Turkey and Russia via email, asking for more Western music. Lord and Patterson started the Internet Underground Music Archive, one of the first major music web sites, offering free MP2s by unknown bands—but they had the foresight to stay away from copyrighted music owned by major record labels.

As internet connections evolved from frustrating to tolerable to enjoyable, Winamp, designed by Justin Frankel, a nineteen-year-old college dropout and programming genius from Sedona, Arizona, became the first standard for playing MP3s online. It was free. Using such tools, voracious music fans started to post MP3s on their web sites—usually well-known songs by artists like Metallica and Madonna. The dam broke in late 1997, when entrepreneur Michael Robertson created MP3.com, a hub for finding free music on the web.* The media started to notice, as "MP3" displaced "sex" as the most-searched-for term through internet search engines such as Yahoo! and AltaVista.

In 1999, the heart of the internet gold rush, there were only two ways for an entrepreneur to get into online music. The first was to play by the rules of copyright. But that meant dealing with the major record labels, whose executives were in no hurry to change their CD-selling model. IBM developed something called the Cryptolope, a locked electronic "envelope" containing music or other content that could be passed around via email or the web. It didn't get anywhere. "A few other companies got into that technology game," recalls Bob Buziak, former president of RCA Records, who went on to consult with AT&T and other high-tech companies. "But the record industry basically said no. They didn't feel they were going to give anybody their content."

---

* In 2000, the RIAA would successfully sue MP3.com after the company bought 45,000 copyrighted CDs and posted them on an internal server for unlimited customer use.

Gerry Kearby started Liquid Audio, a format that included encrypted locks on digital music files, and tried to make licensing deals with the industry. He wound up negotiating with executives like Sony Music's Al Smith, a charming guy who enjoyed meeting with tech people but never committed to a deal. In large part, sources say, that was because he *couldn't*. Tommy Mottola, Michele Anthony, and the rest of the Sony Music brain trust were opposed to licensing content online. "One day in a moment of pure honesty, [Smith] said, 'Look, Kearby, my job is to keep you down. We don't ever want you to succeed,'" Kearby says. "Some of them were more interested in experimenting than others, there's no doubt about it. But they were, in effect, buggy-whip manufacturers, trying to keep the auto at bay as long as they could."

The second way to succeed in online music was through theft—allowing people to download MP3s for free. This was illegal, and dangerous.

The first person in the record industry to notice online song-swapping—officially, anyway—was Frank Creighton, a former computer systems analyst and head of the RIAA's antipiracy division. The files were huge—50-megabyte WAVs took a long time to download, especially over dial-up connections. *This couldn't possibly catch on*, he thought. Then Creighton saw users trading compressed files—MP3s—over file-transfer protocols, chat rooms, and plain old websites. He sent his first cease-and-desist letter to a website in 1997. The pirates ceased and desisted. That approach worked pretty well.

In late summer 1999, Creighton was surfing the 'net and happened across a website with downloadable software. *Napster.com.* He checked it out and peered more deeply into his computer screen. Fans were exchanging messages, just like they did via chat rooms or Internet Relay Channels. Only all the messages were about how they could trade songs for free. And they were actually doing it—*right there*. Hundreds of them at a time. *Thousands* of them! He turned to his boss, Hilary Rosen, then chairman of the RIAA. "You've got to look at this," he said.

"Oh my God," Rosen responded. It was as if vandals had broken the locks on all the record stores and were looting merchandise in bulk.

Creighton sent an email to the registered user for the Napster website. "We're happy to talk with you," responded two names Creighton had never heard of—Shawn Fanning and John Fanning. "We're glad you find our technology interesting and we want to figure out internally who are the right people to sit down with you." Unbeknownst to

Creighton at the time, Napster creator Shawn Fanning and his uncle, John, who controlled most of the company, were stalling. A round of venture-capital financing was about to come through for their business, and the Fannings didn't want to damage it. Creighton received two more responses over the next few weeks, then nothing. He called again. And again. Finally, another name at Napster, Eileen Richardson, returned his call. She said she had no idea why he was calling. When he mentioned his concerns about copyright infringement, she said she'd talk to others within the company and get back to him. He flew to California for business and tried to reach Richardson between meetings. He called several times. No response. That pissed him off.

IN 1996, SHAWN Fanning was a seventeen-year-old hacker. Not the evil-genius kind. Shawn was more the type to hang around in Internet Relay Channels, or IRCs, and absorb as much as he could about computer security at banks and brokerages. He didn't do any of this to make mischief, or so he told friends. It was mostly to learn as much as he could on his own about computers and programming.

When Shawn was born, on November 22, 1980, he lived with his single mother, Coleen, and a rotating cast of her eight brothers and sisters and their families in working-class Rockland, Massachusetts. Within a few years they started moving around, near the projects of Brockton, outside Boston, as Coleen found work as a nurse's aide. She also married a bakery delivery truck driver and ex-Marine, Raymond Verrier, and had four kids with him. Shawn's father was Joe Rando, who at age eighteen started a romance with sixteen-year-old Coleen after performing with his Aerosmith cover band on the Fannings' block. He didn't come around much. "Money was always a pretty big issue," Shawn later told *Business Week* in a Napster cover story. "There was a lot of tension around that." When the Verriers broke up temporarily in the early 1990s, when Shawn was twelve, he and his four younger half-siblings lived for a few months in a foster home. "I told him that I had talked to my wife and we only had a small apartment, but he could come live with us," his uncle, John Fanning, told the *Boston Globe*. "He was just a kid, twelve or thirteen, but he said, 'I guess I've always known that was an option for me, but to tell you the truth, there's no way I can leave my brothers or sisters.'"

In a way, Shawn was lucky. He was shy, but smart and focused. He taught himself how to get good at various things. He played tennis, basketball, and baseball, and hit .650 one year at Harwich High School, in small Harwich Port, part of Cape Cod. And he had an uncle who recognized his talents and became a sort of older-brother-and-mentor figure. John Fanning bought him lavish gifts, like a purple BMW Z3, which would fuel Shawn's lifelong interest in fast cars. In 1996, John also bought Shawn an Apple Macintosh—his first computer. "He set me up with internet access. I was pretty much on the internet right away," Shawn says, in his polite, no-nonsense, borderline self-deprecating way. "I used it for him at his house. I think the first time I used it was to play chess. I was amazed by it. I loved it. Completely sucked in like everybody."

Uncle John was an entrepreneur, a self-made man who had a vocational high school diploma and a few Boston College course credits spread out over eight years. He claimed to have worked as a senior trader at the prestigious Fidelity Investments, but all he really did was take incoming phone calls and route them to actual traders who made actual deals. He tried and failed at two businesses—computer company Cambridge Automation, which he rode to the bottom in the early 1990s, and Chess.net, run by low-paid Carnegie Mellon students he'd recruited personally. On his own, John Fanning was never successful at business by any objective standard, but he had a talent for staving off debt, ignoring creditors, and fighting back in court. Even during his worst periods, he had no problem buying expensive suits and cars for his nephew.

Shawn interned for Chess.net in summer 1997, sleeping on a living room couch in a house rented by the firm's six employees. "We set up a little computer for him in the living room—I think it was something we made with spare parts—and taught him to program. He was fifteen years old," recalls Ali Aydar, a Chess.net employee. "You give him one or two little things and he sort of goes with it from there." Shawn threw himself into hacker IRCs like w00w00, learning about MP3s, and amassing his own digital music collection within weeks. John bought him a second computer, a $7,000 laptop. "I remember having a technical discussion about MP3s online—people explaining compression ratios," Shawn says. "It gained some popularity. I heard quite a bit on IRC." Eventually Chess.net crashed. Most of Fanning's employees took off. John had tens of thousands of dollars in debt. He needed new business—something in the big and moneymaking department.

Shawn badly wanted to attend Carnegie Mellon, from which some of his Chess.net mentors had graduated, but he didn't get in. He settled for Northeastern University, near home. At the time, Shawn didn't much like college. The beginning computer courses were beneath him, so he spent most of his time partying—and hanging out on w00w00. For the next several months, rather than actually attending school, Shawn spent time at his uncle's office, fiddling with the computer.

Looking for a way to trade MP3s online that was faster and less frustrating than web search engines, Shawn was in his dorm room when he conceived the idea for Napster. He was inspired by the easy-to-use format of IRC, in which users' names appeared on the screen when they were logged on, and vanished when they weren't. His plan was to set up a central server, where users would connect, see their log-on names, and view the titles of MP3s they were storing in folders on their hard drives. A search box, set up like Google or AltaVista, would make it easier than ever to find a piece of music by artist or title. The trick was that the central server contained only information on user names and MP3 text information. The actual file sharing took place between individual users' computers. Shawn named his invention after his IRC nickname: Napster. This was a haircut he had as a kid, although by the time he went to Northeastern he already had his familiar look—Marine-doubling-as-Metallica-fan.

As master programmers go, Shawn was a hard worker but not brilliant. He needed help. One of his w00w00 mentors, underachieving geek Jordan Ritter, was intrigued by his online friend's idea. For free, Ritter debugged the code and updated some of Shawn's unsophisticated programming in the C++ language. Some of Shawn's other mentors weren't quite so supportive. "I was living in downtown Chicago, working as a banker," Ali Aydar recalls, "and Shawn popped up on my IM. He started telling me about this software application he was writing and how it was about sharing music and how it was going to work and all this other stuff. I said, 'Stop wasting your time. No one's ever going to share an MP3.' I encouraged him to concentrate on school. Obviously, he didn't listen to me."

One of Shawn's first important IRC contacts was another ambitious teenager, Sean Parker. Like Fanning, Parker grew up with computers. His mom was an infomercial media buyer. His dad was an oceanographer who'd grown up in the Cayman Islands and attended the Massachusetts Institute of Technology. He regaled Parker with stories of computers programmed with punch cards that took up entire rooms, and helped Sean learn to program on the family Atari 800 at an early age. Raised in Herndon, Virginia, outside Washington, DC, Parker had a supportive family and enough money to do the stuff he wanted to do. He was a decent computer programmer—he'd learned languages like Basic and C—but he was far more interested in building a business and making money. In high school, he bought model planes wholesale, then made a few hundred dollars marking up the prices and selling them. He had the gift of gab.

After Parker formed his own security company, Crosswalk, he started to talk with likeminded computer obsessives on IRC, and he soon met Shawn. "We were basically hackers," Parker says. "But we had much broader interests than just technology—we were interested in the consequences of it and building things that people actually wanted to use." But Parker spent only a small portion of his time on IRC. Mostly, he networked. His parents wanted him to go to college, but Parker took a year off to make contacts at business-oriented internet service provider UUNet. He was working there around the same time Shawn Fanning started his freshman year at Northeastern.

By January 1999, second semester, Shawn was working long hours on Napster code and very close to dropping out of college. His mother was disappointed, but John Fanning, by then saddled with tens of thousands of dollars in debt from his two failed businesses and legal fees, encouraged him. Uncle John incorporated Napster Inc. He took 70 percent of the business, giving Shawn 30 percent, despite Shawn's reluctance. That was a slightly better deal than most unknown musicians received when they signed to a major record label, but it was extremely bad business for nineteen-year-old Shawn. He agonized over it for years afterward, but always made the decision not to fight his uncle. As Shawn grew up, they developed a sort of love-hate relationship, squabbling and coming back together at unexpected times. Shawn followed a pattern that would soon be familiar to fellow Napster employees, throwing himself into work during times of stress. Shawn gave the first version of Napster to about thirty friends, mostly hacker types he'd met in the chat rooms, in June. Soon, almost fifteen thousand people had downloaded Napster from the internet. "I had to focus on functionality, to keep it real simple," Fanning later told *Time*. "With a few more months, I might have added a lot of stuff that would have screwed it up. But in the end, I just wanted to get the thing out."

Shawn's head was so filled with code that he didn't have the time or interest to focus on Napster as a business. His uncle took care of that. So did Sean Parker. Through Parker's friend Jonathon Perrelli, who was in charge of hiring for UUNet, he arranged a "practice meeting" with an early potential investor. Parker recalls little about this meeting, but the preparation sticks in his memory. The Fannings flew to his northern Virginia house. "I had been shopping the deal around northern Virginia in order to raise money. Shawn and I had made a lot of progress—building clients, building presentations, we had users, a company in place, all this work in place—and we had never met in person," Parker says. "They landed and took a cab to my house from Dulles Airport. The doorbell rings. I excitedly run to the door. It's Shawn and his uncle. [Shawn] said to me, 'You look exactly like what I expected.' And we immediately got down to running through our pitch." The centerpiece of the pitch was a growth chart with a steep upward bent.

A bit later, Parker lined up the company's first concrete investor—Ben Lilienthal, who had in early 1999 sold his web email service Nascent Technologies to the huge Boston internet holding company CMGI. The internet boom was on. Early investors were put off by debts from John Fanning's failed companies, but Shawn's idea for Napster was too tantalizing to ignore for very long. After talking with Parker, Lilienthal set up a meeting with the Fannings and one of his New York contacts, an "angel investor"—a term for venture capitalists who put in $1 million or less to help a company get started. Lilienthal and Jason Grosfeld flew out to visit the very first Napster office in an old hotel near John Fanning's house in Hull. The investors were shocked—they expected at least an Aeron chair, but all they found were open fast-food containers and Shawn hunched over his laptop on a card table. John Fanning wore shorts and tennis shoes. The investors tried to talk with Shawn, but John kept talking to them, boasting of the important people he knew in Silicon Valley. They were the first of many to realize the best possible way to deal with Napster was by maximizing contact with Shawn and minimizing contact with John. They brought up legal issues. The Fannings acknowledged they hadn't hired an attorney.

Nonetheless, weeks later, the two investors were ready to offer the three-man Napster crew a deal. Parker wrote up a business plan, in which Napster would try to get as much as 10 million users and try to sell them concert tickets and band merchandise. Lilienthal and Grosfeld hooked up a more powerful investor, Reston, Virginia, venture capital firm Draper Atlantic, and two of its executives agreed to meet Grosfeld, Lilienthal, the Fannings, and Parker at Grosfeld's apartment in downtown New York City. The Fannings showed up two hours late in a Z3 convertible with Shawn's Napster server in the backseat. The Draper executives made their offer—$500,000, with Lilienthal as CEO. Draper would take a minority stake in the company. John Fanning wanted more.

Negotiations heated up over the next few months, as both John Fanning and the Lilienthal group frantically researched the legal implications of Napster offering a massive international free market for copyrighted music. But in the end, Fanning kept asking for more and more money—the price went up to $1 million at one point. They were two percentage points of Fanning equity away from a deal when Fanning started saying outrageous things like, "How much do you have?" The investors backed out. That was just the first of many serious investment deals, worth hundreds of thousands of dollars, that derailed at the last minute thanks to Uncle John. "John is a gamer. He carries that over into every aspect of his life," Parker says. "John treats people like objects on a chessboard—they move in completely logical ways. But that's just not the way most people are, especially sophisticated people. It's not that black and white. He would get caught up in the game of it all and rub a lot of people the wrong way."

Miraculously, Parker's contacts and John Fanning's machinations led to a bona fide investor. Yosi Amram was a Tel Aviv–born Harvard Business School student who first encountered John as a chess opponent in the public games at Harvard Square. (At first, Amram says, he was the better chess player, but Fanning practiced for longer hours and caught up.) Amram was smart and cultured, and the style of chess he favored—blitz—was so fast it barely gave the players time to think about their next moves. Amram founded an internet start-up, Individual, with his savings. He set it up for a $200 million initial public offering in 1996, made a lunkheaded purchase of web-surfing software company Freeloader for $38 million, and ran Individual into the ground.

Still, Amram had a lot of money to invest in a start-up. He moved to Silicon Valley to be closer to the action and was soon approached by his old friend John Fanning. Amram didn't consult a lawyer. He didn't check out the legal implications. He made a quick decision—over a period of a few weeks, as he recalls—to invest $250,000 for 1.25 million shares. "This was kind of the height of the internet boom, so money was easy," Amram says. "Today, I would have probably spent more time and effort thinking about making a quarter-million investment." Amram had some conditions: He wanted to pick the CEO, he would serve on a three-member board, and the company would move to Northern California so he could be more involved in its operations.

Shawn Fanning and Sean Parker packed their stuff, boarded planes, and moved to Silicon Valley.

EILEEN RICHARDSON CAME to Napster via a circuitous route. She was born to a poor family in Middletown, New York, with a father who built docks before quitting work for good due to disability, and a staunchly Catholic mother who emigrated from Ireland. Eileen's mother encouraged her to find a husband, and quick. She took the advice, marrying a West Point cadet at age twenty-one. "We got very, very poor, very quickly," Richardson says. "And I realized: I'm a Democrat and he's a Republican, and that didn't make it easy." They had two kids, and while her husband aspired to live in upstate New York, Eileen had broader ambitions. After moving around with him to various military bases after he graduated from West Point, she'd had enough. They divorced. She kept the kids.

Richardson moved to Boston and tried to figure out what to do. She stumbled onto a venture capital company, Atlas, which had been looking for a new employee for nine months. They loved her aggressive, fast-talking personality and agreed to give her a secretarial job and pay for her MBA education. "I did everything," Richardson says. She answered the phone, made coffee, did research, and got promoted—a lot. Within six years, she says, she'd landed deals with Firefly, a start-up with a model of recommending music to internet listeners based on their preferences, as well as Vermeer Technologies, developer of a publishing tool that would become Microsoft's FrontPage. Suddenly other companies, like Forrester Research, heard about her and started trying to hire her away.

Richardson landed at JK&B Capital, a Chicago venture firm that gave her a partnership. Through a young salesman whom she would later hire as a Napster executive, Bill Bales, she snagged a deal with a web content-management company, Interwoven Inc. She convinced JK&B to invest $5.2 million, and it wound up gaining $438 million. Richardson was a first-class networker. One of her contacts in the early

1990s was Yosi Amram. He met with her one day to discuss companies he was working with, like the tech start-up Xtime, then disguised as something called the Palo Alto Coffee Co. She mentioned she might be interested in working as an investor and executive for other companies, and Amram brought up Napster. Richardson went home and checked out the website. She was a music fan—any kind of house or club music, and alt-rockers like Nine Inch Nails—but couldn't hit the clubs due to her two young kids. So Napster made sense, immediately. "What I wanted to do with Napster was never, ever, steal music," she says. "The first idea of ninety-nine cents a song was mine! You could find and buy music for a dollar a song instead of seventeen bucks for sixteen songs that you hate. That was the idea." Amram told Richardson about John Fanning, and how he could be difficult, confounding otherwise easy negotiations and inserting himself into parts of the company where he had very little expertise. Amram promised he could handle Uncle John. Convinced, Richardson bought 333,000 shares from Fanning. She joined Amram and John Fanning on the Napster board.

Meanwhile, Shawn Fanning and Sean Parker were itching to move into real offices. For their first few months in California, they stayed at Russian chess master Roman Dzindzichashvili's house in Sausalito, taking care to be totally silent while he paraded children through the house for chess lessons conducted in his booming voice. "I kind of forgot about that phase," Shawn says today. "It was a really weird experience." Parker and Fanning would soon find an $1,800-a-month San Mateo apartment with a six-foot widescreen television. Like most men in their early twenties, they weren't exactly all-star housekeepers, and more than one visiting reporter observed empty pizza boxes and soda cans lying around the rented furniture. Shawn wasn't especially flamboyant, but he drove a custom Mazda RX-7 and politely shook hands and exchanged greetings with strangers who spotted him at the mall. He was also a gym rat, playing hoops a few times a week and working out frequently.

Napster moved to the top floor of an old bank building in San Mateo. Parker and Fanning were too young to rent cars and had no credit cards, but they were the heads of a company that would ultimately change the world. They were surrounded by executives who were even more enthusiastic than they were, like Richardson and her second-in-command, Bill Bales, newly installed as vice president of business development. "I would put on a presentation for Bill and Eileen, and halfway through, she would start screaming and running around the office, saying, 'We have so much to do!' " Parker told Joseph Menn in the definitive Napster biography, *All the Rave*. "Bill would say, 'That's brilliant! We're going to be a $10 billion company!' And I would say, 'Wait, I'm not finished yet.'" At one point, on Richardson's invitation, former Warner Music high-tech executive Ted Cohen showed up to interview as the next CEO. He walked into the office to find a young man sleeping on the floor with his head on a motorcycle helmet. Cohen woke him up, introduced himself, and asked for Richardson. "Oh, I'm sure they'll be out soon," said the kid, and went back to sleep. That was Shawn Fanning.

It became fairly clear fairly quickly that Napster had no central business plan—other than the obvious, which amounted to "generate a huge user base by allowing fans to trade copyrighted music." The company's top executives disagreed on strategy. Some wanted to charge a monthly subscription fee, like the phone company. Others wanted to sell merchandise. Richardson kept advocating for her charge-by-the-song plan. She figured this would be great exposure for lesser-known artists. "John Fanning absolutely was completely thinking a different thing: 'We will take down the music industry and give away free stuff,'" she recalls. Fanning made comments to that effect in business magazines, which didn't exactly make RIAA people like Hilary Rosen and Frank Creighton very happy. It also didn't put them in the mood to make a deal with Napster.

A week after Creighton first talked to Richardson, she called back. This time, Richardson knew much more about the legal issues. She suggested Napster was totally legal given the US Supreme Court's groundbreaking 1984 decision legalizing Sony's Betamax for home-taping TV shows. She refused to shut down Napster per his request. Rosen got the message. On October 27, 1999, Rosen instructed the RIAA lawyers to draft a complaint.

Richardson recalls her two phone conversations with Creighton. For the first, he was cordial. For the second, she says, "The whole tone changed. It was like, 'Listen, you come talk to us, but I'm telling you right now, you really need to think about shutting things down before we talk.' Then the next conversation was with Hilary." Richardson told Rosen about the plan to charge for music and break new artists over an exciting new medium. Rosen responded: Take down all the signed artists from the site, and we'll talk. Richardson asked for a list. At this point, both women say, the conversation turned ugly.

Rosen remembers Richardson as "either a really bad manipulator or naïve. Because she didn't get it. She really didn't get the piracy aspect of it for several days."

"It was her job to lobby for the record industry and here's this huge, looming thing—*of course* she's going to be a little stern," Richardson says. "I remember seeing someone [in the media] said, 'I'm a bitch to [Rosen].' But believe me, it was vice versa." The RIAA prepared for war.

For Shawn Fanning, the main challenge of running Napster was making sure the servers kept up with the demand. He had help—Jordan Ritter joined the company, as did Ali Aydar and longtime software pirate and IRC regular Jordan Mendelson. As of October 7, 1999, the company had 150,000 registered users, trading 3.5 million files—and was expanding by who-knows-how-much every day. (The numbers were a little skewed, since users could register multiple times, but Napster was unquestionably growing at an extraordinary rate.) Thanks to the efforts of Richardson and Yosi Amram, a new wave of venture capital came in, totaling $2 million, from angel investor Ron Conway as well as internet-boom stars like Excite founder Joe Kraus and Napster's own head of engineering, a new employee named Eddie Kessler.

A former engineer with Quote.com, Kessler hooked up with the Napster crew through a connection. He met one day with Aydar, Ritter, Shawn Fanning, and Sean Parker and came away unimpressed—good idea, he thought, but poor, unstable design. Richardson offered him a job. John Fanning called to tell Kessler he was certain Napster would soon be worth $10 billion. Kessler was hesitant, because he had a wife and four-year-old daughter and was worried about spending too much time in the office during a legendary period of Silicon Valley overworking. Richardson assured him he'd have to work late two days a week and only occasionally on weekends.

What finally sold Kessler was his own tour of the Napster software. He found music he hadn't heard since college, which was only available on hard-to-find vinyl singles. He signed on. The work was great. He liked most of the people, although some didn't like him—according to Menn's *All the Rave*, a few employees complained that Kessler took credit for their work, and he often dragged his feet on deadlines for new versions of the software. In any case, the stress weighed on him. "One of the tragedies of this was I really didn't get to see my family for two years. I would call my home in the early evening and talk to my daughter and she would say, 'Are you going to be home for dinner?'" Kessler says. "I had a BlackBerry and two cell phones. We scheduled seven vacations over two years and all of them got canceled. Everything was clearly insane." Shawn Fanning, still not even twenty-one, with no family of his own, was more equipped for the long hours and endless stress of maintaining Napster. Many employees at Napster recognized Shawn as a compulsive workaholic. "There's no question it was exciting and stressful. We were always at capacity," he says. "Every time they put servers up, they filled with simultaneous users and we hit the capacity again."

The challenges were many and difficult. In November 1999, one of Napster's servers maxed out at a far-too-low 1,000 users. The team kept buying more servers, until somebody figured out the cap was a result of bad code. Once they fixed it, traffic quickly doubled on each server. The Napster crew danced to N.W.A. on company tables. Another time, Shawn found a bug that shrunk users' music files at the last minute, allowing them to share severely damaged songs. He personally worked on that one for two weeks, then came up with a patch for the client software. "One of the most stressful experiences ever," he says. On the rare occasions they took time off from work, Shawn and Parker blew off steam at Bay Area raves.

When the RIAA filed its copyright-infringement lawsuit on December 6, 1999, in US District Court in San Francisco, it surprised no one at Napster. Few of the company's starry-eyed employees thought Napster could possibly lose. When Ted Cohen was interviewing to be Napster's next CEO, he noticed whiteboards all over a Napster conference room. On one was scrawled the phrase: "How to Talk to the Press." Underneath, it said, "If they call to say, 'Don't you know this is illegal?,' say, 'We didn't know it was illegal—we think it's fair use.'" "It was all deflection points," says Cohen, who turned down the Napster job and later went to work as EMI Music's top high-tech executive. "It was basically to convince the press 'we're good guys.' A lot of it wasn't true." Still, the lawsuit had the immediate effect of generating stratospheric publicity for Napster and its young executives. Within a few months, the *Los Angeles Times* and the *New York Times* slotted Napster on the front page, and MTV crews showed up to interview Shawn Fanning and

Parker. The two friends would turn on cable at night and, watching in a surreal daze, see themselves on MTV. The number of total system users grew from 50,000 when the RIAA filed suit to 150,000 by the end of the same month. Shawn Fanning, in his baseball cap, T-shirt, jeans, and blank, aw-shucks expression, was suddenly a rock star, though he didn't think so. "Rock stars and people that play music seriously—they know when they're successful, there's a certain fame associated with that," he says. "When you're writing software, it's the last thing you expected. Long coding sessions don't go well with camera interviews, even back to back." But he had charisma, and Richardson smartly turned Shawn into the face of the company.

Against his will, Fanning became a sort of folk hero. He took on the record labels, which didn't have the best public image. They were always landing in scandals, such as the Mob-connected independent radio promotion imbroglio of the 1980s. For years, label executives had reputations for taking advantage of artists, especially young and inexperienced ones—many of whom didn't even know the labels had been deducting archaic, LP-era "packaging rates" out of their CD royalties for years. But in earlier days, the top execs had been funny, fiery, talkative characters like Walter Yetnikoff of CBS or erudite, well-respected gentlemen like Mo Ostin of Warner Music. They had a knack for changing the agenda, behind the scenes and in the media, whenever an irritating subject like "how much artists get paid" came up. They also had a knack for making talented musicians very, very rich. But in 2000, Yetnikoff and Ostin were gone, replaced with less colorful corporate executives from Seagram and Sony who didn't crave the limelight.

In this new record business environment, Napster had the effect of empowering artists like the irrepressible Courtney Love of Hole. In January 2000, Love declared her Universal Music contract "unconscionable" and announced she wouldn't deliver the records she owed to the company's Geffen Records. Universal sued. She countersued.

This sort of thing happens all the time; usually, the cases are settled and everybody quietly goes home to count their money. Love did so, too, in 2002. But first, she delivered a famous speech at the Digital Hollywood conference, reprinted in Salon.com as "Courtney Love Does the Math." This is how she broke it down: A top band gets a million-dollar advance; the band spends half a million to record its album, $100,000 on a manager, and $50,000 on lawyers and business managers. The four band members then get $180,000 after taxes, or $45,000 per person for a year. Then the band sells 1 million records, and receives no royalties after expenses. According to Love's math, the record label gets $4.4 million.

Yes, Napster users were engaging in theft. But their stick-it-to-the-man righteousness drew much of the public to their side, and major labels were taking the biggest public relations hits they'd ever absorbed. "It just grew and grew. Shawn becomes a cultural phenomenon. Presidential candidates are asked about it in debates," Hilary Rosen says. "The intensity with which the industry was under siege was huge."

Most Napster users were college students. Indiana University tried to ban the software on campus because it sucked up so much bandwidth, but a feisty computer science sophomore, Chad Paulson, chastised the administration on free-speech grounds. IU backed down. Napster supporters reasoned: The record labels have screwed us for years! They charge $18 for two good songs! Backstreet Boys suck! They latched on to Fanning as a symbol, a rebellious David-vs.-Goliath type who invented the coolest slingshot ever.

To some, this spirit reeked of rock 'n' roll—or at least a more efficient way of selling records. At Universal Music, new-media chief Erin Yasgar wore a Napster T-shirt to staff meetings. "Some people got it and there were some laughs," she recalls. "Some people, not so much." Mark Ghuneim, Sony Music's senior vice president of online and emerging technology, spent the 2001 Super Bowl halftime show studying Napster—and noticing a massive surge in tracks by performers Aerosmith, Britney Spears, and the Backstreet Boys. The next day, he walked into work to see about reissuing singles to take advantage of the popularity spike. It turned out to be impossible. Labels didn't put out singles anymore. And they couldn't make any new product available in fewer than twelve to fourteen days. That would have been too late. "Those opportunities met with failure," Ghuneim says, "because everybody was afraid it was going to start a precedent."

With or without major labels, several artists figured out how to harness the power of Napster on their own: In 2000, Radiohead promoted its experimental jazz-rock *Kid A* by secretly releasing tracks to the service, winding up with its first-ever No. 1 album. Dispatch, a young reggae-rock band, flooded Napster with free recordings and, over time, grew its audience—to the point that the band would sell out multiple nights at Madison Square Garden in early 2007. "We were saying, 'It's a new form of radio where people can get music out there, and it doesn't have to have too many strings attached to it,'" recalls Pete Heimbold, the band's bassist. "What we found was it really didn't deter from kids coming to shows and buying CDs. In fact, I think it had the opposite effect—people heard songs off Napster and had a lot of merchandise and CDs."

"I hit a point where I was convinced that there was no next big thing in the music business except technology. It wasn't going to be a sound or a dropped D chord or a new way of looking or a style—it was going to be technology," adds Liz Brooks, a longtime A&R rep who worked at Virgin and Sony before quitting the business to be Napster's vice president of marketing. "Napster was like this cult piece of software—a lot of people in a certain age group were aware of it, and yet nobody else was aware of it." Some bands saw the same thing—Limp Bizkit headlined a Napster-sponsored concert tour in 2000. The Offspring, a Southern California punk band, supported Napster, and its manager, Jim Guerinot, filed an amicus brief in court on Napster's behalf.*

The record industry did its best to turn back the David-vs.-Goliath aspect of the story. This is *theft*, the RIAA kept reminding people. "If you can come up with another way of artists being paid for their work, I'm all for it," says Bill Allen, a Napster opponent who at the time was BMG's director of new technology. "But right now the system we have is copyright. It's only fair that artists get paid for their work." Eminem, the world's biggest rapper, declared: "If you can afford a computer, you can afford to pay $16 for my CD." Dr. Dre sued. So did Metallica, in April 2000, and drummer Lars Ulrich gave heartfelt interviews saying the metal band deserved to get paid for its music. Metallica had a point, but it grossly underestimated its own fans' newfound loyalties to Napster. Suddenly, Metallica, which had made a career of liberally allowing fans to tape its concerts, was Enemy Number One of the People. "Leave Napster alone," declared the online graffiti on Metallica's hacked official website. One Napster fan later created a viral cartoon, "Napster Bad!," depicting singer James Hetfield as a monosyllabic baboon. "Napster spun it cleverly, like 'Metallica is suing their fans,'" recalls Joel Amsterdam, then the band's publicist for Elektra Records. "That was unfortunate. [The band members] certainly hated that part of it."

---

* The mischievous Offspring later offered bootleg T-shirts with Napster's copyrighted kitty-in-headphones logo to fans via its website. Napster sent a cease-and-desist letter. Napster's hypocrisy was duly noted in the media, although both camps agreed to a deal and gave the proceeds to charity.

In May 2000, on advice from his attorneys Howard King and Peter Paterno, Ulrich made the provocative move of calling a press conference at Napster's offices in San Mateo. He showed up in a limo with thirteen boxes full of paper listing the names of Napster users sharing Metallica songs. Napster's executives were prepared. They'd alerted a group of users, who assembled outside the company's offices to protest the press conference. They shouted "Fuck you, Lars!" as he walked from the limo to the building. At Ulrich's side, King demanded that Napster ban all Metallica songs from its service. Afterward the attorney and the drummer rode up the elevator to the company's fourth-floor offices. Employees gathered around and declared themselves fans. Ulrich picked up on the fan-vs.-attorney dynamic and slowly grew less inflammatory and more conciliatory as the events of the day wore on. "I really don't want to sue you," he told the crowd. "All I want is for artists who want to get paid to get paid." Shawn Fanning, Sean Parker, and Ali Aydar were supposed to stay on the fifth floor, away from the circus, but they drifted down, incognito, to check it out. One overzealous Napster employee even approached Ulrich for his autograph. The showdown ended civilly, and Ulrich and King left the building after saying what they had to say. A few days later, Napster announced it would comply with Ulrich's request. The company blocked 317,377 users from a list it received from Metallica.

BY JULY 2000, almost *20 million* users were on Napster. In September, Shawn Fanning introduced Britney Spears at MTV's Video Music Awards; he wore a Metallica T-shirt and joked to VJ Carson Daly about somebody sharing it with him. In October, he hit the cover of *Time* in his trademark bowl-cup headphones. (In the company's crisp, clever logo, a rebellious cartoon cat wore the same headphones.) The same month, he was a presenter at the Rave Awards in San Francisco, sharing the stage with Courtney Love, who flirted with him in her outrageously exaggerated way, calling him "my future husband" and sitting in his lap. Eileen Richardson was constantly on the phone, talking to the likes of Fred Durst of Limp Bizkit, Chuck D. of Public Enemy, and Mike D. of the Beastie Boys, trying to make deals. Guy Oseary, who ran Madonna's label, Maverick, invited Richardson to the Material Girl's office in Los Angeles. As a pregnant Madonna lounged in the background, Oseary discussed a Maverick investment of $1 million. But no major artist ended up investing. "The RIAA went on the huge tour to everyone and opened up their laptops and said, 'Watch this' and 'This will be the end of you,'" Richardson says.

Richardson kept working her old venture capital contacts for more funding. At one point, she had what she describes as "three of the finest and best venture firms"—including Kleiner Perkins Caufield & Byers, where she was dealing with the influential former Intel sales giant John Doerr—lined up to contribute $85 million. "Well, that was not enough for John Fanning," she recalls. To this day, Richardson is convinced Doerr and his connections could have rescued Napster. Instead, she says, John Fanning blew up the deal and went to a smaller financing firm, Hummer Winblad, which quickly agreed to give Napster $65 million for a 20 percent share. Hummer then pushed to replace the excitable Richardson with corporate lawyer Hank Barry. Richardson, who never intended to stay more than six months, quit. Barry's first job at Napster was to deal with the RIAA lawsuit.

He had reason to be optimistic. In the late 1990s, issues involving MP3s, file sharing, and digital copyrights were part of a larger, unexplored legal terrain. A 1984 US Supreme Court precedent seemed perfect for Napster. In *Sony Corp. of America vs. Universal City Studios*—widely known as the "Sony Betamax case"—the court ruled 5–4 that Sony could manufacture VCRs for people to record copyrighted TV shows for their own use. Napster figured the same logic would apply here. Napster itself wasn't actually *infringing* anybody's copyrights. It was merely functional, a middleman, like the VCR. Napster couldn't possibly police the service for copyright violations, just as a telephone company like AT&T couldn't possibly be responsible for whatever illegal plans people made over the phone lines. There was also the Audio Home Recording Act, passed by Congress in 1992, which allowed consumers to make taped copies of their own albums—as long as they didn't sell them. Finally, there was the Digital Millennium Copyright Act of 1998, which gave "safe harbor" to internet service providers as long as they didn't actively encourage illegal behavior. "We felt that they had a pretty good case," Barry says. "When I took this to my partners, we said, 'Look, [Napster] could lose and we could lose all our money. Or they could win and it could be a chance for the first spectacular social networking company.'"

But if the RIAA lawyers could prove that Napster knew about its users pirating copyrighted music, they could easily show the judge that

Napster was hardly an innocent middleman like a VCR manufacturer or an internet service provider. Napster employees were generally careful not to acknowledge its users pirated music—even though surveys showed almost every song shared over the system was copyrighted. When the RIAA attorneys asked for internal Napster documents during a phase of the lawyers' investigation known as the discovery process, they received boxes and boxes. They pored over them for weeks. Finally, after a long day's work, attorney George Borkowski came across an internal email from Sean Parker to Shawn Fanning: "Users will understand that they are improving their experience by providing information about their tastes without linking that information to a name or address or other sensitive data that might endanger them (especially since they are exchanging pirated music)."

Borkowski had to blink at that last part. *Exchanging pirated music?* Parker admitted it, right there in an email, albeit one never intended for outside eyes. Borkowski and partner Russell Frackman, who had worked for years on RIAA piracy cases even though he was so low-tech he didn't even use email himself, couldn't believe it. They deposed Parker the next day. He squirmed. And just like that, the case was all but over.

Hank Barry still had a few cards left to play. He called litigator David Boies, who had represented the US Justice Department in its antitrust trial against heavily favored Microsoft in what many called "the cyber trial of the century." At first, Boies didn't return Barry's call. But later that week he was eating dinner with his family, and three of his sons—two in their early thirties and one in his teens—told him how important the case would be and insisted he take it on. Boies did, but he immediately ran up against Marilyn Hall Patel, US District Judge in San Francisco.

On July 26, 2000, when Patel began the trial in a courtroom packed with hundreds of journalists and Napster supporters and opponents, David Boies tried to make the relevant arguments. He mentioned VCRs and the Audio Home Recording Act. Patel cut him off several times. She cited Parker's "exchanging pirated music" email. After both sides were through, Patel left the bench for half an hour. When she came back, she announced that she'd decided in favor of the recording industry. "Plaintiffs have shown persuasively," she wrote later in her opinion, "that they own the copyrights to more than 70 percent of the music available on the Napster system." Napster had to remove all copyrighted material from its service, essentially shutting down the whole thing, within two days. "Oh my God," Shawn Fanning said to himself, seated in the courtroom. "What in the world is going on here?"

There was a reprieve. Sitting on the three-judge Ninth Circuit Court of Appeals was Alex Kozinski, a President Reagan appointee who fancied himself a cutting-edge technology enthusiast. He wrote columns for the online magazine Slate.com. Kozinski convinced one of his fellow judges, Barry Silverman, to stay Patel's injunction against Napster and hear the case. Napster employees celebrated. "This is like the playoffs," John Hummer, ex-NBA-basketball-player-turned-venture-capitalist, said at the time. "They won the first game, and we won the second game. It's going to seven, and we're going to win it." But Hummer was missing one important piece of information. Kozinski wouldn't be on the Ninth Circuit panel that would rule on Napster's injunction.

UNBEKNOWNST TO MOST people outside Napster or the upper echelons of the record industry, in the days leading up to Judge Patel's decision, Hank Barry had been aggressively using all the wheeling-and-dealing skills he had. At this point, he wasn't sure whether Patel would rule for or against Napster, so he started meeting with the heads of major record labels to try to make a deal. His first call was to Edgar Bronfman Jr., who was, at least in public, one of Napster's strongest opponents. Bronfman, chief executive officer of the Seagram Co., which had purchased Universal Music a few years earlier, had given a speech earlier that year likening Napster to "both slavery and Soviet communism," according to *The Atlantic*. The former songwriter was nonetheless crucial to Barry's purposes, as Universal had grown into the biggest worldwide record label, thanks to hits from Eminem, Dr. Dre, No Doubt, and others. But Bronfman also saw that the labels could make a lot of money if they had direct access to Napster's 22 million users—in addition to selling them music over the internet, they could also figure out what type of music they liked and target them with marketing pitches and sales. He agreed to meet with Barry.

Despite Bronfman's Soviet metaphor, he was not Napster's biggest opponent in the record industry. Neither were other international media moguls whose holdings included major record labels. Sony Corp. co-CEO Nobuyuki Idei was willing to talk, even though he said in later interviews that Japanese law prohibited a service like Napster. So was

Thomas Middelhoff, head of Bertelsmann, which owned BMG Entertainment. Most of the record industry's anti-Napster brigade was a step lower down the executive ladder: Sony Music's Tommy Mottola and Michele Anthony, Universal's Zach Horowitz and Doug Morris, and BMG's Strauss Zelnick, all of whom perceived online music sharing as theft, plain and simple, and had no interest whatsoever in jumping into bed with their sworn enemy. "It became clear that [Bronfman, Middelhoff, and Idei] had very little control over what their record companies ended up doing," says a record industry source. "They basically threw up their hands at their own [subordinate] executives."

Yet Bronfman recalls: "I very much wanted to make a deal with Napster. I thought it made sense for the industry." Bronfman and Barry talked several times—at Universal's office in Los Angeles, at the Seagram Building in New York, at an airport in San Francisco. Behind the scenes, Barry's boss at Hummer Winblad, John Hummer, told Barry to pursue a deal in which the labels would share 10 percent of Napster's future revenues. (Although the company had yet to make revenues from its business plan and was running mostly on venture capital, record company executives could see huge potential profits by selling advertising on the service or even charging users for downloading songs.) Bronfman told Barry to be more creative. The deal on the table, as Barry recalls, was for all five of the major labels to equally share a 60 percent stake in Napster, as well as 90 percent of the voting power over company decisions. "These were business meetings," Barry says. "These weren't like 'OK, you terrible guy.' These were like 'Let's look at the spreadsheets and make this work.'"

These discussions peaked on July 15, 2000, when Barry and Hummer met privately with record executives in Sun Valley, Idaho. Bronfman invited some of his colleagues—Sony's Idei, Bertelsmann's Middelhoff, head of Sony US Howard Stringer, and several aides—to the meeting at investment banker Herb Allen's annual conference of media power brokers. (Executives for Warner and EMI, the other two major labels, were embroiled in merger talks at the time, and Bronfman didn't think it made sense to include them—but they, too, authorized him to speak for their interests.) Middelhoff walked in and noticed immediately that none of the label executives, not even Bronfman, were sitting on the same side of the long table as Napster. He made a joke of squeezing himself into the remaining chair, between Hummer and Barry. After a few awkward seconds, Barry recalls, Bronfman then said, "Thomas, your seat's over *here*"—and Middelhoff dutifully moved to the other side of the table.

By that time, label and Napster executives were even farther apart than they'd started out. As Bronfman recalls, Barry wanted something like a 50–50 split of Napster's future equity, while the record industry wanted more than 90 percent. Although Bronfman recalls a nonetheless friendly, cordial relationship with the Napster people, particularly Barry, Middelhoff says he could tell from the minute he walked into the Sun Valley meeting that the Napster people and the label people didn't really like each other. Bronfman did all the talking. Major players like Idei, Stringer, and Middelhoff said little. Hummer and Barry made their points. After ten minutes, it was over. "This was an unbelievably brief meeting," Middelhoff says, still shocked at the disconnect between the importance of the subject and the length of the discussion. "John Hummer and Hank Barry were not ready to move any of their positions. Neither was Edgar Bronfman." But the meeting was long enough for Napster's business model to make a lasting positive impression on Middelhoff.

The meeting sealed the fate of the whole negotiation. Hummer went "radio-silent" for days, Bronfman remembers, and finally called back later in July with bizarre news. In Bronfman's version of the story, the venture capitalist told him he had another deal on the table—for $2 billion. He wanted to know if Universal Music had a competitive offer. "Please think about it," Hummer said. Bronfman was stunned. "I don't need to think about it, John," he replied, on the spot. "I'm not interested in $2 billion. Frankly, if you get 10 percent [of that], you should celebrate it. Come to think of it, if you get 1 percent, you should celebrate. Good luck." "There was obviously no deal," Bronfman says today. "He was bluffing." Even years later, it's difficult to unravel just where that alleged $2 billion offer came from. Bronfman recalls Hummer strongly implying the source was America Online. Bronfman also spoke with Yahoo!'s Jerry Yang, who said Hummer told him the offer came from AOL. But in an interview for this book, Hummer denies claiming he had such an offer. And George Vradenburg, AOL's general counsel at the time, acknowledges his company was very interested in making a deal for Napster, but no executive ever made an offer— and certainly didn't discuss a number as eye-popping as $2 billion. In any event, negotiations broke down. Days after Bronfman spoke with Hummer for the last time, Judge Patel's injunction came in. Soon after that, Barry proposed a 50 percent ownership split to Napster. But the deal with the labels was dead.

That was the last chance for the record industry as we know it to stave off certain ruin.

To an extent, the opposition from executives at the major labels was understandable. Napster was enabling and encouraging theft, no matter what the internet's "information wants to be free" contingent was saying at the time. The courts, beginning with Judge Marilyn Patel, would consistently rule that file-sharing services trading in illegal music were engaged in copyright infringement. But label chiefs were so bogged down in the file-sharing battleground that they refused to act on the digital future of the business. Many figured they would simply win in the courts and the CD-selling business would go back to normal. As a result, they wasted almost three critical years before agreeing to a functional, legal song-download service.

Several internet-savvy underlings at major labels saw exactly what was about to happen—Albhy Galuten of Universal Music and Mark Ghuneim of Sony Music, to name two. But the majority of executives preferred to cling to the old, suddenly inefficient model of making CDs and distributing them to record stores. In this world, the labels controlled—and profited from—everything. From Michael Jackson's *Thriller* to 'NSync's *No Strings Attached,* the old system made them richer than ever. Also, these executives knew all too well that Napster wasn't *theirs.* The CD, at least, had come from Sony and Philips, two familiar companies with long-standing record industry relationships. This new music distribution system belonged to a snot-nosed punk and his crazy uncle.

Executives also felt they couldn't plunge into a deal with Napster because of their contracts with thousands of artists, song publishers, and retail stores. Publishers, for example, had been getting rich for decades off the mechanical royalties (the seven or eight pennies that go to songwriters for every album sold in a store) from Elvis Presley or Michael Jackson sales. They didn't want to lose their meal tickets, and might have made life difficult for the labels. And many top artists signed to labels had contracts that didn't cover digital music. Most would likely want to renegotiate, especially since their lawyers had dealt with mysterious packaging and new-technology deductions in CD contracts for the past fifteen or twenty years. "It was not what the perception is—it was not ignorance. It was not being caught and bit on the ass by something that was coming. It wasn't any sort of arrogance of maintaining the old way and preventing new things from happening," says Al Smith, a Sony Music VP who became legendary to tech executives as a champion stonewaller. "It's that the whole nature of the copyright business creates issues that are impossible to overcome."

Difficult? Yes. But impossible? When CDs took off in the early 1980s, forever altering labels' contracts with artists, publishers, and retailers, executives had no problem forcing their clients into new deals. And, of course, labels would later jump into a new service with Apple Computer that overcame the very same hurdles Al Smith describes. But in the early 2000s, they simply failed to recognize that the new way of doing business was worth the effort. Had the labels made a deal with Napster, they would have found several immediate advantages: a built-in user base of 26.4 million people, as of February 2001, most of whom were loyal and passionate about both music and the service itself; an efficient way of communicating with their customers, discerning their musical tastes, and aiming pitches for new albums and singles; and the flexibility to set prices at a number of levels, with models ranging from pay-by-the-song to monthly subscriptions. "You can't compete with free," label executives complained at the time, but for many users, *free* was not even the best part of the service. They used Napster to get music whenever they wanted, and could burn it to homemade CDs, play it on their computers, or transfer it to devices like the Rio or, eventually, the iPod. Had the labels charged money for Napster use, a large number of freeloaders would have probably dropped out of the service. But a number would have gladly paid for the privilege, as the huge numbers of iTunes Music Store customers proved a few years later. Yes, it's entirely possible that had the labels licensed Napster, pirate-dominated services like Kazaa and LimeWire would have popped up anyhow and undercut an official Napster store. But the Kazaa and LimeWire services were cluttered with spyware and confusing ads, and were never as clean or easy to use as the original version of Napster.

Any commonsense calculation proves the point. Let's say record labels had jumped in when Napster's user base was at 26.4 million per month. Let's say, conservatively speaking, half don't want to pay and go to Kazaa or LimeWire or some other free service, leaving 13.2 million users. Let's say each uses the official Napster to buy 10 songs for $1 apiece every month. That's record business revenue of $132 million per month, or $15.84 billion a year. Sure, labels would have had to pay artist and publisher royalties out of that, but the overhead of trucks, warehouses, crates, and record stores suddenly gets cut dramatically. And remaining CDs suddenly get a powerful, internet-based marketing and promotional tool. In hindsight, after years of plummeting CD sales and industrywide layoffs and artist-roster cuts, it's clear that making Napster official circa 2001 would have been a huge positive for the record business.

In fairness to the labels, the people who ran Napster weren't exactly open-minded, either. They were rebels by nature. Although Shawn Fanning was an amiable character who would later jump into the digital-music business with major labels via his new company, Snocap, in 1999 and 2000 he wasn't in the position to make Napster deals. He left that function to people like his uncle John, who, as Eileen Richardson recalls, was prone to proclamations like: "We will take down the music industry! And give away free stuff!" Richardson herself was slow and combative in dealing with the RIAA's Frank Creighton and Hilary Rosen. And just as behind-the-scenes negotiations were heating up with the major labels in July 2000, John Hummer appeared in a *Fortune* article headlined "Big Man Against Big Music," declaring, "I am the record companies' worst nightmare." This countercultural bluster was fine for a pirate organization aiming for public attention and users, but it alienated potentially receptive music business partners like Bronfman and Idei. And it pushed less receptive partners even further into fight mode.

Because of this stubbornness—on both sides—the labels had come to the defining fork in the road, and they picked the wrong path. "I feel very strongly about that moment in time, and the labels clearly blew it," says Jeff Kwatinetz, chief executive officer of the Firm, a Los Angeles management company that represents hard-rock bands like Korn and Linkin Park as well as pop star Mandy Moore and rapper Ice Cube. "Something like thirty million-plus music fans were in one spot online. At the time, the idea of all the music you would want for $15 a month was an appealing thing and studies showed most users would've paid it. On top of that, if the site was marketed, in addition to the viral buzz, it goes to fifty to sixty to seventy million users. It's in the billions and billions of dollars that [labels] left on the table by suing Napster. Not to mention the possible advertising dollars that could have been generated.

"Clearly there was a deal to be done, but instead it became the moment that the record labels killed themselves," he continues. "Stealing music became more convenient, and the Napster audience was fragmented all over the internet."

During the Napster era, Hilary Rosen of the RIAA appeared in almost every news story as the anti-Napster, antipiracy spokesperson for the record industry. Aside from Metallica, the flame-haired, tough-talking Rosen was the lightning-rod face of the Napster opposition. *Wired* titled a 2003 profile "Hating Hilary." It described a file-sharing debate at Oxford University at which Rosen represented the music industry's side of the issue—and had to contend with boos and hisses every time she spoke. Daughter of the first woman ever elected to the town council in West Orange, New Jersey, and an insurance broker, Rosen started her career as a bartender-turned-lobbyist in Washington, DC. Her mother provided a connection with then–New Jersey governor Brendan Byrne, and Rosen found herself lobbying for music publishers. She became simultaneously loved and feared. "She can punch you in the face, and you're still smiling after she does it," John Podesta, chief of staff for the Clinton administration, said in the *Wired* piece.

Rosen was publicly infamous among Napster supporters for absolutely refusing to budge from her file-sharing-equals-theft position. In private, however, she argued strenuously for a deal. "Hilary, just stop it," Doug Morris told Rosen at the time. "We have something internally that will solve it all." He was referring to Pressplay, a clunky, poorly reviewed online music store created by Sony and Universal that cost $14.95 a month for a limit of fifty songs. The other "official" service, MusicNet, was planning to use content from EMI, Warner, and BMG, but it never got off the ground despite intense, hard-sell content-licensing meetings between its parent company, RealNetworks, and label executives such as Al Smith of Sony Music. "I think Al Smith enjoyed our meetings because he liked the back and forth," says then-Real executive Alan Citron, who tried everything to get majors to jump aboard. "But it never felt productive. We were going through the motions and had little chance of anything happening."

Today, Rosen, now the political director for the Huffington Post and a familiar Democratic face on CNN, finds the labels' Napster-era foot dragging a tragedy. (Some of her critics left over from the Napster period call Rosen's public flip-flopping disingenuous, wondering how she can square her more liberal new position on file sharing with her unyielding conservatism at the time.) "I say this with the most affection possible—[label executives] had all the wrong reactions. I thought this was a revolution and we should ride the wave," she says. "But they just did not see a business model that was anything but cannibalizing in the worst sense. They needed to jump off a cliff, and they just couldn't."

* * *

THE JULY 2000 Sun Valley meeting did have one positive result: It introduced Thomas Middelhoff to Napster.

With his small spectacles, slicked-back hair, striped ties, impeccable suits, and imposing height, Middelhoff looked the part of the successful German businessman. His career began at his family's textile firm, but he joined Bertelsmann as a management assistant in 1986. At the time, Bertelsmann was under the control of Reinhard Mohn, great-grandson of Carl Bertelsmann, who founded the company as a publisher of religious books in 1835. Mohn was conservative and careful, but he spent the 1960s and 1970s expanding the company, buying Bantam Books and Clive Davis's Arista Records.

Middelhoff rose quickly at Mohn's company, turning around a Berlin printing plant, then managing one of the company's primary factories in Gutersloh. He had a particular affection for new technology—he'd written his PhD thesis in 1983 on a German online service in the early days of CompuServe and Prodigy. As head of strategic planning and multimedia, he spent the 1990s plunging into the internet. One day, a young American internet entrepreneur, Steve Case, contacted him and asked for a meeting; Middelhoff went in thinking he'd disperse some words of media magnate wisdom for a while and leave. Instead, he was blown away by Case's new model and international business plan. He lobbied his bosses to put $100 million into Case's company, America Online. Bertelsmann's top executives thought Middelhoff was crazy, but authorized a $50 million investment nonetheless. In 2000, Bertelsmann sold a stake in AOL Europe for $8.5 billion. This turned Middelhoff into a sort of internet-age business hero—and gave him plenty of Bertelsmann investment money to play with.

Middelhoff may have worked for a conservative company, but he couldn't have been more radical when he first encountered John Hummer and Hank Barry at Sun Valley in 2000. He was impressed with Shawn Fanning's service. He immediately had visions of a peer-to-peer network in which customers would pay $4.95 a month and get unlimited content over the internet—a John Grisham novel (published by Bertelsmann's Random House) here, an Elvis Presley album (owned by Bertelsmann's RCA Music) there. Middelhoff excitedly returned to Germany and authorized his head of e-commerce, Andreas Schmidt, to look into partnering with the company. Like Middelhoff, Schmidt was obsessed with investing in the new economy, but Schmidt took it to an extreme. "He was a charming guy," says Gerry Kearby, who ran Liquid Audio and spent some time negotiating with major labels and with Schmidt in particular. Often, the fast-talking Schmidt mystified Kearby with his incomprehensible ideas. "It was hard to figure out, really. It was the boom time and there was definitely a lack of oxygen in many people's brains. I had no idea, really, what their grand plan was." Kearby was no fan of Napster, which he considered a theft machine that prevented him from making his own deals with labels. But he knew and liked Barry and gave his Napster contact information to Schmidt.

So it was that Bertelsmann got in touch with Barry and proposed a deal—not an investment, but a loan of $60 million, which would give Bertelsmann a majority stake in Napster. In a further attempt to woo Napster's brain trust, Middelhoff took Shawn Fanning out for dinner at the Post House in Manhattan and promised him a new salary of $120,000 and a $60,000 bonus. "He was like the most positive and optimistic person that maybe I've ever worked with," Fanning recalls. "I don't think it was awkward at all. He was just as optimistic privately as he was publicly. He genuinely believed in Napster."

The proposal couldn't have come at a better time for Napster, which was reeling from Patel's injunction and running out of money. But it couldn't have come at a worse time for Strauss Zelnick, head of Bertelsmann's record company, BMG, which had just lost 'NSync to Clive Calder's Zomba Group. Although Middelhoff recalls Zelnick and the rest of BMG's top executives voting to support the Napster investment early on, Zelnick has a different memory. "Without our support or knowledge, Bertelsmann tried to make a deal with Napster," he says. "I said, 'It's illegal.' They said no. I said, 'Moreover, I believe this will turn into a big ugly piece of litigation and will end up costing Bertelsmann hundreds of millions of dollars.' Which it did. It didn't work out so well for Bertelsmann—*in the way I outlined.*" Other label execs were skeptical of the garrulous Middelhoff, interpreting his very public support of high-profile Napster as grandstanding. "Easy way to be in the headlines," Sony Music's Al Smith says today.

On Halloween 2000, while Zelnick's BMG was still involved in the copyright-infringement lawsuit against Napster, forty-seven-year-old Middelhoff stood with nineteen-year-old Shawn Fanning in the Essex House hotel ballroom in New York City. Before an audience of journalists, photographers, and TV crews, they announced Bertlesmann's

$60 million Napster deal. Middelhoff called Fanning a genius. They hugged awkwardly. "When a Napster user is sitting at his PC and he's connected with somebody in Europe or in Latin America or in Asia, then they don't share only the file," Middelhoff told the *New York Times Magazine*. "They are saying, 'Hey, can you remember when this band performed, and what did you do, did you have your first kiss? And by the way, where do you live?' This was Shawn Fanning's genius." Not everybody at Bertelsmann agreed with Middelhoff's investment decision. Less than a week later, Zelnick resigned from BMG, as did the company's chairman, Michael Dornemann.

This bizarre relationship between rebel Napster and the German head of a multinational media corporation that owned a record label that was *suing* Napster was destined to fail. The first blow came in February 2001, when the US Court of Appeals for the Ninth Circuit concurred with Judge Patel. Napster was now officially illegal. On March 6, 2001, Napster engineers followed the judge's order to start blocking file names according to a list provided by the record labels. "It was just terrible—to be so invested in the product and wanting to see it continue to grow and having all these people enjoying using it," Fanning says. "That was a miserable experience. That was when I started to get distraught about the company's future."

Barry contacted the RIAA's Hilary Rosen about making a deal, but the appeals court victory gave the labels all the leverage, and they had little interest in negotiating further. Barry lobbied Congress to try to change the laws to allow music file sharing, and he got some help from an unexpectedly sympathetic source. Orrin Hatch, Republican of Utah, chairman of the Senate Judiciary Committee, was a part-time gospel songwriter who had an interest in getting more of his indie label recordings to the public. He spoke publicly on Napster's behalf. But the RIAA stalled, Senator Jim Jeffords changed his affiliation from Republican to Independent, giving Democrats a majority in the Senate, and Hatch lost his chairman's seat to Senator Patrick Leahy—thereby also losing his best chance to act on his sympathy for Napster.

The recently appointed CEO, Konrad Hilbers, a friend of Middelhoff's installed by Bertelsmann, pushed for more money to keep Napster going as a legal service that specialized in copy-protected music files. He figured $30 million over six months ought to do it. Before long, Bertelsmann was in for $95 million in loans to what was widely perceived as a dying, illegal company. Fanning and Middelhoff secretly decided on a new Napster model: They would allow users to swap files, just like before, only each song would have to go through a filter containing a list of copyright-protected songs—and, of course, only those that weren't protected would be shared. It might have worked. But Bertelsmann's Mohn family lost confidence in Middelhoff and his crazy internet-era wheeling and dealing. They fired him in July 2001.

Napster was out of life preservers. The company declared bankruptcy on May 14, 2002, and all seventy employees were fired. John Fanning had tried a number of things to keep the company running, and to keep his own stake in it. He'd failed. "Essentially, that was the end of the game," recalls Lyn Jensen, the company's chief financial officer and, in essence, final employee. "The judge said, 'Pay everyone and that's it.' From September 5 through the end of November, I kept things going—a one-person, unpaid show."

NAPSTER WENT AWAY, but file sharing did not.

Even as Napster was growing rapidly, in mid-1999, hackers were writing and distributing flawed but operable imitations like CuteMX and iMesh. The most sophisticated new file-sharing service came from Justin Frankel, the onetime hacker extraordinaire who had invented a popular, pre-Napster piece of MP3-playing software called Winamp. Living in San Francisco in 1999, Frankel and Shawn Fanning became friendly, mostly due to their shared interest in speedy cars, and Fanning had an inkling Frankel was about to release something powerful and competitive. Sure enough, Franklin soon introduced a new software called Gnutella. From a user perspective, it worked a lot like Napster—you could plug an artist name or song title into a search engine, then download whatever song happened to come up. The crucial difference was that Gnutella didn't have one central server—it relied on a clever high-tech system in which each user (or "node") functions as his *own* server. There was no central, Napster-like entity or company for record industry lawyers to sue. And unlike Napster, Gnutella was owned by America Online, which had purchased Frankel's small high-tech company Nullsoft. Proud of their Gnutella accomplishment, Nullsoft's employees posted the new software on the AOL website in March 2000. But AOL was in the process of merging with Time Warner, owner of Warner Music, not a fan of file-sharing services—especially ones it couldn't sue. Within two days, after reporters got wind of Gnutella and pressed AOL officials about it, the corporation yanked the software from the service. But the genie, as they say, was out of the bottle; worldwide users had already downloaded the software and were using it to create file-sharing systems such as LimeWire and BearShare.

This was a prominent example of how, after the January 2001 merger, the high-tech, internet-boom visionaries at AOL didn't exactly mesh seamlessly with the old-media guard at Time Warner. At first, Howie Klein, president of Warner-owned Reprise Records, who had been frustrated with the music industry's slow response to the downloading crisis, was excited about this new influx of high-tech experts. He and a few internet-savvy colleagues approached their AOL highers-up with a proposal for a new music-download store, which, as Klein recalls, resembled an early iTunes. "The AOL people said, 'This could be dangerous,' and passed on the idea," he recalls. "As soon as AOL took over, the message was, 'We're paying too much for health insurance for our employees.' And: 'Hey, you're being a pussy with these artists, you're giving them too much and being overly generous and taking away from us.'" Klein quit the company soon after the merger. But an AOL executive who briefly worked on a music deal told Kara Swisher of the *Wall Street Journal* that Warner was the one refusing to innovate: "Neither Warner Music nor anyone else there ever accepted that if we could crack the code, there might be whole new ways to market [online]." Meanwhile, the high-tech portion of the company was more sympathetic to Napster than it let on in public. During an off-the-record interview with Swisher, a top AOL executive pulled a Napster T-shirt out of a drawer. "Napster is good," he said, according to her exhaustive chronicle of the merger, *There Must Be a Pony in Here Somewhere*. "No matter what we say."

For more than two years after Napster died, executives at the major labels meandered, tinkering with Doug Morris's favorite service, Pressplay, as well as MusicNet, but really not coming up with anything. Meanwhile, peer-to-peer file-sharing services like Kazaa and BearShare grew almost as rapidly as Napster. In 2003, labels agreed to work with Napster 2.0, run by Roxio Inc., which had bought Napster's remains for $5 million in bankruptcy proceedings.

But by then it was too late. The labels had already given their digital music business away to Steve Jobs, chief executive officer of Apple Computer.

Big Music's Big Mistakes, Part 6

The Secure Digital Music Initiative

In fall 1998, record industry executives had big plans for digital music: They would . . . *form a committee.* It would be a *really big* committee, with hundreds of the smartest thinkers from Microsoft, Intel, Texas Instruments, Sony, Panasonic and, of course, the five major record labels. They would meet thirty-two times over almost three years, at expensive hotels in exotic places—the Sheraton Park Lane in London, the Radisson Hotel Narita Airport in Tokyo, the Roosevelt in New York, the Hyatt in Maui and, most striking of all, the Villa Castelletti in Florence, Italy. This committee became the Secure Digital Music Initiative, a think tank costing $5 million to $10 million. Its goal was to figure out a standard way to encrypt digital music files so they wouldn't go traipsing around the internet for anybody to download for free. With such a system in place, the industry could set up a sort of legal Napster. It could also work with electronics firms to create the best digital music player ever made.

The meetings began informally, with thirty or forty engineers and other high-tech types at the COMDEX computer-industry convention in Las Vegas. David W. Stebbings from the RIAA was there, and he acknowledged the music business had a little digital problem. Also present was

Gary Johnson of Texas Instruments, who, like other reps of electronics and computer firms, figured he could help—and maybe make some money off a new product as well. They agreed to reconvene the following spring at the Consumer Electronics Show in Vegas.

For the first four months, from the point of view of SDMI members, the committee proceeded like the well-lubricated machine it was designed to be. Albhy Galuten, vice president of interactive programming for the Universal Music Group, was so enthusiastic he bought rock-star T-shirts marked "SDMI World Tour" with a list of dates and cities on the back. The panel created a logo—a bright red checkmark that indicated music players were "SDMI-compliant"—for $200,000. ("It's quite a nice logo!" says panel member Randy Cole, Texas Instruments's manager of digital-audio research and development.) SDMI released 35 pages of portable-device specifications filled with colorful technical diagrams. The document said, in essence: An SDMI-compliant device like a boom box or Walkman would have the power to determine whether an online music file was copy-protected. If not, the music simply wouldn't play. Label reps loved it. Electronics firms hated the idea of making music players designed not to play music, but the record labels wouldn't budge, so reps from these companies were forced into compromise. It wasn't long before every SDMI member realized the process was plagued with conflicting interests, difficult personalities, and a general aversion to making deals.

Two big characters emerged in these meetings of two hundred reps from one hundred companies. The first was Leonardo Chiariglioni, whom the RIAA picked as the committee's executive director. Based in Italy, he was a loud and hyperbolic technology guru who had received his electronic-engineering degree from the Polytechnic of Turin and his PhD from the University of Tokyo. Chiariglioni was a brilliant philosopher and engineer who spoke several languages. He also had a knack for enraging a diverse swath of SDMI, some of whom poke at his regal manner, even today, by calling him "the Famous Leonardo." "Leonardo was essentially a technology socialist," says Talal Shamoon, an executive with audio-encryption firm Intertrust. "He believed there should be a single format for all media."

The other character was Al Smith, the vice president who oversaw technology for Sony Music. A huge man with a booming voice, Smith had a wicked charisma that frequently distracted people from the fact that he said exactly what he was thinking. At one point during an SDMI meeting in Italy, Chiariglioni held court from behind a podium as the other members sat at individual, slightly undersized desks. A witness recalls Smith bending his long legs so that his knees lifted his desk, then absentmindedly unscrewing its legs. ("The meetings were boring sometimes," Smith says today.) After a few minutes the four metal legs dropped to the floor with a thunderous *BONG! BONG! BONG! BONG!* Chiariglioni paused briefly, blankly noted that the disturbance was caused by Smith, and kept talking.

Smith was a powerful guy whose office was part of the inner sanctum of Sony Music, on the thirty-second floor of 550 Madison Avenue in New York City, in a cluster near chairman Tommy Mottola and fellow top label managers Mel Ilberman and Michele Anthony. Smith had started out as a road manager for Blood, Sweat and Tears and Hall and Oates, and after twenty-five years in the music business, he was a loyal Mottola lieutenant who didn't take any crap. During one negotiation between Sony and a music-DVD manufacturer, some hapless lawyer demanded $400,000 up front as well as five cents per disc for his client. When Smith heard about the demand, a source recalls, he barked to his underlings: *"Call their lawyers and say they can shove the $400,000 up their asses."* After a pause he added, *"And tell them they can save room for the per-disc fee!"* Although many SDMI members liked Smith personally, he often irritated the engineers, observers say, asking if it was possible to create encryption for this disc or that digital-music file. No, they would tell him, that's not possible. *"Sometimes,"* he would respond, *"I'm amazed by how much you don't know!"*

All the SDMI tension came to a head in late August at the Villa Castelletti, an opulent hotel in hilly wine country about twenty miles from Florence, Italy. As the executives convened in a courtyard within the villa, they could hear sporadic shotgun blasts in the distance, aimed at scaring birds from the vineyards. The meeting went back and forth, and Al Smith was getting worked up as usual, responding negatively to something chairman Talal Shamoon had said. Finally, Smith walked out. Three seconds later there came a resounding *"Boom!"* from a shotgun. The SDMI members looked at each other uncertainly. Without missing a beat, Shamoon spoke up: "I understand there's an opening at Sony Music."*

In June 2000, SDMI managed to produce one flawed copyright-encryption standard, designed by Boston-area company ARIS, later Verance. Under this system, major labels would inject inaudible digital watermarks into each online track; an electronic device would have to detect it in order to play the music. Pirated songs would be screened out and rejected. The computer and electronics firms hated it.

By this time, it was obvious to frustrated panelists that SDMI was at best unworkable, and most likely doomed. All that was left was the big finish, which Chiariglioni provided in September 2000, with an open letter to hackers, most of whom were sympathetic to Napster. Crack the SDMI watermarking technology in three weeks or less, he wrote, and win

---

* This story has become a sort of legend, with various members of SDMI remembering it in a slightly different way. Randy Cole swears it took place exactly as described in the text, and others confirm his recollection. Talal Shamoon agrees, mostly, but says Smith wasn't angry; rather, he and another Sony Music staffer merely left the tense meeting to strategize and get some air. For his part, Smith, who agreed to several phone interviews for this book, says: "It's probably a true story. I do remember the incident. I remember the shots. I don't remember the humor."

$10,000. Almost 450 hackers took Chiariglioni up on his offer—although some boycotted it completely—and one group succeeded. Edward Felten, a computer science professor at Princeton University, led a team of eight grad students and other experts, some of whom stayed up all night cracking the code. "It was really a race against the clock," Felten recalls.

The team received its $10,000, and the story should have ended there, with SDMI learning from Felten's efforts, improving on the encryption, and moving on. Instead, Felten announced he planned to publish the results of his team's hack. In response, the RIAA's Matt Oppenheim immediately sent Felten a letter saying legal action could result if the professor's team published the material. "We were a bit surprised that they reacted the way they did," Felten says. He sued the RIAA, asking the courts to protect his team's "Hack SDMI" presentation as free speech. The RIAA backed off. Felten's group presented its hack-SDMI paper at a computer conference in August 2001. The next year, he dropped the lawsuit, but the RIAA's clumsy handling of the incident reinforced Napster lovers' beliefs that record executives were hypocrites.

SDMI made almost no progress on encryption, or anything else, after that. In March 2000, Sony came out with one of the few SDMI-compliant digital music players, the Music Clip. It played only copy-protected files—in the ATRAC3 format, which few digital music customers used or knew how to use. Walter Mossberg, influential gadget reviewer for the *Wall Street Journal,* summed up the device—and pretty much the entire SDMI process—in a headline: "Sony Digital Music Clip Is Cool, But Treats Users Like Potential Criminals." The Music Clip, which sold for $300, stiffed. Today, you can buy it on eBay for $37.

SDMI officially disbanded in April 2002. For some members, it wasn't a total loss. "It created the core experts who were involved in digital music," says Cary Sherman, the RIAA's general counsel at the time. "Certainly SDMI contributed in a major way towards getting those people in the same room, week after week, month after month, for a long time." Nonetheless, a huge number of ex-SDMI members recall the panel as a frustrating boondoggle. "It ended up dying a grisly, painful death," says Rob Glaser, chief executive officer of RealNetworks, owner of MusicNet. "It was an incompetently run pipe dream. They were trying to do something technologically that technology wasn't able to do. And as a result, they lost control."

Meanwhile, unbeknownst to most of the panel members, another group of smart, high-tech businesspeople was watching the proceedings very, very carefully. It was Apple Computer, which had been invited to the meetings but conspicuously chose not to attend. "I had conversations with them and they basically said, 'We don't have the bandwidth,'" Sherman recalls. "They weren't in digital music at the time." By 2000, Apple's engineers had studied Sony's Music Clip and the other ridiculously hard-to-use players on the market and decided they could do a far better job.

Chapter 5
2002–2003

How Steve Jobs Built the iPod, Revived His Company, and Took Over the Music Business

ON THE fourteen-hour journey home from secret digital music talks with Sony Corp. executives in Tokyo, Warner Music vice president Paul Vidich looked out the window of his Gulfstream IV jet. Actually, the Gulfstream wasn't *his* jet—it belonged to America Online, which had recently merged with his parent company, Time Warner. Vidich nudged the fellow Warner vice president next to him, Kevin Gage, who was immersed in a novel. They'd changed planes and stocked up on Alaskan king crab in Anchorage, and the Gulfstream was cruising at 39,000 feet over Brandon, Manitoba; it was a beautiful October afternoon. Vidich asked Gage, "Do military jets fly that close to normal airplanes?" Bleary eyed, Gage looked into the sky and saw a Canadian F15 fighter slip some 500 feet below the jet. He woke up William J. Raduchel, AOL's chief technology officer, from snoring a few seats away. "Uh-oh," Raduchel said.

Soon the pilot was standing in the aisle, briefing the suddenly very alert passengers. "We're being diverted to Winnipeg," he said. "Canadian air traffic control heard something in the cockpit. They believe we may be hijacked." It was a mistake. There was no hijacking. But it was October 26, 2001, and North America was still on high alert due to the September 11 attacks. It turned out the Gulfstream's pilot had sent out the wrong transponder signal to air traffic controllers. Vidich had two immediate reactions: *Will I make my 8:00 p.m. dinner reservation with my wife once we get to New York?* and *Why didn't I just stick with the direct reservation my assistant booked from Tokyo to New York?* Sony Music vice president Al Smith characteristically cracked, "Who pays for the extra gas?" Nobody laughed.

The next thing they knew, all six executives on board, as well as three pilots and a flight attendant, were making an unplanned landing at the tiny Brandon Municipal Airport in snow-covered Manitoba farmland. Local police showed up and had them wait on the plane for more than two hours, to give the Royal Canadian Mounted Police and Canadian Customs time to arrive, hand out automatic weapons, and plot a strategy for this unprecedented international incident 60 miles west of Winnipeg. On the plane, Raduchel used his cell phone to reach Time Warner security officials, who quickly discerned what was happening but were too late to do anything about it. The Canadians were well into their antiterrorism procedures. To pass the time, Vidich instructed the flight attendant to break out a bottle of French chardonnay and what was left of the king crab. Vidich and Smith feasted while occasionally glancing out the window at a Canadian sniper squad. Finally, the officers invited the passengers to exit the plane with hands up. They were handcuffed and told to lie on the tarmac. "It was a trip," remembers Smith, the first off the plane, still in disbelief exactly six years later. "There were people with Kevlar outfits with rifles pointed at you. There were dogs." They made Canadian TV news, and the next day, the *Brandon Sun* ran the story lead, with a five-column photo of police cars surrounding the jet and Gage with his hands up.

Later, through Raduchel and the Time Warner security officials, the passengers learned the Canadian authorities believed a hijacked jet with hostages was flying over Manitoba. They issued an urgent plea for all available police officers to head to the Brandon airport. Canadian officials alerted the North American Aerospace Defense Command. President Bush was told of a possible hijacked plane en route to Washington, DC. AOL Time Warner officials later learned the jet would have been shot down had it attempted to enter United States air space. "We had been caught up in a confusing incident with a conflicting chain of command and had been minutes away from being fired upon," Vidich, a prolific fiction writer, would later recall in an unpublished account of the events. But nobody was hurt or arrested, and all the passengers eventually made it to their destination, National Airport in Washington, DC. "We're an old crowd," says Smith, who left Sony Music in 2002 and is now retired. "We flushed our drugs down the toilet on the plane many years earlier."

As for the secret talks with Sony executives in Japan, let's just say the Brandon, Manitoba, jet debacle made for an excellent metaphor.

The talks were code-named "Digital Media X"—that's X for "extreme." Beginning in early 2001, they were an attempt to do almost exactly what the bloated and bureaucratic Secure Digital Music Initiative was in the process of failing to do. Vidich and Gage, Warner Music's vice presidents of strategic planning and technology strategy, respectively, hoped to create music files allowing fans to buy copy-protected songs off the internet. The problem was, millions of CDs had come out for twenty years with no protection whatsoever. The DMX group's solution was to build new "second session" CDs and sell them to the public. This meant adding a second layer of the same songs onto the disc. The first layer would work, as always, in standard car and home-stereo players. The second layer could be ripped to computers, only with restrictions on how many times consumers could copy them or transfer them to Walkman-like devices.

The first DMX meetings were between Vidich, Gage, Raduchel, and others at Warner Music's parent company, the newly formed AOL Time Warner. At this point, the internet bubble had already popped, and once-promising copyright-protection companies such as Liquid Audio and Reciprocal had their own problems and were in no position to bail out the recording industry. Warner's people didn't want to approach Microsoft, which owned the Windows Media audio format, because executives feared the predatory software giant would rope the major record companies into an unfavorable deal. So they picked a longtime partner, Sony Corp., which had had a huge role in creating the original CD. Vidich, Gage, and Raduchel flew all over the world to meet with Sony employees such as Koichi Tagawa—at the Peninsula Hotel near Warner Music in Beverly Hills, at Sony headquarters in Tokyo, and at Sony Music's US headquarters. One such meeting was scheduled for September 11, 2001, in New York City, and after the attacks, shell-shocked Japanese reps realized they were stranded, with nothing better to do than talk about the future of digital music. Gage and Raduchel helped them hang on to their hotel rooms for extra nights, since there was absolutely no way for them to fly back to Tokyo that day.

The secret talks heated up. Vidich and Gage enlisted executives from other companies. Larry Kenswil, the digital-strategy expert at Universal Music, the world's biggest record label, agreed to join. Sony reps insisted on inviting Wally Heijnemans, a senior strategy executive from Philips, because Sony and Philips had a history of working together to create high-tech music products. Sony Music's Al Smith was on board, too. Finally, the Warner group approached James Higa, a vice president at Apple Computer who for years had served as chief executive officer Steve Jobs's number two. (Warner enlisted Apple after a recommendation from Sony, which had been working with the computer company on various projects at the time.) The talks went well, as Gage remembers. The group started to lean toward a new digital music format—Advanced Audio Coding, or AAC, a sort of update to MP3 developed by audio engineers including a team from Fraunhofer Institute in Germany. Unlike MP3, this format made room for copy protection. In Kevin Gage's vision, copy-protected AAC files could have been supported in new digital music stores—and portable players—from AOL, Sony, and Apple. Everybody would have won.

But there was a snag. The reps from Sony Corp. opposed AAC. They preferred their own format, ATRAC3,* for which Sony would have received a CD-like royalty payment, of course. There were other problems, too. Apple's Jobs and Sony's Nobuyuki Idei weren't getting along. They had discussed making Sony's television-focused hardware and Apple's new strategy of combining movies, pictures, music, and other entertainment on the same desktop more compatible. But apparently the technology moguls didn't come out of it as friends. "You know Steve, he has his own agenda," Idei later told ex–*Red Herring* editor Tony Perkins in a website interview. "Although he's a genius, he doesn't share everything with you. This is a difficult person to work with if you are a big company. We started working with them, but it is a nightmare." The Sony-Apple politics trickled down to the DMX group. Al Smith of Sony Music was caught in the middle, wanting to contribute to a new digital music technology but not wanting to alienate his superiors at Sony Corp. The Warner reps who'd started the whole thing, Gage and Vidich, were just frustrated. "There was a certain sense that we have done 99 percent of this work and gotten to this point—and Sony was in a favorable position to hold it up," Gage says. Finally, in early 2002, the talks disintegrated.

A few months later, Vidich was in his office, on the thirtieth floor of 75 Rockefeller Plaza in New York City, when he received a phone call. It was from his boss, Barry Schuler, then president of AOL. Schuler had

---

* In 2006, Sony Corp. opened an online music store, Connect, intending to compete with iTunes. It sold files in the ATRAC format, which worked only with Sony digital players—not iPods or any other devices. The store went nowhere and closed about a year later.

been meeting off and on for months with a colleague—Steve Jobs of Apple Computer—sometimes over dinner at Schuler's house in northern Virginia. At first Schuler was trying to get Jobs to include an AOL platform on the Macintosh computer operating system, which didn't work out. But they started talking about digital music. Jobs showed Schuler a new portable music player Apple had put out called the iPod. At one point, Jobs called Schuler at his AOL Time Warner office, and Schuler pinged Vidich, asking him to join the call. *Of course,* Vidich said. Jobs rambled animatedly for a while. The Apple CEO told Vidich and Schuler the digital music services of the time, Pressplay and MusicNet, had gotten it all wrong. He wanted to talk about something new. Something digital music fans would find more interesting. Vidich listened carefully.

THE MYTHOLOGICAL AURA surrounding Steven Paul Jobs was bright enough to impress even veteran record label executives who were impervious to getting starstruck. His back story rivaled that of Madonna or Bruce Springsteen. Born in 1955, he was adopted as a baby by a South San Francisco couple, Clara and Paul Jobs. His father was a tinkerer who spent weekends fixing and reselling jalopies. He had been a Coast Guard engine room machinist, a handy background for his later work at International Harvester and, when Steve was at elementary school, Spectraphysics. To find work, Paul Jobs moved the family to Mountain View, a quiet town outside Palo Alto where a Hewlett-Packard engineer befriended young Steve and gave him a carbon microphone to play with.

Like his adopted father, Steve was a straight shooter who easily grasped mechanical concepts. Third grade bored him, so he shifted to other pursuits—dropping off live snakes into classrooms and blowing up small homemade bombs. One fourth-grade teacher, Imogene "Teddy" Hill, saw immediately that Jobs was a gifted child and pushed him to skip fifth grade. But he didn't like his hardscrabble junior high, so he convinced his parents to move to Los Altos, heavy with electrical engineers from Lockheed and other companies specializing in electronics and miniaturization. Jobs attended junior high in nearby Cupertino, a place that would later have even more significance in his life, and met a fellow late-1960s geek named Bill Fernandez.

Jobs and Fernandez, an attorney's son, had no interest in sports, unlike the rest of their classmates. But they were obsessed with electronics, and spent endless hours building stuff in their own garages and the garages of friendly local engineers. One of these mentor types was Jerry Wozniak, who worked for Lockheed, and had a son, Stephen, who had spent his one year at the University of Colorado not achieving much by way of academics. Steve Wozniak had earned the wrong kind of attention from the dean of students after programming computers in the campus data center to spit out piles of paper declaring "FUCK NIXON." "The Woz" left CU and returned to Cupertino. Wozniak befriended Fernandez. Conveniently, Fernandez had a nice workbench in his garage.

Wozniak and Fernandez built what they called a "Flair Pen or Cream Soda Computer," on which lights flashed when users flipped switches. Fernandez invited Jobs over to see it, and he was impressed. No other kid in Cupertino knew more about electronics than he did, or so he thought until he met the Woz, who was five years older. They became friends immediately. Both were loners, and while they shared a passion for electronics and computers, it became obvious that Wozniak was purely into the technology while Jobs had higher ambitions for himself. In the meantime, he was happy to meet the Woz's friend John "Captain Crunch" Draper, who showed the misfit electronics prodigies how to "phreak" AT&T telephone technology using something called a "blue box" and make free long-distance calls whenever they wanted.

As Jobs grew older, he went with the times, smoking his share of pot and hallucinating the sounds of Bach in a wheat field during an LSD trip. He enrolled at Reed College in Portland—where James T. Russell, who filed the first patents for the technology leading to the CD, had received his physics degree almost twenty years earlier—and dropped out at age eighteen. It was 1974, and he was living with his parents when he spotted a classified ad from Atari, makers of the hot new video game *Pong*. By then a hippie, dressed in rags, Jobs got the job.*After a brief early hiatus from Atari to track down a baba in India, Jobs

---

* Warner Communications Inc., owner of the Warner Music Group, invested in Atari, then a huge moneymaker, in 1976. Does that mean Steve Jobs was (indirectly) an employee of Warner? No, says Steve Mayer, an Atari and Warner Communications executive of that era, in an interview. But Mayer notes that after the Apple I came out in fall 1976, Warner had an opportunity to buy the Steves' new computer company— and passed. Why? "Because there was no future in personal computers," Mayer deadpans.

returned home and rediscovered his friendship with Wozniak, by then a Hewlett-Packard engineer in Silicon Valley. The Woz was addicted to an Atari driving game, *Gran Track*, and showed up at Jobs's office to play all night on the company's production-room floor. In exchange, Wozniak gave Jobs free, valuable engineering advice. During this time, Atari founder Nolan Bushnell approached Jobs with an idea for a video game, and Wozniak ended up designing the classic *Break-Out* in forty-eight hours while Jobs fetched him candy and Coke. Bushnell paid Jobs his fee of $1,000 for the game, but Jobs told Wozniak he'd received $600—and paid the Woz a lowball $300.

In general, the Steves had very different interests. Jobs delved into Zen Buddhism, and Wozniak was attending meetings of the Homebrew Computer Club in Menlo Park, where he learned to build printed circuit boards that would ultimately drive color displays. He started bringing Jobs to the meetings, and soon they decided to form a company to sell circuit boards to hobbyists who wanted to build their own crude computers. It fell to Jobs to come up with the name, and he decided on Apple. It wasn't because of his favorite band, the Beatles, who owned a famous record label by the same name in London. It was because he had fond memories of working in an apple orchard as a teenager one summer in Oregon. Against his father's wishes—Jerry Wozniak was wary of his son forming a company with a partner who didn't actually invent products—Steve Wozniak agreed to sign a ten-page document forming Apple Computer on April 1, 1976. To generate a budget, Jobs sold his Volkswagen bus for $500, with the price marked down due to a poorly timed engine explosion, and Wozniak sold his HP calculator for $500. Apple's first customer was a new chain of computer stores, the Byte Shop, whose owner liked Wozniak's circuit boards so much he ordered fifty of them for $25,000. The hardware would soon morph into a bona fide computer, the Apple I. "We didn't build the computer in a garage," Wozniak later told *Rolling Stone*. "I built most of it in my apartment and in my office at Hewlett-Packard, where I was working at the time. We just used the garage to assemble the parts toward the end. I don't know where the whole garage thing came from. Maybe it's because Bill Hewlett and David Packard built their machine in a garage, everyone assumed we built ours there, too. But really, very little work was done there." By the end of that year, Apple I sales generated almost $100,000.

Next, the Woz designed the Apple II in his kitchen. Jobs kept hustling up customers, often making sales calls in bare feet and ratty jeans. They recruited employees. Atari's Rod Holt charged $200 a day, which the Steves claimed was no problem even though they had barely any money; Holt came up with a new power supply so Jobs could achieve his Zen Buddhist vision of eliminating the loud fan whirring inside every computer of the era. (Eventually Holt more than made up for his early lost salary, becoming an Apple engineer and taking a 10 percent stake in the company.) Wozniak was busily creating new products. Endowed with equal parts perfectionism and a sense of urgency, Jobs would get a vision in his head of a new product that he knew would excite the personal computer users. Then he would lean incredibly hard on his employees, including Wozniak, to design it quickly and exactly to his specifications. He wanted the casing for the Apple II to look like a popular, boxy dorm stereo called the KLH, for example, and forced his crew to work morning till night improving rejected prototype after rejected prototype. Jobs's relentlessness eventually took its toll on his friendship with Wozniak; within four years, the inventor would leave the company. But in 1977, Apple took more than three hundred orders for Apple IIs. Jobs started to tap into the power of his charisma. His big, slightly goofy nose gave him the look of the gentle electronics geek that was a big part of his personality, while his sharp eyebrows and fierce stare went with the unwavering confidence and bossy precision that sometimes drove his employees crazy.

"You'd work on something all night, he'd look at it in the morning and say, 'That sucks,'" said Steve Capps, a programmer who later quit Apple, then returned to work on the Macintosh team. "He'd want you to defend it. And if you could, then you were doing your job, and Steve respected you. If not, he'd blow you out of the water."

In 1979, Apple Computer sold $7.2 million worth of stock. Jobs was a millionaire at twenty-four. He bought a house in Los Gatos. He combed his hair and occasionally wore suits. In 1980, the week John Lennon was murdered, Apple went public, selling 4.6 million shares in less than an hour, the most successful public offering to date. Jobs was worth $217.5 million. He landed on the cover of *Time* in 1983. A year later, he paid the advertising firm Chiat\Day $1.5 million to create one of the most famous television commercials of all time—"1984," in which a runner destroys a video screen of Big Brother, freeing bald drones in space suits. It ran exactly once, during the Super Bowl, introducing the Macintosh on January 24, 1984. This new personal computer would revolutionize Jobs's industry, but it was a few years ahead of its time. It caught on with artists, designers, and college students, but it led to Jobs's biggest business failure. Mac sales fell far under projections by Christmas 1984. Apple's board voted Jobs out of the company.

For the next decade and a half, independently, Jobs and Apple suffered through extreme highs and lows. Thanks to a $20 million stake from future presidential candidate Ross Perot, Jobs's post-Apple start-up, NeXT, put out a snazzy computer called the Cube. It was a bust, despite a few sexy new ideas, like an efficient magnetic drive rather than an old-school floppy-disc drive, and a sleek, black-box shape. But Jobs recovered from this elaborate setback, aiming the glare of his considerable charisma toward the movie industry—he bought a special-effects company known as the Graphics Group from *Star Wars* director George Lucas for $5 million, and dumped in $5 million of his own money. This was the beginning of Pixar, the computer-animation firm that would create *Toy Story, Finding Nemo,* and *Cars* and wind up with seven Academy Awards. Meanwhile, Microsoft, which over Jobs's protestations had designed the Windows operating system along the same lines as the Macintosh operating system, eclipsed Apple as the world's largest software company by the early 1990s. In turning his company into a monster, just in time for the internet, Bill Gates left Apple behind. "Apple stopped creating," Jobs told *Rolling Stone.* In the fourth quarter of 1995, Apple lost $68 million and laid off 1,300 employees.

Soon a new Apple CEO, Gil Amelio, started nursing the company back to health, taking tax writeoffs for the unsold inventory, securing key loans, and hiring Jobs as a "special adviser." It wasn't enough. Jobs rode back into Apple's Cupertino headquarters as Amelio's replacement in summer 1997. At first he was Interim CEO and made a big deal to the press about his strikingly low salary—$1 a year. He cut costs. He made rules banning outlandish travel expenses. He hired hotshots like NeXT's Jonathan Rubinstein, who took over the hardware division. He was determined to turn Apple around and became irritably focused on the task, barking at employees he encountered in hallways. By the end of Jobs's first year back—in part thanks to Amelio's earlier work—Apple was profitable again.

Apple would slowly crawl back to its 1980s heights with candy-colored iMacs and their portable iBook cousins. But it took one more ahead-of-its-time vision to make Jobs and Apple more successful and famous than ever. The plan, of course, involved digital music.

✵ ✵ ✵

THE FIRST PORTABLE digital music player was the MP3Man, created by a South Korean company, Saehan, which was so tiny it never really registered on the Recording Industry Association of America's radar. Not so the Rio PMP300, a black, rectangular device resembling a walkie-talkie that had shrunk in the dryer. Manufactured by the Chatsworth, California, electronics company Diamond Multimedia, the Rio made its debut in September 1998, promising MP3 fans they could transfer twenty-four songs from their computer to the device and listen through twelve hours of battery power. It was ugly and hard to use. "We were a small company," says David Watkins, then president of Diamond's RioPort division. "We didn't have the funding to build the business the way we wanted to."

Shortly after the Rio PMP300 came out, the RIAA sued Diamond Multimedia, saying the portable player violated the Audio Home Recording Act—which the record industry had lobbied Congress to pass in 1992. But Rio had excellent attorneys. They studied the act and found a gaping loophole. The act required electronics companies—like Sony, for the Digital Audio Tape player—to pay a royalty to record labels every time it made devices that would allow more than one copy of a recording. But it specifically exempted computers. And the only way to transfer an MP3 to a Rio was to rip it onto a computer hard drive.✵ In October 1999, a US District Court judge denied the RIAA's request for a temporary injunction against the Rio. "They were just shocked when they lost," Watkins says. "They had never lost a case before." Diamond sold 200,000 copies of the Rio PMP300 after that.

Meanwhile, over at rapidly recovering Apple Computer, Steve Jobs's latest idea was the "Digital Hub Strategy"—"where the Mac was the center of your lifestyle," as the company's hardware chief, Jonathan Rubinstein, recalls. Digital Hub integrated a number of hip, entertainment-oriented ideas, like iMovie and iPhoto; one blatantly obvious missing piece was the lack of digital music. Apple's brain trust—Jobs, Rubinstein, marketing gurus Phil Schiller and Stan Ng—began discussing how to fill this void.

✵ To clarify, the Audio Home Recording Act exempted *computers* that copied music. It did not exempt file-sharing software services, like Napster or Kazaa, from allowing users to trade copyrighted music files with each other via the internet.

It was serendipitous for ex-Apple engineer Bill Kincaid, who was working with a start-up company on new audio software called Sound-Jam, that he heard a very interesting National Public Radio report as he was driving to a track to do a few laps in his Formula Ford car. The report was about MP3s, which Kincaid had never heard of. It focused on Diamond's Rio player, and the bit that most intrigued Kincaid was its lack of compatibility with Apple's Macintosh system. Kincaid, who had worked for Apple on a Mac operating system in the early 1990s, called Diamond Multimedia the next day about designing hardware to interface between the Rio player and the Macintosh. He needed help with the software, so he contacted Jeff Robbin, one of the best pro-grammers he knew, who had also worked at Apple in the early 1990s. Together they spent months inventing SoundJam, a digital jukebox that made it easy for consumers to organize the MP3s they'd ripped or downloaded to their hard drives and play music over their PC speak-ers. They started selling it through a small software publisher, Casady & Greene, in 1999. "We got that to pretty much be the premiere MP3 player on the Mac," says Robin Casady, the company's co-owner. "And when Apple started looking around for one, they chose ours, and we sold it to them."

At Apple, SoundJam morphed into iTunes, which had a sleek geo-metric screen with a brushed-aluminum look and made organizing music files on a computer seem like the hippest thing in the world. Jobs talked it up in his January 2001 Macworld Conference & Expo key-note.

The next step in Apple's plan was to design a player. The brain trust studied the market. In addition to the PMP300, there was Creative Labs' irritatingly heavy Nomad Jukebox, which had utilized Fujitsu's 2.5-inch hard drive but still relied on a super-slow USB connection to shift songs from the computer to the player. Overall, Apple's Rubinstein remembers, the players were "just awful." With Jobs's unique brand of encouragement ringing in his ears, Rubinstein put his hardware team to work. Through a contact, he found thirty-two-year-old engineer Tony Fadell, who was on a Vail ski-slope chairlift when he took the call. Rubinstein offered him a high-pressure, eight-week contract. Fadell was single. He had plenty of time to work his butt off, Apple-style. By the time he made it to the top of the mountain, although Rubinstein refused to tell him what project he'd be working on, Fadell accepted.

First, Rubinstein and Fadell needed the tiniest hard drive ever made, something that would be affordable to reproduce thousands of times. At the time, nothing small enough to serve their purpose existed. "I basically stalled for a while," Rubinstein recalls. "I told Steve, 'I can't do it yet. It's not time.'" Soon, Toshiba came up with a 1.8-inch, 5-gigabyte disc drive that could carry 1,000 songs and wasn't amazingly expensive. Jobs moved quickly to sign an exclusive deal with Toshiba— shutting out Creative Labs, which was on the brink of releasing its own new player, the Zen. "We had a very sexy player," the company's founder and CEO, Sim Wong Hoo, told *Business 2.0,* animatedly waving his arms in frustration, "but we couldn't ship it." Next, Apple's engineers had to find a much faster way than USB of transferring a digital song from a Mac to the player. The solution was FireWire, a technology Apple had invented in the early 1990s, although at the time it was mostly used with Japanese-built camcorders, not computers. "Once I saw all those technologies, I went to Steve and said, 'Hey, we know how to do this now. We need some funding,'" Rubinstein recalls. "I started hiring a team and we went and built the thing."

The project was a secret. Other than Jobs, Rubinstein, Fadell, and a few other Apple executives, nobody even knew it involved music. The code name was P-68, or, more colloquially, "Dulcimer," which signified nothing more than "an elegant stringed instrument." Working day and night through the course of his contract, Fadell played with cardboard and foam, moving things around in various patterns to show himself what the player might look like. Eventually, he came up with a box the size of a pack of Marlboros with a cell-phone-sized screen at the top and push buttons at the bottom. He weighed down the gadget with fishing weights, to approximate what it might feel like. Then it was time to meet with Jobs. Fadell and Rubinstein knew Jobs liked to get prototypes in groups of three, so they sent up two as "sacrificial lambs," as Steven Levy puts it in his 2006 book *The Perfect Thing.* The third one, they hid under a wooden bowl in the conference room on the fourth floor of Apple's Cupertino offices. It turned out they knew Jobs pretty well. He quickly dismissed the first two, but the third one left him speechless.

At the same meeting, another Apple executive, marketing vice president Phil Schiller, showed his own innovation—the scroll wheel at the center, which would control the gadget in lieu of a keyboard. Jobs turned to Fadell. *We can do it,* Fadell told him.

Fadell sent feelers out to hardware and software companies about manufacturing the device's internal parts in an affordable way. His contacts were, to put it mildly, somewhat confused. "These suppliers were like, 'Apple is calling, that's great. . . . *What* are they doing, exactly?'" Fadell recalls. "Then they're looking at me, going, 'You're a *contractor.* Should I even take this seriously?' And: 'This seems totally foreign to [Apple's] business. Why would they buy this?' It was something non-computer-related." Nonetheless, PortalPlayer, a small company, was thrilled to throw in its lot with Apple Computer, supplying the physical operating system and the external silicon casing. Rubinstein's team then hired Pixo, a software company founded by ex-Apple employee Paul Mercer, to write the programs for running the PortalPlayer chips. "Apple wouldn't even show us what [the final device] looked like," Mercer recalls. "[The working model] had boards and a screen in the corner." Jobs pushed his top lieutenants, who pushed the hardware and software teams, who pushed their subcontractors. The goal was to get the player into stores by Christmas 2001.

They still needed a name. Jobs was vague when *The Perfect Thing* author Levy asked him who thought it up. "It sort of *emerged,*" Levy concluded, adding his speculation that Jobs was impatient and settled for it just before time ran out. Vinnie Chieco, a freelance copywriter who worked regularly at Apple's Cupertino offices at the time, remembers otherwise. One of Apple's creative directors asked Chieco and a couple of other writers to come up with a number of names. The creative director, with help from Chieco, then narrowed down the list, put each name on a huge piece of paper and presented the top sixty or seventy prospects to Jobs in his office. Jobs whittled them down to three. Jobs had come up with one of them himself (Chieco won't say which one it was). Another, *Pod*, was on Chieco's list. Jobs didn't immediately say he liked it, but he stopped holding meetings about the name. In passing, he spoke positively of it to Chieco a couple of times. Then he ran it by Lee Clow, the TBWA\Chiat\Day ad executive who would oversee the iPod "Silhouettes" campaign. Clow liked it, too. "Like everything else at Apple, it was [Jobs's] decision," Chieco says. Jobs added the "i"—as in iMac—and the name stuck.

The first iPod came out in stores on October 23, 2001. Over at Texas Instruments headquarters, in Dallas, intrigued engineers immediately brought one back to the lab and took it apart. They were impressed with the PortalPlayer chips—*two* processors. While TI made similar internal products, Apple had found a smaller, cheaper company to do the same work. The TI engineers liked the integration between iTunes and iPod. They felt it was far superior to what Sony Corp. had done with its clunky Music Clip, the poorly reviewed player that had emerged from the SDMI meetings, and corresponding software a couple of years earlier. And they liked innovations like its scroll wheel and lack of an on-off switch. But Randy Cole, manager of TI's digital audio research and development, was impressed for an even simpler reason. "It just looked *cool*,"* he says.

All Apple needed after that was music—*legal* music—to play on it.

PAUL VIDICH AND Kevin Gage, new-media vice presidents at Warner Music, survived their false-hijacking episode in Brandon, Manitoba. Less than three months later, in January 2002, they faced a scarier ordeal. They had traveled from New York to Cupertino for an appointment at 1 Infinite Loop. They walked into the huge, fanlike glass structure that was the first building at Apple Computer's headquarters, passing underneath the iconic rainbow-colored logo. They met Steve Jobs and a few other Apple executives in a boardroom. Gage started his PowerPoint presentation. Jobs rocked back and forth in his chair, obviously agitated, trying despite himself to be patient. Four slides into Gage's presentation, Jobs interrupted. "You guys are all nuts," he said.

There were a half dozen executives in the room, including AOL's Raduchel and Apple's Higa. Most were in coats and ties. Jobs, true to his image, wore a black turtleneck, jeans, and sneakers. The room went silent. Jobs turned to Vidich, who had spoken with him by phone from New York and was the senior Warner Music executive in the room. "It was almost as if for the first time he was given an audience with a music executive," Vidich says. "And he vented. He vented at the music industry and the ways in which it didn't get it." The major labels, Jobs told Gage and Vidich bluntly, were trying to suck out all the money from digital music for themselves. *His* customers—*Apple's* customers—deserved better. They needed an easy-to-use online music store. His tirade lasted several minutes. "It was kind of awkward," says Gage, who tried to disappear into the blinds behind him.

---

* Rebuttal from country singer-songwriter Shelby Lynne, in the *New York Times Magazine*, January 13, 2008, p. 31: "You can't roll a joint on an iPod."

Finally, Jobs finished skewering Vidich. "Steve," came the response from Warner Music's top technology executive, "that's why we're here. We need some help."

At the time, the iPod was for sale at Apple Stores around the country. Jeff Robbin's iTunes software was available for use on Mac computers. Both were popular, but neither was a smash hit. Consumers were put off by the iPod's initial $399 price—to the extent that critics had given it a new acronym, "Idiots Price Our Devices." An improved version had landed in stores in March 2002, but the market was still limited, as both iTunes and the iPod were still incompatible with Windows-based computers. At the boardroom meeting, there wasn't much to say after Jobs's rant. (Notably, he did not show off the iPod or iTunes to the Warner group at this point.) Neither Jobs nor the Warner people discussed specifics. But it became clear to Vidich that he would have to enlist more powerful officials at their companies to make progress on an Apple deal involving digital music.

Vidich returned to Warner Music's offices in New York. He knew just the executive to contact—Roger Ames, a longtime British record man who'd recently become chairman and chief executive officer. Ames agreed to meet Jobs in Cupertino to move the Apple-Warner digital music talks forward. Vidich and Gage went along, and the technology experts briefed Ames on the plane. So far, the Apple people hadn't mentioned any specifics, so the Warner execs came up with their own agenda. They decided to push the "second session" CDs—the super-secure discs with extra layers of music that had been discussed during the failed DMX sessions.

When they arrived, the Apple CEO turned on the very specific kind of charm he uses to persuade important fellow executives. "Sort of a mogul-to-mogul thing," is how Jonathan Rubinstein describes it. "He never reacted to Roger the same way he reacted to Paul [Vidich] and myself. Put it that way," Gage says. "He ranted on Paul, that first meeting, about the a-holes of the music industry. I got ranted on when I was pushing for digital rights management. But when Roger came into the room, you didn't see any of that. You saw Steve at his brightest and sharpest." Jobs listened patiently to Ames's pitch about super-secure CDs. Then he casually turned around a computer screen to show the Warner executives a new piece of software Apple engineers had been working on for the last few months. It was the iTunes Music Store.

Ames's eyes widened as Jobs demonstrated how the store would work. Like every other digital music fan on the planet, he had been frustrated with half-hearted record industry equivalents like Pressplay and MusicNet. "That's a great piece of software," he told Jobs, sincerely. "It does everything I need—it organizes my music, works very efficiently, it has an efficient mechanism around a credit card. This is exactly what we need." He may as well have simply said, "Sold!"

Vidich and his staff worked out a Warner content-licensing deal with Jobs. The 99-cents-per-song concept came from Warner, Vidich recalls; Jobs had been thinking along similar lines and quickly agreed. "We were looking at a hook, something consumers were going to be interested in," Vidich says. Ames went back to New York and became a sort of unofficial Apple salesman. Not everyone was as sold on Apple as he was. At the time, Jim Caparro headed Warner's powerful distribution company, WEA, and told Ames point-blank that he objected to the pricing structure. Apple would take a 22-cent retailer's cut out of every 99-cent song, leaving just 67 cents for the labels to divide up among artists, publishers, and themselves. Caparro was not naïve about technology: He saw that digital was the future and would quit the major labels entirely within a few years. But he felt Apple was giving the labels a terrible deal, just as MTV had done in scoring videos for free more than twenty years earlier. Within Warner, he suggested a temporary licensing deal, but was overruled. "Ultimately, we could have constructed a far different deal than sixty-seven cents," says Caparro, who today runs the Entertainment Distribution Company, whose biggest client is Universal Music. "Look what happened as a result: The value of Apple has skyrocketed. Roger felt the proposal by Apple was a good one. Steve Jobs was his Jedi."

Undeterred by Caparro's opposition, Ames met with an acquaintance in the record industry, Doug Morris of Universal Music. Morris, one of the most outspoken major label opponents of Napster, was skeptical at first but surprisingly receptive overall. "I don't think we're going to make a lot of money, but [Jobs] is going to sell a lot of iPods," he told Ames. "Doug, I agree, but I don't think we have much choice," Ames responded. "We have to put a legal service in the market. None of us have come up with anything." It took a short time, but Morris was sold, too. He in turn met with one of his top technology vice presidents, Albhy Galuten. "*Of course,* we have to rely on Steve Jobs to do this—we don't have anybody at Universal who knows anything about technology," Morris told Galuten. The remark stung Galuten. "In my group [at

Universal], there was a guy with a Caltech PhD, a guy with a master's in computer science at MIT, and a guy who architected the DirecTV satellite systems," he says today.

Nonetheless, Galuten went to Cupertino. Although Jobs had told Gage and Vidich he vehemently opposed digital rights management— which prevents users from making unlimited copies of the music files they download from the internet—he conceded the point. Jobs could see that Sony Music, owned by Sony Corp., was not about to budge on this. Sony had been instrumental in creating the CD and had invented the popular Walkman cassette player in the 1980s. Its executives were not thrilled about ceding their content to a different computer-and-electronics company. So in an effort to make Sony and the other major labels happy, Apple's engineers came up with FairPlay. This encryption prevented users from playing their protected AAC music files, cousins of the MP3, on more than three different computers. The idea was to stop college students from sharing their files all over the dorm rooms by making sure they still had to buy CDs from an old-fashioned record store once in a while.

Otherwise, to Galuten's surprise, the concessions came mostly from Universal. As the biggest major record label by far, whatever Universal did would ultimately dictate terms for its competitors, especially smaller ones like EMI and BMG. Jobs could not launch the iTunes Music Store without U2, Eminem, and Motown songs from the world's largest label. "We had all the leverage in the world," Galuten says. "I don't know why Doug didn't exercise it." Galuten wanted to fight for a number of points. For example, Jobs insisted that a user must be able to transfer music to an unlimited number of iPods. Galuten saw immediately this would allow people to get as much free music as they wanted. But Morris instructed Galuten to give up this point, as well as several others.* "Doug called and said, 'Just close,'" Galuten recalls. "Doug was not interested in technical details." At Universal, though, Jobs sold his idea to others besides just Doug Morris. He also contacted Jimmy Iovine, head of the company's Interscope Records, which at the time had Dr. Dre, No Doubt, U2, and Eminem and was on the cusp of breaking 50 Cent and Gwen Stefani. Iovine had been worrying about his industry's future for some time but hadn't been impressed with high-tech com-

---

* Morris did not respond to numerous interview requests for this book.

panies' proposed solutions. Also, he liked Jobs. "We just hit it off, what can I say?" he told *The Perfect Thing* author Steven Levy. "Every other company was telling us, 'Give us your licenses and we'll build you a system.' He had a complete thought." Iovine also acknowledged that the persistent rumors at the time of a Universal-Apple merger may have swayed top execs.

For Sony Music executives, price remained a sticking point. Jobs insisted on 99 cents per song. Some at the record labels, such as Warner's Vidich and Sony's Phil Wiser, who had replaced Al Smith as chief technology officer, agreed with the Apple chief. They'd tried $3.99 singles in other formats and customers didn't have any interest whatsoever. Wiser spent a lot of time as a go-between, persuading Sony executives and haggling on the phone with Eddy Cue, Apple's director of iTunes. Finally, Jobs cut through the bureaucracy and called Andrew Lack, then chief executive officer of Sony Music. The other four labels are in, Jobs told Lack, and the iTunes Music Store launches in two months—with or without Sony. Lack took Wiser and Sony Music's US chief, Sir Howard Stringer, with him on a company jet to Cupertino in order to view the iTunes Store with Jobs. After that, Sony was in. Later, Lack would declare, "I don't think it was more than a fifteen-second decision in my mind [to license music to Apple] once Steve started talking."

In reality, the decision most likely took more than fifteen seconds. Since the Napster debacle, Sony Corp., more than any other company, had been wracked with conflict over the new file-sharing technologies. The company that had been the first to profit off the transistor radio in the 1950s and had invented the Walkman in the 1970s was an active member of the Napster-supporting Consumer Electronics Association. But its record label, Sony Music, was simultaneously a member of the RIAA, which, obviously, opposed file sharing. This was a contradiction, as millions of music fans were filling their iPods and other digital music players with songs they'd downloaded illegally. Sony, which sold 19 million Walkmans in fiscal year 2002, wanted to profit from these customers and compete against the iPod. But the company's record label, Sony Music, accounted for 30 percent of the electronics giant's revenues and most of its profits. *Wired* magazine termed this internal conflict "The Civil War Inside Sony." Because of it, the company, which had been so instrumental in developing the CD, merely watched as Apple took over the markets for both digital music players and online songs. Keiji Kimura, a Sony senior vice president in charge of portable products, told *Wired* he admired Apple's device but Sony would not try to compete with it. "We do not have any plans for such a product," Kimura said. "But we are studying it." Sony Corp. reps would not comment on these issues.

With all this static in the background, it was easy for unencumbered Apple to seize the digital music market. Eventually, with the other major labels plunging into iTunes, Sony had no choice. The company gritted its teeth and signed on. "Now Sony Music was going and empowering Steve Jobs and his iPod to take over that business," Wiser says. "It was very controversial and a very difficult move—but it was the right move. No one else in the market was doing anything in digital music at that time."

Why did record executives, who'd stonewalled Rob Glaser's Music-Net and the SDMI process, whoosh into deals with Apple? There are several reasons.* One was Jobs's confidence and charm. At NeXT and Pixar, he'd dealt with Hollywood executives all the time, so he didn't find powerful record people like Roger Ames and Doug Morris particularly intimidating. Another was Apple's tiny market share at the time— just 4 percent or 5 percent of computer users owned Macintoshes, and the iPod–iTunes system was initially incompatible with Windows. "Our smaller market share turned out to be an asset!" Jobs said in *The Perfect Thing*. "We only convinced them to let us do it on the Mac at first. We said, 'Well, if, you know, the virus gets out, it's only going to pollute five percent of the garden here.' And that's probably what, in the end, enabled us to get them to come along with us. Doug Morris, who runs Universal, said, when he was arguing with his own team, 'Look, how—I don't understand how Apple could ruin the record business in one year on Mac. Why shouldn't we try this?'" A third reason was that Jobs told Universal's Galuten that Apple's marketing budget was $15 million to $30 million *every quarter*. This was a free artist-publicity

---

* Executives from major labels had told pre-iTunes digital music services—including Napster and Real—that they couldn't license content because their hands were tied with artist contracts and publisher agreements. There are a number of theories as to how Apple cut through all that: 1) The previous models that labels had discussed were subscriptions, which were more complicated, and iTunes's pay-by-the-song approach was easier to work out; 2) failed early services such as MusicNet (which never went online) and Pressplay had already done much of the heavy lifting as far as haggling with artists, publishers, and attorneys; and 3) label execs were stubborn until they found something they liked, the iTunes Store.

machine on par with MTV. Finally, many executives at record labels believed Microsoft was on the brink of releasing a digital music service that would compete fiercely with iTunes. Surely labels could play the two services off each other. But Microsoft stayed out—until November 14, 2006, when it released the Zune digital music player. Why the long wait? "A lot of people at Microsoft did react quickly, but it took roughly a year to convince the full management chain to act on the knowledge of what was going on with Apple," says Hadi Partovi, who in the early 2000s was general manager of MSN's music and entertainment division, and later cofounded the popular iLike music service on Facebook. "Record labels repeatedly asked us what we were going to do to combat Steve Jobs's marketing budget. Our budget was in the *ones* of millions."

After signing up the major labels, Jobs broadened his support in the record industry. He called Irving Azoff, powerful manager of the Eagles, the aging country-rock superstars who had blocked the use of their music in all other digital music services, and begged. "I've said 'no' to all of them," Azoff told the *Wall Street Journal*. "But I don't like their services, and I liked [Apple's] product." Azoff said yes. In much the same way Sony's CD marketers earned support from big-name artists in the early 1980s, Jobs contacted U2's Bono, the Rolling Stones' Mick Jagger, and Sheryl Crow, among others. "The black iPod is something I coveted—this is a beautiful object," Bono said at an October 2004 press conference, announcing a special-edition iPod that contained U2's entire catalog. (Bono added, "People want to sleep with it.") Jobs invited Dr. Dre, multiplatinum gangsta rapper and masterful Interscope talent scout, who had been a fierce Napster enemy and vowed never to release his music to a digital service, to his office in Cupertino. They tinkered with iTunes for hours. "Man," Dre said afterward, "somebody finally got it right." He gave up the rights.

Not every label executive was thrilled about the sudden rush of Apple excitement. Ted Cohen, who had begun his career as a Bay Area concert promoter and had climbed up the label ladder to be EMI's top new-media executive, was not easily swayed by charisma. He loved Apple products—in a fall 2007 phone interview from his home in Los Angeles, he was in viewing distance of eighteen iPods, five Macintosh computers, and two iPhones. But this was the music executive who'd had the guts to travel with the Sex Pistols during their first and last American voyage, through Texas, in 1977. When

Sid Vicious swung his bass at a rabble-rousing Texan from the stage of a club, he missed and bashed Cohen in the face instead. Although Warner's Roger Ames had called one of EMI's top executives, David Munns, to sell him on the iTunes Store, Munns did not go personally to Cupertino. He sent Cohen, who showed up with other label reps. He was unimpressed.

At one point, Cohen remembers John Rose, then an EMI vice president, writing demographic sales statistics on a thirty-foot-long whiteboard in an Apple conference room. Afterward, Jobs stood up, walked to the whiteboard, which was entirely empty save for the one square foot where Rose had scribbled, and erased it completely. Rose was undeterred by this blatant power maneuver. "John, God bless him, erased what Steve Jobs wrote and wrote something else over that," Cohen recalls. "They were erasing each other's words for about ten minutes. It was funny to watch, but it was very telling—Steve wants to do it his way and that's it." Cohen saw the whiteboard power struggle as a sign of future battles between Jobs and record executives. Shortly after Apple signed up all five of the major record labels—including EMI—Cohen recalls the computer company subtly wriggling out of certain agreements. For example, Cohen says, Coldplay's 2002 smash *A Rush of Blood to the Head* was supposed to sell for $13 on iTunes, but an EMI distribution executive alerted Cohen one day that it was going for $11.88. The distribution rep called Apple. "OK," the Apple contact responded, "you want us to take it down?" The distribution rep was stunned. "Welcome to the world of Apple," Cohen told him. "If you don't like it, they'll stop selling your music." Apple refused to make its executives, including Jobs, available for interviews for this book.*

THE ITUNES MUSIC Store opened on April 28, 2003, with a catalog of 200,000 songs available for 99 cents apiece. And those were *good* songs, from all five of the major record labels, not the local-band dross digital music fans used to find on websites like MP3.com. There were some major holdouts—the Beatles, Led Zeppelin, Radiohead—but top artists mostly supported the iTunes Store. Bob Dylan, U2, and Eminem

---

* Apple's Fadell, who agreed to talk by phone, is a hardware guy who didn't feel qualified to discuss the label deals.

provided exclusive tracks. "This industry has been in such a funk," Sheryl Crow declared, endorsing Apple's system on behalf of rock stars. "It really needs something like this to get it going again."

Crow's vision came true—for Apple. Surprising its record label partners, the iTunes Store crossed over to Windows-based computers in October 2003 and became a mass phenomenon, selling 25 million 99-cent songs. It was a huge success—again, for Apple. In 2003, total iTunes sales were the equivalent of one small blockbuster in the record industry. (By contrast, the hundredth album on the RIAA's Top 100 list of best-selling albums, Green Day's *American Idiot*, had sold 5 million CDs at the time of this writing.) That's a lot, but hardly enough to excite big-spending label executives about a new business model.* Plus, labels made just 67 cents on every 99-cent song, a decent percentage, but far, far inferior to taking roughly $10 to $12 on every $18 CD. (Remember, the labels had to share some of the revenue with artists and songwriters.) For Apple, though, the iTunes Store was absolutely brilliant, because it pushed music fans to buy more and more iPods, for $300 to $500 apiece. In the fourth quarter of 2003, iPods generated about 7 percent of Apple's $1.7 billion in revenue—$121 million overall.

"People think we knew the iPod was just going to be a success," Tony Fadell recalls. "That was the farthest thing from the truth." To his surprise, the iPod changed everything—music, fashion, electronics, computers, the internet. Fans of the Beatles' classic *Sgt. Pepper's Lonely Hearts Club Band* lamented that the iPod, with its irresistible song-shuffling function, would eliminate the album as an art form. The TBWA\Chiat\Day "Silhouettes" ads made it cool to wander college campuses, board buses and trains, jog, and mow lawns while gently swaying to music coming through white earbuds. Vince Carter, superstar dunker for the Toronto Raptors, criticized the National Basketball Association's decision to disallow players from practicing with their iPods. Celebrities from actor Bruce Willis to CNN anchor Aaron Brown to President Bush and Vice President Cheney owned up to making playlists for their iPods. (Bush likes the Knack's "My Sharona"; Cheney prefers the Carpenters.) Thanks to the iPod, music was as exciting and culturally important as ever. That didn't necessarily mean the sound was an

---

* In the May 29, 2008, issue of *Rolling Stone*, Eagles manager Irving Azoff, an enthusiastic early iTunes supporter, told writer Charles M. Young: "We make more money for forty-five minutes of one show in Kansas City than our entire iTunes royalty."

improvement. Over the years, as compressed iTunes files joined MP3s as the standard for online music, and fans started to listen to music on iPods and tinny computer speakers, producers started to compensate in their studios. By 2006, Bob Dylan was complaining to *Rolling Stone* that modern albums "have sound all over them. There's no definition of nothing, no vocal, no nothing, just like—static." In late 2007, prominent rock producer David Bendeth added: "They make it loud to get [listeners'] attention. I think most everything is mastered a little too loud. The industry decided that it's a volume contest."

The majority of fans, however, didn't care about sound quality. Almost immediately, iTunes emerged as the biggest online retailer, taking more than 70 percent of the market and dwarfing later competitors like Napster (whose assets had been purchased by another company, Roxio, and turned into a legal service) and stores from Microsoft, MTV, Sony Corp., and Wal-Mart. By April 2008, the iTunes Music Store had sold more than 4 billion songs around the world. It ranked No. 1, above Best Buy and Wal-Mart, as the top overall music retailer in the United States, according to a survey-research firm called the NPD Group.

Record executives privately started likening Apple to MTV—major labels agreed to give videos to the channel in the early 1980s, when it seemed like a tiny promotional device, and regretted losing all that video revenue when MTV blew up. But this was even worse. Apple had basically taken over the entire music business. Steve Jobs's agenda was not to make money off 99-cent digital songs, although they were a nice additional source of revenue. He used the songs to profit from expensive iPods. Labels made exactly zero dollars for every iPod sale. Not only that, record execs noted ruefully, there was *no chance* music fans were filling their 80-gigabyte iPods with 20,000 songs they'd bought for 99 cents apiece or ripped from their CD collections. Surely pirated music had something to do with the booming iPod sales as well.

"[Jobs's] stock went from $8 billion to $80 billion," recalls Roger Ames, who left Warner Music in 2004 and is today head of EMI North America. "Ours went in reverse.

"Not his fault," Ames hastens to add—but in the five years since the iTunes Music Store, some of Ames's colleagues began to disagree quite vehemently. In a 2005 speech, Warner CEO Edgar Bronfman Jr., who had taken over from Roger Ames, declared some songs worth more than others and called for "variable pricing." Bronfman wouldn't address the subject in an interview for this book, but other executives have come to blame Jobs. It's unfair, they complained, that Apple fixed its song prices at 99 cents. Jobs responded by calling the labels "greedy." He wanted to keep things simple for the consumer, and besides, 99 cents was just the right price. Label executives also howled about Apple's digital rights management, FairPlay, which limited iTunes-purchased tracks to the iPod rather than worthy competitors like Creative Labs's Zen or Microsoft's Zune. In response to these complaints—as well as pressure from European regulators, who in the late 2000s started to accuse Apple of illegally cornering the digital music market—Jobs turned the tables on the labels. He never wanted copy protection, he said. FairPlay came about due to the labels' insistence. He told labels he'd get rid of it if they would. To date, only the smallest major label, EMI, sells unprotected music files via the iTunes Music Store, although others sell MP3s via Amazon and elsewhre.

Early supporters like Doug Morris of Universal and Jimmy Iovine of Interscope also turned against iTunes. Iovine didn't respond to interview requests, but a source who knows him well says, "He feels they got cheated. And he maintains Steve [Jobs] dealt from the bottom of the deck. He talks about it a lot." In May 2007, Universal decided not to renew its contract with Apple, saying it would pull its content any time label executives decided they wanted to. At the time this book went to press, newer online retailers like Amazon's MP3 Store and MySpace Music had yet to challenge Apple's dominance, so Universal-owned music from U2, Gwen Stefani, Motown, and the rest remains available at the iTunes Store. And Apple continues to sell iPods like crazy.

Did Apple really play an unfair game? Not really. Steve Jobs is a businessman. He saw opportunity and went for it. But nobody forced savvy and experienced deal makers like Doug Morris, Roger Ames, and Andrew Lack to sign those Apple contracts in 2002; they were just running out of good choices. The labels had sent stonewalling executives like Sony Music's Al Smith to SDMI meetings rather than truly trying to create a content deal that worked. They didn't support Bertelsmann's Thomas Middelhoff when he tried to turn Napster into a legal song-downloading service. And their international corporate overseers, such as Sony Corp., didn't exactly throw themselves constructively into the Digital Music X talks spearheaded by Paul Vidich and Kevin Gage. By the time Steve Jobs came around, he was the last resort. He was merely smart enough to know it. He played tough, but not any tougher than any lawyer for a major label who had negotiated an artist contract in recent decades.

The post-iTunes years provided a frustrating paradox for record executives. By February 2006, the store sold its 1 billionth download, and digital single sales overall jumped from 19.2 million in 2003 to 844.2 million in 2007. But it was at least four years too late, and way too little. CDs cost $15 to $18. Digital singles cost 99 cents. Executives added up the numbers and realized Jobs had tossed them into a very bad business model. "Stealing music is not [what's] killing music," says Robert Pittman, cofounder of MTV and former chief operating officer of the ill-fated AOL Time Warner merger. "When I talk to people in the music business, most of them will admit the problem is they're selling songs and not albums. I mean, you do the math."

In 2000, shortly after veteran label executive Steve Greenberg started a new label, S-Curve, his band the Baha Men put out the woof-woofing single "Who Let the Dogs Out?" Although Napster was ascendant at the time, music fans were still accustomed to buying CDs—and they plunked down the $15 to $18 for 4 million copies of the Baha Men's album. By contrast, in 2003, S-Curve pushed the American power-pop band Fountains of Wayne's single "Stacy's Mom" onto MTV and radio stations everywhere. The album containing "Stacy's Mom" sold just 400,000 copies. Greenberg blames online piracy for this decline, and he has a point. Thanks to Kazaa, LimeWire, and other inheritors of Napster's peer-to-peer file-sharing approach, 4.3 million people around the world were trading copyrighted songs at any point during September 2003, according to BigChampagne.com. "Stacy's Mom" also sold 520,000 digital singles, mostly through the iTunes Store. It's impossible to track the number of illegal downloads, but it's clear that more people who liked "Stacy's Mom" cherry-picked the song illegally or via the iTunes Store than bought the full album.

Sales of iTunes singles surged, while old-fashioned album sales—and major label revenues—dropped. While CD sales continue to make up the bulk of major labels' profits, iTunes shifted the balance dramatically and quickly. Although this shift is great for consumers, it's a negative for record companies: At least for now, digital music just isn't as profitable as old-fashioned pieces of plastic. Thus, in the post-iTunes world, labels would lay off thousands of people and cut all but the obvious big-selling acts from their artist rosters. Sony and BMG would team up in a questionable merger born of financial desperation. Warner Music would go public for a much-needed cash infusion. Nonetheless, for months after the iTunes Store opened, labels were optimistic about finally gaining a foothold in the digital music market. Their next step was to obliterate the millions of online pirates who showed no signs of breaking their file-sharing habits.

Big Music's Big Mistakes, Part 7

The RIAA Lawsuits

In July 2004, when University of Kansas student Charli Johnson found out the music industry was suing her for illegally trading 592 songs on her campus computer, she did the first thing that came to mind: "I started to cry." Then she called the Recording Industry Association of America and pleaded for a settlement. No problem, its lawyers said. That'll be $3,000.

It wasn't a good time. When she received word of the lawsuit, Johnson, twenty, was about to take a semester off anyhow to save money as a full-time, $6.86-an-hour Wal-Mart cashier. She would have had to earn ten straight weekly paychecks to pay off the RIAA debt. She called her mother, who agreed to pay half. She took out a bank loan for the other half. She called her father, a lawyer in California, who said, "Well, isn't this interesting." She pleaded, and he paid off the loan. "It was pretty stressful," says Johnson, who today is a KU graduate and fourth-grade teacher in Arkansas, Kansas. "Asking my dad for $1,500 is no small task. His reaction was, '*I* didn't download the music.'"

More than 38,000 college students, insurance-company clerks, karaoke DJs, engineers, restaurant owners, flight attendants, and people of all ages, genders, and musical tastes around the US can relate to Johnson's desperation. They've all won the worst lottery in music industry history. Five months after Apple unveiled its iTunes Music Store, allowing major record labels to sell downloaded songs for the first time in a significant way, the Recording Industry Association of America started suing its own consumer base. The first wave involved suits against 261 people. One was Scott Bassett, a Redwood City, California, auto mechanic who had no idea his teenage kids were doing anything wrong. "But I know one thing," he said after he received the lawsuit. "They're not going to be doing it anymore." Another was New York housing-project resident Brianna LaHara, a twelve-year-old in bookish spectacles who made the cover of the *New York Post*. "My stomach is all turning," she declared.

The RIAA was unrepentant. The world needed to know that illegal file sharing was wrong, period. "We knew that the press would find poster children as a result of this program," president Cary Sherman said after the first 261 lawsuits, filed in September 2003. "But you have to choose between your wish to be loved and your wish to survive. The purpose is to get the message out." Most of the lawsuits were for hundreds of thousands of dollars, but as of 2006 the industry had settled roughly 6,000, averaging $3,000 to $4,000 per suit. (Brianna LaHara's family settled for $2,000.)

There were cases of mistaken identity—a grandmother fought back early on, saying she didn't even know how to use a computer, and the RIAA reluctantly dropped its suit. But for the most part, people caught in the act of sharing music files illegally lacked the money or legal firepower to take on the powerful recording industry on legal principles. The association demands $750 per song in copyright-infringement damages, so those accused of sharing 1,500 songs, say, could face $1.125 million in penalties if they take it to court and lose. "These are very nasty one-sided cases, and the people they're suing don't have the resources necessary to fight back," says Ray Beckerman, one of several attorneys who defend RIAA-sued customers and regularly attack the record industry. "There are lots of questions. For us to presume they know what's copyright infringement or not is pretty interesting."

In the post-Napster age, though, label executives felt they had no choice. When the lawsuits began, according to the peer-to-peer—tracking website BigChampagne.com, 4.3 million people around the world were sharing music files illegally at any given time. Also, according to Nielsen SoundScan, CD sales had dropped precipitously, from 943 million in 2000 to 746 million in 2003. Over two or three years, major labels had slipped from their teen pop peak and were laying off hundreds.

Suing was an extreme step, but angry and desperate executives began batting around the idea as early as a 2002 RIAA summit in Washington, DC. Universal Music was especially hell-bent on the lawsuits, sources recall, but Roger Ames of Warner Music was fiercely opposed. By Ames's way of thinking—and the association's then-chairman, Hilary Rosen, agreed with him—it was totally unfair to sue customers for downloading free music when they had no legal way to pay for it online. There were a series of meetings, climaxing with thirteen top label executives at Sony Music's New York offices, and Ames and his subordinates made their case. Warner had to threaten to withdraw its membership from the RIAA in order to get everyone else to back down.

In April 2003, thanks in part to Ames's behind-the-scenes negotiations, Apple Computer's iTunes Music Store went online as the first major legitimate digital music service. So that barrier fell, and Ames and Warner agreed to join the lawsuits. Then a Los Angeles district court ruled one of Napster's harder-to-prosecute successors, Grokster, wasn't responsible for its users' actions—whether they downloaded free porn or free music. Significantly, the key part of the court opinion suggested the users themselves were to blame for their own illegal activities. (The case would go all the way to the US Supreme Court.) After that, Rosen says, "I think everybody was on board with the lawsuits." Recalls another music business source: "Everyone felt like it was too bad that it had to happen and we didn't want it to be our only plan. We didn't want to be suing, but there weren't a lot of alternatives. It's one thing when you're looking from the outside and saying how stupid this is, but it's another thing when you're seeing half your company laid off."

The RIAA's legal and technical teams—actually about twenty lawyers scattered around the US and twenty vendors surfing Kazaa in a Washington, DC, office—picked targets with the most downloading activity. One of those, apparently, was Cindy Lundstrom's sixteen-year-old daughter, Chelsea, a straight-A student and homecoming queen at North Canyon High School near Scottsdale, Arizona. The RIAA sued Cindy Lundstrom in March 2004, accusing her (meaning Chelsea) of downloading 700 hip-hop songs, or total alleged damages of $525,000. The RIAA offered a $3,000 settlement, which Chelsea said she would pay out of her savings from an after-school job at a hair salon, but her mom told her to forget about it. "That is her savings for college," Lundstrom said, shortly after the family settled.

The lawsuits continue to this day with numbing regularity—725 here, 210 there, at least one new wave a month. The industry shifted much of its attention to college campuses in early 2007, because students using their schools' free high-speed internet access were a particularly egregious threat. (Only one case has gone to trial so far: Jammie Thomas, a mother of two from Brainerd, Minnesota, who in October 2007 told a Duluth jury that she didn't do it. Major labels had sued her for infringing the copyrights of twenty-four songs. A jury took less than a day to award the labels $222,000 in damages for "willful" infringement. A year later, Thomas received a mistrial.) In March 2007, the RIAA opted against filing actual lawsuits. The industry chose a cheaper, less cumbersome strategy, sending "prelitigation letters" to colleges. The letters included computer IP addresses with which the schools were supposed to identify file-sharing students and pass the letters along. The students could then make a quick settlement without even dealing with the legal system or cumbersome concepts like "innocent until proven guilty" or "right to due process." "It's effective—at trying to bully people," says Jason Schultz, at the time a staff attorney with the Electronic Frontier Foundation, which opposes the lawsuits. "If your goal is to intimidate people and get them to freak out and write checks, then yeah, it's a great strategy."

In the end, the lawsuit campaign has had little impact on the amount of copyrighted music that is illegally downloaded. Nine million people in fall 2007 were trading files via peer-to-peer services, according to Big-Champagne.com, and 70 percent of that was illegal music. One major label executive believes the suits have been nothing but a costly public-relations debacle. "It seems like the punishment is way disproportionate to the crime," this source says. "Everybody would love it if it knocked piracy down. It doesn't. It costs money. It isn't effective."

To Thomas Middelhoff, the former chairman of Bertelsmann, which invested millions of dollars in Napster only to see the recording industry sue it out of existence, this is madness. He envisioned a future in which the major labels sold music online via Napster—a future that came to pass, instead, through iTunes. "The answer would have been so easy," he says ruefully. "But instead of doing the easy thing, they said, 'We have our business model!'—and sued their customers."

Of course, RIAA executives say, before the lawsuits, consumers weren't sure whether downloading free music was illegal. Now they know.

Certainly Charli Johnson does. The Kansas University graduate and elementary school teacher, who settled with the RIAA for $3,000, has not downloaded a song since receiving her lawsuit. "The lawsuit stopped me from downloading music, but I'm one person," she says. "I can guarantee you my friends still download music. I really cannot see how it's making a huge difference."

Chapter 6
2003–2007

Beating Up on Peer-to-Peer Services Like Kazaa
and Grokster Fails to Save the Industry, Sales
Plunge, and Tommy Mottola Abandons Ship

ON THE blazing hot morning of February 6, 2004, a six-person team
of forensic computer specialists and attorneys pounded on Phil Morle's
door on the outskirts of Sydney, Australia. Phil was at work. His pregnant wife, Kellie, answered, with their two-year-old son at her side.
Flashing a court order, these investigators from the Australian record
industry commenced raiding the Morles' home. Kellie called Phil. He
was unable to return home at the moment because another team was
raiding his Sydney office. The investigators stayed at their house all day
and into the evening, extricating family hard drives, plugging in laptops
to copy the contents, and scouring every room for hidden computers.
"They went under the house to my cellar, where I store my old books
and bits of junk—hardware after years and years. One of the attorneys
called one of the other guys. With glee in their eyes, they figured they
found the Holy Grail—the nerve center, the big red button that controls
everything," Phil recalls. "It was a truly uncomfortable experience."

At the time, Morle was chief technology officer of Kazaa, the ren-
egade peer-to-peer service that had, along with competitors such as
LimeWire and Grokster, taken over the market in illegal music sharing
from Napster. In 2002, Kazaa's worldwide user base totaled 60 million,
including 22 million in the United States. By the time it paid $100 mil-
ion in damages to the recording industry and shut down, three years
later, its software had been downloaded some 370 million times via
Kazaa.com. Working with the RIAA, the Australian Recording Industry Association (ARIA) went after Kazaa's executives like *Law & Order*

prosecutors chasing child molesters. With the help of a smart, ferocious lead investigator, Michael Speck of Music Industry Piracy Investigations, these record-business cops uncovered strange and extravagant private details. (They were able to raid private homes and businesses thanks to an Australian court order known as Anton Piller, which gives copyright holders a lot of power.) Speck's team shadowed owner Kevin Bermeister in the streets of Sydney, using hidden backpack cameras. They discovered he lived in an $8 million mansion with a three-car garage, presumably built with the cash he made from Kazaa's numerous advertisers. In November 2004, nine months after the raids on Morle's home, as well as those of other Kazaa executives, the Kazaa offices in Sydney, and several universities thought to be file-sharing havens, the ARIA finally sued. "It was a tough time," Bermeister says today, as he prepares to put the website back online as a legal service. "The tidal wave of negative publicity was very difficult to defend."

While Napster's executives had been easy to find, ensconced in Silicon Valley offices throughout their copyright-infringement trial, Kazaa's executives were cagier. Kazaa's owner was the mysterious Sharman Networks, based in Vanuatu, a South Pacific island country and tax haven; its servers were in Denmark; its Kazaa.com internet domain was registered by an Australian firm, LEF Interactive (which stands for *"liberté, égalité, fraternité,"* in case anybody was unclear about the company's anti-establishment spirit); and its twenty-person staff, including Morle, worked in Sharman's Sydney offices. When *Wired* reporter Todd Woody was given a rare glimpse of the company's nerve center, he found a dozen people typing on computers surrounded by whiteboards covered with elaborate technical scrawls. "I hired actors to come in here," Morle joked at the time.

The first lawsuit against Kazaa had taken place in October 2001, in US District Court in Los Angeles. A twenty-eight-company coalition of major record labels and Hollywood studios sued Kazaa and fellow peer-to-peer services Grokster and StreamCast, owner of Morpheus. In *MGM v. Grokster et al.*, attorneys referred to the three file-sharing services as a "21st-century piratical bazaar" and argued that "the sheer magnitude of this haven for piracy is overwhelming and unknowable." They demanded $150,000 for each copyrighted song shared over the networks—which would potentially put damages in the billions of dollars. StreamCast and Grokster chose not to hide. They paid lawyers and fought back in court. With the help of the Electronic Frontier Foundation, a group of San Francisco lawyers funded by Grateful Dead lyricist John Perry Barlow, as well as Mark Cuban, high-tech billionaire and Dallas Mavericks owner, they argued an MGM victory in the case would have discouraged high-tech innovation from US entrepreneurs.

Swedish entrepreneur Niklas Zennström and his Danish partner, Janus Friis, had introduced Kazaa in 2000. The inventors met at a European telecom, Tele2, and were inspired by Napster's file-sharing model—which they interpreted not as a tool for piracy but as a revolutionary new technology, like radio and the videocassette recorder. In 2001, the founders linked Kazaa to another one of their inventions, the FastTrack protocol. Unlike Napster, which used a central server, Kazaa was able to rely on a series of "supernodes," essentially allowing users to create their own servers. These decentralized nodes had the advantage of making the company difficult to track. But Zennström and Friis had no stomach to fight a legal battle against the record industry.

Three months after the entertainment industry filed *MGM v. Grokster*, Zennström disappeared. Kazaa.com went offline (temporarily). Before lawyers could figure out what was going on, Kazaa's code belonged to a new company, Blastoise, which had two locations, one on an island off the British coast, the other in Estonia, a longtime pirate "safe harbor." Then the founders sold their company, Consumer Empowerment, to an even more mysterious outfit known as Sharman Networks. (Zennström and Friis would go on to release Skype, the internet free-phone service, in 2003; two years later, they sold it to eBay for a Clive Calder–esque $2.5 billion.) The new owner was Kevin Bermeister, a Sydney high-tech entrepreneur who had become a multimillionaire through a series of companies, beginning with the Australian software distributor Ozisoft in the early 1990s. When Kazaa came along, Bermeister was running Brilliant Digital Entertainment, which had made a deal involving 3-D internet ads with another file-sharing service, Morpheus. Through connections with his Brilliant board members and Morpheus employees, he tracked down Zennström and Friis and bought their company.

And that's when the major record labels were introduced to Nikki Hemming. Born in England, Hemming had been an employee of former record mogul Richard Branson, establishing Virgin Interactive offices in various European countries before moving to Sydney in the late 1990s. She and Bermeister worked together on an Australian theme park known as Segaworld, which lost some $60 million but nonetheless established a long-term business relationship between the two. In 2002, the forceful and charismatic Hemming, in her late thirties at the time, became the CEO of Sharman Networks. For the public face of a company, though, she was surprisingly inscrutable, emerging from her Sydney offices for press interviews only on rare occasions. She quickly replaced Shawn Fanning and the Napster crew as the international recording industry's most notorious enemy. But her employees were loyal and admiring. "She has done things the hard way," says Morle, who considers Hemming a mentor. "She has just crawled and pushed herself to the level she was at."

To Hemming, Kazaa's peer-to-peer model was not a piracy enabler but a revolutionary new way to distribute music, movies, and video games at low costs. "We are a utility," she told Australia's *The Age* in March 2003. "We are an effective, efficient utility that can be used to distribute myriad content." Hemming's employees concurred. "I knew the powers of peer-to-peer, I knew it was going to be the way of the future and I was excited to be part of the pioneering team," says Mick Liubinskas, Kazaa's former director of marketing.

Record executives weren't exactly fond of Napster, but they *hated* Kazaa. Around 2003, Eric Garland of BigChampagne.com presented his data on peer-to-peer file-sharing at a Warner Music boardroom. Afterward, a crowd of enthusiastic employees, who saw they could take this data to radio stations to help break new acts, gathered around Garland to ask questions. In a dramatic interruption from the back of the room, Jeff Ayeroff, the label's creative director, asked if there was a way to encode music files with copy protection that would snake through broadband cables, destroy pirates' computers, and melt their iPods. (Of course, Ayeroff knew full well that such a plan was technologically impossible. Out of frustration, and with Kazaa very much on his mind, he was speaking sarcastically.*)

"Shawn Fanning was genuinely a kid with a great idea," says Cary Sherman, who replaced Hilary Rosen as the public face of the RIAA. "The second generation of peer-to-peer operators were definitely in this for the money and not because they were kids with good ideas." Adds another industry source: "These were pornographers and bad guys who

---

* Ayeroff agreed to be interviewed at length for this book on a range of topics. He insists, counter to Garland's recollection, that the exchange in question took place not in 2003 but before the iPod was even in the marketplace.

were making millions of dollars of profit. This was almost an underworld business, using the lure of free music for other, darker uses."

Yes, users of Kazaa, LimeWire, and the rest weren't just downloading music and movies. Some were exchanging kiddie porn. (As with Napster, Kazaa operators had no knowledge or control over what users were sharing; that was part of the appeal of the anonymous service.) The US Senate Judiciary Committee took up the case. In a single search using Kazaa's service, one director working for the US General Accounting Office found 543 titles and file names that had to do with child pornography. Capitol Hill held hearings. The National Center for Missing & Exploited Children sent experts to testify. The music industry trotted out executives such as Andrew Lack, Sony Music's chief executive, to tell the *New York Times*: "As a guy in the record industry and as a parent, I am shocked that these services are being used to lure children to stuff that is really ugly." "It was one of the big propaganda positions in the public relations battle at the time," responds Kazaa's Morle. "They just kept throwing it up—that it was all about child pornography, just to damage our reputation, rather than being based on fact." In the end, Congress did nothing. There was no evidence that Kazaa or LimeWire distributed any more pornography than the internet at large.

But it's hard to blame a record executive for feeling like a victim in the early 2000s. Peer-to-peer services were popping up like Whack-a-Mole, to use a popular industry metaphor of the time. Grokster may have been fighting for its life in US court, but its owner, a family company in the West Indies, was smart enough to hire an old-school record industry PR man to generate exposure. "Being an old press guy, I knew how to get free advertising. I knew I could sit there and say anything I want. And the more outrageous I was the more coverage I would get," says Wayne Rosso, who started his career cleaning toilets at a United Artists record warehouse in the 1970s. "It would spread every time I was on TV or in print. Our downloads would go up. And that's how we made money. It was all conceived." Audiogalaxy, started in 1998 by a University of Texas computer science student named Michael Merhej, took the quality-over-quantity approach, building a music-geek–friendly interface and becoming what the *Austin Chronicle* called "the best music file-sharing service" in 2003. There were others, big and small, with ever more playful names: LimeWire, eDonkey, Soulseek, Aimster, BearShare, OiNK.

For a while, it looked bad for the record industry. The US Supreme

Court had ruled in 1984 that it wasn't Sony's fault that people made copies of movies and TV shows with the company's Betamax technology. Kazaa, Grokster, and Morpheus used the same Napster-style argument: *We're just the service. We can't control what people do with it.* They were careful not to create "smoking guns" the way Napster's Sean Parker had—nobody in these companies was inexperienced enough to admit, even in private emails, that their services were marketed to music pirates. A District Court in California originally dismissed the case, citing the Betamax decision, and the Ninth Circuit Court of Appeals agreed. But in 2005, the record industry earned a huge victory in the US Supreme Court. In a unanimous decision, the justices ruled that Grokster, Morpheus, and Kazaa violated copyrights "on a gigantic scale." On the one hand, the court preserved *Universal City Studios v. Betamax,* reaffirming viewers' rights to tape programs for personal use. On the other, the justices added the concept of "inducement to infringe," punishing companies that encourage copyright violation. In other words, even without evidence that there was knowledge and approval of piracy, like Parker's Napster emails, a business model implicitly based on customers stealing copyrighted material is illegal.

Within months, Grokster, Morpheus, and Kazaa stopped distributing their file-sharing software. But a day after the ruling, ex–RIAA chairperson Hilary Rosen was reluctant to celebrate. "I've been cautioning people in the industry not to be too euphoric over this—because no matter what the courts ever say, the courts can't keep up with technology," she said at the time. She was right. Immediately after the decision, 5.2 million to 5.4 million people continued to trade illegal music over peer-to-peer networks, according to BigChampagne.com. That number has only increased since then. "Kazaa lost. 'Recording Industry Defeats Kazaa,' went the headlines," recalls Eric Garland of BigChampagne.com. "Then what happened? *Nothing.* That became a really difficult point in the news cycle for the RIAA. They had every journalist pile on: 'Why didn't it solve the problem?' Why didn't iTunes sales go through the roof? Everybody thought the Supremes would rule, Grokster would be found liable, and 'we'll wipe our hands of this.' That was exactly the expectation of Napster and Kazaa. It's always the same: 'Oh, this is going to end the piracy.'"

With the courts sympathetic but ineffective, the major labels had only a few tools left to fight piracy. One tool was known as spoofing. They spent hundreds of thousands of dollars a year, sources say, on flooding peer-to-peer services from Kazaa to LimeWire with fake or

damaged files. By 2007, MediaDefender had become the biggest company to provide this service, charging major labels $4,000 to stave off
online-piracy activity for an individual album and $2,000 for a track.
The company opened in 2000, immediately landing big-fish clients from
Hollywood studios to Universal Music and becoming so prominent that
Condé Nast Portfolio would later call it "the online guard dog of the
entertainment world." From its inception in 2000 to late 2006, Media-
Defender had more than doubled its revenue, to $15.8 million, with
profit margins of roughly 50 percent. "The hope is, you make the experience so poor, it's not worth [a user's] time anymore. It helps deter it
enough where you turn people off to one system and maybe they move
to another," says Cory Llewellyn, ex-vice president of digital marketing
and promotion for Sony BMG–owned Epic Records. "You're looking
for a Nirvana track—ten spoofs and 'I'm going to go out and buy it.'"

The stakes were especially high at major labels for prerelease piracy.
Under this scenario, hot albums "leak" into the public's hands, usually
through studio or label underlings or journalists who receive advance
copies. This has been a problem since before Napster, with albums by
artists from U2 to Lil Wayne leaking before the all-important Tuesday
record-store release date. Some artists have turned such breaches into
marketing: Radiohead deliberately leaked 2000's *Kid A* to fan-operated
websites and reaped a word-of-mouth publicity bonanza. Most artists
and labels, however, can't stand these breaches; they feel they kill an
album's sales potential before it even begins.

Disaster struck MediaDefender in late 2006. A high school hacker—
called "Ethan" in a 2008 *Condé Nast Portfolio* article—had taken to
staying up all night in his father's Macintosh-strewn home office. Ethan
first broke through MediaDefender's website firewall during Christmas break, accessing secret internal files from Time Warner, Universal,
News Corp., and other media giants. Over the coming year, Ethan and
his hacker friends started to release pages and pages of internal emails
from "Monkey Defenders," as they began to call the company, through
the Swedish peer-to-peer service the Pirate Bay. "In the beginning, I
had no motivation against Monkey Defenders," Ethan told *Condé Nast
Portfolio.* "It wasn't like, 'I want to hack those bastards.' But then I
found something, and the good nature in me said, 'These guys are not
right. I'm going to destroy them.'" Taking advantage of a hole in Media-
Defender's online security, Ethan reportedly hacked into employee Jay
Maris's gmail account, gaining access to thousands of business-related

emails, as well as personal email addresses and phone numbers and outlines of company strategy.

Ethan then found someone to help him distribute this material: Peter Sunde, one of three people who run the Pirate Bay. Sunde, himself the target of May 2006 antipiracy raids in his home country, Sweden, was no fan of the major labels. "This is a stupid industry that thinks they're above the law and they're above evolution," he says. Long before he met Ethan, Sunde had figured out how to block MediaDefender's identifying computer IP addresses. He created a program to send a database error every time a MediaDefender employee tried to upload a damaged or corrupted file intended to throw users off the track of a copyrighted song. After Ethan got in touch, Sunde was happy to publicly circulate a 700-megabyte file containing crucial bits of Media-Defender operating procedures. Some were routine, like Universal executives authorizing "decoys" for Sum 41's *Underclass Hero* or Timbaland's *Shock Value*. Others were meatier: MediaDefender employees had been meeting with the US Justice Department to track down child pornographers who used peer-to-peer sites, and the same employees planned to erect their own fake peer-to-peer service, MiiVi, to create a valuable user list. "This is really fucked. Let's pull MiiVi offline," Media-Defender cofounder Randy Saaf, wrote to a company developer on July 3. Saaf was unaware that Ethan was about to intercept even this email and circulate it publicly.

Ethan's attacks came at a bad time for MediaDefender. ArtistDirect had bought the company in 2005 for $42.5 million, turning Saaf and cofounder Octavio Herrera into twenty-nine-year-old millionaires. They received roughly $700,000 a year to keep working for the company. As of this writing, MediaDefender was still operable; its employees did not respond to interview requests.

For many at major record labels, the public MediaDefender debacle was just another blow to company morale. Spoofing was one of their last tools in the war against online music piracy. "Whenever you brought up something like Napster, it was absolutely, 100 percent 'the enemy.' All we really knew about it was, at the time, our product's getting stolen. The only thing we kept thinking was, 'How do we defensively fix this?' And that was spoofing and suing," says Llewellyn, who lost his Epic Records job during a round of Sony BMG layoffs in late 2007 and is now a consultant for the label. "I thought there wasn't really wiggle room to try to figure out a new business."

But many others, working quietly in new-media departments within every major label, had spent years and years trying to figure out the new internet business. The sad fact was employees at major record labels largely downplayed the internet as a marketing tool—even a decade after Napster and a half-decade after iTunes. In part this was due to corporate policy. For example, major labels' new-media marketers and certain artists and managers had pushed for years to give away unprotected MP3s, for free or very cheap, to generate hype and publicity online and regain credibility with young, tech-savvy music fans.

In 2000, the Offspring, a Columbia Records punk band, attempted to release a free album in MP3 form as part of an MTV promotion. But label attorneys threatened a lawsuit, the Offspring threatened one right back, and the artist-vs.-label press coverage made Columbia look petty and out of touch. (In the end, the Offspring and Columbia compromised, agreeing to release just a few songs in MP3 form instead of a full album.) Label lawyers feared authorizing MP3 giveaways would legitimize the Kazaas and LimeWires of the world and damage the industry's prospects for winning their copyright-infringement cases.

Not everybody at labels felt this way. Fiercely competitive Don Ienner at Columbia, for example, followed an old CBS Records mantra, "Whatever it takes." Ienner barely knew how to work a computer, but he knew how to sell records. As quoted in the *Los Angeles Times,* he once referred to label promotion sessions as "war meetings" and added, "We devise a plan of attack where we figure out . . . how bloody we expect the battles to be." If that battle was on the internet, and the weapons were MP3 promotions, so be it. But hardly anyone else at the top of a label agreed. What really demoralized the Napster-sympathizing employees of label new-media departments was a corporate culture that valued traditional marketing like video and radio above anything else.

"Certainly, that was the attitude of majors across the board," recalls Mark Williams, Interscope Records's head of A&R until he accepted a buyout in 2007. "The people that were in the online and new-media areas—it felt like, for a long time, the niche people instead of the leading people. The focus was still on radio and high big-box retail. That was where the bulk of the sales and income was still being driven from day to day. You couldn't look so far in the future that you would lose what you had right in front of you. You had to work within a system that was still there. It was getting broken, but it hadn't broken at that point."

Some new-media executives refused to succumb to this attitude. If ever there was a person in the record business equipped to take advantage of the internet, it was Robin Bechtel. She was from Texas, and everyone knew it. She wore cowboy boots, spoke in an excitable drawl, favored folksy expressions like "well-behaved women rarely make history," and had a knack for experimenting with radical ideas without going through channels first to get permission. Like a select few employees of major labels who had computers and knew how to use them in the 1990s, she discovered the internet early on and immediately thought, *New marketing tool!* As an employee at Capitol Records, she set up one of the first artist websites in 1994, for metal band Megadeth. Drawing from her background working for a greeting card shop in Austin, she came up with a community concept for the site: "Megadeth, Arizona," a reference to the band's home state. It included a chat room called the MegaDiner, where singer Dave Mustaine showed up from time to time. The website also contained a radio station called K-Deth 101. The band couldn't believe how much attention its website was getting. CNN covered it, as did numerous magazines, and before long Bechtel had established herself as a one-woman new-media department at Capitol.

It wasn't easy for Bechtel or the numerous kindred new-media spirits at major labels—Erin Yasgar at Universal, Mark Ghuneim at Columbia, Ty Braswell at Capitol—who formed a sort of fraternity as the Napster era began. Even after iTunes went online in 2003, using peer-to-peer services as marketing tools was strictly forbidden, and God help a label marketer who proposed releasing a free MP3 as a promotional device. As a new-media executive for the independent label Wind-Up Records, Syd Schwartz had the leeway to build a successful internet marketing campaign for the rock band Creed in 1997—the band released a free online single via several retailer and radio websites. "I basically built Creed's online fan base one fan at a time," Schwartz says. Word spread, radio picked up on the internet buzz, and the band would go on to sell 24 million albums. But when Schwartz moved up in the world, taking a similar job at EMI, he quickly realized corporate policy prevented him from doing anything remotely close to the Creed campaign. "I remember, one of my first days of work, being sat down by a senior executive who shall remain nameless and being told that MP3s are the tool of the pirate. 'We don't do that here,'" Schwartz recalls.

Through their own determination, many of these new-media executives persevered, using the internet to sell records no matter what their bosses said. Bechtel, who switched to Warner Music in 2001, was among the best at navigating corporate culture in this manner. "Show her a brick wall, and she'll find a way to build a ladder, smash through it, levitate over it—she's going to find a way to get around that wall," says Ty Braswell, a vice president for new media at Virgin Records from 1999 to 2003. "If there's a lawyer or business-affairs person that's locked in a time warp, she's going to figure out a way with the leadership so people can grow from it."

Bechtel was prepared when YouTube and MySpace came along. The former, founded by three ex-PayPal employees in early 2005, gave online-video enthusiasts an easy, central hub to watch and post clips. It didn't catch on until after Christmas that year, when fans of NBC's *Saturday Night Live* posted a previously aired hip-hop spoof video called "Lazy Sunday," which quickly went viral. Fans watched it more than 5 million times through February 2006. Some of the music videos that popped up in YouTube's early days were extraordinary finds, like the original black-and-white Motown audition clip starring a tiny Michael Jackson fronting the Jackson 5, or John Lennon and Bob Dylan speaking incomprehensible hipster-ese in the back of a limousine in the late 1960s. Some owners of this copyrighted content reacted in much the same way they did to Napster: After the "Lazy Sunday" exposure died down, NBC Universal lawyers asked YouTube's founders to pull down the clip, which they did. (Like Napster, YouTube was free, but its employees pulled materials off the website if the copyright owners complained.) But Warner's Bechtel was among the first in the music business to see a marketing opportunity. "When YouTube came up, it was illegal," she recalls. "It was putting up a bunch of illegal clips. But our company was like, 'This is a huge consumer habit. This site is going to be huge.'" It was exactly the reaction marketers at major labels should have had when Napster popped up some eight years earlier.

YouTube turned out to be an extraordinarily efficient place to break new singles and acts. In fall 2005, the Chicago rock quartet OK Go spent $4.99 on its goofy-dancing "A Million Ways" video and posted it on YouTube. Fans would ultimately download it 9 million times, transforming the band from journeymen to superstars and leading to lucrative gigs in Moscow and South America. "The funny part is we don't get paid anything for it—that's the thing for our record company [EMI] that's sort of baffling," the band's manager, Jamie Kitman, said at the time. "It resulted in a lot of income for the band, yet it's all indirect. It's really a perfect example of the unfolding new music economy, wherein you don't make your money from selling records, particularly." Rather than suing YouTube, acts from Panic! at the Disco to Justin Timberlake figured out how to use it as a sort of self-critique, gauging fans' reactions to recent live concert footage. In September 2006, Bechtel's company, Warner Music, made a deal to distribute its large music video catalog on YouTube in exchange for a portion of the company's advertising revenues. A month later, Google Inc. bought YouTube for $1.65 billion in Google stock. Universal, too, would find gold in YouTube exposure, making a deal with the company and taking in $20 million in annual online-video revenues over the past few years.

MySpace began in 2003 as an improvement on the early social networking website Friendster. Like YouTube, the website soon became an internet phenomenon, racking up more than 100 million accounts within three years. Although artists from middle-of-the-road pop singer Colbie Caillat to one-man band Secondhand Serenade would soon break after generating tons of publicity through their MySpace pages, major record labels initially reacted in a familiar way. In 2006, Universal Music sued the company, alleging it encouraged users to infringe their song and video copyrights by providing free music.

But label executives, seeing just how much publicity a familiar or unknown act can generate by providing free music on its MySpace page, changed their attitudes over the next few years. "We've had relationships with [the labels] since the beginning of MySpace, but we never came up with a concrete business plan that we could present to them that shows a big win for our users that also makes sense for the music business," Chris DeWolfe, one of the company's founders, said in early 2008. "We needed to create this utopian service in such a way that the music companies are starting to make money. That took a little while to do. Attitudes have definitely changed over the years, and music companies are wanting to experiment more. They're more daring and more creative." In April 2008, Universal dropped its lawsuit, and three of the four major labels partnered with MySpace Music later that year, selling downloads and streaming songs for free. At the time this book went to press, EMI Music, reeling from layoffs and a corporate takeover, was expected to join the partnership, too. In the social networking world, MySpace competitors like Facebook and Last.fm also relied heavily on music, and labels made deals with them, too. In spring 2008, venerable rock band R.E.M. released its comeback, *Accelerate,* for free via iLike, Facebook's music application. It sold 115,000 copies of the album (that's combined sales of CDs plus online albums) in its first week, hitting No. 2, R.E.M.'s highest chart debut since 1996. Later in 2008, iLike made a deal with the Rhapsody subscription service to stream millions of major-label-owned songs for free via Facebook.

"When we started out in 2002, the major labels didn't take our calls—there was panic about anything having to do with the word MP3 or online music generally," says Martin Stiksel, cofounder of Last.fm, which CBS bought in 2007 for $280 million. "It took until about 2006 to see services like ours as something other than an enemy." In part, this was because the attitudes of major label executives changed, over time, as they saw CD sales dropping no matter how aggressively they tried to stop online piracy. But in part, it's because what Robin Bechtel, Syd Schwartz, Ty Braswell, and others were saying for years in meetings with their bosses about the importance of the internet finally started to catch on.

DURING THE 1990S—THE heart of the CD boom—Sony Music Entertainment chairman Tommy Mottola built the most bulletproof hit machine in the record business. Sony sold more than 50 million of Mariah Carey's records in the US alone, and 11 million of Céline Dion's *Titanic* soundtrack. With the help of Sony, little-known Seattle punk bands Pearl Jam and Alice in Chains turned into the world's biggest rock stars. The Sony team shared one overwhelming philosophy: It takes money to make money. "If a record wasn't selling, they would apply a little bit of muscle to get it in the front of a store—and it would start selling," says Randy Sosin, a longtime executive at competitor Interscope Records. "It was a little bit of old school." Sony routinely spent $1 million on a new artist, knowing full well that few of these artists would come close to making money. The ones that did paid for the ones that didn't—and Sony's team was masterful at boosting the odds. Like almost every other major label, Sony lost ground to Clive Calder's nimble Zomba Music Group in the era of boy bands and Britney. But as always, Mottola's team fought back: For singer Jessica Simpson's 2001 CD release, Mottola threw a swanky party on a yacht in the East River near New York City. "He did spend a ton of money," says Barbara O'Dair, party attendee and editor-in-chief of *Teen People*. Simpson made a respectable third-place showing in the teen-diva arena, after Spears and Christina Aguilera.

However, the "It takes money to make money" philosophy works only if a company is *making money*. After ripping and burning, Napster, online piracy, and the industry's hamhanded response to it all, US album sales were down 17 percent in 2002. By early 2003, Mottola's bottom line looked shockingly ordinary. Sony Music lost $132 million during the first half of that fiscal year. The label's American market share dropped from 16.6 percent in 1998 to 15.7 percent in 2002—and would fall to 13.7 percent in 2003.

Ordinarily, none of this would have fazed Mottola. He had endured a similar sales dip in the early 1990s. The difference this time was that while Mottola had been so deft at manipulating Norio Ohga and other Sony Corp. executives to wrest power away from Walter Yetnikoff, by 2003 his heart just didn't seem into the politics. At age fifty-three, his attention was elsewhere. He'd survived a divorce from Mariah Carey after five years of marriage.* He remarried, to the golden-haired singer and Mexican soap-opera beauty Thalia, and built a $4 million villa for her in Miami.

By 2002, the tolerant Ohga had left the company. His replacement, Nobuyuki Idei, was not so easily impressed by flashy American record executives. Moreover, Mottola had an uneasy relationship with his direct boss at Sony Corp., CEO Sir Howard Stringer, a Welshman with a tough-minded business reputation. Stringer was an active hobnobber and skilled party host, remembering his guests' names and showering them with hugs. But just as Yetnikoff had referred to his superiors with crude bon mots like "the Jew Upstairs," Mottola's nickname for Stringer was "the Buffoon." He kept Stringer away from Sony stars, refusing to dole out good seats at concerts and never inviting him to Grammy Awards parties. "Tommy didn't 'manage up' well with regards to Howard Stringer. He didn't include him enough and operated independently. And he was just on a roll—for years and years, he couldn't be touched," says a major label source. "As soon as the company started losing money, they used that opportunity to get rid of him. [Mottola]

---

* Neither Mottola nor Carey would talk about their divorce in public. But Carey's "Honey" video was fairly simple to deconstruct—in it, the singer escapes house arrest by jumping off a balcony into a pool. And after she escaped Mottola, she shrewdly took off from his company as well. It seems a music snippet she had licensed wound up on label mate Jennifer Lopez's CD. Rather than suing, Carey's people reportedly used this sticking point to break her contract. (Both parties denied that this was true.) She fled to EMI.

didn't massage the relationship. If he had let Howard Stringer play in his sandbox, and had him up in the pictures with his artists and vetted him at awards shows, he'd still be there."

Stringer frequently complained to his brother, Rob, a Sony UK executive who'd risen through the ranks on his own, according to *New York*: "Why the fuck am I dealing with this guy? Why the fuck are we paying this guy? Tell me what this guy does. Tell me what this guy does. *Tell me what this guy does*." Why, indeed? Mottola announced in 2002 he wanted a new contract, but got no response from his superiors. Idei stopped inviting him to Japan. Stringer started to make public hints that Sony would not renew Mottola's contract. Finally, not wanting Mottola to make an embarrassing public scene, as Clive Davis had done earlier in the decade with BMG, Sony bought out his five-year contract. Mottola's fall finally went public on January 9, 2003, in the form of a faxed press release.

The rest of the music business was shocked. "The Tommy-Donnie-Michele management structure was viewed by everybody, without question, as the most stable management structure in the business," says Jim Guerinot, a former A&M executive who manages Gwen Stefani, Nine Inch Nails, and others. "They got a lot of momentum and strength from that stability. Those guys had been in place a long time. Nobody seemed more invulnerable. They really appeared omnipotent." And then Mottola was gone.

Within a day, his replacement had been named—and it wasn't Donnie Ienner, his heir apparent. Stringer went outside the company, to an old friend who'd worked with him at CBS, making documentary films in the 1970s: Andrew Lack, fifty-five-year-old president of NBC. Lack had no experience whatsoever in the music business, a fact that was even more conspicuous at a major like Sony, where for decades the powers-that-be had artist-centered pedigrees stretching back to Hall and Oates, Blood, Sweat and Tears, even Elvis. As a bone to the Mottola-team remnants, Stringer made Ienner president of Sony Music US. Frustrated with his high responsibility but low autonomy and prestige, Ienner turned around and created some politics of his own. Within months, the longtime Columbia exec indulged his rivalry with sibling label Epic and purged many of its holdover employees, sources say.

The power shift was symbolic. Tommy Mottola represented the heart of the spend-money-to-make-money CD boom. That's not to say there were no CEOs left with this philosophy—the music industry's grand old man, Clive Davis, was still spending lavishly at BMG.* Antonio "LA" Reid jumped from Arista to Island Def Jam, taking his private jets and legendary artist payouts with him. (Reid's son Aaron was a star of MTV's *My Super Sweet 16*, throwing a lavish party including a concert from hot Island Def Jam rapper Kanye West and an appearance by Diddy. His invitations to guests came via MP3 player.) But in the post-Napster world, these old-school record men started to give way to new-school cost cutting—layoffs, dropping artists, even the dreaded scaling back of expense accounts. Sony Music had already started shrinking, from 17,700 employees in 2000 to 13,400 in 2003. And Tommy Mottola wouldn't be around to ride the hydrogen bomb down to the ground, like Slim Pickens in *Dr. Strangelove*. In a press release, Stringer called him "an icon of the music industry" and referred to his "legacy to be envied." Mottola would restart a record label with a familiar name—Casablanca, the disco label whose excesses almost killed the entire industry in the late 1970s. Casablanca signed actress Lindsey Lohan and had a few hits, but as of this writing, Mottola's career as a hit maker is over. "It was the end of an era," says a record company source. There was no longer enough money left in the record business to support Tommy Mottola.

One of the first things Andrew Lack did as head of Sony Music was something his predecessor almost certainly would have never done: He started a friendship with a rival. Rolf Schmidt-Holtz was chairman of BMG, which, not so long ago, had fought like a prize fighter against Sony and the other major labels. Schmidt-Holtz had been a journalist and political talk-show host before becoming a media executive in Germany. Lack had been president of NBC, overseeing *Today* and *NBC Nightly News*. Both were outsiders, shifting from TV to music. Both were cutting costs from their record labels at a time when online piracy and CD ripping and burning had ravaged a gigantic business. "We speak

---

* Davis and his reported $10-million-a-year salary finally succumbed to stark music business reality in May 2008, when Sony BMG removed him from the BMG chairmanship and shifted him to "chief creative officer." Davis's allies in the business, including Rod Stewart's manager, Arnold Stiefel, insisted the move was Davis's idea and that he'd be working as closely with artists as ever. Other sources, however, said more germane factors were Davis's large salary at a time of cost cutting and his refusal, at age seventy-six, to name a successor. Sony BMG's replacement for Davis was Barry Weiss, forty-nine, who had taken over as president of Zomba after Clive Calder left the company, and continued to break hit CDs from the likes of Chris Brown and T-Pain despite the industry's ongoing sales problems.

the same language," Schmidt-Holtz told the *Wall Street Journal.* "Personal trust allowed us to overcome a number of obstacles."

Bertelsmann, the German publishing company that owned BMG, had survived its misadventures with Thomas Middelhoff and Napster, but just barely. Teen pop, its music mainstay in the late 1990s, was over. Reeling from a drop in CD sales, Bertelsmann was merger-happy. In 2003, its executives approached AOL Time Warner, whose own merger was on the verge of catastrophe, and offered a 50–50 deal to combine BMG with Warner Music. Warner was interested, but both sides immediately grew stubborn. AOL Time Warner insisted its catalog of Madonna, Frank Sinatra, and Led Zeppelin tunes was far more valuable than BMG's catalog of Elvis Presley and the Dave Matthews Band. Bertelsmann's offer was $100 million, but Warner demanded an extra $150 million—too much for the German company. That's when Schmidt-Holtz and his superiors turned to Sony, using Lack as their initial connection and conduit. After weeks of talks, Schmidt-Holtz met with Sony's Nobuyuki Idei and Sir Howard Stringer and Bertelsmann chief executive Gunter Thielen for ninety minutes at a New York airport in October 2003 and hashed out a merger. Regulators were concerned Sony BMG would form a cartel and violate international antitrust laws. But they ultimately agreed Big Music wasn't so big anymore and the major labels didn't control as much money as they used to. They approved the deal in July 2004.

On paper, the new Sony BMG looked like a powerhouse. They had Bruce Springsteen *and* Britney Spears, Barbra Streisand *and* Elvis Presley. Combined, their market share, at least in the US, added up to around 30 percent, a few points above even dominant Universal Music. The only bad news was a few thousand layoffs, but that's the price of making two companies stronger, right? But the executives miscalculated. Sony's Lack and BMG's Schmidt-Holtz may have been pals, but in the ranks underneath them, some of the fiercest competitors in music industry history were suddenly partners, conducting business with tight smiles. Clive Davis, who had started his career nurturing Bob Dylan and Streisand at Columbia and had discovered Whitney Houston with Arista Records in the 1980s, was the head of BMG. Don Ienner, a Sony Music company man who had been one of Tommy Mottola's loudest and most cutthroat loyalists, was in charge of Columbia and Epic. Making matters worse, Ienner had worked for Davis in the early 1980s at Arista, and had no intention of taking a subservient role this time. Things were uneasy whenever they found themselves at meetings together. "One side of the room was Clive and his people. The other side was Donnie and his people," recalls Joe DiMuro, executive vice president of the merged company's strategic marketing group until he left in late 2006. "There was a level of cordiality, but you could tell there was a dividing line. It was palpable."

Lack, who had been appointed boss of the newly merged company, found himself in a no-win position smack in the middle of these two suspicious cultures. He might have made it work if he'd had the clout and charisma of a Davis or a Mottola, but his lack of record business experience rankled the more seasoned executives below him. One of those was Michael Smellie, a BMG executive since the mid-1990s who'd worked his way up to chief operating officer in the merged company. "The two of them, in many cases, were like oil and water," DiMuro says. "Michael, at times, was reporting to Andy, and Michael became frustrated and disenchanted. There was a level of noncommunication. They shut down at times." (Some on the Sony side believed the competitive Smellie did everything he could to set up Lack for a fall.)

Lack was no technology expert—his comments before Congress likening peer-to-peer services to child pornographers weren't exactly forward-thinking—but he was smart enough to grasp that technology represented the future of the business. For a time around 2003, Lack developed an interest in selling songs through those very same peer-to-peer services—this time using "fingerprinting" technology that could separate the customers from the pirates. He started contacting people who knew about this kind of technology—Talmon Marco, head of iMesh, which the RIAA had sued in 2003; Vance Ikezoye of Audible Magic; and Wayne Rosso, the cigar-smoking record-business veteran who, as head of Grokster, had likened record executives to Josef Stalin. Rosso spent some time with Lack, introducing him to the key players and acting as a go-between for meetings with Sony executives. "Andy was the key mover and shaker in loosening things up," Rosso says. "He was trying to do the right thing. He met with resistance all the way through." Lack's efforts failed, as did his other clumsy high-tech innovations. He flooded stores with new releases using the CD-plus-DVD DualDisc format. They didn't help sales, and the format basically disappeared. What cut off his head at Sony, though, was a very traditional decision—Lack resigned Bruce Springsteen, who was inarguably past his prime in selling new albums—for $100 million.

Lack could have been the greatest record executive in the world, and he still wouldn't have been able to pump up Sony BMG's bottom line as piracy and iTunes cannibalized CD sales. He kept cutting costs, which stopped the bleeding somewhat but didn't exactly improve employees' spirits. Publicists, for example, watched budgets for artist photo sessions drop from $25,000 to $5,000 in just two or three years. No longer could they spend more than $5,000 to fly an artist to New York or Los Angeles for a prominent late-night TV appearance. Instead of giving away thirty tickets to a concert, they could give away eight. And their coworkers kept losing their jobs, day after day. Sony's US market share dropped from 30 percent to 27 percent in 2005. Finally, Sir Howard Stringer decided he'd had enough.

In early 2006, he switched the jobs of Schmidt-Holtz and Lack, giving Schmidt-Holtz chief executive power over the entire company, and turning Lack into a "nonexecutive chairman" with relatively little power. Although he remained with the company, Lack was, for all intents and purposes, done as a record mogul. By summer, so were Don Ienner and Michele Anthony, the two primary holdovers from the Tommy Mottola era, who couldn't stand it anymore and left. Their replacement was Stringer's younger brother, Rob. Within a few short years, the Mottola team of experienced, hard-nosed music executives was gone. Some in the business mourned the departure of the classic record men. Others wondered why it took so long to get rid of Tommy Mottola's team, which was about as far as the record industry could get from technology gurus.*

THEN THINGS GOT really bad.

In the iTunes era, old-school distribution and manufacturing were suddenly relics. Since the early 1970s, record-making plants had been cash cows for major labels. So had complex shipping networks of warehouses and branch offices around the world. But in 2004, EMI closed CD-manufacturing plants in Jacksonville, Illinois, and Uden, in the Netherlands, and laid off 900 workers. Around that time, AOL Time Warner sold the company's once-mighty CD-distribution arm, WEA,

---

*In August 2008, Bertelsmann bailed out of the Sony-BMG merger, selling its 50 percent stake to Sony in a deal valued at $900 million.

to a Canadian company called Cinram International for $1.05 billion—analysts called it a steal, until CD sales dropped 15 percent in 2007. Later, with backing from a wireless company called Glenayre Technologies, former Warner and Island Def Jam executive Jim Caparro formed the Entertainment Distribution Company and bought what was left of Universal Music's plants and warehouses, plus the employees who worked in them, for $122 million. The deal worked great for a few years, until the company posted a net loss of $11.4 million, forcing Caparro to step down in 2008. "Darwinian evolution took hold," Caparro says of the record industry, which he lambastes for not embracing digital music quickly enough. "Things changed." As for CD-manufacturing plants, some remain open, including Sony's pioneering one in Terre Haute, Indiana. It survives not on CDs but DVDs. But maybe not for long. Even US DVD sales dropped 3.6 percent in 2007—although Sony executives have said the movie industry's adoption of the Blu-ray format in February 2008 may lead to expansion of the 1,200-employee Terre Haute plant.

Old-school marketing fell just as hard. For as long as anybody in the business could remember, labels relied on MTV, radio, and record stores for exposure. Push the gatekeepers at those places aggressively enough—in some cases, bribe them—and you've got a hit. The first to go was MTV. Beginning in the late 1990s, the channel's executives realized they could snag higher ratings with self-produced reality shows like *The Real World* and *Road Rules* than by actually playing music videos. Labels went from spending $1 million on a typical video for an MTV-worthy artist in the early 2000s to $100,000 or $200,000 in 2007. "It's a very precarious and somewhat unfortunate development," says Randy Sosin, Interscope's senior vice president of music video production until he lost his job in late 2007. "The cost of making a film has gone up, but the dollars that they're spending have gone down." MTV still breaks artists like emo-pop band Paramore and rapper Common, but often through tiny commercial snippets in the middle of shows like *A Shot at Love with Tila Tequila*.

Then the major labels' long-standing relationship with radio stations hit a cataclysmic snag. For decades, they relied on independent promoters to "persuade" radio programmers to add their singles to their playlists. By the 1990s, the big indies were corporate, clean-image types like Bill Scull and Jeff McClusky, who figured out they could make the most money by hooking up with one big radio company, like Clear

Channel or Entercom. By 2001, the mathematics of indie promotion looked like this, according to Eric Boehlert of Salon.com: Of 10,000 commercial US radio stations, 1,000 were the tastemakers that broke hits and moved CDs; those stations added roughly three new songs per week; labels paid indies like Scull and McClusky between $1,000 and $8,000 to add a song to a station's playlist. So the top indies, a handful of entrepreneurs including Scull, McClusky, and Bill McGathy, received roughly $3 million *every week*.

This lucrative relationship lasted as long as major labels had that kind of money to spend. But in the early 2000s, as McClusky remembers, "Costs start becoming more of a consideration." They stopped wanting to pay independent promoters—for real this time. It helped that senators such as Democrat Russ Feingold started to look into "legal payola," finding it uncomfortably close to *actual* payola. Congress pressured the big media companies, like Clear Channel Communications, which owned 1,225 stations and received millions of dollars a year from major labels through indie promoters. In 2003, just before the Federal Communications Commission voted on a measure to relax rules for radio,* the San Antonio company turned against indie promo. Most of the other big radio companies followed. Thus did onetime power players like Scull and McClusky resign themselves to, well, making less than millions of dollars per week. "We were too greedy," Scull says today, with resignation.

It was nice, for the bean counters at major labels, to give up a budget item of millions of dollars every year. It was not so nice for label promotion departments with singles to break. They decided to keep up the pressure on radio programmers—only without the middlemen who knew what they were doing. They went back to $50 handshakes or their modern equivalents. At one point, an Epic Records executive spent $5,000 on New York–to–Miami trips to get rock bands Franz Ferdinand and Good Charlotte on the air. Another time, two Epic executives wrote a memo to programmers listing "fixed billing rates" of $500 to $1,000 for 75 or more airings of a record, or "spins," on a station. One

---

* On June 3, 2003, the FCC did, in fact, relax media-ownership rules. The commission lifted a twenty-eight-year rule disallowing a newspaper from owning a TV or radio station in the same market and allowed other broadcast companies to own more stations in general. This decision benefited Clear Channel, along with other large media companies.

especially indiscreet Epic promotions director asked a Clear Channel radio station employee in an email: "WHAT DO I HAVE TO DO TO GET AUDIOSLAVE ON WKSS THIS WEEK?!!? Whatever you can dream up, I can make it happen!!!" In another email, a Top 40 program director for a Rochester, NY, station wrote: "I'm a whore this week. What can I say?" Some labels paid radio programmers thousands of dollars in cash, Las Vegas airline tickets, laptops, and Walkmans to push artists from Audioslave to J. Lo into heavy rotation.

This bald-faced bribery continued until Eliot Spitzer, attorney general of New York, found himself a new campaign issue. A Democrat who had successfully crusaded against investment-banking researchers over their Wall Street conflicts of interest, Spitzer was on the path to becoming governor, and payola was the perfect issue for him. It was secret and widespread, fit snugly into headlines, and made important people like FCC commissioners and US senators good and angry. Spitzer subpoenaed all of New York's major record labels, as well as the big radio companies. He demanded emails and documents, and they complied. His staff interviewed tons of people. His evidence was enough to strong-arm the major labels. They settled. Sony BMG was first, coughing up $10 million in July 2005. Sony Music's top executives, Don Ienner and Charlie Walk, fired sacrificial lamb Joel Klaiman, head of radio promotions for Epic Records, allowing Spitzer to say he drew blood from the record business. But shortly after Spitzer's investigation became public, the *Los Angeles Times* broke an extraordinary story based on anonymous sources, reporting that Walk and Ienner "condoned or participated in pay-to-play." One source claimed to the paper: "Donnie would tell you: 'Do whatever it takes. Get the song played.'" Another source added that Ienner would say, "I've approved $50,000 this year for that [program director], and when we're developing this baby band, we get nothing. Tell him if we don't get spins, we're cutting his support." Ienner and Walk denied the allegations to the *Times* and did not respond to interview requests for this book. In any case, after the Sony BMG settlement came Warner, later that year, paying $5 million; EMI, Universal, and several big radio companies added more millions later to New York charities devoted to music education.

Spitzer, of course, would bring a few secrets of his own to the governor's mansion in New York. As most of the world knows by now, this crusader against corruption was disgraced in early 2008 when he was caught paying for a high-priced prostitute. Ironically, the woman, Ashley Alexandra Dupré, was an aspiring singer-songwriter, and after the Spitzer scandal broke, she received more than 7 million hits on her MySpace page. The resulting 98-cent song downloads, according to the *New York Daily News*, added up to more than $206,000 in pure profit.

But hookers and political scandals aside, the Spitzer-led payola settlements suddenly left major labels without a crucial radio tool beginning in 2005. Soon, promotion executives at labels noticed stations around the US were becoming more conservative, adding fewer new singles, repeating more of the old, popular ones, and keeping their label contacts at arm's length. For the first half of 2006, *Radio & Records,* a trade magazine that uses computers to study airplay, noticed newly added radio singles were dramatically down—in most of the big formats, from rock to hip-hop to country to adult contemporary. Spitzer's investigation made programmers paranoid. Radio companies made their vice presidents of operations sign a form whenever a programmer received a box of CDs. "Songs aren't just getting on the radio as quickly as they did before," says Doug Podell, operations manager for Detroit rock station WRIF, adding that the bands Flyleaf, Powerman 5000, and Army of Anyone were victims of this new conservatism. "The labels are scrambling," a source at a major label said at the time, "and we're all freaking out." Radio was still the most reliable way to break an international hit—hard-rock band Flyleaf, R&B star Chris Brown, and pop acts James Blunt and Maroon 5 broke on the air over time—but this key promotional outlet was no longer a sure thing for big-spending major labels like it had been in the 1980s and 1990s.

With MTV and radio changing, only one huge, reliable promotional outlet remained: record stores. Surely, thought label executives, chains like Tower, Wherehouse, and Sam Goody would push new music like they had since the 1940s. Unfortunately, during the CD boom, labels had shifted their resources away from these steady music-only chains and towards mega-sellers such as Best Buy, Wal-Mart, and Target— which were in the mood to slash prices and cut CD shelf space. Hundreds of record stores went out of business. In January 2006, Musicland went bankrupt, taking the venerable Sam Goody chain with it into anachronistic oblivion.

And then came the fall of Tower Records, the red-and-yellow chain that had become an institution. Founder Russ Solomon, a big music fan, first began selling records in 1941 in the back of his father's drugstore in Sacramento. He opened his first store in Sacramento in 1960, and emphasized deeper catalogs than his competitors. He started branching into other cities in the late 1960s, notably San Francisco, where he stumbled onto a Fisherman's Wharf "for rent" sign while nursing a hangover. He leased the space, opened a store, and turned it into a hangout for Haight-Ashbury musicians such as Carlos Santana, Steve Miller, and members of Jefferson Airplane. Its most famous location, on the Sunset Strip in Los Angeles, opened in 1970, and it became a local music centerpiece—Axl Rose of Guns N'Roses once worked there as a night manager, and the store opened early for Michael Jackson to shop by himself during the *Thriller* era. Elton John and the Beach Boys' Brian Wilson were among the best-known customers, and the Hollywood location took on its own mythology. Rose's onetime bandmate Slash has a childhood photo of himself in the store, begging his record-collecting parents for certain albums in the aisle. A few years later, he was arrested for stealing cassettes. Still later, he worked with a crew of big-haired metalheads at the video store across the street. "We happened to be funny-looking, but met the right requirements," he recalls. "It was something they should have made a movie out of, like *Clerks*, but a little bit more rock 'n' roll and a little bit more mayhem."

Like the rest of the music industry, Tower boomed in the 1980s and 1990s, as music fans replaced their LPs with CDs. But at the peak, in the mid-1990s, Solomon expanded a bit too aggressively—by his own recollection—opening stores in expensive retail spaces all over the world. "I lost a lot of money in Argentina and Mexico, even England and Taiwan and Hong Kong," he says. Like a lot of people in the record business, Solomon figured the good times would last forever. But Tower filed for bankruptcy in 2004. Solomon and his family lost their controlling stake. A new CEO, Allen Rodriguez, rubbed Solomon and other longtime Tower employees the wrong way. "What these cuckoo, MBA-style managers did—they tried to turn Tower into a chain store," Solomon says. "Every single inch of space [in the store] is taken up by who's paying for it—price and position and signs and shit. Everything was wrong." For years, the company worked on a prototype for an iTunes-style online retailer, but that never went anywhere. "Russ Solomon didn't believe in digital music," recalls Lisa Amore, who handled publicity for Tower for many years. In 2006, the company finally succumbed, holding going-out-of-business sales, closing its 89 stores, and laying off 3,000 employees.

Executives at the major labels had unwittingly planted the seeds for

Tower's demise. They could only watch helplessly as Tower fell. The following year, in 2007, US CD sales dropped almost 15 percent. All year, label sources promised blockbusters for the all-important holiday shopping season—Eminem! U2! Madonna! Green Day! Metallica! None of them materialized, save one from R&B singer Alicia Keys, a heavily hyped album-release rivalry between rappers Kanye West and 50 Cent, and the first new studio album in twenty-eight years from the Eagles, who bypassed record labels completely and sold *Long Road Out of Eden* exclusively through Wal-Mart. In 2007, Wal-Mart reduced its shelf space by 20 percent, dropping the number of music titles at the chain's biggest stores to about 4,000, and Best Buy cut its music space as well. The following year, sources at major labels predicted Wal-Mart would cut back another 20 percent on music titles.

That meant more pain. EMI Music, owner of the lucrative Beatles and Beach Boys catalogs, took the brunt of it. A British equity firm, Terra Firma, bought the company for $5 billion in May 2007 with the intent of cutting costs and turning things around. But by September, Terra Firma's chief executive officer, Guy Hands, was calling the major label "the worst business . . . in the most challenged sector." One source who does business with EMI predicted a "bloodbath" for the label in 2008. The famous EMI-owned Capitol Records tower in LA, shaped like a stack of records and built in 1956 as a testament to the vibrancy of the record industry, was sold to a New York condominium developer in late 2006, although what was left of Capitol's staff continued to work there.

Also reeling was Warner Music, which for decades had been the ideal record label, with well-respected top executives from Ahmet Ertegun to Joe Smith to Mo Ostin signing career megastars like Neil Young, Jimi Hendrix, Prince, R.E.M., and Metallica. When Time and Warner merged in the early 1990s, Warner Music was generating tons of money and was an industry powerhouse. After a series of corporate changes and post-Napster malaise, the music division had grown into exactly the opposite. The sad fact was Warner Music never really recovered from the AOL Time Warner merger in 2000. By the time the merger imploded in 2003, and Time Warner reestablished control of the company, the music division was in trouble. Time Warner spent months trying to dump its music division.

Finally, Edgar Bronfman Jr. led a group of investors to buy the label. He was coming off problems of his own. Having purchased MCA and PolyGram and created Universal Music in the late 1990s, the Seagram

Co. heir sold Seagram's stock for $42 billion in shares in media giant Vivendi International in 2000. At the time, the head of Vivendi was Frenchman Jean-Marie Messier, who quickly ran the company into the ground. Bronfman's family fortune dropped from $6.5 billion to $3 billion, and he resigned as a Vivendi director. He tried and failed to buy Vivendi Universal, and failed to hang on to the company's US entertainment assets. But he recovered. "I remember my mother saying as I was a kid, 'It's not a question of being thrown from the horse—it's whether you get back on,'" Bronfman said in a 2007 interview. "And I think that's true in life as well. The question is, Are you going to climb up on another horse?"

Still enamored of the record business, Bronfman found a new horse. He put together a group of investors who bought Warner Music for $2.8 billion in 2004. As he'd done at Universal during better times, he assembled a halfway decent team—including Lyor Cohen, who had started out as Run-D.M.C.'s road manager and risen through the music industry to become head of Island Def Jam Records. Warner's new brain trust refashioned themselves as futurists, pushing employees at every level of the company to think digitally. At first, it almost worked—the Red Hot Chili Peppers gave fans a chance to preorder concert tickets after downloading their double-CD *Stadium Arcadium* via iTunes in 2006, and stars from rockers Green Day to rapper T.I. created custom ringtones to go with their latest CDs. Bronfman also cut costs and took the company public, and its stock price initially went up. "Technology allows more people to get more music in more places than ever before—I just have no question in my mind that that bodes positively for the content businesses," Bronfman said. "I just think you take a snapshot of the business in 2000, and take a snapshot in 2010, you'll see a picture of a healthy business. In between, it's not so great."

"Not so great" is exactly how investors would describe some of Warner's business decisions after Bronfman bought the company. Warner wrote off $18 million in 2007 for an investment in Bulldog Entertainment Group, which put on $3,000-a-ticket summer concerts in the Hamptons by Billy Joel, Prince, Tom Petty, and others. The company also paid $73 million to buy hard-rock hitmaker Nickelback's independent label, Roadrunner Records, just to inherit the two or three albums the band had left on its contract—and watch the band sign with concert promoter Live Nation in mid-2008. Warner's stock dropped more than 50 percent in 2007, to a little more than $8 a share, and the company reported a $37 million loss in the second quarter of 2008. The label spent 2007 laying off 400 employees, including talented A&R people like Atlantic's Leigh Lust, who signed Jet and many other hit acts over the course of his seventeen-year career. "This industry is like George W. Bush getting elected to a third term," says Steve Gottlieb, president of independent label TVT Records, which broke Lil Jon and other hip-hop stars before succumbing to legal problems of its own in early 2008 and filing for Chapter 11 bankruptcy. "We can't undo past mistakes without the industry's current administration getting voted out." Yet Bronfman and other top Warner executives continue to pay themselves exceedingly well. Bronfman's earnings in fiscal year 2007 were $1 million in salary and $2.4 million in stock dividends; Lyor Cohen drew a $1.5 million salary, $1.5 million in bonuses, and almost $1.4 million in stock. These lavish salaries and bonuses may explain why the top executives at major labels have taken so long to develop a new business model.

FOR A LONG time, one major record label escaped the carnage: the Universal Music Group.

The company's success began with Bronfman, who bought MCA and PolyGram and merged them into one superlabel in the late 1990s. He had no music business experience other than his own small songwriting successes, but he turned out to be good at finding executives to do the dirty work. He made two smart decisions right away.

The first was hiring chairman and chief executive officer Doug Morris, who had a lifelong track record of building hits, from writing the Chiffons' "Sweet Talkin' Guy" in 1966 to working with the Rolling Stones and Led Zeppelin as the head of Atlantic and Warner.

The second was buying Interscope, the hip-hop record label that flourished in the 1990s thanks to gangsta rap. Interscope was available to Bronfman because its previous owner, Warner Music, had certain image issues. In the wake of the Ice-T "Cop Killer" controversy, Time Warner shareholders railed that too much hip-hop was profane. C. DeLores Tucker, head of the National Political Congress of Black Women, made it a personal crusade to prevent Interscope's next album, Tha Dogg Pound's *Dogg Food*, from coming out. (It was actually quite a tame album, by gangsta rap standards, although it did contain a song subtitled "Bitch Azz Niggaz.") Bob Dole, then a US senator and Republican presidential candidate, accused Time Warner of putting out musical "nightmares of depravity." Time Warner caved. It divested from Interscope.

That left Interscope on the free market, and Bronfman's company scooped it up. Bronfman got lucky. The head of Interscope was Jimmy Iovine. Born in Brooklyn, Iovine was the son of a longshoreman. He'd started his career in the music business at age nineteen, as a gofer in a Times Square studio—and was fortunate enough to befriend John Lennon early on. "If you bring somebody tea one hundred times and get it right each time, they get to like you," Iovine liked to say. He used his connections to get close to Jon Landau, Bruce Springsteen's well-connected manager. Iovine was a hardworking engineer for a demanding singer in the process of agonizing over his classic 1975 album *Born to Run*. Iovine survived the experience and parlayed it into important studio gigs with U2, Tom Petty and the Heartbreakers, and Dire Straits. Iovine talked fast, tough, and funny. When members of Interscope band U2 told him one day the band wanted to make house music, he responded, "You don't want to make *house music*. You want to make music to *buy a house with*."

In the 1980s, Iovine had befriended Ted Field, heir to the Marshall Field family, who had moved to Hollywood to open a film production company. With an initial stake of $15 million from Field, the pair founded Interscope Records in 1990. Two fortuitous events made Interscope a player: Marion "Suge" Knight founded Death Row Records, and he recruited Andre "Dr. Dre" Young from the Compton, California, gangsta rap group N.W.A. Knight was pure muscle. In order to release Dr. Dre from his contract with his old label, N.W.A. member Eric "Eazy-E" Wright's Ruthless Records, Knight and some friends allegedly showed up at the Ruthless offices with pipes and bats. (Knight has denied this.) Later, in September 1996, video cameras in a Las Vegas hotel lobby captured Knight and one of his artists, megastar rapper Tupac Shakur, beating a rival from another gang. (Shakur was not a gang member; Knight had been affiliated with a sect of the Bloods dating to his roots in Compton.) About two hours after the beating, in an incident that may or may not have been related, Shakur was shot and mortally wounded in the passenger seat of a BMW sedan. (Knight was driving.) Knight's assault, a parole violation, ultimately landed him in prison for five years.

In the early days of Interscope, nobody wanted to touch Knight's label, even though it was about to release a sure hit, Dre's solo debut *The Chronic*. But Iovine entered into a distribution agreement with Death Row. Of course, Iovine himself never engaged in Suge Knight's questionable business practices, but there's no question he made a lot of money off them. "He did a deal with the devil," says a music business source. Ultimately, the Death Row–Interscope connection gave Iovine a working relationship—and lifelong friendship—with Dr. Dre, who turned out to be a hip-hop production genius and talent scout extraordinaire. Thanks to Dre, Iovine signed Eminem, 50 Cent, G-Unit, and D12 to his Aftermath label, whose products were distributed by Interscope. By 2005, these artists had sold a combined 61.6 million albums in the United States.

Universal was the House That Dre Built, and it was a big house. In the post-iTunes era, when almost everybody else was reeling, the label became the hit machine Warner, Sony BMG, and EMI had once been and were unlikely to be again. Its market share hovered around 30 percent in the US, more than double that of its competitors—although Sony and BMG came close to catching up after the merger. "Many people say these [record] companies are a bunch of ugly ducklings," Doug Morris said in 2005, less than a year after his company released holiday season blockbusters by Eminem, U2, Gwen Stefani, and Shania Twain. "I don't feel that way. I feel our company is a Tiffany company."

Universal was the most obvious and widespread success in the post-iTunes era, but there were others. Fox's hit reality show *American Idol* was a starmaking machine, turning unknowns like Kelly Clarkson, Clay Aiken, Carrie Underwood, and Daughtry into CD-sales juggernauts for Clive Davis's J and Arista labels. Disney took a page from Lou Pearlman's book and created a new wave of teen pop superstars, building the *High School Musical* soundtrack into 2006's best-selling CD and following up with recording stars such as Ashley Tisdale of *High School Musical*, Miley Cyrus of *Hannah Montana*, and the Jonas Brothers. And it turned out the internet, despite its unfortunate tendency to enable worldwide piracy, was a pretty good marketing tool. YouTube and MySpace broke numerous artists, including OK Go, for EMI, and pop singer Colbie Caillat, for Universal. TV commercials—taboo for pop and rock musicians for years until Sting sat in a Jaguar in the late 1990s—started to pay off. Newer acts can make roughly $2,500 per TV or movie license, while veterans routinely pull in as much as $3,000 for TV shows, $100,000 for movies, and $25,000 for commercials. Video games from *Madden NFL* to *Guitar Hero* generate the same kinds of paydays, with a promise of even greater exposure, since players can listen to these same songs a collective 1 billion times or more. *Guitar Hero* and *Rock Band* sold a combined 14.8 million copies in 2008. Fans have paid two dollars each to download roughly 44 million songs, by artists from Aerosmith to Mötley Crüe, during the brief history of those games. Universal's partnership with Apple Computer led to publicity via iPod and iTunes ads and extra sales for U2, the Black Eyed Peas, and Mary J. Blige.

If these opportunities were good news during a dismal time, ringtones were extraordinarily good news. With cell phone users all around the world using customized snippets of music as fashion accessories, worldwide ringtone revenues jumped from $3.2 billion in 2004 to $4 billion in 2005, according to Juniper Research. Crazy Frog's "Axel F" hit No. 1 on the British music charts—as a ringtone.

But the malaise finally caught up to Universal. Eminem retired. Jay-Z retired. Then he came back, but without the same sales power. (Jay-Z stepped down in early 2008 from his post as president of Universal's Def Jam Records; according to the *New York Times*, the label did not want to boost his previous salary, which had amounted to a total of $10 million.) Watching the *Billboard* pop charts every week started to feel like counting the dead. An album thought to have smash-hit potential would make a strong first-week debut, then plunge the following week—such as Alicia Keys's *As I Am*, which hit record stores before Thanksgiving 2007, sold 742,000 copies in its first week, then dropped by 53 percent the following week. And when there were no Alicia-level hits? Well, those weeks were just ugly.* In one week in January 2007, the *Dreamgirls* soundtrack sold 66,000 copies, the lowest for a No. 1 album since SoundScan started keeping track of these things in 1991. For Universal, Christmas 2007 was a disaster. Expected hits from Eminem, the Pussycat Dolls' Nicole Scherzinger, and Mariah Carey (who by now had relocated from her post–Tommy Mottola label, EMI, to Antonio "LA" Reid's Island Def Jam) failed to materialize.

---

* In the October 2008 *Blender*, Oasis's Noel Gallagher talked trash on this subject: "Can I just point out that [1997's] *Be Here Now* did sell 9.5 million copies? If any band sells 9.5 million albums this year, I'll fucking shit in my trousers."

Labels began to drop their facade of sunny optimism. In a late 2007 conference call announcing that Warner Music Group's fourth-quarter profits had plunged an astonishing 58 percent, Bronfman declared it "a year of real challenge in the recorded music industry" and announced CD sales were rough and digital sales were slower than expected.

Universal laid off more employees after that. Island Def Jam Records fired a dozen or so people, including a onetime rock savant, A&R man Rob Stevenson, who had signed hit bands like Fall Out Boy and the Killers, which suffered through sophomore slumps during a critical business period in 2007. Geffen, Interscope, and Sony BMG followed with dozens more layoffs. And as of this writing, EMI was rumored to be hacking dozens more employees. "Going into a major record label is like you've just boarded a plane where the pilot is at 30,000 feet and announces you're going to be making a water landing. And everybody has their heads between their knees," says Jamie Kitman, manager of OK Go, which records for the EMI-owned label Capitol Records. "I mean, it's grim." From 2000 to 2007, the music business laid off 5,000 employees.

Many have adapted to this carnage. Simon Baeyertz lost his job as head of international affairs for V2 Records when the company restructured in 2007; today he and his wife are building El Blok, a 22-room hotel and bar in Vieques, an island off Puerto Rico. Robert Wieger was vice president of marketing for Atlantic Records until he was downsized in the AOL Time Warner merger in 2001; as door captain at the Bacara Resort & Spa, in Santa Barbara, California, he occasionally encounters hotel guests he used to work with, such as singer Barry Manilow. Barry Feldman, who used to oversee blues and jazz reissues at record labels from Verve to Columbia, perceived no future in the music business after the 2004 Sony-BMG merger and quit to become a full-time financial adviser.

Then there's Debbie Southwood-Smith, whose indoctrination into the record business began when she was a promotional secretary at MCA Records in the 1980s. She moved up the old-fashioned way—scouring dingy New York City nightclubs for the best talent, finding a few worthy candidates, and turning them into hits. One of them—Blessid Union of Souls, a Cincinnati rock band—caught on when its hit "I Believe" dominated radio playlists in the early 1990s. The success gave her a golden ticket for A&R jobs at major record labels. She was good at finding and nurturing bands, and over a twenty-year career with EMI, A&M, and Interscope, she worked with Uncle Tupelo, the Yeah Yeah Yeahs, Queens of the Stone Age, and Monster Magnet. She loved it, holding court at concerts in her spiky blond hairdos, Chuck Taylors poking out from underneath her dresses. It was what she was meant to do.

One of the last things Southwood-Smith did as an A&R executive at Interscope was sign TV on the Radio, a spacey, experimental, electronic rock band she was always convinced could turn into the next R.E.M. given time, resources, and patience. She never got to finish the project, though, because her boss, A&R executive Mark Williams, badgered her to meet with him one day in November 2005. When they finally sat down in her office, he closed the door and said, "We have to talk." She rolled her eyes and said, "Now what?" He laid her off. "Rock records aren't selling," he said, "so we're firing rock A&R people." By December 2007, Williams was gone, too. "I was a woman who could find, like, *art* artists and make them commercially viable," Southwood-Smith says. "And there wasn't room for that too much anymore."

So what do you do when you work for the record business and the record business collapses? "If you spent twenty years in the music business, like I did—I started as a kid, and I'm forty-four now—we're not trained in anything else. That's our skill set," she says. "But I'm lucky. I only have an English professor boyfriend, and we only have, like, cats and dogs."

Southwood-Smith enrolled at Fairleigh-Dickinson University to get her education degree and, in September 2008, was to become an English teacher at Ferris High School in Jersey City, New Jersey. It turns out even a forty-four-year-old woman can speak to teenagers if she has spent her adult life signing bands that appeal to teenagers. "Maybe something will come along in the entertainment field that will speak to me," she says. "But if that happens or not, I still need something to fall back on."

Big Music's Big Mistakes, Part 8

Sony BMG's Rootkit

The Bad Plus, a jazz trio that turns rock and pop hits like Nirvana's "Smells Like Teen Spirit" into bebop workouts, never planned to sign to a major record label. But when a Columbia Records scout caught a concert at the Village Vanguard in 2002 and offered a contract, the band went for it. At first, the deal went perfectly. The Bad Plus's Columbia debut sold 53,000 copies. The follow-up did a respectable 34,000. In 2005, the band released what it regarded as its best record, *Suspicious Activity?*, and hit a very hard wall.

That wall was called a *rootkit,* a series of files that would infiltrate a computer's registry, the internal brain that allows Windows to operate a computer. A rootkit, according to *Technology Review,* is "software that tricks an operating system into overlooking worms, viruses, and any other files a hacker might want to conceal inside a user's computer." When rootkit files work successfully, they provide a passageway for outside hackers to install viruses and other malicious programs onto somebody else's system. To the shock of the Bad Plus—as well as other artists such as veteran singer-songwriters Neil Diamond and Burt Bacharach, Trey

Anastasio of Phish, and Southern rockers Van Zant—Sony BMG released 4.7 million CDs containing rootkits between January and November 2005. Many of these problematic discs actually allowed malicious programs, like a Trojan horse called Troj/Stinx-E, to hide themselves on computers. But most computers merely slowed down, crashed, or wound up with unworkable CD drives.

How could Sony BMG have let this happen? The simple answer is that the label's high-tech executives wanted to limit illegal copying and online piracy. The newly merged label's tech executives had hired two companies, First 4 Internet and SunnComm, to install copy protection on fifty-two CD titles so consumers who tried to pirate them or make excessive copies would hit a speed bump. First 4 Internet, a British company, achieved this with a program called extended Copy Protection, or XCP. This was the heart of the issue: XCP installed the rootkit without informing users first.

At first, when the CDs came out in record stores, few noticed the software's presence. But Mark Russinovich, a computer security expert in Austin, Texas, realized his computer was performing oddly, dug up the files from deep within the registry, and posted reports on his blog. Thanks to the tech-news website Slashdot, Sony BMG's use of rootkits quickly blew up in the company's face. Hundreds of consumers posted complaints on Amazon message boards, many of which reflected this sentiment from a Neil Diamond fan: "My sister and I will no longer buy any

Sony products because of this blatant abuse of her trust. Neil, she's not buying any more of your music, either, unless you switch companies." Taken by surprise, Sony BMG's top executives handled the crucial early damage control exactly wrong. Thomas Hesse, president of the label's global digital business, said in a National Public Radio interview: "Most people, I think, don't even know what a rootkit is, so why should they care about it?" *Because it damages our computers!* thousands of CD buyers must have said to themselves. This lack of empathy reinforced Napster-era beliefs that the music industry was more interested in suing and punishing its customers than catering to them. Sony BMG stars like the Dave Matthews Band and Foo Fighters rushed to decry the rootkit-infected CDs on their websites, and Johnny Van Zant and Switchfoot bassist Tim Foreman expressed their hurt and confusion in media interviews.

Eventually, Sony BMG backed off from Hesse's smug position, apologizing and issuing a patch for users to fix the problem. But the damage had been done. Music fans distanced themselves from the rootkit-infected titles, wreaking havoc on their sales figures. Neil Diamond's *12 Songs* had made its debut on the pop charts at No. 4 the week before the rootkit story broke, and its sales never recovered. "It was the highest debut of Neil's career, off to a great start. But Columbia—it was some kind of corporate thing—had put spyware on the CD," the album's producer, Rick Rubin, who later became Columbia's president, told the *New York Times Magazine*. "We came out on a Tuesday, by the following week the CD was not available. Columbia released it again in a month, but we never recovered. Neil was furious."

"It seemed to us that the record was just tainted on some basic level," adds Ethan Iverson, pianist for the Bad Plus, which has since left Columbia. "We expected some of the attention paid to our previous two releases to be paid to it and instead it just had this patent of evil to it. The record company didn't push it at all. How could they, really?"

To really understand why Sony BMG allowed the rootkit debacle to happen, you have to understand the history of copy protection itself. Since Napster, major labels had spent countless amounts of money trying to prevent fans from bootlegging their CDs. "If you shed a tear for every dollar spent, you could fill the Pacific," says Talal Shamoon, head of a digital rights management company called Intertrust, which once worked closely with labels on copy protection. The labels' first few attempts were failures—a Céline Dion CD crashed in 2002 whenever fans tried to load it into their computer drives, and some hackers later claimed they could overcome a certain copy protection by drawing on the disc with a marker. So technologists on Sony BMG's staff felt pressured to do an even better job. "That's why the technology was used," says a source familiar with the situation. "Anything less than that could be defeated by a marker and the companies look stupid." When they hired the British company First 4 Internet, Sony BMG executives hadn't intended to go as far as rootkit, but they did want to use "something deep," according to the source.

It's not clear exactly who at Sony BMG authorized the rootkit—and it's not clear whether First 4 Internet installed the hidden files on purpose. The company's job was simply to equip the CDs with copy protection. Security experts quoted in *Technology Review*, however, insist the company's programmers had to have known what they were doing.

Bill Whitmore, chief executive officer at SunnComm at the time, later said his company worked with new-media staffers at BMG (before its merger with Sony) to arrange a workable copy-protection technology called MediaMax. SunnComm, Whitmore argued, did thorough testing and due diligence, ensuring nothing would go wrong on consumers' computers once MediaMax came out. Then came the Sony-BMG merger, in 2004, and suddenly the two technology departments started competing with each other. In Whitmore's recollection, certain Sony employees, acting arrogant and competitive, rushed to make an alternative deal with First 4 Internet. Whitmore insisted that's what caused the problems, but his theory is somewhat disingenuous. While he was correct that the SunnComm CDs did not employ a rootkit, per se, MediaMax did install other potentially harmful software on users' computers even if they clicked "no" on a licensing agreement. These files, while not as damaging, behaved similarly to the rootkit, potentially allowing hackers to take over computers. Anyway, regardless of the differences between the two types of software, the rootkit fiasco lumped SunnComm and First 4

Internet together in the eyes of copy-protection opponents. "It took our revenue stream right out from under us and [made us susceptible] to the media barrage," Whitmore said. "We got sucked into this vortex."

Whereas Whitmore laid the fault with Sony employees, a music industry source blamed BMG-side executives such as Thomas Hesse and then—chief operating officer Michael Smellie, who took the copy-protection issues out of the label's hands and executed them at the top, within the merged company's new Global Digital Business department. "When we found out the Neil Diamond record had rootkit technology and was being pulled out of stores, we were devastated and upset—and wanted to know who was responsible," added Steve Greenberg, then president of Sony BMG-owned Columbia Records. "It wasn't like *we* did it." Neither Smellie nor Hesse responded to interview requests; Sony BMG spokespeople refused to comment, and First 4 Internet did not return calls or emails.

Even Sony BMG insiders came to realize the rootkit aftershock was devastating to the company, and the industry at large. In the short term, Sony BMG recalled a total of 4.7 million CDs, costing the company $2 million to $4 million. In the long term, the company wound up settling fifteen class actions, costing the company another $50 million. And in the even longer term, CD copy protection, which had been a central part of major labels' digital strategies since before Napster, was suddenly dead, tainted with the stink of rootkit. "They don't do it anymore," Greenberg says. "I would actually point to that as the beginning of the mind-shift that led to the abandonment of digital rights management." At the very least, label execs stopped tossing dollars into the ocean of copy protection, and started thinking about how to profit from music with no copy protection. It was a good change, but much too late.

Chapter 7
The Future

How Can the Record Labels Return to the Boom Times? Hint: Not by Stonewalling New High-tech Models and Locking Up the Content

THE REST of the record business thought Eric Nicoli was nuts. And maybe he was. Or maybe he just had nothing to lose. The chief executive officer of EMI Group, the seventy-six-year-old major label that was home to pop superstars from the Beatles to Radiohead, called an April 2, 2007, press conference at his company headquarters in London. Wearing an open-necked light-pink shirt tucked into his slacks, Nicoli sat in an atrium with Steve Jobs, chief executive officer of Apple Computer, at his side in his trademark black turtleneck and jeans. A British band, the Good, the Bad, and the Queen, performed two songs. Employees crowded onto glass balconies overlooking the stage. Nicoli then announced that after almost a decade of doing everything it could think of to lock up songs so consumers couldn't rip them into MP3s or trade them over the internet, the smallest of the four major labels would release most of its catalog online with no copyright protection whatsoever. These songs would be available via Jobs's iTunes Music Store at a slightly higher price—$1.29 rather than the standard 99 cents—allowing consumers to play them on a Microsoft Zune, Creative Labs Zen, or whatever instead of just an iPod. "In all of our research, consumers tell us overwhelmingly that they would be prepared to pay a higher price for a digital music file that they could use on any player," Nicoli declared. "It's clear to us that interoperability is important to music buyers and is the key to unlocking and energizing the digital business."

Nicoli, fifty-six at the time, had a reputation for shaking up major industries. He began his career as a physicist, then shifted to the food service industry in England in the early 1970s. As a twenty-six-year-old marketer for British confectioner Rowntree's, he noticed a niche in the chocolate marketplace and invented the Yorkie and the Lion Bar, both of which turned into best-sellers. But Nicoli was merely the figurehead for EMI's decision to sell MP3s. The person behind the scenes was Barney Wragg, who started his career booking Happy Mondays shows in Manchester, England, in the late 1980s. He worked for a while as an A&R man but shifted to a microprocessor company because the pay was better, and he wound up making music-business contacts at SDMI meetings. With this double-barreled background, he became a senior vice president for digital music at Universal Music in 2001.

For a time, Wragg bought into the record industry's conventional wisdom. He went along as the industry attempted to upgrade from the CD format to difficult-to-pirate, high-audio-quality SACD or DVD-Audio albums. When that didn't work, Wragg went along with digital rights management, the copyright protection allowing consumers to buy a song online but play it only on certain devices or stereos. Yet he watched helplessly as music fans, despite the industry's efforts to stop them, continued to rip CDs and download MP3s by the millions.

Wragg left Universal in 2005, spent a half year thinking and came up with this conclusion: "I realized that as an industry we'd kind of been smoking crack." Wragg was hardly the first in the business to think this way. After almost eight years of stonewalling MP3s and Napster, major label employees gradually accepted the fact that freely selling digital music was the blueprint for survival. EMI's decision to sell MP3s was a step in this direction—as would be Amazon's MP3 Store, MySpace Music, and the Radiohead model of giving away music online. But labels were still a long way from overcoming their outdated ideas. They clung stubbornly to long-held beliefs that selling millions of pieces of plastic would return them to massive profits.

With this in mind, in summer 2006, Wragg took a job as head of digital for EMI. Storied history aside, EMI had been struggling since 2001. That was the year Mariah Carey, who'd escaped Tommy Mottola and Sony Music and landed with EMI-owned Virgin Records, put out her catastrophic movie *Glitter*, then withdrew from public view with what she called a nervous breakdown. Carey's antics shell-shocked Virgin to the extent that the label handed her $28 million just to leave. Not only that, one of the label's most promising artists, R&B and movie star Aaliyah, died in a plane crash, taking with her several label executives who'd been her traveling companions. More than any other label, EMI seemed bedeviled by piracy and the lack of a profitable internet business model.

But unlike at Universal, EMI's executive staff was small and nimble enough to change its long-standing digital-music policies. Wragg went to work. He did research and conducted studies about consumers' preferences, started a partnership with Apple and spoke regularly with Steve Jobs and iTunes executive Eddy Cue, made deals with digital retailers, and finally presented his plan to EMI's board. The board quickly agreed.

EMI's big announcement may not have seemed like much to fans of online music. What was the big deal? Napster had taught an entire generation of kids to rip the digital music from their totally unprotected compact discs and swap the resulting MP3s for free online. But within the record industry, EMI's decision was like dropping a bomb. Until that point, the most forward-thinking top record executive had been Edgar Bronfman Jr. of Warner Music, and his speeches at the time were filled with phrases like "there is no logical reason to abandon DRM," or digital rights management. If the movie industry could protect DVDs from sailing willy-nilly over the internet, so, then, could the record labels, Bronfman argued. Many of his colleagues privately agreed. "In a moment of desperation, [EMI] enabled the eight-hundred-pound gorilla that really didn't need enabling," declared a source at another major label.

In fact, the results of the MP3 decision weren't very impressive. EMI's digital album sales went up less than 1 percent from 2006 to 2007, according to Nielsen SoundScan, and its digital song sales dropped by roughly the same amount. Industry-wide, digital sales rose 46 percent in 2007, a big jump, but not if you consider they went up 65 percent the previous year. Less than four months after Eric Nicoli's big announcement, the British equity firm Terra Firma bought EMI for almost $5 billion. Nicoli was out, accepting a buyout package of almost $6 million. Terra Firma's Guy Hands, a specialist in buying failing companies and turning them around, was in. After he took over, Hands circulated a memo to investors accusing Nicoli of being the most flamboyant kind of old-school record executive. According to the memo, while Nicoli headed the company, he spent almost $12 million on a rarely used three-bedroom townhouse in Park Lane, London, as well as some $40,000 supplying his Los Angeles apartment with candles and flowers. The memo accused Nicoli of spending $400,000 annually on flowers and fruit for the company's London headquarters and said his management cost EMI roughly $200 million a year. (Both before and after he left, Nicoli refused requests for interviews.) Wragg was out, too, leaving the company in 2008 for reasons he wouldn't divulge.

Then a weird thing happened. The rest of the major labels *joined* EMI in doing the same thing they swore they would never do. Steve Jobs was responsible for their decision.

In early 2007, Apple controlled 70 percent of the digital music market through the iTunes Music Store. Jobs was still irritated, though, that labels had forced him into a digital rights management scheme when he'd made his first content deals five years earlier. What he *didn't* say was that FairPlay—the copy protection that comes embedded in iTunes digital downloads, preventing users from playing their music on more than five computers and so forth—benefited Apple far more than it benefited the labels. It had the effect of locking iTunes customers into iPod portable music players; thanks to FairPlay, somebody who bought a Microsoft Zune or a Creative Labs Zen couldn't buy or store music on iTunes and transfer it to the foreign player. European regulators complained that Jobs was using this scheme to corner the digital music market unfairly. Jobs responded by blaming the labels. He posted an 1,800-word manifesto on apple.com, arguing for a music world free of DRM. "The music industry might experience an influx of new companies willing to invest in innovative new stores and players," Jobs wrote. "This can only be seen as a positive by the music companies."

It took a while, but ultimately the labels took Jobs's advice and used it to create competition for iTunes. Jobs was rigid about certain things—99 cents for a single, no sales of songs bundled together—but he could get away with that only if he controlled the market. Labels wanted competing stores, like Amazon, to take some of Jobs's control away. Then they would have the clout, perhaps, to raise online prices or sell songs as bundles. In this spirit, Universal Music made a huge swath of its catalog, from U2 to Eminem to Motown, available with no digital rights management. When Universal's contract expired with iTunes, the company reupped, but only on a month-to-month basis. By summer 2007, the executives threw their support behind Amazon's new MP3 Store. Warner Music was next, announcing in late December 2007 that it would reverse course on DRM and make its entire catalog available, too, via Amazon. Within a few weeks, Sony BMG realized it had no choice and sent its catalog to the online bookseller as well. Suddenly, Amazon was in the digital music game, offering a one-of-a-kind retail experience—

a store where 3 million MP3s, for 79 to 99 cents each, supplemented through-the-mail CD sales. And it had all the big names, from 50 Cent to Madonna. "My instinct is it will beef up the digital sales pretty significantly. I've used it a hell of a lot," says Ian Rogers, general manager of Yahoo! Music until he stepped down in early 2008. "I bought eight Zeppelin albums over the weekend and it took no time at all to drop eighty bucks. It just hasn't been that easy in the past. You have to ask yourself for the first time: 'Do I want to buy it or do I want to steal it?'"

Rogers is no fan of the iTunes Music Store, which he dismisses as a "spreadsheet that plays music." But Amazon's MP3 Store has given him newfound optimism, not just for the selling of digital music but also for a shift in long-standing major label behavior. "All the stuff we've been saying is going to happen, the last ten years, now is finally happening," he says. "The record companies are all realizing they're not in the CD business anymore. The fact that that's not a controversial thing for me to say anymore is incredible."

In June 2008, Rhapsody, the subscription service, also began selling MP3. Surreally, for high-tech experts who've been dealing with executives at major labels since Napster, the response they started getting in 2007 was no longer a simple, polite "*No*."

The overwhelming mantra at major labels has become *digital*. "Digital isn't the future—it's today. And we're evolving very quickly because of it," said Tom Corson, general manager and executive vice president of the RCA Music Group, which puts out music by Alicia Keys, Christina Aguilera, and others. "People became very fluent in digital. As the industry contracted and the digital business grew, you have a situation where you're either a digital person or you're gone, on some level." As a result, when BMG released Keys's hit album *As I Am* in late 2007, it wasn't solely in the CD format—there were digital singles and albums for iTunes and Rhapsody, 30-second snippets for mobile phone ringtones, shorter snippets for ringbacks, images for background "wallpaper" on phone screens, and certain digital video tracks distributed both for free on YouTube and MySpace and for sale via iTunes. As of July 2008, *As I Am* had rebounded from its poor second week and sold more than 3.5 million copies (CDs and digital albums combined).

Warner's Bronfman, ever the optimist, gave frequent speeches playing up these new revenue streams. He sees huge potential for ringtone sales in underdeveloped markets like South Korea and Malaysia. He envisions a massive business in which music fans download entire songs, not just ringtones, onto iPhones, LG Shines, Samsung Juke U470s, or Nokia N81 Blues. In December 2007, Nokia announced an extraordinary partnership with Universal Music, something that would have been unthinkable just a year or two before. Subscribers to the cell phone carrier's "Comes with Music" program outside the US were to be able to download all the music they wanted, via certain types of mobile phones, for a year, beginning sometime in late 2008. (Sony BMG and Warner later joined Nokia's program.) The music would come with digital rights management, meaning it would be extremely difficult for users to transfer songs from their phones to an iPod or other device—or burn the music to a blank CD. But it's still a forward-thinking idea for a major label that had spent the past decade with extreme allergies to free online music.

For record labels, mobile music is a far less dangerous animal than online music. It's difficult, if not impossible, to hack a cell phone and liberate the copyrighted music inside for anyone to share. As a result, executives at record labels have become accustomed to big, easy profits from stuff people buy through their cell phones. At first, in the late 1990s, ringtones were a profit center exclusively for the song-publishing industry, which received a royalty every time a cell phone user bought one of those tinny-sounding, computerized tones. The major labels, which own most of the master recordings for familiar hit records, plunged into the market in the early 2000s. This was when the technology advanced to "real tones," or high-fidelity snippets of actual recordings. Over the last five or six years, labels' A&R departments have participated far more heavily in creating tones out of their song catalogs. This market initially seemed limitless. Ringtone revenues jumped from $68 million in 2003 to $600 million in 2006, according to BMI. "We see no sign of it slowing down right now, that's for sure," Rio Caraeff, vice president of Universal's US mobile division, said in late 2006. "The bottom line is the business is exploding day upon day, week upon week."

Thus, labels have spent the last few years sending their biggest artists into the studio to make generous side dishes of ringtones to go with what is still the main course—the compact disc. Green Day was among the first to make ringtones while working on its 2004 CD, *American Idiot*. 50 Cent, Paul Wall, and Pretty Ricky soon followed, with Mariah Carey and Mary J. Blige creating original ringtones as part of a 2006 Pepsi-Motorola promotion. Hip-hop has been especially ripe for ringtone exposure—Dem Franchize Boyz, Soulja Boy, and Hurricane

Chris even co-opt tiny, ringtone-style hooks into their musical styles. Black Eyed Peas' "My Humps" has sold more than 2 million ringtones, helping the hip-hop band's *Monkey Business* CD reach 6.5 million copies; Dem Franchize Boyz started putting out tones in July 2006, selling 1.5 million not long before their CD *On Top of Our Game* debuted on the *Billboard* charts at No. 5. The Zomba Record Group sold 2.3 million copies of R&B singer and rapper T-Pain's "Buy U A Drank" in 2007; the resulting publicity and cross-marketing helped his CD debut at No. 1 on the charts that year. Even longtime ringtone holdouts such as AC/DC, Led Zeppelin, and the Dave Matthews Band finally agreed to put out their music in this format in late 2007.

"You're doing it for the person who's in the mall and their phone rings. You have to be conscious about how to translate to a phone and how it translates to a melody in a clear way," says will.i.am, producer and frontman for Black Eyed Peas. "It's a new way for people to listen to music and appreciate it. It's another way for people to hear it."

Warner's Bronfman and others believe ringtones are one primary reason major labels will ultimately turn their business around. Ringtone sales are especially strong outside the United States, in countries such as South Korea, where Warner created a joint venture with the country's primary telecom service, SK Telecom, in 2006. One of the first celebrity guinea pigs for this experiment was South Korean pop star Baek Ji Young, who put out 416 separate digital products, from ringtones to album art. In countries like China, where the government ignores US copyright laws and looks the other way when people and companies engage in bootlegging and piracy, labels see potential for a huge expansion in the piracy-resistant ringtone market. And in countries like Brazil, where far more people use mobile phones than personal computers, labels see potential for selling even more ringtones. Puerto Rican pop star Ricky Martin took advantage of this market in early 2007 when his label, Sony BMG, offered his album for sale via memory card loaded onto a mobile phone just before he performed at sold-out stadiums throughout Latin America. Juanes offered his latest album, *La Vida Es . . . Un Ratico*, a similar way, selling 6 million digital tracks (including ringtones and digital singles) the week before the official release hit stores. "It is a huge, huge, huge piece of the business and it's growing rapidly," says an industry source. "Any executive watching their stock and what they're selling is going to be completely all over this stuff."

But the explosive ringtone market carries the disturbing whiff of fad. Studies from Jupiter Research and M:Metrics indicate monthly purchases are down in both the US and Europe, and huge ringtone companies such as Berlin's Jamba and Paris's Musiwave have diversified into video games and graphics. "It doesn't seem like anything that's going to have a long-term sustained growth," says Peter Paterno, attorney for Metallica and Dr. Dre. "I mean, what's wrong with a [traditional] ring?" The idea of buying a 30-second snippet of a song for $2.99 when the entire song is available on iTunes for 99 cents has appealed to mobile-phone enthusiasts since roughly 2003. Can it last? "People say, 'Ringtones are fashion,'" says Mark Donovan, a senior analyst for M:Metrics. "That makes some sense, but it's not clear it will carry [record labels] into the future." Another big problem: Services like XingTone, which allow music fans to fashion their own tones out of digital songs rather than buying readymade ones, are getting easier and easier to use.

So why sell just snippets of songs over the phone? Why not sell the whole song? The iPhone was a blockbuster hit throughout 2007 and 2008, even though its music-playing capabilities weren't nearly as impressive as those of the iPod. In addition, Nokia and Sony Ericsson announced they would open mobile-music stores in 2008. Moreover, several phone devices have emerged on the market that sync with internet radio stations, and subscription services such as Napster and Rhapsody are available via mobile as well. Some in the music industry salivate over such massive potential—why even put up with Steve Jobs and his iThings when a record label can shift its mobile-music market to some of the 991 million portable phones sold worldwide in 2006? But much of this remains theoretical. "I don't think the research indicates, at least that I've seen, that people are using their mobile phones the way they're using their iPods or other music devices," says a major label source. "The number of mobile phones may greatly outweigh the number of iPods—but consumers may not care." This source adds that cell phones could conceivably take over the music market from the iPod, but labels and high-tech companies need to work out some thorny issues first—like the fact that an internet download sells for 99 cents while a full mobile song goes for $2 or $3. There's also the issue of changing consumer behavior—people *like* their iTunes libraries. Why would they switch to a model where they'd have to buy new songs on the phone? For now, labels focus on ringtones, and new ideas like embedding music into wireless games.

Here's another industry-saving sales model, at least according to people in the industry: subscriptions. But subscriptions aren't exactly a new idea. Rhapsody, Yahoo! Music, and others have for years offered some version of this type of service whereby music fans pay a monthly fee of anywhere from $9 to $16 for an unlimited number of songs, and pretty much anything they could ever want would be available. "It's mind-blowing—I'm listening to music constantly," Rick Rubin, the veteran producer who took over as Columbia Records president in early 2007, told *Rolling Stone*. (The article also included endorsements from U2 manager Paul McGuinness and Lollapalooza cofounder Marc Geiger.) "I had been talking about the subscription model based on theory, and now I will tell you that in practice it is even better." Rubin said he favored Rhapsody, which cost between $13 and $15 for a catalog of 4.5 million songs, as well as the Sonos service, which streamed music through speakers scattered throughout the house. "If you're a massive music fan, the 99-cent-per-song thing doesn't work, because it creates this barrier to discovery: 'Well, I might like that artist, but I'm going to have to pay 99 cents,'" added Ted Cohen, the influential former high-tech executive at EMI. "Whereas I'm a massive fan of Rhapsody and I think there'll be a better version: I want to hear Todd Rundgren *right now*, I type in 'Todd Rundgren,' and get it *right now*. And based on that, it throws the New Radicals at me. It's about recommendations and filters and playlists and music being presented to me for my enjoyment continually. It's really about overserving me with music that I like." Universal is betting high on the idea; in late 2007, the company floated Total Music, a subscription plan in which the label would license music to other services and compete with Apple and iTunes. Universal executives were hoping to get hardware companies and cell phone carriers to absorb the cost of a $5 subscription, so customers wouldn't have to deal with the increase. Nokia's Comes with Music phones were to be part of this program, although neither Universal nor Nokia spokespeople would comment on the terms of the deal.

The catch: Subscription services, as they stand, are rental models. You can listen to the stuff you buy on certain cell phones or portable players, like Microsoft's Zune, but you can't transfer it to your permanent collection. That's a big hurdle for consumers, especially the old folks who grew up actually buying LPs and CDs in stores. Another huge minus is that Jobs has never been a fan, which means there's no subscription model that works on the iPod.*

The subscription service Rhapsody is Exhibit A in *The Long Tail*, the best-selling 2006 book by *Wired* editor-in-chief Chris Anderson. In the book, Anderson envisions a snake-shaped vision of the market, with the "short head" containing *Thriller* or the latest smash Justin Timberlake album. The long tail contains endless obscurities, serving every possible subculture and obsessive interest. Anderson outlines what will almost certainly be a profitable model for selling and marketing songs and records. But it's not what the record industry wants to hear. "I passed out twenty copies of Chris's book," said Erin Yasgar, who, when *The Long Tail* came out, was head of new media for Universal-owned Interscope Records. "Some of the people read it and said, 'That's not us. That's not our model.'"

Rather than clinging to *Thriller*-style hits beloved by everyone, Anderson suggested, the record industry ought to embrace a new idea: Music companies should profit by selling millions of small, niche items. In the digital world, huge hits, chained as they are to dwindling physical shelf space in stores like Wal-Mart, would become less important. Meanwhile, online services such as Rhapsody, Netflix, and Amazon carry countless millions of titles, all profitable with low-cost distribution.

Terry McBride, manager of Canadian stars Barenaked Ladies, Sarah McLachlan, and Avril Lavigne, has high hopes for this vision of the future. Digital sales, he insisted, are potentially far more profitable than CDs ever were. They carry almost no overhead expenses in warehouses, crates, or record stores; McBride predicted that once record labels allow their prices to drop even farther, to something like 25 cents, there will be another music business boom. "You want to take a record label profitable quickly? Don't sign any new artists. Just sell the catalog. You will be instantly profitable," he says. "Now it's much easier for someone to find something they basically want. It's not like the old days,

---

* In early 2008, a story landed in the *Financial Times*, citing unnamed sources, speculating that Jobs had come around to the idea of subscription sales. Apple refused to comment, and several sources interviewed for this book speculated that the *Times* article was a trial balloon floated by record executives. Regardless, as of mid-2008, Apple had yet to act on the subscription idea.

where you had to talk to the person behind the counter at Tower with a Mohawk and you wanted to find a jazz album."

Five years ago, according to McBride, almost all the executives at major record labels refused to listen to such evil talk. Their goal was to protect the old model—what *The Long Tail*'s Anderson calls "the tyranny of geography," in which consumers have access only to the limited shelf space within a few miles of their homes. In that economic model, a CD that costs $15 in a physical record store makes a nice profit. A digital track for 99 cents, whether it's by Timberlake or the late R&B singer and sax man Eddie "Clean Head" Vinson, does not. Napster could have been a perfect case study of Anderson's *Long Tail* model. Had the labels taken over this kind of service, charging music fans $20 a month for, say, a maximum of 200 tracks, they could have owned the long-tail music model. Sure, fans would have purchased all the Led Zeppelin and Beyoncé tracks they could find in their first few months, but within ten years, they would have dug down to the deepest corners of the major labels' most obscure catalog items. And, the theory goes, they would continue to find music to buy for all eternity.

Rhapsody offers this kind of *Long Tail* promise—a user can stream an unlimited number from a pool of 2.5 million songs. But according to consumer research firm NPD in 2007, Rhapsody-style subscription services attract just 2.5 percent of music consumers. By comparison, iTunes's own-the-song model is at 17 percent. So far, at least, music fans still want to *collect* music. That could change, as kids who grew up with hard drives stuffed with songs rather than shelves of records or CDs in their bedrooms start to dominate the marketplace. When that happens, many say, the record industry better be prepared for the shift. "It's getting better," McBride says. "Some of the senior execs get it, but some of the people who hold power within the corporation don't. They're still fighting it."

Today's version of a Napster-style ownership model, as opposed to a Rhapsody-style rental model, is BitTorrent, a peer-to-peer file-sharing service invented by reclusive Manhattan-born programmer Bram Cohen. His innovation was allowing users to share tiny pieces of music or movie files, which come together as a whole at the end of the download process. It's therefore more efficient and harder to track—and BitTorrent has grown into one of the most popular peer-to-peer services. But a strange thing happened with BitTorrent. Unlike Napster or Kazaa, it didn't receive legal summonses from major record labels or

Hollywood studios. Instead, in early 2007, several big movie companies made a deal with BitTorrent to release their films online as a promotional tool. Ashwin Navin, a former Yahoo! executive who hooked up with Cohen to be a deal maker and media-friendly company spokesperson, then went to the labels to do the same with music. The answer was a 1999-style "*No*." "The music companies were just paralyzed. No one inside these companies was able to make distinctions between good and bad technology," Navin says. "We had one record label tell us, after probably a year of being at their doorstep, they had to wait for the courts to decide on the precedent of another peer-to-peer company before they could engage with us. They were very heavily dependent on litigation, rather than making decisions on their businesses that would allow them to thrive."

By early 2008, the death of the old music business model was almost impossible to miss. When the Nielsen SoundScan sales figures came out for 2007, almost every major number had dropped dramatically, but digital sales were a notable exception to that trend. The top album, Josh Groban's *Noel*, sold just 3,699,000 CDs, about 20,000 fewer than the previous year's best-seller, the *High School Musical 2* soundtrack. Album sales (including CDs and digital albums) were down 15 percent, with steep declines in every genre, from hip-hop to rock to alternative. And that was just the beginning. Tower Records is dead. Some 2,700 music retailers have closed since 2003. Best Buy and Wal-Mart are drastically reducing music shelf space. Virgin Megastore closed its outlet in West Hollywood, California, reducing its number of US stores to just ten. "We're trying to reposition the business," Simon Wright, the chain's chief executive officer in North America, told the Associated Press in late 2007, "and a lot of our stores are too big for the future, primarily due to the drop in music sales."

Radio's future isn't quite as dire as that of record stores, but it's getting there. In the old days—with the help of independent promoters, of course—major labels could count on help from radio programmers to break a range of new artists and use the exposure to sell millions of records. But from fall 1998 to summer 2007, the average number of people listening to US radio has dropped by more than 18 percent, according to Arbitron, with especially precipitous declines in rock formats. Old-school label executives see this trend as crippling for any future model—especially one revolving around low-profit iTunes singles rather than CDs. "It's going to be difficult to make a lot of money off a singles market. You usually record a lot [of music] to get that single—what you usually record for an album. There are ten or nine cuts you paid for," says retired executive Joe Smith, who began his career accepting payola as a DJ in the 1950s before joining the record business and rising to the top of Warner, Elektra, and EMI.

In the end, digital revenue streams and pie-in-the-sky high-tech ideas are unlikely to bring the industry back to its CD-based profit margins of a decade ago. So in 2007, desperate label executives began talking about something called a *360-degree deal*. In this new contractual mode,* rather than just putting out an artist's CD, a label would partner with the artist and take a cut of touring, merchandise, publishing, and maybe even something like a perfume company, if the artist happens to be Gwen Stefani or Madonna. One of the first guinea pigs for this new-fangled type of record deal was Paramore. When the emo-pop band from Franklin, Tennessee, was ready to sign a big-time contract with Atlantic Records in 2005, Paramore had two choices. It could make like just about every other band in the world and share a portion of CD sales with the label, while keeping the profits from concert tickets, tour sponsorship, T-shirt sales, and song publishing purely for itself. Or the band could share everything with Atlantic, so even if CD sales continued to drop, the label would still make money off the band—and still have an incentive to push its singles to radio stations and shell out marketing money. Paramore signed the second kind of deal with Atlantic as well as its longtime partner, Fueled by Ramen, an innovative independent label that sets up successful online merchandise stores and other profitable ventures for its acts. "You have to sacrifice to get somewhere. You have to give up pieces of something to get back something from your work," says singer Hayley Williams. "We've been lucky. It really does feel like a great partnership." In the two and a half years after the band signed its 360-degree deal, Paramore grew into one of the hottest young rock bands in America, playing the Warped main stage in summer 2007, getting MTV airplay at a time when MTV barely ever plays videos, and selling more than 350,000 copies of its *Riot!* CD.

---

* The 360-degree deal isn't exactly new—indies from Motown to Zomba to Wind-Up have participated in a range of revenue streams beyond records for decades. But they've never been standard practice at the biggest record labels, which until recently didn't really need new revenue streams, given the strength of CD and LP sales.

Lawyers for major labels were thrilled about this new development. They rewrote standard contracts to take a piece of these revenue streams. "Say I was considering being the sole investor in a new Italian restaurant being opened by a talented chef," says Steve Greenberg, a former Columbia Records president who today runs Fountains of Wayne's label, S-Curve Records. "And suppose the chef told me that in exchange for putting up all the money and doing all the work marketing the restaurant, he'd share with me the revenue from pizza sales—but not the revenue from sales of pasta, meat, fish, beverages, or anything else on the menu. I can't imagine anyone investing under those terms."

Some artists plunged into 360-degree deals—young bands like Cartel, Cinder Road, American Bang, and Operator figured it was their best shot to make it while major labels still had the clout to influence big-time radio stations and retail stores. "It gives the label more incentive to work hard," says Chris Black, manager of Cartel, which signed with Epic Records. "It gives you that peace of mind to know the label's behind you for financial reasons." Bigger stars started to take this approach as well, only they had more leverage for bigger advances—in 2005, metal stars Korn partnered with EMI and, later, the concert promotion company Live Nation—and received a $25 million payment for a 30 percent stake in all profits. Some in the music business are absolutely convinced this model will float the major record labels for the foreseeable future. "They're going to have to use 360 deals to maintain their status," says Chris Lighty, a longtime hip-hop manager who represents superstars such as 50 Cent, Missy Elliott, and Busta Rhymes. Lighty predicts that, as ever, the record label will be a base for which major music stars will build their brands, using sponsorship deals and appearances in movies and commercials to keep making the big money. To make it in the music business, Lighty says, "You have to have the mind of a record company, the heart of a manager, and almost the soul of an advertiser. It can't just be 'I'm a record man, through and through.' The days of just being a record man aren't putting food on the table."

But the 360-degree model rests on the idea that artists and labels trust each other in a broad, revenue-sharing partnership. And after years of the labels taking mysterious packaged-goods deductions from artists' CD sales and abandoning promising acts that don't make it after the first or second album, artists and their managers are a wee bit mistrustful. The most suspicious ones, such as singer-songwriter Aimee Mann, who has complained to reporters for years about her bad deals from major labels, are going it alone. These days, Mann uses recording technology that is cheaper than ever and makes licensing deals with major distribution companies simply to put her records in stores and post them on iTunes. She gets to keep control of her master recordings and makes every creative decision about what does and doesn't go on the record. "A lot of artists don't realize how much money they could make by retaining ownership and licensing directly," her manager, Michael Hausman, told ex–Talking Head David Byrne in *Wired*. "If it's done properly, you get paid quickly, and you get paid again and again. That's a great source of income."

Thus do many stars, including outspoken Dixie Chicks singer Natalie Maines, scoff at 360-degree deals. Jamie Kitman, manager of OK Go, says one of his acts, Ann Arbor, Michigan, indie-pop band Tally Hall, turned down such an offer from a major label in 2006: "It's easy to see why bands would resist." Adds Jordan Kurland, manager of Death Cab for Cutie and the Postal Service: "My knee-jerk reaction would be 'no way,' because that's something that's been sacred for so long. A lot of bands, aside from an advance from a record deal, might not see money for a very, very long time, even if things go well—aside from touring and merchandise."

So in 2008, label executives and prominent artist managers floated an alternate idea, one that could return them to 1990s-style profits: The labels could simply ask internet service providers, like Verizon or Comcast, to start charging their users a fee for all the free music-trading they facilitate. Jim Griffin, a former Geffen Records technology executive, has been pushing this approach for years, and in 2007, Warner Music hired him as a consultant to work on this and other ideas. "ISPs, telcos, and tech companies have enjoyed a bonanza in the last few years off the back of recorded music content," U2's manager, Paul McGuinness, said in an early 2008 industry speech. "It is time for them to share that with artists and content owners." Griffin's proposal involves dumping the newfound ISP-tax money in a pool, then divvying it among labels, songwriters, and artists. Many in the business can't resist doing the math: If ISPs pay labels an extra $10 for each of 90 million users every month, a loose estimate of how many people pirate music, that's $10.8 billion in yearly profit. Easy money. But can it work? "Never gonna happen," says Gary Stiffelman, attorney for Justin Timberlake, Eminem, and others. "There's no motivation for the ISPs to come up with the money."

Unless such a big-money idea actually comes to fruition, it looks like the record business is doomed. The *music* business, however, has a bright future.

In 2007, Madonna announced she was leaving Warner Music, her major label of twenty-five years, to sign with the world's biggest concert promoter, Live Nation. If anything pointed to the dire prospects of major record labels, it was this: *Madonna* was leaving. And she was going not to another label, but to a concert company—one that spun off from monolithic Clear Channel Communications, which made its money off radio and billboards. The Material Girl signed with Live Nation for $120 million—sharing revenue for music sales, performances, merchandise, and the rights to her name. Everybody in the concert business knew this deal was all about touring revenue, which has boomed over the past decade. At forty-nine, when she agreed to the Live Nation deal, Madonna was no longer at her peak as a recording star. In 2005, her *Confessions on a Dance Floor* CD sold just 1.6 million copies in the US, while her subsequent worldwide tour grossed $193 million. In April of the following year, hip-hop star Jay-Z announced he'd leave his long-time label, Def Jam Records—the same label at which he had recently been the president—to sign a Madonna-like deal with Live Nation. Jay-Z's haul was reportedly $150 million, for a decade's worth of recordings, tours, and an unnamed entertainment business venture. Nickelback and Shakira, longtime hitmakers for major labels, made similar deals with Live Nation in summer 2008.

At the time Madonna announced her new deal—on October 10, 2007, to be exact, which *SPIN* magazine later called "a day that will live in infamy in the hearts of major-label executives"—Radiohead decided to avoid record labels entirely and release its *In Rainbows* album as a digital download. Even more radically, the band asked fans to pay whatever they wanted for the album. The people who paid averaged $6, which amounted to a total of $2.26 per album—or more than $2.7 million in profits for Radiohead. Radiohead's experiment—concocted by managers Chris Hufford and Bryce Edge "when they were a bit stoned," guitarist Jonny Greenwood later said—was a stunning success. Although the band refused to say how many fans bought *In Rainbows* online, or for how much, comScore estimated close to 1.2 million downloaders. "It felt very liberating to take complete control," singer Thom Yorke said. "If I die tomorrow, I'll be happy that we didn't carry on working within this huge industry that I don't feel any connection with."

Radiohead's plan was so unique that it generated tons of media coverage, and regardless of its revenue success, it drummed up publicity for its 2008 summer tour. The band later delivered a CD version of the album to record stores—and, as it turned out, the album hit No. 1 on the *Billboard* charts during the first week of 2008, selling more than 122,000 copies. Marketing scheme or not, the band pocketed most of those profits.

Who needs a major record label? Earlier that same year, Paul McCartney put out a new album, *Memory Almost Full*, without the help of his (and the Beatles') longtime label Capitol Records. He released it through Starbucks, which expanded its purview in the early 2000s to include a specialty music label and distributed CDs from Ray Charles to Bob Dylan to Joni Mitchell to a completely unknown singer-songwriter named Hilary McRae. (In an attempt to revitalize its business, the coffee giant announced in 2008 it would start deemphasizing music to focus on, you know, coffee.) Tellingly, McCartney's last Capitol album, 2005's *Chaos and Creation in the Backyard*, sold 540,000 copies; the Starbucks release, as of late 2007, was up to 562,000. This lesson was not lost on the Eagles, who in fall 2007 distributed their first new studio album in twenty-eight years, *Long Road Out of Eden*, directly and exclusively to Wal-Mart, with no record company involvement. (The band sold the album digitally, through official Wal-Mart and Eagles websites, but not on iTunes, Amazon, or elsewhere.) The strategy paid off—the Eagles sold 711,000 copies in their first week and, by mid-December, more than 2 million.

In the same year, another huge rock act, Nine Inch Nails, announced it would no longer work with its longtime label, Jimmy Iovine's Interscope. "I'm truly saddened because I think music has been devalued, so that it's just a file on your computer, and it's usually free," Trent Reznor told *New York*. "But we can't change that. What we can do is try to offer people the best experience that we can provide them. Will it work? I don't know. But I think it's a great way to get music out to people who are interested. At the end of the day, all I care about is the integrity of the music, and that the feeling of those who experience it is as untainted as possible. I'd rather it not be on an iPod commercial. I'd rather it not be a ringtone that you have to get with a free cell phone or any of that bullshit." Reznor backed up his talk in early 2008 by self-releasing an instrumental album, *Ghosts I-IV*, in $5 downloadable chunks, or for $10 to $300 for fans who preferred the CD format and more elaborate packaging. Unlike Radiohead, in March 2008, NIN told the world how much revenue the band took in by releasing *Ghosts I-IV* on its own: $1.6 million. The band's manager, Jim Guerinot, estimated NIN made more than five times as much profit off this release compared to what it would have made under the traditional industry system. In May, the band released a full-album download, *The Slip*. Ian Rogers, former general manager of Yahoo! Music, helped start a new company, Topspin Media, later in 2008, to help artists release music directly to fans, Radiohead-style.

For veteran artists, this newfound independence from major record labels means a shocking, liberating new world. They began their careers when labels had just about every bit of leverage possible in the star-making process. An artist who wanted to make a record needed studio time—and that cost money, which meant a sizable loan from a label. An artist who wanted to get a single onto a radio playlist needed connections—and that usually meant a label executive who had the money to hire an independent promoter. An artist who wanted to sell millions of copies of a record needed a big-time distributor with the clout to push CDs into big stores like Best Buy or Target—and that meant one of the major label's own subsidiaries, like WEA or CEMA. Today, it's not necessary to hook up with a label to do all these things. An artist can make a record cheaply, and professionally, using software like Pro Tools. An artist can forgo the radio, building buzz and exposure online via do-it-yourself websites like MySpace, viral videos on YouTube, or any number of social networking services from Facebook to Garageband.com. As for distribution, who needs crates, trucks, warehouses, stores, or even the discs themselves? Artists can follow Radiohead's example and simply distribute the music essentially free online.

"You see these articles about the disaster in the music business," James Mercer, lead singer for the Shins, told *SPIN*. "When you think about how unhealthy the business has been, this is like lancing the fucking boil and cleaning it out. It's not a fucking disaster to regular bands out there. It's now more likely I'll be able to start my own label, release my work, profit from it, and have a more lucrative career. For a band at our level, it's all a bowl of cherries."

Although the Shins recently departed from the record company that made them famous, Sub Pop Records in Seattle, these kinds of independent labels are proving that they can navigate industry problems with far more nimbleness and creativity than multinational corporations like Warner and EMI. They're unencumbered, for example, with the baggage that goes with producing one or two multimillion-selling CDs in order to pay for the smaller releases. The smaller labels don't have to show quarterly results to shareholders or corporate boards of directors. They can just put out music they like, experimenting with internet marketing and various new paths. In his *Wired* piece, David Byrne cited the example of his own label, Warner-owned Nonesuch, which has a bare-bones staff of twelve people to release and market medium-selling music by Wilco, Philip Glass, and k. d. lang. On the web page for twenty-year-old Chapel Hill, North Carolina, indie Merge Records, there's a "listen/watch" link, allowing fans to stream video and audio from a wide range of acts. It's the same idea as radio: drum up free publicity so fans will buy the records. Acts from singer-songwriters Ryan Adams and James McMurtry to new-wave fixtures B-52's and rock hitmakers Coldplay have put out free online singles to promote their albums over the past year. Prolific rapper Lil Wayne is a master of this approach, releasing free, high-quality online mixtapes over the past several years. Artists signed to major labels can't go very far with it, though, because many top record executives still consider free music a recipe for online piracy and a threat to profits. "The mixtapes were obviously very concerning to us as a label," Sylvia Rhone, president of Universal Motown, told *Rolling Stone* in June 2008, just before her label released Lil Wayne's smash *Tha Carter III* in partnership with Cash Money Records. "It really goes counter to what we would like our artists to do."

This major-label attitude strikes many in the music business as anachronistic. "The idea of fighting it still seems silly. I've always felt like major labels blaming downloading for their declining sales is just somewhat wishful thinking. It's like a scapegoat—they wish it was that and not 'they've been putting out terrible records for a long time,'" says Mac McCaughan, frontman for punk band Superchunk and founder of Merge, whose roster includes Arcade Fire and Spoon. "I'm sure people download albums that come out on Merge and don't pay for them all the time. But for the most part people who are our hardcore fans like music and want to support the artists and the labels that put out records they like. We're all in the music business, but it's like we're two different businesses."

So where does this leave the major record labels? Streaming songs for free as promotional items may be well and good for Mac McCaughan of Superchunk, but Doug Morris, chief executive officer of Universal Music, made a total of $14.46 million in salary and bonuses as recently as 2005. These gigantic companies need serious revenues. They can't afford to tinker with small-time experiments.

And that's exactly why major labels are failing in the digital age. For decades, they relied on long-term artist-development plans, breaking stars such as Bruce Springsteen and U2 over a period of four or five records, betting their investments would pay off with huge hit albums. But that process has become a luxury in today's record business. Signing a weird, unknown act like R.E.M. or TV on the Radio and waiting years for it to manufacture a hit is simply unprofitable. In late 2007, major labels started letting go the executives who were experts at exactly that—like Rob Stevenson, the veteran A&R talent scout who discovered rock bands Fall Out Boy and the Killers, then lost his Island Def Jam job in a round of layoffs. Or Mark Williams, longtime A&R man for Interscope, who helped Gwen Stefani transform from No Doubt punk rock frontwoman to glamorous solo diva in 2004, then allowed his contract to expire and left the label three years later. For labels to survive and maintain an executive staff of top talent, they need faster hits than ever before.

A few days before he left Interscope, just before Christmas 2007, Williams was reflective. He was tired of forcing developing artists into the studio with big-name producers in order to manufacture a big hit right away. He was tired of pressure from top executives to tinker with an artist's vision until it became diluted. He was starting to second-guess his own instincts. "If I could just make records and work with artists, I'd do it forever. But it just doesn't work that way," he says. "There's always pressure. 'Is this the best it can get?' 'Will people like it?' 'It's not there yet.' 'Can we spend more money?' The overall focus [at major labels] is one of desperation to have hits. When the climate is one of desperation, it tends to not work so well.

"People at the majors for some time have been looking for an answer. The obvious answer is 'there is no answer.' Big labels are going to become smaller and smaller," Williams continues. "But it's going to affect the other side—small opportunities for releasing music are going to rise up. It's like, drop a globe and it shatters into a million pieces. It's going to be like in the '50s and '60s, when you had hundreds and hundreds of small labels. It's going to be a lot of trial and error. None of us know whether it'll work right. I laugh when people say, 'We're going to try to fix it.' They can try, but there's no real answer. It's over. It's just done."

Under the management of new CEO Guy Hands, EMI employees recently invited a group of teenagers to the label's company headquarters and instructed them to help themselves to a huge table full of free CDs. The kids turned up their noses. Hands has yet to figure out how to replace the CD, but his first job is to make the company leaner and more flexible, through layoffs and cuts in the artist roster. "The recorded music industry as a whole has not positioned itself well for the changing environment over the last ten years and has failed to anticipate or adapt to the new marketplace," he wrote in a letter to employees.* It's working so far: In mid-July 2008, Hands announced that EMI revenues rose 61 percent in the first quarter, according to Reuters.

Other major labels are starting to think along the same lines. Even Universal, the powerhouse company run by Morris and Iovine, with superstars from U2 to Eminem to Gwen Stefani, has hit a prolonged weak spot. In its Securities and Exchange Commission filings from 2006, Universal's parent company, Vivendi SA, acknowledged as much: "The recorded music market has been declining and may continue to decline." Many label executives think they know the formula for recovery: *hits.* Sound familiar? Yes, even after a decade of Napster and Kazaa, YouTube and MySpace, iTunes and Amazon, the record industry clings to its time-honored model of selling a large number of shiny plastic discs. As of midyear, major labels were planning to roll out albums by some of their biggest names in 2008: Eminem, Beyoncé, and Metallica. In July, rapper Lil Wayne's *Tha Carter III* became the first album since 50 Cent's *The Massacre* in early 2005 to sell 1 million copies in its first week. Coldplay's EMI album *Viva La Vida* followed the next week, with 721,000 copies. But this boomlet was short lived. Both albums' sales declined precipitously in their subsequent weeks, and overall industry sales were down 11 percent by late July, compared with the same period in 2007.

The last time the record industry went through a slump of this magnitude was in the early 1980s, immediately after disco crashed. CDs and MTV would ultimately save the industry, but before they kicked in, what turned things around was, of course, Michael Jackson's *Thriller*. Ahmet Ertegun, the late Atlantic Records founder who discovered

---

* As of mid-2008, Hands has made more news for hiring than firing, appointing high-tech experts like ex–Google executive Douglas Merrill and Second Life online-community pioneer Cory Ondrejka to top EMI posts.

Ray Charles, Led Zeppelin, Kid Rock, and dozens of other superstars, brought this point home in a 1982 meeting that has turned into a sort of industry legend. Fredric Dannen retold it in his classic investigative book *Hit Men*, and Doug Morris mentioned it in a 2005 interview. In Morris's version of the story, after a not-so-great year, superiors at Warner Communications, Atlantic's parent company, asked Ertegun and then-president Morris to report to a strategy-planning meeting first thing in the morning. Morris showed up on time. Ertegun straggled in twenty minutes late with bloodshot eyes and a stained suit. The Warner executives asked, pointedly, what Ertegun and Morris would do to turn things around in the coming year.

Ertegun stood up. "Doug and I," he said, "are going to try to get more hits." Then he sat down again.

"The truth is, that's what it's all about," says Morris, chairman and chief executive officer of the Universal Music Group. "It comes down to hits and developing artists. And it's still the same. Nothing has changed."

He's wrong. Everything has changed. *Thriller* won't save the record business this time. Thinking differently will. And unless Morris and his colleagues stop fiercely protecting the old model of selling pieces of vinyl or plastic to as many consumers as possible and start hiring digital music executives trained to build the next Napster or the next iTunes or the next *Long Tail* service or the next music-equipped cell phone or whatever particular shape the future might take,* the labels will become an anachronism. The biggest ones may survive, by manufacturing a few Beyoncé-level, 2- or 3-million-copy blockbusters every year. They may still make money licensing their catalogs to movies, commercials, TV shows, and video games. But if they can't figure out, soon, how to make greater profits via digital downloads or other means, struggling majors like EMI may have to sell their lucrative catalogs to other companies.

---

* One interesting but radical vision for the music business' future comes from McGill University visiting scholar Sandy Pearlman, once a prominent producer for Blue Oyster Cult, the Clash, the Dictators, and others. He talks about the "paradise of infinite storage." As computer data storage continues to grow in capacity and shrink in size, he believes, every music fan will simply carry a tiny chip filled with every song ever recorded. Once that happens, the record business as we know it is over. But he believes it will be possible for artists and labels to levy some kind of tax on the devices and generate a new business model. Unsurprisingly, today's label employees consider Pearlman a bit of a wacko. "I've brought this up," he says in an interview, "and it's always very disturbing to people who work in music."

Maybe these new companies will follow Terry McBride's prescription: Stop messing around with any type of digital rights management, stop suing customers, drastically reduce digital-track prices, cut unnecessary overhead like warehouses and crates, and thereby return to 1980s-style profits. It's also possible that major labels such as Universal or Warner will come to this conclusion on their own—the Amazon MP3 Store and MySpace Music are tiny steps in this direction. Maybe, some in the business suggest, Apple or Microsoft or some other visionary company with money to burn will buy up the assets and, finally, start running the major record labels as high-tech content houses.

But continuing to build an entire business that relies on another *Thriller* is simply not viable. Hits are getting smaller and smaller, and they just don't have the healing power they had in 1982. Whether this reality finally prompts record executives to overhaul their business model in some profitable new way or destroys their entire business, buggy-whip style, remains to be seen. But in late 2008, it sure feels like the end is near.

Notes

All author interviews were conducted between August 2006 and July 2008 except where noted.

Prologue 1979–1982: Disco Crashes the Record Business, Michael Jackson Saves the Day, and MTV *Really* Saves the Day

1   Early Dahl background from "Shocked Jock: His Partner Dumped Him. His Station Demoted Him. His Listeners Deserted Him. Will Steve Dahl Survive?" *Chicago Tribune*, November 6, 1994, p. 14. Steve Dahl quotes in this section are from an author email interview except where noted.

2   "still-Hawaiian-shirt-wearing": More recent personal Dahl description comes from author research for Knopper, Steve, "'Subtler' Steve Dahl Still Rocks Chicago," *Billboard*, March 7, 1998, p. 68.

2   Description of Disco Demolition comes from the following sources: Johnson, Steve, *Chicago Tribune*, November 6, 1994, p. 14; Sullivan, Paul, "July 12, 1979: Who Knew So Many People Hated Disco This Much?" *Chicago Tribune*, October 28, 1997, p. 2; Sullivan, Paul, "Looking Back on a Record-Breaking Night at Comiskey," *Chicago Tribune*, July 12, 1989, p. 1; Behrens, Andy, "Disco Demolition: Bell-bottoms Be Gone!" ESPN.com *Page 3*, August 11, 2004; Steinhardt, Simon, "Disco Demolition Night," *Swindle*, December 2006, pp. 122–129; and "Disco Demolition 25th Anniversary: The Real Story" DVD (TeamWorks Media, 2004, executive produced by Steve Dahl et al.).

2   "I loathed disco": From Sullivan, Paul. *Chicago Tribune*, July 12, 1989, p. 1.

4   "I loved disco music back then!": Author interview with Michael Clarke Duncan.

4   July 1979 Top 10 analysis: From Greenberg, Steve, "Sugar Hill Records," *The Vibe History of Hip-Hop*, Alan Light, ed. (New York: Three Rivers Press, 1999), pp. 24–25, as well as author interview with Steve Greenberg.

5   "Most DJs never stopped": Author interview with Steve "Silk" Hurley in 1999. Unpublished notes for Knopper, Steve, "The Day Disco Died?" *Chicago*, July 1999, p. 21.

5   "People were trying to murder it": Author interview with Gloria Gaynor.

5   "The labels should have lost *more* money": Author interview with Nicky Siano.

6   Sales plummeted that year by almost 11 percent: Industry sales statistics come from the Recording Industry Association of America or Nielsen SoundScan.

6   Dannen, Fredric, *Hit Men* (New York: Random House, 1990), pp. 161–171. Dannen's chapter on Casablanca Records is the definitive statement on the company. The Elephant's Memory recollection: Author interview with Ron Weisner, a former Buddah executive. "Almost anything could have happened": Author interview with Bill Aucoin.

7   "being used for nonsocial purposes": Author interview with David Braun. The Angel pods detail comes from a recollection by Leland Rucker, who reviewed

one of the band's shows in the late 1970s for the *Kansas City Star*. The "$30 million mess" is based on Braun's estimate. PolyGram market share figures: From *Hit Men*, pp. 161–171.

7 Casablanca imploded, and so did the industry: Most of the details in this paragraph, including the Walter Yetnikoff quote, come from Knoedelseder, William, *Stiffed* (New York: HarperCollins, 1993), pp. 19–20. Also author interview with Susan Blond.

8 Walter Yetnikoff's personal background information: From Yetnikoff, *Howling at the Moon* (New York: Broadway, 2005).

8 to win the respect of Mick Jagger: From Ibid., p. 138.

9 outrageous tantrums: From Dannen, *Hit Men*, pp. 316–317 (Tisch), 123–124 (Simon). George Vradenburg quotes from author interview.

9 to make Springsteen happy: From Yetnikoff, *Howling at the Moon*, p. 133.

9 "If anything" . . . "I became more defiant": From Ibid., p. 188.

9 By the end of 1981: From Dannen, *Hit Men*, pp. 226–228.

9 "I told you I'd do it": Jackson-Yetnikoff exchange from Yetnikoff, *Howling at the Moon*, p. 154.

10 "*Thriller* was like Moses": Author interview with Lee Solters.

11 "taking black people back 400 years" as well as J. J. Jackson material and other MTV background: From Anson, Robert Sam, "Birth of an MTV Nation," *Vanity Fair*, November 2000, p. 231.

11 "I was the instigator, I guess": Author interview with Ron Weisner.

11 "I'll give you my story": Author interview with Robert Pittman.

12 MTV background involving Tom Freston, John Sykes, and Van Halen: From Anson, *Vanity Fair*, pp. 206–216.

12 Pittman background: From Acker, Steve, "From MTV, Nick-at-Nite, Six Flags to Century 21," *The Mississippi Business Journal*, August 7, 1995, p. 1.

12 MTV background and quotes: From Anson, *Vanity Fair*, pp. 206–216, 233. Quotes from Joe Smith and Robert Pittman are from author interviews.

13 "Like everything else, when the tide comes in": Author interview with Dick Asher.

14 David Braun quotes and recollections from author interview.

Chapter 1 1983–1986: Jerry Shulman's Frisbee: How the Compact Disc Rebuilt the Record Business

15 The bulk of the James T. Russell material comes from author interviews with James T. Russell and Barbara Russell. Quotes from Kees Immink and Michael Rackman are from author interviews. Supplementary sources were Dudley, Brier, "Scientist's Invention Was Let Go for a Song," *Seattle Times*, November 29, 2004; Holdorf, Adam, "The Discoverer," *Reed Magazine*, November 2000; *Optical Recording Corporation vs. Time Warner Inc. and WEA Manufacturing Inc.*, US District Court, District of Delaware, June 23, 1992; documents from the US Patent Office, such as Russell, James T., "Photographic Records of Digital Information and Playback Systems Including Optical Scanners," filed November 26, 1971, patented April 23, 1974; and "Time Warner Is Told to Pay $30 Million for Patent Violations," *Wall Street Journal*, June 24, 1992, p. B10. Immink points out another pre-CD pioneer, David Paul Gregg, who first envisioned an optical disc for video in the late 1950s and earned two patents for it in the 1960s. Official Sony Corp. history quote is from various authors, *Genryu* (Sony, 1996), p. 216.

19 Details about John Adamson, Optical Recording Corp., and its patent negotiations with Sony and Philips come from Adamson, John, "Time Warner Inc. and

the ORC Patents," Ivey Management Services, Richard Ivey School of Business, the University of Western Ontario, 2001, pp. 1–20; Adamson clarified some details via email. Finally, Lawrence B. Goodwin, who represented Optical Corp. in the Time Warner trial, confirmed trial details in two author interviews, although he is no longer affiliated with the firm that participated in the case.

20   Early Philips-Sony history of the CD: From Nathan, John, *Sony* (Boston: Mariner Books, 2001), pp. 116–121, 137–140; *Genryu*, pp. 216–225.

21   "Ohga had a long discussion with Morita": Author interview with Michael Schulhof.

22   "The meetings were absolutely fantastic": Author interview with Kees Immink.

22   Later CD history, including Sony-Philips cooperation on lenses and players: From Nathan, *Sony*, p. 141.

22   "Hostile. Very hostile": Author interview with Jan Timmer. Description of *Billboard* conference in Athens: From Nathan, *Sony*, p. 143.

23   "I made a bit of a small statement": Author interview with Jerry Moss.

23   Business climate for Philips and Sony: From Nathan, *Sony*, p. 143, and "Philips: An Electronics Giant Rearms to Fight Japan," *Business Week*, March 30, 1981, pp. 86–87.

24   Ohga and the first CD plant: From Nathan, *Sony*, p. 143.

24   CD meeting in which the late Jay Lasker grills Jac Holzman: Author interview with Joe Smith, confirmed in email from Jac Holzman.

25   "It was a guaranteed showstopper": Author interview with Marc Finer.

25   Yetnikoff's resistance: From Nathan, *Sony*, p. 169, as well as author interviews with John Briesch, Marc Finer, and Jerry Shulman.

25   "Super Goy": From Dannen, *Hit Men*, p. 204.

25   "[Yetnikoff] was pretty tough": Author interview with John Briesch.

26   "I have no idea what they're talking about": Author interview with Jerry Shulman.

26   Clive Davis's resistance: Author interview with John Briesch. Confirmed by Jan Timmer. EMI's resistance: Author interview with Joe Smith.

26   "The expense of digital-music equipment is horrendous": From Foti, Laura, "Digital Cost Deters Studio Commitment," *Billboard*, February 13, 1982, pp. 1, 44.

26   Musicians Against Digital and "the mind has been tricked": From Nathan, *Sony*, p. 145.

26   "We had a number of major acts": Author interview with Alan Perper.

26   "The retailers' point of view": Author interview with Jerry Shulman.

27   Beard and Yes album detail: From Mark Knopper, my brother, who by coincidence was a friend of Simonds's during this period. "I was the first one of the people that I knew" and biographical information about Rob Simonds: Author interview with Simonds.

28   Jan Timmer background and Warner seeing the CD as the future: Author interview with Jan Timmer. Some description of Timmer from Dannen, *Hit Men*, pp. 253–254.

28   Steve Ross's fondness for video games: From Bruck, Connie, *Master of the Game* (New York: Penguin, 1994), p. 165.

28   Hamburg meeting: Author interviews with Elliot Goldman, Jan Timmer, and Stan Cornyn. (Holzman did not respond to email questions on this subject.) Also Cornyn, *Exploding: The Highs, Hits, Heroes, and Hustlers of the Warner Music Group* (New York: Harper Collins, 2002), p. 303.

29   The royalty stands today: Author interview with Jim Caparro.

30   "the CD marketing guys kept pushing": Information in this paragraph comes from author interviews with Marc Finer and John Briesch; McCullaugh, Jim, "Compact Disc Seen Boosting Music Industry," *Billboard*, April 3, 1982, pp. 1,

74; Spahr, Wolfgang, "Compact Disc Officially Debuted; Timmer Stresses System's Standardization Benefits," *Billboard*, August 28, 1982, pp. 10, 41; Penchansky, Alan, "Digital Seen as Audio's Future," *Billboard*, September 18, 1982, p. 51.

30 Stevie Wonder and other stars: Author interview with John Briesch. Toshitada Doi and Stevie Wonder: From Nathan, *Sony*, pp. 145–146. "It was what I was wanting to happen": Author interview with Phil Ramone.

31 Compact Disc Group background: Author interviews with Marc Finer, John Briesch, and Alan Perper. "We ran around the country like a bunch of vagabonds": Author interview with Alan Perper. MTV lobbying: Author interview with Robert Pittman.

31 Shizuoka Prefecture plant information: From Fujita, Shig, "Japan CD Demand Outstripping Supply," *Billboard*, January 22, 1983, pp. 1, 56. Capitol Record Shop: From Lichtman, Irv, "Compact Disc Spins On," *Billboard*, March 12, 1983, p. 1. Sony executive (Michael Schulhof): From Horowitz, Is, "Momentum Builds for US CD Bow," *Billboard*, December 18, 1982, pp. 1, 64.

31 Windham Hill: from Sutherland, Sam, "Windham Hill Pacts for CD Pressing," *Billboard*, March 26, 1983, p. 6.

31 *Rolling Stone* printed: Booth, Stephen A., January 20, 1983, p. 55.

31 $16.95 opening CD price: From Horowitz, Is, "PolyGram Advances CD Bow; WEA Enters," *Billboard*, March 5, 1983, p. 1.

32 They also saw the CD as a chance to rejigger artists' contracts: Author interviews with Jay Cooper and Josh Grier. Note that the artist rate per disc is a hypothetical example based on a then-standard 12 percent royalty rate. To avoid confusion, I've calculated the rates based on the list price at record stores rather than the wholesale prices that labels change. Wholesale prices tend to fluctuate from store to store, making broad calculations difficult.

32 "They did it under the guise": Author interview with Cooper.

32 "That's not an insignificant reason": Author interview with Michael Schulhof.

33 CD price increases and "Every year they'd do this": Author interview with Russ Solomon.

33 CBS plant closings: From "Slow Year for CBS Records & Parent, Too," *Billboard*, February 20, 1982, pp. 4, 78; Lichtman, Irv, "CBS Records to Close Plant in Terre Haute," *Billboard*, October 23, 1982, pp. 1, 78.

34 "The environment is totally controlled": Author interview with Jim Frische. Most of the Terre Haute plant information comes from author interview with Jim Frische. Other helpful sources were Schumacher-Rasmussen, Eric, "20 Years Burning Down the Road: Sony Disc Manufacturing Celebrates, Rolls Out SACD Hybrid Production," *eMediaLive*, July 1, 2003, and Chambers, John, "Sony DADC TH Facility Is Company's Largest North American Plant," *Tribune-Star*, Terre Haute, Indiana, September 20, 2005, p. A1.

34 The plant had cost $20 million: From Horowitz, Irv, "Momentum Builds for US CD Bow," *Billboard*, December 18, 1982, pp. 1, 64; Reuters, "Sony-CBS Deal," October 19, 1985. Half from Sony, and half from CBS: Author interview with Jim Frische; Chambers, *Tribune-Star*, September 20, 2005, p. A1.

34 "Ten million *fucking* dollars for *this*?": Confidential source. Yetnikoff did not respond to multiple interview requests.

34 CBS profits: From "CBS Records '82 Profits Down: Revenues Also Dip; Domestic 'Reorganization' Cited," *Billboard*, February 19, 1983, p. 4.

34 "I had been predicting": Yetnikoff, *Howling at the Moon*, p. 145.

34 Terre Haute plant growth: From Schumacher-Rasmussen, *eMediaLive*, July 1, 2003; record industry profits, from RIAA; players, from Murphy, Liz, "Compact Discs Sing a Hi-Tech Success Story," *Sales & Marketing Management*, Feb. 4, 1985, p. 34.

35   Rykodisc growth: From Morse, Steve, "Amazing Little CD Firm That's Really Rocking," *Boston Globe*, April 2, 1989, p. B1; anecdotal information from author interview with Rob Simonds.

35   "Suddenly, everybody had to go in": Author interview with Howie Klein.

Big Music's Big Mistakes, Part 1: The CD Longbox

36   Terry Friedman . . . 10,000 to 20,000 trees: From Rosen, Craig, "Ban-the-Longbox Bill Passes State Assembly in California," *Billboard*, July 6, 1991, p. 65.

36   "This went on for *years*": Author interview with Jordan Harris.

37   $9,000 to $10,000 for every 5,000-album store: Estimate from Steve Orbach, sales rep from postlongbox packaging company Sensormatic, cited in Paige, Earl, "Retailers Grapple with Post-Longbox Life: Some Find New Opportunities During Transition," *Billboard*, May 8, 1993, p. 50. Background on retailers' opposition, as well as the efforts of Henry Droz and Paul Smith: Author interview with Russ Solomon.

37   "We're not insensitive": Harry Losk quote from Lichtman, Irv, "PolyGram Mulls Long CD Box: 'Augmented' Package Is Showcased at RIAA Meets," *Billboard*, January 20, 1983, p. 1.

37   Mike Bone and Ban the Box: From Stark, Phyllis, "Majors, Retail Cool Toward Ban-the-Longbox Group," *Billboard*, May 5, 1990, p. 9. "This is garbage," Raffi and Peter Gabriel: From Goldstein, Patrick, "So Long, Box: Long-Awaited Move Makes Some Ask, 'Who Will Pay?'" *Los Angeles Times*, March 10, 1992, p. 1. Spinal Tap: From Selvin, Joel, "Spinal Tap Concert Is a Backbreaker; Parody Band Reunites for Gag-Heavy Live Shows," *San Francisco Chronicle*, June 3, 1992, p. E1.

38   "Why We Should Keep": From Licata, Sal, "Size, Graphics Are Major Pluses: Why We Should Keep the CD Longbox," *Billboard*, December 2, 1989, p. 9.

38   "It would cost retailers a *fortune*": Author interview with Jeff Gold.

Chapter 2 1984–1999: How Big Spenders Got Rich in the Post-CD Boom

40   Gil Friesen's biography based mostly on three author interviews with Friesen and two with Jerry Moss. Description of Friesen's house is from author observation, details from Friesen himself, and Giovannini, Joseph, "Modernism Revisited: A Pair of Additions Elevate a 1953 Los Angeles House," *Architectural Digest*, July 2003, pp. 114–121, 171.

42   archaic American network of mom-and-pop distributors: From Dannen, *Hit Men*, pp. 63–64.

42   "There was a period of time at A&M there": Author interview with Al Cafaro.

43   "They're the most exciting innovation": From Pond, Steve, "Gil Friesen: The President of A&M Records Talks About the Issues Confronting the Music Business," *Rolling Stone*, December 17, 1987, pp. 103–106.

43   $1.45 million purchase price and $4.9 million in additional value: From Los Angeles County Assessor's Office.

43   "The business grew pretty dramatically": Author interview with Bob Buziak.

44   Barbra Streisand deal: From Cox, Meg, "Sony Corp. Is Said Near to Signing New Streisand Deal," *Wall Street Journal*, May 12, 1992, p. A1. Michael Jackson deal: From Fabrikant, Geraldine, "Sony Music's Mr. Big Spender," *New York Times*, December 1, 1991, p. A1. ZZ Top deal: From Cox, Meg, "ZZ Top Negotiates RCA Records Deal for Up to $40 Million—Deal with Bertelsmann Unit Would Include 5 Records from Trio in Their Early 40s," *Wall Street Journal*, June 17, 1992, p. B2. Janet Jackson deal: From Walker, Michael, "It's as Easy as SBK:

SBK Records Takes Unknowns and Spends Big to Make Them Known. (Hey, It Worked with Wilson Phillips and Vanilla Ice)," *Los Angeles Times*, March 10, 1991, p. 6.

44 "People would say, 'How can you do that to the companies?'": Author interview with Donald S. Passman.

44 Video costs and "An average budget for me was maybe close to $1 million": Author interview with Dave Meyers, 2005.

44 There is a scene: From Lee, Tommy, Mick Mars, Vince Neil, Nikki Sixx, and Neil Strauss, *The Dirt: Confessions of the World's Most Notorious Rock Band* (New York: HarperCollins, 2002), pp. 224–225.

45 Wilson Phillips was spending $7,000 on hair and makeup: From Goodman, Fred, "Wilson Phillips: The Crash," *Entertainment Weekly*, November 27, 1992, pp. 40–42. $500,000 advance, as well as personal details about Charles Koppelman: From Walker, *Los Angeles Times*, p. 6.

45 "CDs were selling like crazy": Author interview with Charles Koppelman.

45 Wilson Phillips's budget: Author interview with Arma Andon.

46 "You've got to understand": Ibid.

46 Koppelman's $50 million buyout: Lichtman, Irv, "Koppelman Among Top Exec Departures: EMI Music Overhauls Its N. American Operations," *Billboard*, June 7, 1997, p. 1.

46 "I spent money!": Author interview with Michael Alago.

47 "They're bastions of indie rock": Author interview with Debbie Southwood-Smith.

47 "The all-vinyl business had its ups and downs": Author interview with Bob Merlis.

47 Yetnikoff, Tisch, and "the Evil Dwarf": From Nathan, *Sony*, p. 172.

48 "When Larry got in" and "[Tisch] thought the business relied too much": Author interview with George Vradenburg.

48 Yetnikoff's idea for Sony to buy CBS: From Nathan, *Sony*, p. 172; Yetnikoff, *Howling at the Moon*, pp. 209, 240.

48 "The noncreative side" and Schulhof background: Author interview with Michael Schulhof.

49 "Whatever you discussed with [Schulhof]": From Nathan, *Sony*, p. 170. Ohga answered some email questions for this book but would not agree to a full interview.

49 "I called Morita at home": Author interview with Michael Schulhof. Mayfair Regis and Bill Paley detail as well as MiniDisc/DAT theory: From Nathan, *Sony*, pp. 173–174.

50 "He said, 'If the company was worth $2 billion yesterday'": Author interview with Michael Schulhof. "Install me as Super Czar and make me superrich": From Yetnikoff, *Howling at the Moon*, p. 209.

50 Thomas D. Mottola biography: From Anson, Robert Sam, "Tommy Boy: Even by the Standards of the Wild and Wooly Music Industry, Tommy Mottola, Chairman of the $5.9 Billion Sony Music Entertainment, Plays by His Own Rules," *Vanity Fair*, December 1996, pp. 288–294, 313–314.

51 "Al was a Harvard MBA": Author interview with Bob Sherwood.

52 Jon Landau and Bruce Springsteen detail: From Griffin, Nancy, and Kim Masters, *Hit & Run: How Jon Peters and Peter Guber Took Sony for a Ride in Hollywood* (New York: Simon & Schuster, 1997), pp. 289–291.

53 "Once they blow me out, Walter's vulnerable": Author interview with Frank Dileo.

53 $25 million settlement: From Griffin and Masters, *Hit & Run*, p. 290.

53 Detail about Yetnikoff's fall, including Ohga quote and "Count my money": From Yetnikoff, *Howling at the Moon*, pp. 260–261.

53 "He was riding that job for all it was worth": Confidential source. Aerosmith, Mariah Carey, and mansion spending: From Anson, *Vanity Fair*, pp. 314–316.

54 "The eight-hundred-pound gorilla in the room": Author interview with Bob Sherwood.

54 Michael Jackson called . . . Schulhof: From Anson, *Vanity Fair*, p. 315; confirmed by Schulhof.

54 This was unacceptable: From Fabrikant, *New York Times*, December 1, 1991, p. A1. "I wouldn't sign a rock act with Sony if my life depended on it": From Philips, Chuck, "Charting Sony Music's Future; for Tommy Mottola (Yes, the One Married to Mariah Carey), the Next Step Is to Take the No. 2 Firm to the Top," *Los Angeles Times*, May 5, 1996, p. 1.

55 "Nobody likes to overspend": Author interview with Michael Schulhof.

55 Mottola's personal expenses and "famiglia": From Eaton, Phoebe, "Tommy Mottola Faces the Music," *New York*, March 3, 2003, p. 42. "These guys were very aggressive": Author interview with Jeff Ayeroff.

55 "I didn't look at the financials": Author interview with Michael Goldstone.

55 "a real oligarchy": From Eaton, Phoebe, *New York*, p. 42. "They wanted to move Columbia": Author interview with Bob Sherwood.

56 "Mo loved talent magnets": From Cornyn, Stan, *Exploding*, p. 272.

56 "He trusted my instincts": Author interview with Michael Alago.

56 Steve Ross biography, as well as Warner–Seven Arts deal and Sinatra's role in it: From Bruck, *Master of the Game*, pp. 48–57.

57 "There were many people there in key positions": Author interview with Jorge Hinojosa.

57 "At Time Warner, the record company was, cash on cash, the best business in the company": Author interview with Michael Fuchs. Financial details of Time Warner merger: From Bruck, *Master of the Game*, pp. 246–272, and Cornyn, *Exploding*, p. 345.

57 "It was a pretty benign place": Author interview with Jeff Gold.

58 "the fucking 'Cop Killer' fuse gets lit": Author interview with Jorge Hinojosa.

59 Time Warner picketers and Charlton Heston: From Cornyn, *Exploding*, pp. 366–368. Details about Ice-T presenting Warner executives with *Home Invasion* and leaving the label via letter: Author interview with Jorge Hinojosa.

59 "balanced and coherent": From Hames, William, *Time*, May 3, 1993, p. 81.

59 "No one ever replaced": Author interview with Danny Goldberg.

60 "To observers, it was like tacking a happy ending": From Cornyn, *Exploding*, pp. 394–395, 402–415.

60 "When I got there": Author interview with Michael Fuchs.

61 "[Warner Music] couldn't take the heat": Author interview with Roger Ames.

61 "Big advances were starting to be more of a key fix" and detail about David Fine: Author interview with Jerry Moss.

62 "We had the opportunity to get fresh new repertoire in the company": Author interview with Jan Cook.

62 Moss-Friesen feud: Author interviews with Jerry Moss, Gil Friesen, Al Cafaro, and several confidential sources. "From my perspective, Gil was a terrific leader": Author interview with Cafaro.

62 Friesen resigned under pressure: From Shiver, Jube, Jr., "A&M President Resigns After 25 Years," *Los Angeles Times*, April 3, 1990, p. 3.

62 "We had a different philosophical approach" and "All of a sudden I had a new boss": Author interviews with Jerry Moss.

63 "As far as I know, the board at Seagram": Author interview with Edgar Bronfman Jr.

64 Alain Levy and the film business: Author interviews with Jan Cook and Al Cafaro. "Levy took the position": Author interview with Cafaro.

64 "I don't think [Boonstra] had Alain Levy much in the loop": Confidential source.
64 "We were certainly taken by surprise" and other Jan Cook quotes: Author interview.
65 "They swallowed up my company, and I was gone": Author interview with Mark Kates.
65 "These are record men like the old days": Author interview with Bob Buziak.

Big Music's Big Mistakes, Part 2: Independent Radio Promotion

66 "social exchanges between friends are not payola": From Dannen, *Hit Men*, p. 45.
66 Background on DiSipio: Ibid., pp. 197–199.
67 Labels spent $40 million a year on independent promoters, 30 percent of pretax profits: Ibid., p. 15.
67 Dick Asher's Floyd experiment: Ibid., pp. 3–11.
67 "I wasn't a whistleblower": Author interview with Dick Asher.
68 *NBC Nightly News* report detail and Yetnikoff's reaction: From Dannen, *Hit Men*, pp. 272–278.
69 "I'm not saying no indie [radio promoter] ever did anything wrong" and schmooze detail: From Lombardi, John, "King of the Schmooze," *Esquire*, November 1986, p. 128.
69 Early Bill Scull history: Author interviews with Bill Scull, Craig Diable, and Tim Hurst. "He's always doing promotion, no matter what it is": Author interview with Diable.
69 Disipio quickly disappeared: From Dannen, *Hit Men*, p. 290, and Philips, Chuck, "Is It Lucky Timing?" *Los Angeles Times*, July 6, 2007, p. E-1.
70 "I thought, 'There's no independent promotion person in Cincinnati'": Author interview with Scull.
71 "an earnest, non-blustery, teetotaling family man": From Kot, Greg, "Arranged by Jeff McClusky: As an Independent Record Promoter, He Makes Friends So He Can Make Hits," *Chicago Tribune*, November 28, 1999, p. 10. McClusky contacting attorneys and likening the business to grocery stores: Author interview with Jeff McClusky.
72 Clear Channel, Citadel, and Cumulus owned 60 percent: From Boehlert, Eric, "Pay for Play: Why Does Radio Suck? Because Most Stations Play Only the Songs the Record Companies Pay Them To. And Things Are Going to Get Worse," *Salon*, March 14, 2001 (60 percent), and Manning, Jason, "Revolutions in Radio," *PBS Online NewsHour*, May 4, 2005 (top three companies).
72 Cumulus' $1 million deal with McClusky: From Boehlert, *Salon*, March 14, 2001, and Cumulus Media Inc. 10-K Securities and Exchange Commission filing, March 31, 2003.
72 Bill McGathy's $3.25 million bid: From Boehlert, Eric, "The 'Bootylicious' Gambit: Can a Hot New Single from Destiny's Child Help Columbia Records Crack the Indie Promoters' Control of Pop Radio?" *Salon*, June 5, 2001.
72 "Drugs and hookers are out; detailed invoices are in": From Boehlert, *Salon*, March 14, 2001.
72 take as much as *$300 million*: From Kot, Greg, "We Haven't Seen the Last of Pay-for-Play," *Chicago Tribune*, April 13, 2003, p. 1.
72 McClusky paying for Backstreet Boys tickets out of his own pocket: From Kot, Greg, *Chicago Tribune*, November 28, 1999.
73 It was not uncommon for: Author interview with Bill Scull. DiSipio making $27 million: This estimate comes from a quote by Danny Davis, the longtime label promotion man who'd worked for Casablanca and Motown. Davis said to singer Al Martino, who played Johnny Fontane in *The Godfather*: "What do you figure

he's got, Al? Joe [Isgro] tells me he's got $17 million." Al Martino says, "Danny, add *ten* to it" (Dannen, *Hit Men*, p. 198).

73 "From the mid-'80s to the late '90s, the labels were really, as we say, 'donkey strong'": Author interview with Scull.

73 "Probably [labels'] biggest expense was indie promotion": Author interview with Tim Hurst.

Big Music's Big Mistakes, Part 3: Digital Audio Tape

75 $270 billion a year: From Haring, Bruce, "Trade Groups Sound Renewed Piracy Alarm: Issue Warnings on Korea, Taiwan, Saudi Arabia," *Billboard,* December 2, 1989, p. 4.

75 Raid in Bell, California: From Thackrey, Ted Jr., "Printing Shop Raid Yields Bogus Record Labels," *Los Angeles Times,* July 30, 1985, p. 2.

76 $1,000 to $1,500 costs for early DAT players: From Takiff, Jonathan, "DAT Units to Arrive Sooner Than Expected," Knight-Ridder Newspapers wire service, published in *Chicago Tribune,* February 6, 1987, p. 78.

76 "They proceeded to claim that DAT": Author interview with John Briesch.

76 the "Maneuver in Vancouver": From Takiff, *Chicago Tribune,* February 6, 1987. Other description of this meeting, including "the Japanese" walking out, from author interview with Joe Smith.

77 Background on Serial Copy Management System: From Hunt, Dennis, "How Digital-Recording Pact Will Affect Consumers: The Royalty Accord Won't Raise Prices Soon, If at All, But It Will Lead to Introduction of New Software, a Major Factor in the Acceptance of the New Format," *Los Angeles Times,* July 22, 1991, p. 8, as well as author interviews with Marc Finer, John Briesch, and Mark Viken.

77 Sammy Cahn and publishers' lawsuit: From Pollack, Andrew, "Music Publishers' Suit Reopens DAT Question," New York Times News Service, published in *Chicago Tribune,* July 29, 1990, p. 10D.

77 "We killed the DAT machine": Author interview with Joe Smith.

78 Audio Home Recording Act: Author interviews with Jim Burger, David Leibowitz, and Marc Finer.

78 "I said, 'Here's the deal'": Author interview with Burger.

78 "They blew it": Author interview with Finer.

78 Albums on the Hill description: Author interview with Andy Schneidkraut.

79 "It was like a knife in my back": Ibid.

79 "It was clear that the computer companies": Author interview with Steve Gottlieb.

Chapter 3 1998–2001: The Teen Pop Bubble: Boy Bands and Britney Make the Business Bigger Than Ever—But Not for Long

80 "It was *maniacal*": Author interview with Erik Bradley.

80 "We were like, 'All right, they seem to have a track record'": Author interview with Tom Calderone.

81 "People keep asking me, 'What are you going to do'": From Leeds, Jeff, "That Awkward Phase: Britney and Pals Are Maturing. Sales Are Slowing. But Kid Pop Feeds a Media Establishment That Won't Give Up on the Genre Easily," *Los Angeles Times,* December 2, 2001, p. F8.

82 "You have the huge infrastructure of people": Author interview with Lyor Cohen, 2005.

82 "As busy as [Calder] was": Author interview with Gary Stiffelman.

83   "Clive was more no-frills": Author interview with David McPherson.

83   Early Clive Calder biography and "There are many cities in South Africa": From Scott, Ajax, "Clive Calder: Zomba's $500m Mystery Man Thinks Big," *Music Business International*, August 1996, page number unknown.

83   "Fanatically self-disciplined" and tax manuals: From Malan, Rian, "The $3 Billion Man: Say Goodbye (for Now) to Clive Calder, the Mystery Mogul Who Sold His Baby, Jive Records, and Set the World's-Record Pop-Music Payday," *Rolling Stone*, July 25, 2002, pp. 26–28.

83   Calder, EMI, and Malawi: From Malan, *Rolling Stone*, July 25, 2002, pp. 26–28.

84   Theory on Calder's "ears": Author interview with David McPherson.

84   "South Africa was segregated": Author interview with Jonathan Butler.

84   "We were politically very much opposed": Author interview with Ralph Simon.

85   "slightly off the pace": From Malan, *Rolling Stone*, July 25, 2002, pp. 26–28.

85   Henri Belolo . . . Village People: From Scott, *Music Business International*, August 1996, page number unknown, confirmed by Ralph Simon. Calder and Simon agreed they had to keep as much control of Zomba as possible: Author interview with Simon.

85   Clive Davis role: Author interview with Simon. $225 million and fifty companies: From Malan, *Rolling Stone*, July 25, 2002, pp. 26–28.

85   "The Jive offices were crummy, cardboard desks": Author interview with Gary Stiffelman.

85   "very bad" falling-out and "For a variety of reasons": Author interview with Ralph Simon.

85   "has a ruthlessness that knows no boundaries": From Kafka, Peter, and Brett Pulley, "Jive Talking," *Forbes*, March 19, 2001, p. 138.

86   Barry Weiss and Hy Weiss: Author interview with Barry Weiss, Jive Records company biographies. $50 handshake: From Sisario, Ben, "Hy Weiss, 84, Music Executive from Rock 'n' Roll's Early Days, Dies," *New York Times*, March 31, 2007, p. A16.

86   "Do you know any rappers?" and Weiss-Calder relationship: Author interview with Barry Weiss.

86   Early Whodini background and "We had rooms next to each other": Author interview with Barry Weiss.

86   "I never had been on a plane in my *life*": Author interview with Jalil Hutchins.

87   Lou Pearlman biography and quotes: From Pearlman, Lou, with Wes Smith, *Bands, Brands, & Billions: My Top 10 Rules for Making Any Business Go Platinum* (New York: McGraw-Hill, 2003), pp. 3–17, 97–99.

88    $250,000 in savings detail: From Lipner, Maxine, "More Than Hot Air," *Nation's Business*, March 1993, p. 16

88   "You could tell the alternative age was over": Author interview with Paris D'Jon.

89   Backstreet Boys auditions: From Pearlman, *Bands, Brands, & Billions*, pp. 115–125.

89   "We were living in Orlando in a nondescript office park" and other Jay Marose quotes: Author interview with Marose.

89   Donna Wright's voicemail and biography of David McPherson, "He was like, 'You know what?'" and other McPherson quotes: Author interview with McPherson.

90   Mercury bought out the Backstreet Boys' contract: Author interview with Barry Weiss.

91   Stuart Watson's Asia publicity plan: Author interview with Watson.

91   Girls screamed: Author interview with Barry Weiss.

91   "They brought them to Chicago": Author interview with Erik Bradley.

91   "Unlike rock bands, these bands were perfect": Author interview with Bill Scull.

92 "We were looking for a Debbie Gibson": Author interview with Steve Lunt.

92 "When Clive heard that in the A&R meeting": Ibid.

93 "We at Jive said, 'This is a fuckin' smash'": Ibid.

93 "We go out in the parking lot": Author interview with Michael Steele.

93 his public company, International Ltd.: From Boucher, Geoff, "The Making of Heartthrobs Inc.: First Came the Backstreet Boys, Then 'NSync, and Now a Fleet of More Contenders for Pop Idolization," *Los Angeles Times*, January 24, 1999, p. 4.

93 $12 million mansion, neighbor Shaquille O'Neal, and Rolls-Royce: From Palmeri, Christopher, "From Starmaker to Scammer? Boy Band Svengali Lou Pearlman Is Accused of Running a Ponzi Scheme," *Business Week*, March 19, 2007, p. 46. Jet skis, Windemere mansion, Republican donations, Orlando Predators, and Rolex: From Huntley, Helen, "Unmasking Lou Pearlman: The Promoter Who Loved the Limelight Has Retreated to the Shadows. Left in the Dark Are the Investors," *St. Petersburg Times*, June 3, 2007, p. 1D.

93 "He was arrogant and thought he was the smartest guy in the room": Author interview with Bob Jamieson.

93 "You can't make money on an airline": From Boucher, Geoff, *Los Angeles Times*, January 24, 1999, p. 4.

94 'NSync audition: From Pearlman, *Bands, Brands, & Billions*, pp. 233–237 (Pearlman's version), and Lynn Harless affidavit, *Trans Continental Records Inc. et al. vs. Zomba Recording Corp. et. al*, November 2, 1999 (Harless's version).

94 "We brought in another brother and they saw it as an abandonment": From Boucher, *Los Angeles Times*, January 24, 1999, p. 4.

94 Backstreet Boys lawsuit, meeting, Johnny Wright quote, "name-calling," "indentured servants," and "It would be nice to have them as my five sons": From Reilly, Patrick M., "The Impresario Behind Boot Camp for Pop-Music Idols," *Wall Street Journal*, January 22, 1999, p. B1.

95 "Here were some guys that sold twenty-plus million albums": Author interview with Peter Katsis.

95 Backstreet Boys tour numbers: From Evans, Rob, "Backstreet Boys Cash In on Unorthodox Ticket Sales Plan," LiveDaily.com, August 19, 1999.

95 JC Chasez's realization and $10,000 advance: From JC Chasez affidavit, *Trans Continental vs. Zomba*, November 2, 1999.

96 Ritholz on Trans Continental numbers: From Adam Ritholz affidavit, *Trans Continental vs. Zomba*, November 2, 1999. 'NSync's meeting with Pearlman: Author interview with Ritholz.

96 "He said to me, 'I have a certain principled way of doing things'" and other Ritholz quotes, as well as detail about "inducement letter" and Ariola contract: Author interview with Adam Ritholz.

97 Early Strauss Zelnick–Clive Calder friendship: Author interview with Zelnick.

97 Adam Ritholz–Clive Calder phone conversation: Author interview with Ritholz.

97 Strauss Zelnick background, including "Mr. Know-It-All" and Tyrese and Pink anecdotes: From Roberts, Johnnie L., "BMG: Behind the Music," *Newsweek*, May 15, 2000, p. 46. "I had virtually no record business experience": Author interview with Zelnick.

98 Barbecue sauce: From Landman, Beth, and Mitchell, Deborah, "Intelligencer," *New York*, July 20, 1998.

98 BMG sales increased 7 percent, to $4.6 billion: From Pulley, Brett, "Ballad of the BMG Blues," *Forbes*, December 27, 1999, p. 56.

98 Strauss Zelnick–Clive Davis background, and Barry Manilow quote: From Pulley, Brett, *Forbes*, December 27, 1999, p. 56.

98 "As Bertelsmann's board knew well" and Davis's not grooming a successor: Confidential source.

99 "Lou is a bad guy. He treated the guys badly. But BMG had a deal with him": Confidential source.

99 "Justin and I were texting each other about our suits": Author interview with Jay Marose.

99 "That was the most stressful time of my career": Author interview with Bob Jamieson.

99 Clive Calder's "put option": From Benoit, Bertrand, "Media Chief Keen on Zomba," *Financial Times*, December 17, 2001, p. 19.

99 Details of Calder's plan: Confidential source.

100 AOL-Bertelsmann deal: From Waters, Richard, "The Price of Britney: The Sale of Zomba to Bertelsmann Raises Doubts About the Financial Health of the Industry," *Financial Times*, June 13, 2002, p. 21.

100 Blackwell, Geffen, and Branson sale prices: From Malan, *Rolling Stone*, July 25, 2002, pp. 26–28.

100 "The most impressive man ever in the music business": Author interview with Peter Katsis.

100 Ralph Simon used the word *ruthless* in the context of Clive Calder in *Forbes*; Malan used it in *Rolling Stone*, July 25, 2002, pp. 26–28; Scott used it in *Music Business International*, August 1996, page number unknown; and a confidential source used it in an author interview.

100 "Anyone who knew him": Author interview with Steve Lunt.

101 "He was never hands-on": Author interview with Raul Molina (and the other two members of C Note).

101 "Watch, at the end of the next song": From Boucher, *Los Angeles Times*, January 24, 1999, p. 4.

101 Puerto Rican parade details: Author interview with Raul Molina.

101 "He's one of these salesmen": Ibid.

102 Employee Investment Savings Accounts and Steven Sarin detail: From Palmeri, *Business Week*, March 19, 2007, p. 46.

102 Joseph Chow background, $14 million payment, and "He was certainly very friendly": Author interview with Jennifer Chow.

102 "He told us he had 412 airplanes" and other details from David Mathis: From Huntley, Helen, *St. Petersburg Times*, June 3, 2007, p. 1D.

103 Steven Sarin's family and Mathis's $2.8 million, Ibid., p. 1D. Chow's death and family: Author interview with Jennifer Chow.

103 He pleaded guilty: From "Boy Band Mogul Lou Pearlman Admits Role in Ponzi Scheme," Associated Press, March 5, 2008. Pearlman sentencing details and "I'm truly sorry, your honor": From Leusner, Jim, and Willoughby Mariano, "Boy-Band Mogul Lou Pearlman Sentenced to 25 Years in Federal Prison," *Orlando Sentinel*, May 21, 2008. *Vanity Fair* revelations and Alan Gross quotes: From Burrough, Bryan, "Mad About the Boys," *Vanity Fair*, November 2007, pp. 252–268.

104 "Karma's a bitch": From Soll, Lindsay, "Monitor," *Entertainment Weekly*, June 29, 2007, p. 28. Members of the Backstreet Boys and 'NSync refused interview requests.

104 Zelnick-Middelhoff friendship: Author interview with Thomas Middelhoff. Zelnick felt blindsided and "How could the music group not know about this?": From Menn, Joseph, *All the Rave: The Rise and Fall of Shawn Fanning's Napster* (New York: Crown Business, 2003), pp. 263–265.

Big Music's Big Mistakes, Part 4: Killing the Single

105 Terry McManus biography: Author interview with McManus. "Here is where the North American music industry made its greatest mistake": From McManus, Terry, "Singles Are Key to the Record-Buying Habit," *Billboard*, December 27, 1997–January 3, 1998, p. 10.
105 "If you think about water": Author interview with McManus.
106 "Very simple" and "The industry was looking for excuses": Author interview with Jim Caparro.
106 "They tried everything": Author interview with Stan Goman.
107 "It's no coincidence": Author interview with Steve Gottlieb.
107 "If you only sold hand lotion in five-gallon bottles": Author interview with Albhy Galuten.

Big Music's Big Mistakes, Part 5: Pumping Up the Big Boxes

108 Hegewisch Records description and Beatles *Anthology* prices: From author observation and Knopper, Steve, "Small Stores Use Strategy to Survive," *Post-Tribune*, Gary, Indiana, March 31, 1996, p. E4. More on competition from Best Buy: From Knopper, Steve, "Slash and Burn: When Record Stores Go to War, It's Survival of the Biggest," *SPIN*, September 2000, p. 72.
108 Best Buy started selling CDs . . . in 1986: Author interview with Gary Arnold. Best Buy carrying 40,000 to 60,000 titles: From Schmeltzer, John, "A New Tune: Price Cuts, Listening Posts Change Pitch of Music Retailing," *Chicago Tribune*, August 14, 1994, p. 1.
109 "The reality is all of our businesses": Author interview with Gary Arnold.
109 The chain demanded $40,000 to $50,000: Author interviews with Stan Goman and Robb Nansel, president of Saddle Creek Records. "Frigging Best Buy!": Author interview with Goman.
111 Newbury Comics prices: From Peers, Martin, and Evan Ramstad, "Prices of CDs Likely to Drop, Thanks to FTC," *Wall Street Journal*, May 11, 2000, p. B1.
111 "The MAP thing was great": Author interview with Terry Currier.
111 "Nobody ever explained that to us": Author interview with Gary Arnold.
112 FTC overpayment estimate of $480 billion: From Morris, Chris, "Consumers Sue Majors Over MAP Policies," *Billboard*, May 27, 2000, p. 7.
112 Label settlements, library donations, and "It's better than a poke in the eye": From Knopper, Steve, "Unwanted Music," *Rolling Stone*, August 5, 2004, p. 28.
112 More than 65 percent of all the CDs: From Smith, Ethan, "Can Music Survive Inside the Big Box?: Wal-Mart, Target, Best Buy Tighten Their Grip on CDs as Sales, Choices, Decrease," *Wall Street Journal*, April 27, 2007, p. B1. Confirmed in author interview with Jim Caparro.

Chapter 4 1998–2001: A Nineteen-Year-Old Takes Down the Industry—with the Help of Tiny Music, and a Few Questionable Big Music Decisions

113 "There's no one in the record industry that's a technologist": From Mnookin, Seth, "Universal's CEO Once Called iPod Users Thieves. Now He's Giving Songs Away," *Wired*, December 2007, pp. 202. Morris did not respond to numerous interview requests, although he granted one to the author for *Rolling Stone* in 2005, cited later in the book.
113 "There were only like forty people trying to get Doug's attention": Author interview with Erin Yasgar. Background on Albhy Galuten and Courtney Holt from author interviews with Galuten and Holt.

114 Cornyn's small staff included Ted Cohen, who went on to be an important high-tech executive at EMI in the 2000s, and Steve Greenberg, later president of Columbia Records.

114 Joni Mitchell ad, the Record Group, and "Bill Gates came by my office": From Cornyn, *Exploding*, pp. 116, 309–310.

114 Early internet marketing by Jeff Gold and Marc Geiger: Author interviews with Gold and Geiger; "Fantastic . . . but don't forget your real job": Author interview with Gold. Mo Ostin did not respond to an interview request.

114 The Madison Project: Author interview with Paul Vidich. Sony Music's investment in eUniverse and "A lot of those investments wound up being very successful": Author interview with Fred Ehrlich.

115 "I met with people until I was blue in the face": Author interview with John Grady.

115 RealNetworks background and Rob Glaser meeting with major-label executives: Author interview with Rob Glaser.

116 Professor Dieter Seitzer's role: From "The Story of MP3," Fraunhofer Institute for Integrated Circuits, http://www.iis.fraunhofer.de/EN/bf/amm/mp3history/mp3history01.jsp, interview with Seitzer for "The MP3 Inventors," dir. Gerd Brohasga, Petra Wagner, Fraunhofer-Gesellschaft documentary, 2007, available in YouTube snippet, and author interviews with Bernhard Grill, Rocky Caldwell, and Karlheinz Brandenburg.

116 "Everybody contributed ideas": Author interview with Karlheinz Brandenburg. Psychoacoustics: From Schmid, John, "German Creators of MP3 March to Different Tune," *International Herald Tribune*, November 5, 2001, p. 11.

116 Haas effect: From Wilburn, Thomas, "The AudioFile: Understanding MP3 Compression," *Ars Technica: The Art of Technology*, www.arstechnica.com, October 3, 2007.

116 This was complicated: From Schmid, *International Herald Tribune*, November 5, 2001, p. 11; Heingartner, Douglas, "Patent Fights Are a Legacy of MP3's Tangled Origins," *New York Times*, March 5, 2007, p. C3; Wilburn, Thomas, "The AudioFile: Understanding MP3 Compression: From Anonymity to Ubiquity," *Ars Technica: The Art of Technology*, arstechnica.com, October 3, 2007; author interview with Talal Shamoon, who tied much of this information together and reviewed technical passages; and author interviews with Harald Popp and Bernhard Grill, who filled in some of the blanks.

117 "In 1988 somebody asked me what will become of this": From "MP3 Creator Speaks Out: MP3 Is Well-Known to Millions of the World's Teenagers But Its Mere Mention Sends Shivers Down the Spines," BBC News Online, July 13, 2003.

117 Moving Picture Experts Group: From "The Story of MP3," Fraunhofer Institute, and Heingartner, Douglas, *New York Times*, March 5, 2007, p. C3.

118 "It's not a straightforward story, unfortunately": Author interview with Bernhard Grill.

118 "There was not that much interest at that time": Ibid.

119 Rob Lord and Jeff Patterson detail: From Menn, *All the Rave*, pp. 30–31, and author interview with Lord.

119 "A few other companies got into that technology game" and Cryptolope: Author interview with Bob Buziak.

120 "One day in a moment of pure honesty": Author interview with Gerry Kearby.

120 Frank Creighton background: Author interview with Creighton; and Menn, *All the Rave*, pp. 161–163.

120 Creighton-Rosen exchange: Author interview with Hilary Rosen.

120 Frank Creighton conversations with John Fanning, Shawn Fanning, and Eileen Richardson: Author interview with Creighton and Menn, *All the Rave*, p. 163.

121 In 1996, Shawn Fanning: From Menn, *All the Rave*, pp. 13–17.

121 "Money was always a pretty big issue": From Ante, Spencer, "Shawn Fanning's Struggle: An Uncle Helped the Troubled Teen Find His Way—and He Went On to Create the Smash Napster Program," *Business Week*, May 1, 2000, p. 197.

121 "I told him that I had talked to my wife": From Gorov, Lynda, "Hi, I'm Napster," *Boston Globe*, June 11, 2000, p. A1.

122 Harwich High School, purple BMW, and Macintosh: From Menn, *All the Rave*, pp. 13–17. "He set me up with internet access": Author interview with Shawn Fanning, 2000 (for Knopper, Steve, "Napster Creator Wonders What All the Fuss Is About," *Chicago Tribune*, April 10, 2000, Tempo section, p. 1).

123 Uncle John was an entrepreneur, John Fanning background, and Shawn's internship at Chess.net: From Menn, *All the Rave*, pp. 52–55.

123 "We set up a little computer for him": Author interview with Ali Aydar. IRCs and w00w00: From Menn, *All the Rave*, pp. 34–35. $7,000 laptop: From Ante, *Business Week*, May 1, 2000, p. 197. "It gained some popularity": Author interview with Shawn Fanning, 2000. John Fanning's debt: From Menn, *All the Rave*, p. 54.

123 Shawn Fanning at Northeastern: From Menn, *All the Rave*, pp. 34–37, 53–54.

123 "I was living in downtown Chicago": Author interview with Ali Aydar.

123 One of Shawn's first important IRC contacts: Sean Parker biography, from Menn, *All the Rave*, pp. 23–27.

124 "We were basically hackers": Author interview with Parker.

124 Fanning's 70–30 split: From Menn, *All the Rave*, p. 54. Confirmed by Eileen Richardson.

124 Fifteen thousand people had downloaded Napster: From Ante, *Business Week*, May 1, 2000, p. 197. "I had to focus on functionality, to keep it real simple": From Greenfeld, Karl Taro, "Meet the Napster," *Time*, October 2, 2000, p. 60.

125 "practice meeting" and "I had been shopping the deal around northern Virginia": Author interview with Sean Parker.

125 Ben Lilienthal investor meeting detail: From Menn, *All the Rave*, pp. 57–71.

126 "John is a gamer": Author interview with Sean Parker. John Fanning did not respond to interview requests.

126 Yosi Amram biography: From Menn, *All the Rave*, pp. 78–85.

126 "This was kind of the height of the internet boom": Author interview with Amram.

127 Eileen Richardson biography and quotes: Author interview with Richardson.

128 A few details, such as the Palo Alto Coffee Co. description and Richardson's purchase of 333,000 Napster shares: From Menn, *All the Rave*, pp. 87–93, 98.

128 Shawn Fanning at the chess master's house: From Menn, *All the Rave*, p. 86. Fanning and Parker apartment details, Mazda, and gym rat: From Gorov, Lynda, *Boston Globe*, June 11, 2000, p. A1. "I kind of forgot about that phase": Author interview with Shawn Fanning, 2007.

128 "I would put on a presentation for Bill and Eileen": From Menn, *All the Rave*, p. 100.

129 Shawn Fanning–Ted Cohen encounter and "Oh, I'm sure they'll be out soon": Author interview with Ted Cohen.

129 "John Fanning absolutely was completely thinking a different thing": Author interview with Eileen Richardson.

129 Richardson exchanges with Creighton and Rosen: Author interview with Richardson. "Either a really bad manipulator or naïve": Author interview with Rosen.

130 "It was her job to lobby": Author interview with Richardson.

130 150,000 registered users: From Menn, *All the Rave*, p. 101; $2 million financing, Ibid., p. 116.

130 Eddie Kessler biography and quotes: Author interview with Kessler.

131 Shawn Fanning as compulsive workaholic: Author theory based on Fanning's publicly known work habits, confirmed by confidential source. "There's no question it was exciting and stressful": Author interview with Fanning, 2007.

131 In November 1999 (server fix): From Menn, *All the Rave*, p. 120. N.W.A. detail: Confidential source. "One of the most stressful experiences ever": Author interview with Shawn Fanning, 2007.

131 "If they call to say, 'Don't you know this is illegal?'": Author interview with Ted Cohen.

132 "Rock stars and people that play music seriously": Author interview with Shawn Fanning, 2007.

132 Love, Courtney, "Courtney Love Does the Math": From *Salon,* June 14, 2000.

133 "It just grew and grew": Author interview with Hilary Rosen.

133 Chad Paulson: From Menn, *All the Rave*, pp. 134–135. "Some people got it": Author interview with Erin Yasgar.

133 Super Bowl and "Those opportunities met with failure": Author interview with Ghuneim.

133 "We were saying, 'It's a new form of radio'": Author interview with Pete Heimbold.

134 "I hit a point": Author interview with Liz Brooks.

134 "If you can come up with another way": Author interview with Bill Allen. "If you can afford a computer": Quoted in Menn, *All the Rave*, p. 141.

134 "Napster spun it cleverly": Author interview with Joel Amsterdam.

135 Lars Ulrich goes to Napster: From Menn, *All the Rave*, pp. 144–145. Napster employee asking for autograph: Author interview with Liz Brooks.

135 "my future husband": Love quoted in Menn, *All the Rave*, p. 258. Eileen Richardson meets Guy Oseary and Madonna and "The RIAA went on the huge tour": Author interview with Richardson.

136 "three of the finest and best venture firms" and Doerr details: Author interview with Eileen Richardson.

136 "We felt that they had a pretty good case": Author interview with Hank Barry.

137 George Borkowski and Sean Parker's email: From Menn, *All the Rave*, p. 230.

137 David Boies biography and participation: Author interview with Boies.

137 "Plaintiffs have shown persuasively": From *A&M Records Inc. et al. vs. Napster Inc.*, US District Court, Northern District of California, August 10, 2000. "Oh my God": Quoted in Menn, *All the Rave*, p. 246.

138 Alex Kozinski background and "This is like the playoffs": From Menn, *All the Rave*, pp. 248–249.

138 Edgar Bronfman Jr.'s distaste for Napster: From Mann, Charles C., "The Heavenly Jukebox: Rampant Music Piracy May Hurt Musicians Less Than They Fear," *The Atlantic*, September 2000, pp. 39–59. Bronfman also saw that the labels could make a lot of money: Author interviews with Bronfman and Hank Barry.

138 Idei . . . said in later interviews that Japanese law prohibited a service like Napster: From "Interview with Nobuyuki Idei—'We Have to Believe That We'll Be Out of the Darkness Someday'," *Tech-On!*, April 9, 2001.

139 Anti-Napster brigade and "It became clear": Confidential source.

139 "I very much wanted to make a deal with Napster": Author interview with Edgar Bronfman Jr.

139 "These were business meetings": Author interview with Hank Barry.

139 Sun Valley meetings and presence of Idei, Stringer, Middelhoff, and aides: Author interviews with Edgar Bronfman Jr., Hank Barry, Thomas Middelhoff, and John Hummer. Middelhoff squeezed himself between Hummer and Barry:

From author interview with Middelhoff. "Thomas, your seat's over *here*": Author interview with Barry. Bronfman says he doesn't remember but doubts anybody refused to sit next to anybody.

140 Bronfman recalls a . . . friendly, cordial relationship with the Napster people: Author interview with Bronfman. Napster and label execs didn't like each other and "This was an unbelievably brief meeting": Author interview with Thomas Middelhoff.

140 Hummer went "radio-silent," called Bronfman, and mentioned AOL's $2 billion offer: Author interview with Bronfman. "Please think about it": Bronfman-Hummer exchange from author interview with Bronfman.

140 Hummer denies claiming: Author interview with Hummer. AOL was interested but didn't make an offer: Author interview with George Vradenburg. Barry proposed a 50 percent: Author interview with Barry.

141 "It was not what the perception is": Author interview with Al Smith.

142 Napster's peak of 26.4 million users in February 2001: This widely used estimate comes from Jupiter Media Metrix, "Global Napster Usage Plummets, but New File-Sharing Alternatives Gaining Ground," July 20, 2001.

143 "We will take down the music industry": Quote from John Fanning comes from author interview with Eileen Richardson. "I am the record companies' worst nightmare": John Hummer quote from Tully, Shawn, "Big Man Against Big Music," *Fortune*, August 14, 2000, p. 186.

143 "I feel very strongly about that moment in time": Author interview with Jeff Kwatinetz.

144 "Hating Hilary," the Oxford debate, Rosen's personal background, and John Podesta quote: From Bai, Matt, "Hating Hilary," *Wired*, February 2003, pp. 94–96.

144 "Hilary, just stop it": Author interview with Hilary Rosen.

144 "I think Al Smith enjoyed our meetings": Author interview with Alan Citron.

144 Criticism of Rosen as disingenuous: Confidential sources.

144 "I say this with the most affection possible": Author interview with Hilary Rosen.

145 Thomas Middelhoff biography: From Gunther, Marc, "Bertelsmann's New Media Man," *Fortune*, November 23, 1998, p. 176, and Kirkpatrick, David D., "Thomas Middelhoff Has A Hunch," *New York Times Magazine*, June 10, 2001, pp. 72–77.

146 "He was a charming guy": Author interview with Gerry Kearby.

146 a loan of $60 million: From Menn, *All the Rave*, p. 264.

146 Middelhoff recalls Zelnick: Author interview with Middelhoff. "Without our support or knowledge": Author interview with Zelnick.

146 "Easy way to be in the headlines": Author interview with Al Smith.

146 $120,000 salary and $60,000 bonus: From Menn, *All the Rave*, p. 265. "He was like the most positive and optimistic person": Author interview with Shawn Fanning, 2007.

146 Essex House detail and "When a Napster user is sitting at his PC": From Kirkpatrick, *New York Times Magazine*, June 10, 2001, pp. 72–77.

147 "It was just terrible": Author interview with Shawn Fanning, 2007.

147 [Hilbers] figured $30 million: From Menn, *All the Rave*, p. 284. $95 million: Ibid., p. 289. Fanning and Middelhoff secret plan: Ibid., p. 301.

148 "Essentially, that was the end of the game": Author interview with Lyn Jensen.

148 CuteMX and Gnutella background: From Menn, *All the Rave*, pp. 170–175.

149 "The AOL people said, 'This could be dangerous'": Author interview with Howie Klein. "Neither Warner Music nor anyone else there": Anonymous AOL executive from Swisher, Kara, *There Must Be a Pony in Here Somewhere* (New York: Three Rivers Press, 2003), p. 187. "Napster is good": Ibid., p. 186.

Big Music's Big Mistakes, Part 6: The Secure Digital Music Initiative

150   SDMI itinerary provided by Randy Cole. $5 million to $10 million, from Harris, Ron, "Whatever Happened to SDMI?," *Salon*, April 29, 2002, which reports that each of the 200 participating companies paid $20,000 to be on the panel. That comes out to $4 million. Some former SDMI members say the costs were higher.

150   The meetings began informally: Author interviews with Gary Johnson, Randy Cole, and David W. Stebbings.

151   SDMI T-shirts: Author interview with Albhy Galuten. $200,000 logo and "It's quite a nice logo!": Author interview with Randy Cole, who provided a picture of the logo.

151   SDMI . . . portable-device specifications: From Secure Digital Music Initiative, "SDMI Portable Device Specification, Vol. 1," July 8, 1999. Label reps loved it. Electronics firms hated: This is the opinion of several SDMI members, including David W. Stebbings, Randy Cole, Gary Johnson, and others.

152   Leonardo Chiariglioni background: From chiariglioni.org and author interview with Chiariglioni. "the Famous Leonardo": Author interview with Randy Cole. "Leonardo was essentially a technology socialist": Author interview with Talal Shamoon.

153   Al Smith biography and anecdotes: Confidential source, confirmed by Smith.

155   "It was really a race against the clock": Author interview with Edward Felten.

156   "It ended up dying a grisly, painful death": Author interview with Rob Glaser.

156   Apple Computer employees watching SDMI carefully: Author interview with Talal Shamoon, who theorizes, "A lot of the plumbing in iTunes is definitely contemplated in SDMI. The iPod itself is very, very close to something that would comply with the [SDMI] portable device specifications." Apple didn't attend: Author interview with Cary Sherman, then general counsel of the RIAA. Sony Digital Clip: From Mossberg, Walter S., "Sony Digital Music Clip Is Cool, But Treats Users Like Potential Criminals," *Wall Street Journal*, March 2, 2000, p. B1. They could do a far better job: Paraphrasing from Levy, Stephen, *The Perfect Thing: How the iPod Shuffles Commerce, Culture, and Coolness* (New York: Simon & Schuster, 2006), p. 53, as well as author interview with Jonathan Rubinstein.

Chapter 5 2002–2003: How Steve Jobs Built the iPod, Revived His Company, and Took Over the Music Business

157   Much detail about the Gulfstream IV jet incident comes from a 2,150-word, unpublished memoir by Paul Vidich, a prolific fiction writer and member of the *Poets & Writers* board. "Do military jets fly that close to normal airplanes?": Author interview with Kevin Gage.

158   Detail about Brandon, the airport, and the police forces, as well as photo of police cars: From Pritchard, Dean, and Rod Nickel, "Hijack Scare Grounds Jet," *Brandon Sun*, October 27, 2001, p. A1. Confirmation Gage is the figure in the photo with his hands up: Author interview with Gage.

158   "It was a trip" and "We're an old crowd": Author interview with Al Smith.

159   The talks were code-named "Digital Media X": Author interviews with Kevin Gage, Paul Vidich, Al Smith, and William J. Raduchel. Talks breaking down due to Sony Corp. problems with AAC format: Author interview with Gage.

160   There were other problems, too, Jobs-Idei tension, and "You know Steve, he has his own agenda": *MacWorld* staff, "Apple 'a nightmare'—Sony CEO," *MacWorld U.K.*, macworld.co.uk, March 11, 2003.

160 Al Smith . . . was caught in the middle: Author interview with Smith. "There was a certain sense that we have done 99 percent of this work": Author interview with Gage.

161 Barry Schuler–Steve Jobs talks: Author interview with Schuler. Jobs's remarks to Paul Vidich on the phone: Author interview with Vidich.

161 Steve Jobs biography: From Young, Jeffrey S., and William L. Simon, *Icon: Steve Jobs, The Greatest Second Act in the History of Business* (New York: Wiley, 2005), pp. 9–57.

162 "FUCK NIXON" detail: From Butcher, Lee, *Accidental Millionaire: The Rise and Fall of Steve Jobs at Apple Computer* (Paragon House, 1988), p. 37.

163 "We didn't build the computer in a garage": Steve Wozniak quoted in Goodell, Jeff, "The Rise and Fall of Apple Inc.," *Rolling Stone*, April 4, 1996, p. 51.

165 "Apple stopped creating": Steve Jobs quoted in Goodell, Jeff, "The Rise and Fall of Apple Inc., Part Two: The Techno Dreamers vs. the Marketing Pods," *Rolling Stone*, April 18, 1996, p. 59. Jobs refused interview requests for this book.

166 Background on Saehan and MP3Man: From Levy, *The Perfect Thing*, p. 49. Depiction of Rio's attorneys: From author interview with Ron Moore, then general counsel for Diamond Multimedia. "We were a small company": Author interview with David Watkins.

166 "They were just shocked when they lost": Watkins interview.

166 "where the Mac was the center of your lifestyle" and early digital-music discussions at Apple: Author interview with Jonathan Rubinstein.

167 Background on Bill Kincaid: From Levy, *The Perfect Thing*, pp. 48–49. Background on SoundJam: Ibid., pp. 49–52.

167 "We got that to pretty much be the premiere MP3 player on the Mac": Author interview with Robin Casady.

167 Background on Nomad Jukebox: From Kahney, Leander, "Straight Dope on the iPod's Birth," Wired.com, October 17, 2006. "just awful": Author interview with Jonathan Rubinstein. Background on Tony Fadell: Author interview with Fadell.

168 "I basically stalled for a while": Author interview with Jonathan Rubinstein.

168 "We had a very sexy player": Sim Wong Hoo quoted in Sloan, Paul, "What's Next for Apple: Steve Jobs Won't Ever Tell You—But We Will. Here's What a Trail of Intriguing Evidence Reveals About Where the World's Hottest Company Is Going," *Business 2.0*, April 1, 2005, p. 68. Background on Toshiba drive and FireWire: From Levy, *The Perfect Thing*, pp. 56, 58. "Once I saw all those technologies": Author interview with Rubinstein.

168 Rubinstein, Fadell, and their teams building the iPod prototype and presenting it to Jobs: From Levy, *The Perfect Thing*, pp. 58–62.

169 "These suppliers were like, 'Apple is calling, that's great'": Author interview with Tony Fadell.

169 Background on PortalPlayer: From Levy, *The Perfect Thing*, pp. 64–68. "Apple wouldn't even show us what it looked like": Author interview with Paul Mercer.

169 Jobs was vague: From Levy, *The Perfect Thing*, pp. 68–69. Vinnie Chieco's version of the iPod story: Author interview with Chieco.

170 Texas Instruments engineers and "It just looked *cool*": Author interview with Randy Cole.

170 Paul Vidich and Kevin Gage at Apple headquarters detail: Author interview with Gage.

170 "It was almost as if for the first time he was given an audience": Author interview with Vidich. Jobs's tirade and "It was kind of awkward": Author interview with Gage. "Steve, that's why we're here": Vidich quoted in Sloan, *Business 2.0*, April 1, 2005, p. 68.

171 $399 and "Idiots Price Our Devices": From Burrows, Peter, "Show Time!: Just as the Mac Revolutionized Computing, Apple Is Changing the World of Online Music," *Business Week*, February 2, 2004, p. 56.

171 Paul Vidich and Roger Ames: Author interviews with Vidich and Ames.

171 "Sort of a mogul-to-mogul thing": Author interview with Jonathan Rubinstein. "He never reacted to Roger": Author interview with Kevin Gage.

172 "That's a great piece of software": Author interview with Roger Ames.

172 99-cents-per-song and "We were looking at a hook": Author interview with Paul Vidich.

172 Jim Caparro's opposition, breakdown of iTunes wholesale price, and "Ultimately, we could have constructed a far different deal": Author interview with Caparro.

172 Roger Ames–Doug Morris conversation and "I don't think we're going to make a lot of money": Author interview with Ames.

172 "*Of course,* we have to rely on Steve Jobs": Author interview with Albhy Galuten.

173 Galuten went to Cupertino, negotiation detail: Ibid.

173 "We had all the leverage in the world" and "Doug called and said, 'Just close'": Ibid. "We just hit it off": Jimmy Iovine quoted in Levy, *The Perfect Thing*, p. 151.

174 Phil Wiser's Apple negotiations: Author interview with Wiser. "I don't think it was more than a fifteen-second decision in my mind": Andy Lack quoted in Leonard, Devin, "Songs in the Key of Steve," *Fortune*, May 12, 2003, p. 54.

174 Sony Corp.–Sony Music politics and "We do not have any plans for such a product": From Rose, Frank, "The Civil War Inside Sony," *Wired*, November 2003, p. 100.

175 "Now Sony Music was going and empowering Steve Jobs": Author interview with Phil Wiser.

175 "Our smaller market share turned out to be an asset!": Steve Jobs quoted in Levy, *The Perfect Thing*, p. 150. Jobs told Albhy Galuten about $15 million to $30 million marketing budget: Author interview with Galuten. "A lot of people at Microsoft": Author interview with Hadi Partovi.

176 "I've said 'no' to all of them": Irving Azoff quoted in Tam, Pui-Wing, Bruce Orwall, and Anna Wilde Mathews, "Going Hollywood: As Apple Stalls, Steve Jobs Looks to Digital Entertainment—His New Online Music Service Faces Tough Competition; Pixar's Prickly Disney Ties—Courting the Eagles, No Doubt," *Wall Street Journal*, April 25, 2003, p. A1. "The black iPod is something I coveted": Bono quoted in Levy, *The Perfect Thing*, p. 106. "Somebody finally got it right": Dr. Dre quoted in Leonard, *Fortune*, p. 54.

176 Ted Cohen and Apple battles: Author interview with Cohen. Sex Pistols details: From Monk, Noel, *12 Days on the Road: The Sex Pistols in America* (Harper Paperbacks, 2002), pp. 132–133.

178 "This industry has been in such a funk": Sheryl Crow quoted in Leonard, *Fortune*, May 12, 2003, p. 54.

178 In 2003, total iTunes sales and Apple revenue: From Wingfield, Nick, and Smith, Ethan, "Apple Sells Over 25 Million Songs on the Internet," *Wall Street Journal*, December 16, 2003, p. D5.

178 "People think we knew the iPod was just going to be a success": Author interview with Tony Fadell.

178 Vince Carter, Dick Cheney, Aaron Brown, George W. Bush using iPods: From Levy, *The Perfect Thing*, pp. 26, 28–29, 31, 33.

179 Bob Dylan and David Bendeth quotes: From Levine, Robert, "The Death of High Fidelity," *Rolling Stone*, December 27, 2007, pp. 15–18.

179 sold more than 4 billion songs: NPD Group retail study, from apple.com.

179 Record executives privately started likening Apple to MTV: Confidential source.

179 "[Jobs's] stock went from $8 billion to $80 billion": Author interview with Roger Ames.
180 "He feels they got cheated": Confidential source.
181 "Stealing music is not [what's] killing music": Author interview with Robert Pittman.
181 "Who Let the Dogs Out?" vs. "Stacy's Mom": Author interview with Steve Greenberg.

Big Music's Big MIstakes, Part 7: The RIAA Lawsuits

183 Charli Johnson background: From author interview with Johnson as well as Knopper, Steve, "RIAA Will Keep on Suing: The Music Industry Has Targeted 11,456 Illegal Downloaders—Has It Done Any Good?," *Rolling Stone*, June 9, 2005, p. 26.
183 More than 38,000: From RIAA, as of late 2008.
184 "But I know one thing": Scott Bassett quoted in Knopper, Steve, "261 Music Fans Sued: Record Biz Busts Everyday People," *Rolling Stone*, October 16, 2003, p. 25. "My stomach is all turning": Brianna LaHara quoted in Mongelli, Lorena, "Music Pirate: N.Y. Girl, 12, Sued for Web Songs Theft," *New York Post*, September 9, 2003, p. 1.
184 "We knew that the press would find poster children as a result of this program": Cary Sherman quoted in Knopper, *Rolling Stone*, October 16, 2003, p. 25. Settlement figures, from RIAA.
185 "These are very nasty one-sided cases": Author interview with Ray Beckerman.
185 BigChampagne.com peer-to-peer numbers courtesy of Eric Garland.
185 Roger Ames's opposition: Author interview with Hilary Rosen, confidential source, Leeds, Jeff, "Warner Strategy Set Pace for Action on Downloaders," *Chicago Tribune*, September 14, 2003, p. 9. Series of meetings in New York and Sony Music headquarters: Author interviews with three confidential sources.
186 "I think everybody was on board with the lawsuits": Rosen quoted in Knopper, *Rolling Stone*, June 9, 2005, p. 26. "Everyone felt like it was too bad": Confidential source, Ibid. Chelsea and Cindy Lundstrom, Ibid.
188 "It's effective—at trying to bully people": Jason Schultz quoted in Knopper, Steve, "RIAA's Campus Crackdown," *Rolling Stone*, April 5, 2007, p. 15.
188 "It seems like the punishment is way disproportionate to the crime": Confidential source.
188 "The answer would have been so easy": Author interview with Thomas Middelhoff.
189 "The lawsuit stopped me from downloading music": Charli Johnson quoted in Knopper, *Rolling Stone*, June 9, 2005, p. 26.

Chapter 6 2003–2007: Beating Up on Peer-to-Peer Services Like Kazaa and Grokster Fails to Save the Industry, Sales Plunge, and Tommy Mottola Abandons Ship

190 Raid on Phil Morle's home and office: Author interview with Morle.
190 60 million, including 22 million in the United States: From Woody, Todd, "The Race to Kill Kazaa: The Servers Are in Denmark. The Software Is in Estonia. The Domain Is Registered Down Under, the Corporation on a Tiny Island in the South Pacific," *Wired*, February 2003, p. 104. Downloaded some 370 million times: From Rosenbush, Steve, "Skype: On the Block: The Web Phone Service Has Discussed a $3 Billion Deal with News Corp., but an IPO May Be the Most Likely Scenario," businessweek.com, August 10, 2005. [S]hadowed owner Bermeister, backpack cameras, and an $8 million mansion: From Montgom-

ery, Garth, "When the Music Stops," *The Age*, March 23, 2005, page number unknown. "It was a tough time": Author interview with Bermeister.

191 Kazaa background and "I hired actors to come here": From Woody, *Wired*, February 2003, p. 104.

191 "21st-century piratical bazaar" and "the sheer magnitude of this haven for piracy is overwhelming and unknowable": From *Metro-Goldwyn-Mayer Studios Inc. et al. vs. Grokster Ltd. et al.*, US District Court, Central District of California, October 2, 2001.

192 Niklas Zennström and Janus Friis background: From Woody, *Wired*, February 2003, p. 104, and "How Skype and Kazaa Changed the Net," BBC News, June 17, 2005 (how they met at a British telecom).

192 Nikki Hemming background, including Segaworld and $60 million loss: From Montgomery, *The Age*, March 23, 2005, page number unknown. "She has done things the hard way": Author interview with Phil Morle.

193 "We are a utility": Nikki Hemming quoted in Johnston, Chris, "Pirate Queen: Cyber-boss Nikki Hemming Is Defiant. Her Landmark Case Against Hollywood and the Music Industry Will Be a Bloody Battle. But She Says She'll Win," *The Age*, March 5, 2003, page number unknown. "I knew the powers of peer-to-peer": Author interview with Mick Liubinskas.

193 Jeff Ayeroff and melting users' iPods: Author interview with Eric Garland. Confirmed by Ayeroff, although his recollection of the exchange is slightly different, per the footnote in the chapter.

193 "Shawn Fanning was genuinely a kid with a great idea": Author interview with Cary Sherman. "These were pornographers and bad guys": Confidential source.

194 543 peer-to-peer file titles having to do with child pornography: From US General Accounting Office, GAO-03-351, report to the Chairman and Ranking Minority Member, Committee on Government Reform, House of Representatives, "File-Sharing Programs: Peer-to-Peer Networks Provide Ready Access to Child Pornography," February 2003, p. 1.

194 "As a guy in the record industry and as a parent": Andrew Lack quoted in Hansell, Saul, "Aiming at Pornography to Hit Music Piracy," *New York Times*, September 7, 2003, p. 1. "It was one of the big propaganda positions": Author interview with Phil Morle.

194 "Being an old press guy": Author interview with Wayne Rosso. "[T]he best music file-sharing service": From Chamy, Michael, "I Want My MP3s: Audiogalaxy, Austin's Onetime File-Sharing Supernova," *Austin Chronicle*, January 31, 2003, p. 50. Merhej's next project, based on the same peer-to-peer platform and software, was FolderShare, which he sold to Microsoft in 2005. He works for Microsoft to this day.

195 "on a gigantic scale" and other background on Grokster case: From US Supreme Court, *Metro-Goldwyn-Mayer Studios Inc. et al. vs. Grokster Ltd. et al.*, June 27, 2005.

195 "I've been cautioning people in the industry": Author interview with Hilary Rosen, 2005.

195 File-sharing numbers from BigChampagne.com.

195 "Kazaa lost": Author interview with Eric Garland.

196 MediaDefender charged major labels $4,000 to protect an album and $2,000 for a track: From leaked MediaDefender emails and Paul, Ryan, "Leaked Media Defender E-mails Reveal Secret Government Project," arstechnica.com, September 16, 2007. "[T]he online guard dog of the entertainment world" and MediaDefender revenues: From Roth, Daniel, "The Pirates Can't Be Stopped," *Condé Nast Portfolio*, February 2008, p. 98. "The hope is, you make the experience so poor": Author interview with Cory Llewellyn.

196 "In the beginning, I had no motivation against Monkey Defenders" and background on "Ethan": From Roth, Daniel, *Condé Nast Portfolio*, February 2008, p. 98. Details of Ethan's hack into MediaDefender email accounts: Author interview with "Forrest F.," who helped circulate the emails via the Pirate Bay.

197 "This is a stupid industry": Author interview with Peter Sunde. Details about the Pirate Bay's role in leaking the MediaDefender emails, from Roth, Daniel, *Condé Nast Portfolio*, February 2008, p. 98. Sum 41 and Timbaland titles: From leaked emails, posted on mediadefender.com, as of January 2008. "This is really fucked," Randy Saaf's email quoted in Roth, Ibid.

197 ArtistDirect purchase of MediaDefender and founder salaries: Ibid.

197 "Whenever you brought up something like Napster": Author interview with Cory Llewellyn.

198 Offspring promotion: Author interview with Jim Guerinot.

198 Don Ienner receptive to internet marketing and "Whatever it takes": Confidential source. "War meetings" and "We devise a plan of attack": Ienner quoted in Philips, Chuck, "Passion for Music Drives Columbia Chief to Make Plenty of Industry Noise," *Los Angeles Times*, January 29, 2001, p. C1.

198 "Certainly, that was the attitude of majors across the board": Author interview with Mark Williams.

199 Robin Bechtel background: Author interview with Bechtel, and Bechtel, Robin, "The Internet Is a Fad: How the World Wide Web Changed Music," *Flaunt*, May 2007, pp. 94–97.

199 "I basically built Creed's online fan base one fan at a time": Author interview with Syd Schwartz.

200 "Show her a brick wall": Author interview with Ty Braswell.

200 "When YouTube came up": Author interview with Robin Bechtel.

200 "The funny part is we don't get paid anything for it": Author interview with Jamie Kitman, 2006. Panic! at the Disco using YouTube: From Hancock, Noelle, "YouTube Rocks," *Rolling Stone*, July 13, 2006, p. 40. Justin Timberlake using YouTube: Author interview with Timberlake's manager, Johnny Wright, 2006. Universal, too, would find gold: From Graham, Jefferson, "Q&A with Universal Music's Rio Caraeff." *USA Today*, October 2, 2007, p. B2.

201 "We've had relationships with [the labels] since the beginning of MySpace": Author interview with Chris DeWolfe.

202 "When we started out in 2002": Author interview with Martin Stiksel.

202 "If a record wasn't selling": Author interview with Randy Sosin.

202 Jessica Simpson party and "He did spend a ton of money": Author interview with Barbara O'Dair.

203 Sony lost $132 million: From Eaton, *New York*, March 3, 2003, p. 42. Album sales and market share figures from Nielsen SoundScan.

203 Mottola's $4 million mansion and marriage to Thalia: From Eaton, *New York*, March 3, 2003, p. 42.

203 Mottola-Stringer relationship: Ibid.

203 "Tommy didn't 'manage up' well": Confidential source.

204 "Why the fuck am I dealing with this guy?": From Eaton, *New York*, March 3, 2003, p. 42.

204 "The Tommy-Donnie-Michelle management structure": Author interview with Jim Guerinot.

205 Sony Music shrinking and employee numbers: From analysis of Securities and Exchange Commission reports from Sony, Vivendi Universal, EMI, and Warner, 2000 to 2004, compiled by Bill Werde and Charley Rogulewski. Used with permission.

205 "icon of the music industry": Press release quoted in Eaton, *New York*, March 3, 2003, p. 42. "It was the end of an era": Confidential source.

205 "We speak the same language": Howard Stringer quoted in Smith, Ethan, "Two Cost-Cutting TV Executives Will Run Music Monolith," *Wall Street Journal*, November 7, 2003, p. B1.

206 AOL Time Warner-Bertelsmann merger talks: From Peers, Martin, "Bertelsmann, AOL Continue Music-Deal Talks," *Wall Street Journal*, September 18, 2003, p. B8. New York airport meeting: From Smith, Ethan, *Wall Street Journal*, November 7, 2003, p. B1.

206 30 percent combined market share: Calculations based on Nielsen SoundScan data.

207 "One side of the room was Clive and his people": Author interview with Joe DiMuro.

207 Sony employees' skepticism of Smellie: Confidential source.

207 Andrew Lack's peer-to-peer ideas and "Andy was the key mover and shaker": Author interview with Wayne Rosso.

208 Publicists . . . watched budgets: From author interview with Lisa Markowitz, then-Epic publicity executive.

208 EMI plant closings: From Timmons, Heather, "EMI to Cut Artist Roster and Close 2 CD Plants," *New York Times*, April 1, 2004, p. W1. Cinram International purchase of Warner manufacturing: From "AOL Time Warner Agrees to Sell Its DVD/CD Manufacturing and Physical Distribution Businesses to Cinram International for $1.05 Billion," AOL Time Warner news release, July 18, 2003. Glenayre buying Universal plants and warehouses: From "Glenayre Announces Acquisition Agreements," Glenayre Technologies news release, May 9, 2005. Entertainment Distribution Company posts $11.4 million loss: From company earnings conference call transcript, August 7, 2007.

209 "Darwinian evolution took hold": Author interview with Jim Caparro. DVD sales: From Digital Entertainment Group. Blu-ray's possible impact on Terre Haute plant: From "Sony May Be Expanding Terre Haute Operations," *Tribune-Star*, Terre Haute, Indiana, January 7, 2008, verified by Jim Frische.

209 Label spending on videos and "It's a very precarious and somewhat unfortunate development": Author interview with Randy Sosin.

209 mathematics of indie promotion: From Boehlert, *Salon*, June 25, 2002.

210 "Costs start becoming more of a consideration": Author interview with Jeff McClusky. Clear Channel's 1,225 stations and reversal on indie promotion: From Boehlert, *Salon*, June 25, 2002. "We were too greedy": Author interview with Bill Scull.

211 Eliot Spitzer's payola investigation, including Audioslave and J. Lo details and Epic email detail: From Knopper, Steve, "Payola Probe Rocks Biz," *Rolling Stone*, August 25, 2005, p. 12.

211 "condoned or participated in pay-to-play" and details about Don Ienner and Charlie Walk in *Los Angeles Times* investigation: From Duhigg, Charles, "Hitmakers Implicated in 'Pay for Play' Plans; Investigators Looking into the Corruption Charges Found Evidence Against Two Sony BMG Senior Executives, Sources Say," *Los Angeles Times*, December 4, 2005, p. A1.

211 Ashley Alexandra Dupré receiving more than $206,000 via MySpace song downloads: From Lemire, Jonathan, "Hooker's an Online Hit—to the Tune of $200G," *New York Daily News*, March 15, 2008.

212 *Radio & Records* 2006 "adds" data: Courtesy of the magazine and John Fagot. "Songs aren't just getting on the radio as quickly as they did before": Author interview with Doug Podell, 2006. "The labels are scrambling": Confidential source, 2006.

212   Tower Records bankruptcy background and "We happened to be funny-looking": From Knopper, Steve, "Tower Records Shuts Its Doors," *Rolling Stone*, November 2, 2006, p. 16.

213   "I lost a lot of money in Argentina and Mexico": Author interview with Russ Solomon, 2006. "Russ Solomon didn't believe in digital music": Author interview with Lisa Amore.

214   Wal-Mart cutting shelf space by 20 percent, and label sources predicting another 20 percent in 2008: From Knopper, Steve, "Wal-Mart Demands CD-Price Cut," *Rolling Stone*, April 3, 2008, p. 16.

214   "the worst business . . . in the most challenged sector": EMI internal email from Guy Hands, provided by confidential source. "Bloodbath": Confidential source.

214   Bronfman, Messier, and Seagram: From Smith, Ethan, and Martin Peers, "Cost Cutting Is an Uphill Fight at Warner Music," *Wall Street Journal*, May 24, 2004, p. B1. $42 billion sale price: From "Music Tycoon Continues to Deal in Entertainment Industry," *Sunday Business*, London, circulated on Knight Ridder Tribune Business News wire service, November 30, 2003. Family fortune dropping from $6.5 billion to $3 billion: From Adler, Stephen J., "Facing the Digital Music," *Business Week*, May 22, 2006, p. 64. "I remember my mother saying as I was a kid": Author interview with Edgar Bronfman Jr.

215   "Technology allows more people to get more music": Author interview with Edgar Bronfman Jr.

216   Warner Music laid off 400 employees: From Christman, Ed, "Taking Stock," *Billboard*, May 19, 2007, p. 11. Leigh Lust background: Confidential source. "This industry is like George W. Bush": Author interview with Steve Gottlieb. Lyor Cohen and Edgar Bronfman Jr. salaries: From Warner Music Group Corp. Schedule 14A filing with Securities and Exchange Commission, January 25, 2008.

217   Jimmy Iovine background and "if you bring somebody tea one hundred times": From Trachtenberg, Jeffrey A., "Jimmy Iovine Spins More Gold at Interscope," *Wall Street Journal*, February 22, 1996, p. B1. "You don't want to make *house music*": Confidential source.

217   Ted Field and $15 million: From Roberts, Johnnie L., "Field Marshal: The Man Behind Gangsta Rap Is Mild-Mannered, Old-Money, and Into Politics. Is Interscope Records' Ted Field a Menace to Society?" *Newsweek*, February 10, 1997, p. 44. Marion "Suge" Knight and Death Row Records background, including Knight's affiliation with the Bloods: From Boucher, Geoff, "Suge's Next Act? The Rap Mogul's Empire Has Dwindled, but He Sees Only Possibilities," *Los Angeles Times*, December 4, 2002, p. E1.

218   "He did a deal with the devil": Confidential source.

218   "Many people say these [record] companies are a bunch of ugly ducklings": Author interview with Doug Morris, 2005.

218   Revenue estimates from TV, movie, and video game licenses: From Goodman, Fred, "Rock's New Economy: Making Money When CDs Don't Sell," *Rolling Stone*, May 29, 2008, pp. 22–24. *Guitar Hero* and *Rock Band* sales: From Halperin, Shirley, "Rock Game Nation," *Entertainment Weekly*, September 5, 2008, pp. 38–40.

219   Worldwide ringtone revenues: From Juniper Research. Will.i.am hiring engineers: From author interview with will.i.am, 2006.

219   Jay-Z's $10 million salary as president of Def Jam: From Leeds, Jeff, "Jay-Z to Quit His Day Job as President of Def Jam," *New York Times*, December 25, 2007, p. C3.

220   "Going into a major record label": Author interview with Jamie Kitman. Labels'

5,000 layoffs: From Eliscu, Jenny, "Labels' Unhappy Holiday," *Rolling Stone*, January 24, 2008, pp. 9–10.

220 Details on Simon Baeycrtz, Robert Wieger, and Barry Feldman: From Knopper, Steve, "Rock & Roll Refugees," rollingstone.com, July 22, 2008.

220 Debbie Southwood-Smith background and quotes: Author interview with Southwood-Smith.

Big Music's Big Mistakes, Part 8: Sony BMG's Rootkit

222 "software that tricks an operating system": From Roush, Wade, "Inside the Spyware Scandal: When Sony BMG Hid a 'Rootkit' on Their CDs, They Spied on You and Let Hackers into Your Computer. What Were They Thinking?" *Technology Review*, May 2006, pp. 48–57. Sony BMG released 4.7 million CDs containing rootkits, and 52 titles: From Smith, Ethan, "Sony BMG Pulls Millions of CDs Amid Antipiracy-Software Flap; Recall Could Dent Sales of Artists and Retailers During Key Holiday Season," *Wall Street Journal*, November 17, 2005, p. D5.

223 "My sister and I will no longer buy any Sony products": Quoted in Zeller, Tom Jr., "Railing at Sony BMG, Disguised as a Review," *New York Times*, November 21, 2005, p. C3. "Most people, I think, don't even know what a rootkit is": Thomas Hesse on National Public Radio broadcast, quoted in Mitchell, Dan, "The Rootkit of All Evil," *New York Times*, November 19, 2005, p. C5.

224 "It was the highest debut of Neil's career": Rick Rubin quoted in Hirschberg, Lynn, "The Music Man," *New York Times Magazine*, September 2, 2007, pp. 26–50.

225 "It seemed to us that the record was just tainted": Author interview with Ethan Iverson.

225 "If you shed a tear for every dollar spent": Author interview with Talal Shamoon.

225 "That's why the technology was used" and "something deep": Confidential source.

226 Security experts quoted in *Technology Review*: From Roush, *Technology Review*, May 2006, pp. 48–57.

227 SunnComm recollections and "It took our revenue stream right out from under us": Author interview with Bill Whitmore.

227 Blaming Thomas Hesse and Michael Smellie: Confidential source. "When we found out the Neil Diamond record had rootkit technology": Author interview with Steve Greenberg.

227 Recall costing $2 million to $4 million: From Smith, *Wall Street Journal*, November 17, 2005, p. D5. Fifteen class-action suits, $50 million settlement: Estimate in Smith, Ethan, "Sony BMG Agrees to Settle 15 Suits Over CD Software," *Wall Street Journal*, December 30, 2005, p. A14. "They don't do it anymore": Author interview with Steve Greenberg.

Chapter 7 The Future: How Can the Record Labels Return to the Boom Times? Hint: Not by Stonewalling New High-tech Models and Locking Up the Content

229 Eric Nicoli background: From Martinson, Jane, "Eric Nicoli: Music Boss Who Went from Choc to Rock," *The Guardian*, January 27, 2006, p. 31.

229 "In all of our research": Eric Nicoli quoted in EMI news conference, audio webcast from April 2, 2007; other details about the press conference come from this source.

230 Barney Wragg background: Author interview with Wragg.

230 "I realized that as an industry we'd kind of been smoking crack": Ibid.

230 Analysis of EMI struggles: Paraphrased from author interview with Ty Braswell.

231 Barney Wragg did research and worked with Steve Jobs and Eddy Cue: From author interview with Wragg.

231 "In a moment of desperation": Confidential source.

231 Eric Nicoli's spending: From Dugan, Emily, "Money to Burn: How EMI's Profligate Bosses Filled a House with £20,000 Worth of Candles," *The Independent*, November 30, 2007, p. 27.

231 Wragg . . . leaving the company for reasons he wouldn't divulge: Author interview with Wragg.

232 Steve Jobs's manifesto and quotes: From Jobs, Steve, "Thoughts on Music," apple.com, February 6, 2007.

233 "My instinct is it will beef up the digital sales pretty significantly": Author interview with Ian Rogers.

233 "spreadsheet that plays music": Ian Rogers quoted in "Convenience Wins, Hubris Loses and Context vs. Context, a Presentation for Some Music Industry Friends," October 6, 2007, blog post, fistfulayen.com "All the stuff we've been saying": Author interview with Ian Rogers.

233 "Digital isn't the future—it's today": Author interview with Tom Corson. Alicia Keys list of formats: Provided by BMG.

234 Ringtone revenues: From BMI. "We see no sign of it slowing down right now": Author interview with Rio Caraeff, 2006.

235 "You're doing it for the person who's in the mall and their phone rings": Author interview with will.i.am, 2006.

235 Edgar Bronfman Jr. speech, including Baek Ji Young and SK Telecom: From Convergence 2.0 Symposium keynote address, September 17, 2007, transcript.

235 Ricky Martin detail: Confidential source. Juanes promotion: From Cobo, Leila, and Ayala Ben-Yehuda, "Digital Business Heats Up for Latin Music," Reuters/*Billboard*, December 17, 2007. "It is a huge, huge, huge piece of the business": Confidential source.

236 Jupiter Research and M:Metrics studies: From Morrison, Dianne See, "WMG Reports Fall in Ringtone Sales; Mobile Remains Soft, *mocoNews*, February 7, 2008. "It doesn't seem like anything that's going to have a long-term sustained growth": Author interview with Peter Paterno, 2006. "People say, 'Ringtones are fashion'": Author interview with Mark Donovan.

236 "I don't think the research indicates": Confidential source.

237 "It's mind-blowing—I'm listening to music constantly": Rick Rubin quoted in Hiatt, Brian, "Biz Bets on Subscriptions," *Rolling Stone*, December 13, 2007, pp. 17–18.

237 "If you're a massive music fan": Author interview with Ted Cohen. Total Music detail: From "Universal Music Takes On iTunes: Universal Chief Doug Morris Is Enlisting Other Big Music Players for a Service to Challenge the Jobs Juggernaut," *Business Week*, October 22, 2007.

238 Steve Jobs may be coming around to subscriptions: From Hiatt, *Rolling Stone*, December 13, 2007, pp. 17–18.

238 Description of *The Long Tail* theories: From Anderson, Chris, *The Long Tail: Why the Future of Business Is Selling Less of More* (New York: Hyperion, 2006). "I passed out twenty copies of Chris's book": Author interview with Erin Yasgar.

238 "You want to take a record label profitable quickly?": Author interview with Terry McBride.

239 Rhapsody/iTunes percentages from NPD Group study: Cited in Hiatt, *Rolling Stone*, December 13, 2007, pp. 17–18. "It's getting better": Author interview with Terry McBride.

239 BitTorrent, discussions with movie and record companies: Author interview with Ashwin Navin.

240 "The music companies were just paralyzed": Ibid.

240 Some 2,700 music retailers have closed since 2003: From the Almighty Institute of Music Retail. "We're trying to reposition the business": Simon Wright quoted in "Steep Rent Forces Closure of LA-area Virgin Megastore," Associated Press, December 27, 2007.

240 Radio listenership: From Arbitron.com.

240 "It's going to be difficult to make a lot of money": Author interview with Joe Smith.

241 Paramore deal and "You have to sacrifice to get somewhere": From Knopper, Steve, "Reinventing Record Deals," *Rolling Stone*, November 29, 2007, p. 13.

242 "Say I was considering being the sole investor": Author interview with Steve Greenberg.

242 "It gives the label more incentive to work hard": Author interview with Chris Black.

242 "They're going to have to use 360 deals": Author interview with Chris Lighty.

242 Aimee Mann detail and "A lot of artists don't realize how much money they could make": From Byrne, David, "The Fall and Rise of Music: The CD? It's Dead," *Wired,* January 2008, pp. 124–129.

243 "It's easy to see why bands would resist": Jamie Kitman quoted in Knopper, *Rolling Stone*, November 29, 2007, p. 13. "My knee-jerk reaction would be 'no way'": Jordan Kurland quoted in Ibid.

243 Jim Griffin's tax-the-ISP plan, as well as Paul McGuinness quote (from speech) and Gary Stiffelman quote: From Knopper, Steve, "Best Plan to Save the Record Biz: Bill the ISPs, Make File-Sharing Legal," *Rolling Stone*, May 1, 2008, p. 51.

244 "A day that will live in infamy": From Peisner, David, "The October Surprise," *SPIN*, January 2008, pp. 82–86.

244 Radiohead quotes and comScore numbers: From Binelli, Mark, "The Future According to Radiohead," *Rolling Stone*, January 23, 2008, p. 57.

245 "I'm truly saddened because I think music has been devalued": Trent Reznor quoted in Westhoff, Ben, "Trent Reznor and Saul Williams Discuss Their New Collaboration, Mourn OiNK," newyork.com, October 30, 2007.

246 "You see these articles about the disaster in the music business": James Mercer quoted in Peisner, *SPIN*, January 2008, pp. 82–86.

247 David Byrne and Nonesuch: From Byrne, *Wired*, January 2008, pp. 124–129.

247 "The mixtapes were obviously very concerning": From Serpick, Evan, "How Lil Wayne became a Superstar," *Rolling Stone*, June 26, 2008, p. 15.

247 "The idea of fighting it seems kind of silly": Author interview with Mac McCaughan.

247 Doug Morris's salary: From Vivendi S.A. Form 20-F filing with US Securities and Exchange Commission, June 29, 2006.

248 "If I could just make records and work with artists": Author interview with Mark Williams.

249 Guy Hands information and quotes: From Langley, William, "Profile: Guy Hands," telegraph.co.uk, January 20, 2008.

249 "The recorded music market has been declining and may continue to decline": From Vivendi S.A., Form 20-F, US Securities and Exchange Commission, June 29, 2006.

249 Ahmet Ertegun anecdote: From Dannen, *Hit Men*, p. 252.

250 Doug Morris's retelling and "the truth is, that's what it's all about": Author interview with Morris, 2005.

Acknowledgments

First, thanks to the more than 230 executives, scouts, publicists, artists, lawyers, technologists, authors, teachers, inventors, managers, and DJs who shared their recollections of working in this bizarre and colorful industry, which, as Frank Dileo says, is in "a confusion of flux, a flux of confusion." A small portion of them spoke anonymously or off the record; most of the rest are named in the endnotes if not in the text. I'm especially indebted to those who agreed to multiple interviews—Gil Friesen, Jerry Moss, Joe Smith, Marc Finer, Bob Jamieson, Bob Buziak, Bill Scull, Bob Sherwood, Stan Cornyn, Jim Caparro, Jim Guerinot, Randy Cole, Al Smith, Paul Vidich, Kevin Gage, David W. Stebbings, Howie Klein, Roger Ames, John Briesch, James T. Russell, Talal Shamoon, David Leibowitz, Michael Schulhof, and others I'm sure I've missed.

Eric Garland of BigChampagne.com saved my butt a number of times—he suggested a rough outline at a critical, last-minute point in the pitch process, revealed important sources, and lightly pointed out when I was wandering aimlessly in the wrong direction. I owe him numerous Shiner Bocks at the top of a parking garage someplace in Austin. Several sources were kind enough to review technical passages, including the professorial James T. Russell, the good-humored Talal Shamoon, and my older brother, Mark Knopper, who in addition to inventing the internet (more or less) was (through his coincidental friendship with a pre–Rykodisc Rob Simonds) the first person I ever knew with an actual CD player. Garland, Steve Greenberg, Jenny Eliscu, and my old Colorado Coalition pal and bullshit-detector Leland Rucker volunteered their time as readers; all made thoughtful comments, some of which led to drastic restructurings of entire chapters.

Wylie O'Sullivan, my editor, inherited this project, and turned out to be the absolute perfect person for it. She was gentle and patient, critical and pointed, adaptable and receptive—all at the right times, and all in an encouraging way. Daniel Lazar, my agent, happened across a "funny little article" (as he calls it) I wrote in *Wired* about attempting to kill a cheapo PC with viruses and spyware. Six ideas, three months, and eight proposal rewrites later, thanks to his savvy, perseverance, and connections, I had a book deal. This book wouldn't have been possible without Maris Kreizman, who held Wylie's post at Free Press before leaving for another opportunity in early 2007. I regret never getting the chance to truly work with her. Thanks to Dominick Anfuso for believing in this project all along. In the UK, I'm grateful to Dan's counterpart, Dorie Simmonds, as well as Andrew Gordon for signing the book, and Angela Herlihy and Katherine Stanton for seeing it to fruition. Patty Romanowski Bashe is a former *Rolling Stone* editor who knows her Hall from her Oates; I was lucky to get her as copy editor.

About forty interview subjects did not wind up in the text, mostly for space reasons. They were knowledgeable and insightful and shared their valuable time—particularly Davitt Sigerson (who turned me on to Andrew S. Grove's book), Bob Divney, Dave Richards, Steve Wozniak, Tim Sommer, Jim McGuinn, Konrad Hilbers, Russell Frackman, Milt Olin, Tom DeSavia, Gilles Boccon-Gibod, F. Joseph Gormley, Asif Ahmed, James Diener, David Pakman, Lucas Mann, Bruce Flohr, Fred von Lohmann, and Fred Goldring.

Enthusiastically setting up interviews, suggesting sources, or just being kind when I needed it were Lisa Stone in Gil Friesen's office, Sunnie Outlaw in Strauss Zelnick's office, Michelle Burt in Jeff Ayeroff's office, Annie Meaher in Tom Corson's office, Nathaniel Brown, and Lisa Lake (for hooking me up with Joe Smith and Marc Finer). Also helpful with connections, interviews, recollections, running interference, or tracking down clippings: George Boyd, Ann Morfogen, Jeff White, Diana D'Angelo, Marianne Hasselbach, Will Tanous, Amanda Collins, Debbie Densil, Hannah Pantle, Stephanie Gold, Sara Christensen, Mary Van Daele, Bobby Ewing, Michael Zager, Molly Schoneveld, Kathryn Litsas, Bill Bentley, Jim Kloiber, Christian Algar, Joanne Dant, Lauren Harris, Fernando Aguilar, Stephan Weikert, Wendy Washington, Brian Lucas, Yvonne Gomez, Sohayla Cude, Karen Allen, Joerg Howe, Marc Pollack, Alfonso Alvarez, Marnie Black, Patti Conte, Peter Lofrumento, Chad Goonan, Vera Salamone, Jacqueline Park, Rich LaMagna, Kay Lyn Byrne, Matt Graves, Matthias Rose, Nakia Fowler, Susan Gordon, Doug Wyllie, Ilka Becker, Carrie Davis, Ricki Seidman, Isabelle Caldenbach, Cathy Arthur, Laura Ormes, Jennifer Stryd-Donahue, Steve Karas, Jeannie Kedis, Steven Strosser, Sue Turner, Nadia Rogers, Anna Vrechek, Leyla Turkkan, Sarah Weinstein,

Theola Borden, Christina Rentz, Jocelyn Johnson, Andy Greene, Carol Chisholm, Diane Retiand, Gary Morgenstern, and Bob Kostanczuk.

Anna Loynes provided sales numbers from Nielsen SoundScan; Jonathan Lamy did the same from the Recording Industry Association of America. Mark Coleman, author of the excellent book *Playback*, was friendly enough to respond when I came across his name on the I Love Music board and (in somewhat confused manner) sought his advice.

My editors at *Rolling Stone*—especially Jason Fine and Jonathan Ringen, but also Joe Levy and Jann S. Wenner behind the scenes—have since 2002 given me the best possible journalistic platform to observe the cataclysmic shifts in the music industry. They were also kind enough to keep the work coming as I trudged through this book. My colleagues Brian Hiatt and Evan Serpick gave important insights at key times. Other editors who offered encouragement or at least looked the other way when I stopped pitching to them (temporarily!): Adam Rogers of *Wired*; Josh duLac of *The Washington Post*; Greg Kot, Carmel Carrillo, and Kevin Williams of the *Chicago Tribune*; Genetta Adams, Kevin Amorim, and Glenn Gamboa of *Newsday*; Tina Maples of the Milwaukee *Journal Sentinel*; and Joe Rassenfoss and Mark Brown of the *Rocky Mountain News*.

Special thanks to Gloria Gaynor for her patience.

My friends and family have always enthusiastically supported this project, even when they became understandably sick of hearing about free-goods allowances and compression schemes: Dorothy Knopper, Doug, Abbie, and Benjamin Knopper, Don and Peggy Ramsdell, Jonathan Boonin, Larry Gallagher, Michael McKelvey, Maynard Eaton, David Menconi, Jim DeRogatis, Tim Riley, and fellow idiot Mark Bliesener. Gary Graff met me at a Detroit-area hotel buffet on a gray Christmas Day 2006 and gave a crucial bit of advice he probably doesn't even remember.

Finally, my father, Morton P. Knopper, died August 3, 2008. Thanks, Dad. I hope you can get books up there.

Index

About the Author

Steve Knopper is a *Rolling Stone* contributing editor who has covered the music business since 2002. Since beginning his career in 1989, as an obituary writer and concert reviewer for *The Richmond* (Virginia) *News Leader,* he has contributed to such publications as *Wired, SPIN, Esquire, National Geographic Traveler, Billboard, Newsday,* the *Chicago Tribune,* and the *Rocky Mountain News.* He lives in Denver with his wife and six-year-old daughter.